Praxis II

Elementary Education: Content Knowledge for Teaching (7801) Exam Part 1 of 2

SECRETS

Study Guide

Your Key to Exam Success

MW00723784

Praxis II Test Review for the
Praxis II: Subject Assessments

Dear Future Exam Success Story:

First of all, **THANK YOU** for purchasing Mometrix study materials!

Second, congratulations! You are one of the few determined test-takers who are committed to doing whatever it takes to excel on your exam. **You have come to the right place.** We developed these study materials with one goal in mind: to deliver you the information you need in a format that's concise and easy to use.

In addition to optimizing your guide for the content of the test, we've outlined our recommended steps for breaking down the preparation process into small, attainable goals so you can make sure you stay on track.

We've also analyzed the entire test-taking process, identifying the most common pitfalls and showing how you can overcome them and be ready for any curveball the test throws you.

Standardized testing is one of the biggest obstacles on your road to success, which only increases the importance of doing well in the high-pressure, high-stakes environment of test day. Your results on this test could have a significant impact on your future, and this guide provides the information and practical advice to help you achieve your full potential on test day.

Your success is our success

We would love to hear from you! If you would like to share the story of your exam success or if you have any questions or comments in regard to our products, please contact us at **800-673-8175** or **support@mometrix.com**.

Thanks again for your business and we wish you continued success!

Sincerely,
The Mometrix Test Preparation Team

Need more help? Check out our flashcards at: http://MometrixFlashcards.com/PraxisII

Copyright © 2019 by Mometrix Media LLC. All rights reserved.
Written and edited by the Mometrix Exam Secrets Test Prep Team
Printed in the United States of America

TABLE OF CONTENTS

Introduction

Thank you for purchasing this resource! You have made the choice to prepare yourself for a test that could have a huge impact on your future, and this guide is designed to help you be fully ready for test day. Obviously, it's important to have a solid understanding of the test material, but you also need to be prepared for the unique environment and stressors of the test, so that you can perform to the best of your abilities.

For this purpose, the first section that appears in this guide is the **Secret Keys**. We've devoted countless hours to meticulously researching what works and what doesn't, and we've boiled down our findings to the five most impactful steps you can take to improve your performance on the test. We start at the beginning with study planning and move through the preparation process, all the way to the testing strategies that will help you get the most out of what you know when you're finally sitting in front of the test.

We recommend that you start preparing for your test as far in advance as possible. However, if you've bought this guide as a last-minute study resource and only have a few days before your test, we recommend that you skip over the first two Secret Keys since they address a long-term study plan.

If you struggle with **test anxiety**, we strongly encourage you to check out our recommendations for how you can overcome it. Test anxiety is a formidable foe, but it can be beaten, and we want to make sure you have the tools you need to defeat it.

Copyright © Mometrix Media. You have been licensed one copy of this document for personal use only. Any other reproduction or redistribution is strictly prohibited. All rights reserved.

Secret Key #1 – Plan Big, Study Small

There's a lot riding on your performance. If you want to ace this test, you're going to need to keep your skills sharp and the material fresh in your mind. You need a plan that lets you review everything you need to know while still fitting in your schedule. We'll break this strategy down into three categories.

Information Organization

Start with the information you already have: the official test outline. From this, you can make a complete list of all the concepts you need to cover before the test. Organize these concepts into groups that can be studied together, and create a list of any related vocabulary you need to learn so you can brush up on any difficult terms. You'll want to keep this vocabulary list handy once you actually start studying since you may need to add to it along the way.

Time Management

Once you have your set of study concepts, decide how to spread them out over the time you have left before the test. Break your study plan into small, clear goals so you have a manageable task for each day and know exactly what you're doing. Then just focus on one small step at a time. When you manage your time this way, you don't need to spend hours at a time studying. Studying a small block of content for a short period each day helps you retain information better and avoid stressing over how much you have left to do. You can relax knowing that you have a plan to cover everything in time. In order for this strategy to be effective though, you have to start studying early and stick to your schedule. Avoid the exhaustion and futility that comes from last-minute cramming!

Study Environment

The environment you study in has a big impact on your learning. Studying in a coffee shop, while probably more enjoyable, is not likely to be as fruitful as studying in a quiet room. It's important to keep distractions to a minimum. You're only planning to study for a short block of time, so make the most of it. Don't pause to check your phone or get up to find a snack. It's also important to **avoid multitasking**. Research has consistently shown that multitasking will make your studying dramatically less effective. Your study area should also be comfortable and well-lit so you don't have the distraction of straining your eyes or sitting on an uncomfortable chair.

The time of day you study is also important. You want to be rested and alert. Don't wait until just before bedtime. Study when you'll be most likely to comprehend and remember. Even better, if you know what time of day your test will be, set that time aside for study. That way your brain will be used to working on that subject at that specific time and you'll have a better chance of recalling information.

Finally, it can be helpful to team up with others who are studying for the same test. Your actual studying should be done in as isolated an environment as possible, but the work of organizing the information and setting up the study plan can be divided up. In between study sessions, you can discuss with your teammates the concepts that you're all studying and quiz each other on the details. Just be sure that your teammates are as serious about the test as you are. If you find that your study time is being replaced with social time, you might need to find a new team.

Copyright © Mometrix Media. You have been licensed one copy of this document for personal use only. Any other reproduction or redistribution is strictly prohibited. All rights reserved.

Secret Key #2 – Make Your Studying Count

You're devoting a lot of time and effort to preparing for this test, so you want to be absolutely certain it will pay off. This means doing more than just reading the content and hoping you can remember it on test day. It's important to make every minute of study count. There are two main areas you can focus on to make your studying count:

Retention

It doesn't matter how much time you study if you can't remember the material. You need to make sure you are retaining the concepts. To check your retention of the information you're learning, try recalling it at later times with minimal prompting. Try carrying around flashcards and glance at one or two from time to time or ask a friend who's also studying for the test to quiz you.

To enhance your retention, look for ways to put the information into practice so that you can apply it rather than simply recalling it. If you're using the information in practical ways, it will be much easier to remember. Similarly, it helps to solidify a concept in your mind if you're not only reading it to yourself but also explaining it to someone else. Ask a friend to let you teach them about a concept you're a little shaky on (or speak aloud to an imaginary audience if necessary). As you try to summarize, define, give examples, and answer your friend's questions, you'll understand the concepts better and they will stay with you longer. Finally, step back for a big picture view and ask yourself how each piece of information fits with the whole subject. When you link the different concepts together and see them working together as a whole, it's easier to remember the individual components.

Finally, practice showing your work on any multi-step problems, even if you're just studying. Writing out each step you take to solve a problem will help solidify the process in your mind, and you'll be more likely to remember it during the test.

Modality

Modality simply refers to the means or method by which you study. Choosing a study modality that fits your own individual learning style is crucial. No two people learn best in exactly the same way, so it's important to know your strengths and use them to your advantage.

For example, if you learn best by visualization, focus on visualizing a concept in your mind and draw an image or a diagram. Try color-coding your notes, illustrating them, or creating symbols that will trigger your mind to recall a learned concept. If you learn best by hearing or discussing information, find a study partner who learns the same way or read aloud to yourself. Think about how to put the information in your own words. Imagine that you are giving a lecture on the topic and record yourself so you can listen to it later.

For any learning style, flashcards can be helpful. Organize the information so you can take advantage of spare moments to review. Underline key words or phrases. Use different colors for different categories. Mnemonic devices (such as creating a short list in which every item starts with the same letter) can also help with retention. Find what works best for you and use it to store the information in your mind most effectively and easily.

Copyright © Mometrix Media. You have been licensed one copy of this document for personal use only. Any other reproduction or redistribution is strictly prohibited. All rights reserved.

Secret Key #3 – Practice the Right Way

Your success on test day depends not only on how many hours you put into preparing, but also on whether you prepared the right way. It's good to check along the way to see if your studying is paying off. One of the most effective ways to do this is by taking practice tests to evaluate your progress. Practice tests are useful because they show exactly where you need to improve. Every time you take a practice test, pay special attention to these three groups of questions:

- The questions you got wrong
- The questions you had to guess on, even if you guessed right
- The questions you found difficult or slow to work through

This will show you exactly what your weak areas are, and where you need to devote more study time. Ask yourself why each of these questions gave you trouble. Was it because you didn't understand the material? Was it because you didn't remember the vocabulary? Do you need more repetitions on this type of question to build speed and confidence? Dig into those questions and figure out how you can strengthen your weak areas as you go back to review the material.

Additionally, many practice tests have a section explaining the answer choices. It can be tempting to read the explanation and think that you now have a good understanding of the concept. However, an explanation likely only covers part of the question's broader context. Even if the explanation makes sense, **go back and investigate** every concept related to the question until you're positive you have a thorough understanding.

As you go along, keep in mind that the practice test is just that: practice. Memorizing these questions and answers will not be very helpful on the actual test because it is unlikely to have any of the same exact questions. If you only know the right answers to the sample questions, you won't be prepared for the real thing. **Study the concepts** until you understand them fully, and then you'll be able to answer any question that shows up on the test.

It's important to wait on the practice tests until you're ready. If you take a test on your first day of study, you may be overwhelmed by the amount of material covered and how much you need to learn. Work up to it gradually.

On test day, you'll need to be prepared for answering questions, managing your time, and using the test-taking strategies you've learned. It's a lot to balance, like a mental marathon that will have a big impact on your future. Like training for a marathon, you'll need to start slowly and work your way up. When test day arrives, you'll be ready.

Start with the strategies you've read in the first two Secret Keys—plan your course and study in the way that works best for you. If you have time, consider using multiple study resources to get different approaches to the same concepts. It can be helpful to see difficult concepts from more than one angle. Then find a good source for practice tests. Many times, the test website will suggest potential study resources or provide sample tests.

Copyright © Mometrix Media. You have been licensed one copy of this document for personal use only. Any other reproduction or redistribution is strictly prohibited. All rights reserved.

Practice Test Strategy

When you're ready to start taking practice tests, follow this strategy:

Untimed and Open-Book Practice

Take the first test with no time constraints and with your notes and study guide handy. Take your time and focus on applying the strategies you've learned.

Timed and Open-Book Practice

Take the second practice test open-book as well, but set a timer and practice pacing yourself to finish in time.

Timed and Closed-Book Practice

Take any other practice tests as if it were test day. Set a timer and put away your study materials. Sit at a table or desk in a quiet room, imagine yourself at the testing center, and answer questions as quickly and accurately as possible.

Keep repeating timed and closed-book tests on a regular basis until you run out of practice tests or it's time for the actual test. Your mind will be ready for the schedule and stress of test day, and you'll be able to focus on recalling the material you've learned.

Copyright © Mometrix Media. You have been licensed one copy of this document for personal use only. Any other reproduction or redistribution is strictly prohibited. All rights reserved.

Secret Key #4 – Pace Yourself

Once you're fully prepared for the material on the test, your biggest challenge on test day will be managing your time. Just knowing that the clock is ticking can make you panic even if you have plenty of time left. Work on pacing yourself so you can build confidence against the time constraints of the exam. Pacing is a difficult skill to master, especially in a high-pressure environment, so **practice is vital**.

Set time expectations for your pace based on how much time is available. For example, if a section has 60 questions and the time limit is 30 minutes, you know you have to average 30 seconds or less per question in order to answer them all. Although 30 seconds is the hard limit, set 25 seconds per question as your goal, so you reserve extra time to spend on harder questions. When you budget extra time for the harder questions, you no longer have any reason to stress when those questions take longer to answer.

Don't let this time expectation distract you from working through the test at a calm, steady pace, but keep it in mind so you don't spend too much time on any one question. Recognize that taking extra time on one question you don't understand may keep you from answering two that you do understand later in the test. If your time limit for a question is up and you're still not sure of the answer, mark it and move on, and come back to it later if the time and the test format allow. If the testing format doesn't allow you to return to earlier questions, just make an educated guess; then put it out of your mind and move on.

On the easier questions, be careful not to rush. It may seem wise to hurry through them so you have more time for the challenging ones, but it's not worth missing one if you know the concept and just didn't take the time to read the question fully. Work efficiently but make sure you understand the question and have looked at all of the answer choices, since more than one may seem right at first.

Even if you're paying attention to the time, you may find yourself a little behind at some point. You should speed up to get back on track, but do so wisely. Don't panic; just take a few seconds less on each question until you're caught up. Don't guess without thinking, but do look through the answer choices and eliminate any you know are wrong. If you can get down to two choices, it is often worthwhile to guess from those. Once you've chosen an answer, move on and don't dwell on any that you skipped or had to hurry through. If a question was taking too long, chances are it was one of the harder ones, so you weren't as likely to get it right anyway.

On the other hand, if you find yourself getting ahead of schedule, it may be beneficial to slow down a little. The more quickly you work, the more likely you are to make a careless mistake that will affect your score. You've budgeted time for each question, so don't be afraid to spend that time. Practice an efficient but careful pace to get the most out of the time you have.

Copyright © Mometrix Media. You have been licensed one copy of this document for personal use only. Any other reproduction or redistribution is strictly prohibited. All rights reserved.

Secret Key #5 – Have a Plan for Guessing

When you're taking the test, you may find yourself stuck on a question. Some of the answer choices seem better than others, but you don't see the one answer choice that is obviously correct. What do you do?

The scenario described above is very common, yet most test takers have not effectively prepared for it. Developing and practicing a plan for guessing may be one of the single most effective uses of your time as you get ready for the exam.

In developing your plan for guessing, there are three questions to address:

- When should you start the guessing process?
- How should you narrow down the choices?
- Which answer should you choose?

When to Start the Guessing Process

Unless your plan for guessing is to select C every time (which, despite its merits, is not what we recommend), you need to leave yourself enough time to apply your answer elimination strategies. Since you have a limited amount of time for each question, that means that if you're going to give yourself the best shot at guessing correctly, you have to decide quickly whether or not you will guess.

Of course, the best-case scenario is that you don't have to guess at all, so first, see if you can answer the question based on your knowledge of the subject and basic reasoning skills. Focus on the key words in the question and try to jog your memory of related topics. Give yourself a chance to bring the knowledge to mind, but once you realize that you don't have (or you can't access) the knowledge you need to answer the question, it's time to start the guessing process.

It's almost always better to start the guessing process too early than too late. It only takes a few seconds to remember something and answer the question from knowledge. Carefully eliminating wrong answer choices takes longer. Plus, going through the process of eliminating answer choices can actually help jog your memory.

Summary: Start the guessing process as soon as you decide that you can't answer the question based on your knowledge.

Copyright © Mometrix Media. You have been licensed one copy of this document for personal use only. Any other reproduction or redistribution is strictly prohibited. All rights reserved.

How to Narrow Down the Choices

The next chapter in this book (**Test-Taking Strategies**) includes a wide range of strategies for how to approach questions and how to look for answer choices to eliminate. You will definitely want to read those carefully, practice them, and figure out which ones work best for you. Here though, we're going to address a mindset rather than a particular strategy.

Your chances of guessing an answer correctly depend on how many options you are choosing from.

How many choices you have	How likely you are to guess correctly
5	20%
4	25%
3	33%
2	50%
1	100%

You can see from this chart just how valuable it is to be able to eliminate incorrect answers and make an educated guess, but there are two things that many test takers do that cause them to miss out on the benefits of guessing:

- Accidentally eliminating the correct answer
- Selecting an answer based on an impression

We'll look at the first one here, and the second one in the next section.

To avoid accidentally eliminating the correct answer, we recommend a thought exercise called **the $5 challenge**. In this challenge, you only eliminate an answer choice from contention if you are willing to bet $5 on it being wrong. Why $5? Five dollars is a small but not insignificant amount of money. It's an amount you could afford to lose but wouldn't want to throw away. And while losing $5 once might not hurt too much, doing it twenty times will set you back $100. In the same way, each small decision you make—eliminating a choice here, guessing on a question there—won't by itself impact your score very much, but when you put them all together, they can make a big difference. By holding each answer choice elimination decision to a higher standard, you can reduce the risk of accidentally eliminating the correct answer.

The $5 challenge can also be applied in a positive sense: If you are willing to bet $5 that an answer choice *is* correct, go ahead and mark it as correct.

Summary: Only eliminate an answer choice if you are willing to bet $5 that it is wrong.

Copyright © Mometrix Media. You have been licensed one copy of this document for personal use only. Any other reproduction or redistribution is strictly prohibited. All rights reserved.

Which Answer to Choose

You're taking the test. You've run into a hard question and decided you'll have to guess. You've eliminated all the answer choices you're willing to bet $5 on. Now you have to pick an answer. Why do we even need to talk about this? Why can't you just pick whichever one you feel like when the time comes?

The answer to these questions is that if you don't come into the test with a plan, you'll rely on your impression to select an answer choice, and if you do that, you risk falling into a trap. The test writers know that everyone who takes their test will be guessing on some of the questions, so they intentionally write wrong answer choices to seem plausible. You still have to pick an answer though, and if the wrong answer choices are designed to look right, how can you ever be sure that you're not falling for their trap? The best solution we've found to this dilemma is to take the decision out of your hands entirely. Here is the process we recommend:

Once you've eliminated any choices that you are confident (willing to bet $5) are wrong, select the first remaining choice as your answer.

Whether you choose to select the first remaining choice, the second, or the last, the important thing is that you use some preselected standard. Using this approach guarantees that you will not be enticed into selecting an answer choice that looks right, because you are not basing your decision on how the answer choices look.

This is not meant to make you question your knowledge. Instead, it is to help you recognize the difference between your knowledge and your impressions. There's a huge difference between thinking an answer is right because of what you know, and thinking an answer is right because it looks or sounds like it should be right.

Summary: To ensure that your selection is appropriately random, make a predetermined selection from among all answer choices you have not eliminated.

Copyright © Mometrix Media. You have been licensed one copy of this document for personal use only. Any other reproduction or redistribution is strictly prohibited. All rights reserved.

Test-Taking Strategies

This section contains a list of test-taking strategies that you may find helpful as you work through the test. By taking what you know and applying logical thought, you can maximize your chances of answering any question correctly!

It is very important to realize that every question is different and every person is different: no single strategy will work on every question, and no single strategy will work for every person. That's why we've included all of them here, so you can try them out and determine which ones work best for different types of questions and which ones work best for you.

Question Strategies

Read Carefully

Read the question and answer choices carefully. Don't miss the question because you misread the terms. You have plenty of time to read each question thoroughly and make sure you understand what is being asked. Yet a happy medium must be attained, so don't waste too much time. You must read carefully, but efficiently.

Contextual Clues

Look for contextual clues. If the question includes a word you are not familiar with, look at the immediate context for some indication of what the word might mean. Contextual clues can often give you all the information you need to decipher the meaning of an unfamiliar word. Even if you can't determine the meaning, you may be able to narrow down the possibilities enough to make a solid guess at the answer to the question.

Prefixes

If you're having trouble with a word in the question or answer choices, try dissecting it. Take advantage of every clue that the word might include. Prefixes and suffixes can be a huge help. Usually they allow you to determine a basic meaning. Pre- means before, post- means after, pro - is positive, de- is negative. From prefixes and suffixes, you can get an idea of the general meaning of the word and try to put it into context.

Hedge Words

Watch out for critical hedge words, such as *likely, may, can, sometimes, often, almost, mostly, usually, generally, rarely*, and *sometimes*. Question writers insert these hedge phrases to cover every possibility. Often an answer choice will be wrong simply because it leaves no room for exception. Be on guard for answer choices that have definitive words such as *exactly* and *always*.

Switchback Words

Stay alert for *switchbacks*. These are the words and phrases frequently used to alert you to shifts in thought. The most common switchback words are *but, although*, and *however*. Others include *nevertheless, on the other hand, even though, while, in spite of, despite, regardless of*. Switchback words are important to catch because they can change the direction of the question or an answer choice.

Copyright © Mometrix Media. You have been licensed one copy of this document for personal use only. Any other reproduction or redistribution is strictly prohibited. All rights reserved.

Face Value

When in doubt, use common sense. Accept the situation in the problem at face value. Don't read too much into it. These problems will not require you to make wild assumptions. If you have to go beyond creativity and warp time or space in order to have an answer choice fit the question, then you should move on and consider the other answer choices. These are normal problems rooted in reality. The applicable relationship or explanation may not be readily apparent, but it is there for you to figure out. Use your common sense to interpret anything that isn't clear.

Answer Choice Strategies

Answer Selection

The most thorough way to pick an answer choice is to identify and eliminate wrong answers until only one is left, then confirm it is the correct answer. Sometimes an answer choice may immediately seem right, but be careful. The test writers will usually put more than one reasonable answer choice on each question, so take a second to read all of them and make sure that the other choices are not equally obvious. As long as you have time left, it is better to read every answer choice than to pick the first one that looks right without checking the others.

Answer Choice Families

An answer choice family consists of two (in rare cases, three) answer choices that are very similar in construction and cannot all be true at the same time. If you see two answer choices that are direct opposites or parallels, one of them is usually the correct answer. For instance, if one answer choice says that quantity x increases and another either says that quantity x decreases (opposite) or says that quantity y increases (parallel), then those answer choices would fall into the same family. An answer choice that doesn't match the construction of the answer choice family is more likely to be incorrect. Most questions will not have answer choice families, but when they do appear, you should be prepared to recognize them.

Eliminate Answers

Eliminate answer choices as soon as you realize they are wrong, but make sure you consider all possibilities. If you are eliminating answer choices and realize that the last one you are left with is also wrong, don't panic. Start over and consider each choice again. There may be something you missed the first time that you will realize on the second pass.

Avoid Fact Traps

Don't be distracted by an answer choice that is factually true but doesn't answer the question. You are looking for the choice that answers the question. Stay focused on what the question is asking for so you don't accidentally pick an answer that is true but incorrect. Always go back to the question and make sure the answer choice you've selected actually answers the question and is not merely a true statement.

Extreme Statements

In general, you should avoid answers that put forth extreme actions as standard practice or proclaim controversial ideas as established fact. An answer choice that states the "process should be used in certain situations, if..." is much more likely to be correct than one that states the "process should be discontinued completely." The first is a calm rational statement and doesn't even make a

Copyright © Mometrix Media. You have been licensed one copy of this document for personal use only. Any other reproduction or redistribution is strictly prohibited. All rights reserved.

definitive, uncompromising stance, using a hedge word *if* to provide wiggle room, whereas the second choice is a radical idea and far more extreme.

Benchmark

As you read through the answer choices and you come across one that seems to answer the question well, mentally select that answer choice. This is not your final answer, but it's the one that will help you evaluate the other answer choices. The one that you selected is your benchmark or standard for judging each of the other answer choices. Every other answer choice must be compared to your benchmark. That choice is correct until proven otherwise by another answer choice beating it. If you find a better answer, then that one becomes your new benchmark. Once you've decided that no other choice answers the question as well as your benchmark, you have your final answer.

Predict the Answer

Before you even start looking at the answer choices, it is often best to try to predict the answer. When you come up with the answer on your own, it is easier to avoid distractions and traps because you will know exactly what to look for. The right answer choice is unlikely to be word-for-word what you came up with, but it should be a close match. Even if you are confident that you have the right answer, you should still take the time to read each option before moving on.

General Strategies

Tough Questions

If you are stumped on a problem or it appears too hard or too difficult, don't waste time. Move on! Remember though, if you can quickly check for obviously incorrect answer choices, your chances of guessing correctly are greatly improved. Before you completely give up, at least try to knock out a couple of possible answers. Eliminate what you can and then guess at the remaining answer choices before moving on.

Check Your Work

Since you will probably not know every term listed and the answer to every question, it is important that you get credit for the ones that you do know. Don't miss any questions through careless mistakes. If at all possible, try to take a second to look back over your answer selection and make sure you've selected the correct answer choice and haven't made a costly careless mistake (such as marking an answer choice that you didn't mean to mark). This quick double check should more than pay for itself in caught mistakes for the time it costs.

Pace Yourself

It's easy to be overwhelmed when you're looking at a page full of questions; your mind is confused and full of random thoughts, and the clock is ticking down faster than you would like. Calm down and maintain the pace that you have set for yourself. Especially as you get down to the last few minutes of the test, don't let the small numbers on the clock make you panic. As long as you are on track by monitoring your pace, you are guaranteed to have time for each question.

Copyright © Mometrix Media. You have been licensed one copy of this document for personal use only. Any other reproduction or redistribution is strictly prohibited. All rights reserved.

Don't Rush

It is very easy to make errors when you are in a hurry. Maintaining a fast pace in answering questions is pointless if it makes you miss questions that you would have gotten right otherwise. Test writers like to include distracting information and wrong answers that seem right. Taking a little extra time to avoid careless mistakes can make all the difference in your test score. Find a pace that allows you to be confident in the answers that you select.

Keep Moving

Panicking will not help you pass the test, so do your best to stay calm and keep moving. Taking deep breaths and going through the answer elimination steps you practiced can help to break through a stress barrier and keep your pace.

Final Notes

The combination of a solid foundation of content knowledge and the confidence that comes from practicing your plan for applying that knowledge is the key to maximizing your performance on test day. As your foundation of content knowledge is built up and strengthened, you'll find that the strategies included in this chapter become more and more effective in helping you quickly sift through the distractions and traps of the test to isolate the correct answer.

Now it's time to move on to the test content chapters of this book, but be sure to keep your goal in mind. As you read, think about how you will be able to apply this information on the test. If you've already seen sample questions for the test and you have an idea of the question format and style, try to come up with questions of your own that you can answer based on what you're reading. This will give you valuable practice applying your knowledge in the same ways you can expect to on test day.

Good luck and good studying!

Copyright © Mometrix Media. You have been licensed one copy of this document for personal use only. Any other reproduction or redistribution is strictly prohibited. All rights reserved.

Copyright © Mometrix Media. You have been licensed one copy of this document for personal use only. Any other reproduction or redistribution is strictly prohibited. All rights reserved.

English Language Arts

Literacy

Literacy is commonly understood to refer to the *ability to read and write*. UNESCO has further defined literacy as the "ability to identify, understand, interpret, create, communicate, compute, and use printed and written materials associated with varying contexts." Under the UNESCO definition, understanding cultural, political, and historical contexts of communities falls under the definition of literacy. While **reading literacy** may be gauged simply by the ability to read a newspaper, **writing literacy** includes spelling, grammar, and sentence structure. To be literate in a foreign language, one would also need to have the ability to understand a language by listening and to speak the language. Some argue that visual representation and numeracy should be included in the requirements one must meet to be considered literate. Computer literacy refers to one's ability to utilize the basic functions of computers and other technologies. Subsets of reading literacy include phonological awareness, decoding, comprehension, and vocabulary.

Phonological Awareness

A subskill of literacy, **phonological awareness** is the ability to perceive sound structures in a spoken word, such as syllables and the individual phonemes within syllables. **Phonemes** are the sounds represented by the letters in the alphabet. The ability to separate, blend, and manipulate sounds is critical to developing reading and spelling skills. Phonological awareness is concerned with not only syllables, but also **onset sounds** (the sounds at the beginning of words) and **rime** (the same thing as rhyme, but spelled differently to distinguish syllable rime from poetic rhyme). Phonological awareness is an auditory skill that does not necessarily involve print. It should be developed before the student has learned letter to sound correspondences. A student's phonological awareness is an indicator of future reading success.

Activities That Teach Phonological Awareness

Classroom activities that teach **phonological awareness** include language play and exposure to a variety of sounds and contexts of sounds. Activities that teach phonological awareness include:

- Clapping to the sounds of individual words, names, or all words in a sentence
- Practicing saying blended phonemes
- Singing songs that involve phoneme replacement (e.g., The Name Game)
- Reading poems, songs, and nursery rhymes out loud
- Reading patterned and predictable texts out loud
- Listening to environmental sounds or following verbal directions
- Playing games with rhyming chants or fingerplays
- Reading alliterative texts out loud
- Grouping objects by beginning sounds
- Reordering words in a well-known sentence or making silly phrases by deleting words from a well-known sentence (perhaps from a favorite storybook)

Alphabetic Principle and Alphabet Writing Systems

The **alphabetic principle** refers to the use of letters and combinations of letters to represent speech sounds. The way letters are combined and pronounced is guided by a system of rules that establishes relationships between written and spoken words and their letter symbols. Alphabet

Copyright © Mometrix Media. You have been licensed one copy of this document for personal use only. Any other reproduction or redistribution is strictly prohibited. All rights reserved.

writing systems are common around the world. Some are **phonological** in that each letter stands for an individual sound and words are spelled just as they sound. However, there are other writing systems as well, such as the Chinese **logographic** system and the Japanese **syllabic** system.

Development of Language Skills

Children learn language through interacting with others, by experiencing language in daily and relevant context, and through understanding that speaking and listening are necessary for effective communication. Teachers can promote **language development** by intensifying the opportunities a child has to experience and understand language.

Teachers can assist language development by:

- Modeling enriched vocabulary and teaching new words
- Using questions and examples to extend a child's descriptive language skills
- Providing ample response time to encourage children to practice speech
- Asking for clarification to provide students with the opportunity to develop communication skills
- Promoting conversations among children
- Providing feedback to let children know they have been heard and understood, and providing further explanation when needed

Relationship Between Oral and Written Language Development

Oral and written language develops simultaneously. The acquisition of skills in one area supports the acquisition of skills in the other. However, oral language is not a prerequisite to written language. An immature form of oral language development is babbling, and an immature form of written language development is scribbling. **Oral language development** does not occur naturally, but does occur in a social context. This means it is best to include children in conversations rather than simply talk at them. **Written language development** can occur without direct instruction. In fact, reading and writing do not necessarily need to be taught through formal lessons if the child is exposed to a print-rich environment. A teacher can assist a child's language development by building on what the child already knows, discussing relevant and meaningful events and experiences, teaching vocabulary and literacy skills, and providing opportunities to acquire more complex language.

Print-Rich Environment

A teacher can provide a **print-rich environment** in the classroom in a number of ways. These include:

- **Displaying** the following in the classroom:
  - Children's names in print or cursive
  - Children's written work
  - Newspapers and magazines
  - Instructional charts
  - Written schedules
  - Signs and labels
  - Printed songs, poems, and rhymes
- Using **graphic organizers** such as KWL charts or story road maps to:
  - Remind students about what was read and discussed

Copyright © Mometrix Media. You have been licensed one copy of this document for personal use only. Any other reproduction or redistribution is strictly prohibited. All rights reserved.

    - Expand on the lesson topic or theme
    - Show the relationships among books, ideas, and words
- Using **big books** to:
    - Point out features of print, such as specific letters and punctuation
    - Track print from right to left
    - Emphasize the concept of words and the fact that they are used to communicate

Benefits of Print and Book Awareness

Print and book awareness helps a child understand:

- That there is a **connection** between print and messages contained on signs, labels, and other print forms in the child's environment
- That reading and writing are ways to obtain information and communicate ideas
- That **print** runs from left to right and from top to bottom
- That a book has **parts**, such as a title, a cover, a title page, and a table of contents
- That a book has an **author** and contains a **story**
- That **illustrations** can carry meaning
- That **letters and words** are different
- That **words and sentences** are separated by spaces and punctuation
- That different **text forms** are used for different functions
- That print represents **spoken language**
- How to **hold** a book.

Facts Children Should Know About Letters

To be appropriately prepared to learn to read and write, a child should learn:

- That each letter is **distinct** in appearance
- What **direction and shape** must be used to make each letter
- That each letter has a **name**, which can be associated with the shape of a letter
- That there are **26** letters in the English alphabet, and letters are grouped in a certain order
- That letters represent **sounds of speech**
- That **words** are composed of letters and have meaning
- That one must be able to **correspond** letters and sounds to read

Decoding

Decoding is the method or strategy used to make sense of printed words and figure out how to correctly pronounce them. In order to decode, a student needs to know the relationships between letters and sounds, including letter patterns; that words are constructed from phonemes and phoneme blends; and that a printed word represents a word that can be spoken. This knowledge will help the student recognize familiar words and make informed guesses about the pronunciation of unfamiliar words. Decoding is not the same as **comprehension**. It does not require an understanding of the meaning of a word, only a knowledge of how to recognize and pronounce it. Decoding can also refer to the skills a student uses to determine the meaning of a **sentence**. These skills include applying knowledge of vocabulary, sentence structure, and context.

Copyright © Mometrix Media. You have been licensed one copy of this document for personal use only. Any other reproduction or redistribution is strictly prohibited. All rights reserved.

Teaching of Reading Through Phonics

Phonics is the process of learning to read by learning how spoken language is represented by letters. Students learn to read phonetically by sounding out the **phonemes** in words and then blending them together to produce the correct sounds in words. In other words, the student connects speech sounds with letters or groups of letters and blends the sounds together to determine the pronunciation of an unknown word. Phonics is a commonly used method to teach **decoding and reading**, but has been challenged by other methods, such as the whole language approach. Despite the complexity of pronunciation and combined sounds in the English language, research shows that phonics is a highly effective way to teach reading. Being able to read or pronounce a word does not mean the student comprehends the meaning of the word, but context aids comprehension. When phonics is used as a foundation for decoding, children eventually learn to recognize words automatically and advance to decoding multisyllable words with practice.

Role of Fluency in Literacy Development

Fluency is the goal of literacy development. It is the ability to read accurately and quickly. Evidence of fluency includes the ability to recognize words automatically and group words for comprehension. At this point, the student no longer needs to decode words except for complex, unfamiliar ones. He or she is able to move to the next level and understand the **meaning** of a text. The student should be able to self-check for comprehension and should feel comfortable expressing ideas in writing. Teachers can help students build fluency by continuing to provide: reading experiences and discussions about text, gradually increasing the level of difficulty; reading practice, both silently and out loud; word analysis practice; instruction on reading comprehension strategies; and opportunities to express responses to readings through writing.

Role of Vocabulary in Literacy Development

When students do not know the meaning of words in a text, their comprehension is limited. As a result, the text becomes boring or confusing. The larger a student's **vocabulary** is, the better their reading comprehension will be. A larger vocabulary is also associated with an enhanced ability to **communicate** in speech and writing. It is the teacher's role to help students develop a good working vocabulary. Students learn most of the words they use and understand from listening to the world around them (adults, other students, media, etc.) They also learn from their reading experiences, which include being read to and reading independently. Carefully designed activities can also stimulate vocabulary growth, and should emphasize useful words that students see frequently, important words necessary for understanding text, and difficult words such as idioms or words with more than one meaning.

Teaching Techniques Promoting Vocabulary Development

A student's **vocabulary** can be developed by:

- Calling upon a student's **prior knowledge** and making comparisons to that knowledge
- **Defining** a word and providing multiple examples of the use of the word in context
- Showing a student how to use **context clues** to discover the meaning of a word
- Providing instruction on **prefixes, roots, and suffixes** to help students break a word into its parts and decipher its meaning
- Showing students how to use a **dictionary and a thesaurus**
- Asking students to **practice** new vocabulary by using the words in their own writing

Copyright © Mometrix Media. You have been licensed one copy of this document for personal use only. Any other reproduction or redistribution is strictly prohibited. All rights reserved.

- Providing a **print-rich environment** with a word wall
- Studying a group of words related to a **single subject**, such as farm words, transportation words, etc. so that concept development is enhanced.

Affixes, Prefixes, and Root Words

Affixes are syllables attached to the beginning or end of a word to make a derivative or inflectional form of a word. Both prefixes and suffixes are affixes. A **prefix** is a syllable that appears at the beginning of a word that, in combination with the root or base word, creates a specific meaning. For example, the prefix "mis" means "wrong." When combined with the root word "spelling," the word "misspelling" is created, which means the "wrong spelling." A **root word** is the base of a word to which affixes can be added. For example, the prefix "in" or "pre" can be added to the root word "vent" to create "invent" or "prevent," respectively. The suffix "er" can be added to the root word "work" to create "worker," which means "one who works." The suffix "able," meaning "capable of," can be added to "work" to create "workable," which means "capable of working."

Suffixes

A suffix is a syllable that appears at the end of a word that, in combination with the root or base word, creates a specific meaning. There are three types of suffixes:

- **Noun suffixes** – There are two types of noun suffixes. One denotes the act of, state of, or quality of. For example, "-ment" added to "argue" becomes "argument," which is defined as "the act of arguing." The other denotes the doer, or one who acts. For example, "-eer" added to "auction" becomes "auctioneer," meaning "one who auctions." Other examples include "-hood," "-ness," "-tion," "-ship," and "-ism."
- **Verb suffixes** – These denote "to make" or "to perform the act of." For example, "-en" added to "soft" makes "soften," which means "to make soft." Other verb suffixes are "-ate" (perpetuate), "-fy" (dignify), and "-ize" (sterilize).
- **Adjectival suffixes** – These include suffixes such as "-ful," which means "full of." When added to "care," the word "careful" is formed, which means "full of care." Other examples are "-ish," "-less," and "-able."

Strategies to Improve Reading Comprehension

Teachers can model in a read-aloud the strategies students can use on their own to better comprehend a text. First, the teacher should do a walk-through of the story **illustrations** and ask, "What's happening here?" Based on what they have seen, the teacher should then ask students to **predict** what the story will be about. As the book is read, the teacher should ask open-ended questions such as, "Why do you think the character did this?" and "How do you think the character feels?" The teacher should also ask students if they can **relate** to the story or have background knowledge of something similar. After the reading, the teacher should ask the students to **retell** the story in their own words to check for comprehension. This retelling can take the form of a puppet show or summarizing the story to a partner.

Role of Prior Knowledge in Determining Appropriate Literacy Education

Even preschool children have some literacy skills, and the extent and type of these skills have implications for instructional approaches. Comprehension results from relating two or more pieces of information. One piece comes from the text, and another piece might come from **prior knowledge** (something from a student's long-term memory). For a child, that prior knowledge comes from being read to at home; taking part in other literacy experiences, such as playing

Copyright © Mometrix Media. You have been licensed one copy of this document for personal use only. Any other reproduction or redistribution is strictly prohibited. All rights reserved.

computer or word games; being exposed to a print-rich environment at home; and observing examples of parents' reading habits. Children who have had **extensive literacy experience** are better prepared to further develop their literacy skills in school than children who have not been read to, have few books or magazines in their homes, are seldom exposed to high-level oral or written language activities, and seldom witness adults engaged in reading and writing. Children with a scant literacy background are at a disadvantage. The teacher must not make any assumptions about their prior knowledge, and should use intense, targeted instruction. Otherwise, reading comprehension will be limited.

Using Puppetry in the Classroom

Using puppets in the classroom puts students at ease and allows them to enjoy a learning experience as if it were play. The purpose of using puppetry is to generate ideas, encourage imagination, and foster language development. Using a puppet helps a child "become" the character and therefore experience a different **outlook**. **Language development** is enhanced through the student interpreting a story that has been read in class and practicing new words from that story in the puppet show. Children will also have the opportunity to practice using descriptive adjectives for the characters and the scene, which will help them learn the function of adjectives. **Descriptive adjectives and verbs** can also be learned by practicing facial expressions and movements with puppets. The teacher can model happy, sad, eating, sleeping, and similar words with a puppet, and then ask students to do the same with their puppets. This is an especially effective vocabulary activity for ESL children.

Using Drama or Story Theater in the Classroom

Drama activities are fun learning experiences that capture a child's attention, engage the imagination, and motivate vocabulary expansion. For example, after reading a story, the teacher could ask children to act it out as the teacher repeats the story. This activity, which works best with very young learners, will help children work on listening skills and their ability to pretend. The best stories to use for this passive improvisation are ones that have lots of simple actions that children will be able to understand and perform easily. Older children can create their own improvisational skits and possibly write scripts. **Visualization** also calls upon the imagination and encourages concentration and bodily awareness. Children can be given a prompt for the visualization and then asked to draw what they see in their mind's eye. **Charades** is another way to act out words and improve vocabulary skills. This activity can be especially helpful to encourage ESL students to express thoughts and ideas in English. These students should be given easier words to act out to promote confidence.

Classroom Practices Benefiting Second Language Acquisition

Since some students may have limited understanding of English, a teacher should employ the following practices to promote second language acquisition:

- Make all instruction as **understandable** as possible and use simple and repeated terms.
- Relate instruction to the **cultures** of ESL children.
- Increase **interactive activities** and use gestures or non-verbal actions when modeling.
- Provide language and literacy development instruction in **all curriculum areas**.
- Establish **consistent routines** that help children connect words and events.
- Use a **schedule** so children know what will happen next and will not feel lost.
- Integrate ESL children into **group activities** with non-ESL children.
- Appoint bilingual students to act as **student translators**.

Copyright © Mometrix Media. You have been licensed one copy of this document for personal use only. Any other reproduction or redistribution is strictly prohibited. All rights reserved.

- Explain actions as activities happen so that a **word to action relationship** is established.
- Initiate opportunities for ESL children to **experiment** with and practice new language.
- Employ multisensory learning.

Theories of Language Development

Four theories of language development are:

- **Learning approach** – This theory assumes that language is first learned by imitating the speech of adults. It is then solidified in school through drills about the rules of language structures.
- **Linguistic approach** – Championed by Noam Chomsky in the 1950s, this theory proposes that the ability to use a language is innate. This is a biological approach rather than one based on cognition or social patterning.
- **Cognitive approach** – Developed in the 1970s and based on the work of Piaget, this theory states that children must develop appropriate cognitive skills before they can acquire language.
- **Sociocognitive approach** – In the 1970s, some researchers proposed that language development is a complex interaction of linguistic, social, and cognitive influences. This theory best explains the lack of language skills among children who are neglected, have uneducated parents, or lives in poverty.

Teaching Strategies to Promote Listening Skills of ESL Students

Listening is a critical skill when learning a new language. Students spend a great deal more time listening than they do speaking, and far less time reading and writing than speaking. Two ways to encourage ESL students to listen are to:

- Talk about topics that are of **interest** to the ESL learner. Otherwise, students may tune out the speaker because they don't want to put in that much effort to learn about a topic they find boring.
- Talk about content or give examples that are **easy** to understand or are **related** to a topic that is familiar to ESL students. Culturally relevant materials will be more interesting to ESL students, will make them feel more comfortable, and will contain vocabulary that they may already be familiar with.

Considerations Relevant to ESL Students Related to Learning by Listening

Listening is not a passive skill, but an **active** one. Therefore, a teacher needs to make the listening experience as rewarding as possible and provide as many auditory and visual clues as possible. Three ways that the teacher can make the listening experience rewarding for ESL students are:

- Avoid **colloquialisms** and **abbreviated or slang terms** that may be confusing to the ESL listener, unless there is enough time to define them and explain their use.
- Make the spoken English understandable by stopping to **clarify** points, **repeating** new or difficult words, and **defining** words that may not be known.
- Support the spoken word with as many **visuals** as possible. Pictures, diagrams, gestures, facial expressions, and body language can help the ESL learner correctly interpret the spoken language more easily and also leaves an image impression that helps them remember the words.

Copyright © Mometrix Media. You have been licensed one copy of this document for personal use only. Any other reproduction or redistribution is strictly prohibited. All rights reserved.

Top-Down and Bottom-Up Processing

ESL students need to be given opportunities to practice both top-down and bottom-up processing. If they are old enough to understand these concepts, they should be made aware that these are two processes that affect their listening comprehension. In **top-down processing**, the listener refers to **background and global knowledge** to figure out the meaning of a message. For example, when asking an ESL student to perform a task, the steps of the task should be explained and accompanied by a review of the vocabulary terms the student already understands so that the student feels comfortable tackling new steps and new words. The teacher should also allow students to ask questions to verify comprehension. In **bottom-up processing**, the listener figures out the meaning of a message by using "**data**" obtained from what is said. This data includes sounds (stress, rhythm, and intonation), words, and grammatical relationships. All data can be used to make conclusions or interpretations. For example, the listener can develop bottom-up skills by learning how to detect differences in intonation between statements and questions.

Listening Lessons

All students, but especially ESL students, can be taught **listening** through specific training. During listening lessons, the teacher should guide students through three steps:

- **Pre-listening activity** – This establishes the purpose of the lesson and engages students' background knowledge. This activity should ask students to think about and discuss something they already know about the topic. Alternatively, the teacher can provide background information.
- **The listening activity** – This requires the listener to obtain information and then immediately do something with that information. For example, the teacher can review the schedule for the day or the week. The students are being given information about a routine they already know, but need to be able to identify names, tasks, and times.
- **Post-listening activity** – This is an evaluation process that allows students to judge how well they did with the listening task. Other language skills can be included in the activity. For example, this activity could involve asking questions about who will do what according to the classroom schedule (Who is the lunch monitor today?) and could also involve asking students to produce whole sentence replies.

Helping ESL Students Understand Subject Matter

Speaking

To help ESL students better understand subject matter, the following teaching strategies using spoken English can be used:

- **Read aloud** from a textbook, and then ask ESL students to **verbally summarize** what was read. The teacher should assist by providing new words as needed to give students the opportunity to practice vocabulary and speaking skills. The teacher should then read the passage again to students to verify accuracy and details.
- The teacher could ask ESL students to explain why the subject matter is important to them and where they see it fitting into their lives. This verbalization gives them speaking practice and helps them relate to the subject.
- Whenever small group activities are being conducted, ESL students can be placed with **English-speaking students**. It is best to keep the groups to two or three students so that the ESL student will be motivated by the need to be involved. English-speaking students should be encouraged to include ESL students in the group work.

Copyright © Mometrix Media. You have been licensed one copy of this document for personal use only. Any other reproduction or redistribution is strictly prohibited. All rights reserved.

Reading

There are supplemental printed materials that can be used to help ESL students understand subject matter. The following strategies can be used to help ESL students develop English reading skills.

- Make sure all ESL students have a **bilingual dictionary** to use. A thesaurus would also be helpful.
- Try to keep **content area books** written in the ESL students' native languages in the classroom. Students can use them side-by-side with English texts. Textbooks in other languages can be ordered from the school library or obtained from the classroom textbook publisher.
- If a student lacks confidence in his/her ability to read the textbook, the teacher can read a passage to the student and have him or her **verbally summarize** the passage. The teacher should take notes on what the student says and then read them back. These notes can be a substitute, short-form, in-their-own-words textbook that the student can understand.

General Teaching Strategies to Help ESL Students

Some strategies can help students develop more than one important skill. They may involve a combination of speaking, listening, and/or viewing. Others are mainly classroom management aids. General teaching strategies for ESL students include:

- **Partner** English-speaking students with ESL students as study buddies and ask the English-speaking students to share notes.
- Encourage ESL students to ask **questions** whenever they don't understand something. They should be aware that they don't have to be able to interpret every word of text to understand the concept.
- Dictate **key sentences** related to the content area being taught and ask ESL students to write them down. This gives them practice in listening and writing, and also helps them identify what is important.
- **Alternate** difficult and easy tasks so that ESL students can experience academic success.
- Ask ESL students to **label** objects associated with content areas, such as maps, diagrams, parts of a leaf, or parts of a sentence. This gives students writing and reading experience and helps them remember key vocabulary.

Impact of Reading Skills on Student Success

The ability to read is not simply one academic area; it is a basic skill set underlying all academic activity and determines whether students fail or succeed in school. Research shows that of first-graders with poor **reading skills**, 88% still read poorly in fourth grade. By this time, most information that students require is provided in text form. For this reason, the focus shifts from *learning to read* in the earlier grades, to *reading to learn* by fourth grade. Consequently, students with poor reading skills can find it harder to access and interact with the content in their schools' curricula. Moreover, reading abilities that are delayed or disordered usually are identified in higher elementary grades. Yet research finds remediation attempts then could be too late, because children acquire language and have literacy experiences from birth. Phonemic awareness, the alphabetic principle, and print awareness normally develop in early childhood. Children missing such early experiences will fall behind peers without extra instruction. This means elementary school teachers must give these children **literacy-rich environments**.

Copyright © Mometrix Media. You have been licensed one copy of this document for personal use only. Any other reproduction or redistribution is strictly prohibited. All rights reserved.

Reading Comprehension

The whole point of reading is to **comprehend** what someone else is trying to say through writing. Without comprehension, a student is just reading the words without understanding them or increasing knowledge of a topic. Comprehension results when the student has the vocabulary and reading skills necessary to make sense of the **whole picture**, not just individual words. Students can self-monitor because they know when they are comprehending the material and when they are not. Teachers can help students solve problems with comprehension by teaching them strategies such as pre-reading titles, sidebars, and follow-up questions; looking at illustrations; predicting what's going to happen in the story; asking questions to check understanding while reading; connecting to background knowledge; and relating to the experiences or feelings of the characters.

Review Video: Predicting What Will Happen in a Story
Visit mometrix.com/academy and enter code: 288778

Review Video: Predictions
Visit mometrix.com/academy and enter code: 437248

Review Video: Reading Comprehension Tips
Visit mometrix.com/academy and enter code: 280215

Skills Needed to Develop Literacy

According to studies by the National Reading Panel, for children to develop **literacy**, they must have developed skills in phonemic awareness, phonics, vocabulary, comprehension, and fluency. A prerequisite to developing these five skill areas is having an understanding of how literacy works, what it does, and how it is used. While young children exposed to spoken and printed language interactions from birth often develop this understanding of the functions and applications of literacy in a natural way, children with language and learning disabilities may not. A **literacy-rich environment** is defined as one that provides students having disabilities with stimulation to take part in activities involving language and literacy during their everyday life routines. Stimulating such participation in and integration of language and literacy into daily living is an effective way to help disabled students begin to develop understanding of how spoken and printed language function and are used. Teaching strategies to establish literacy-rich environments can not only remediate language and literacy deficits, but also benefit all elementary-level students.

Literacy-Rich Environment in Elementary School Classrooms

An elementary classroom constituting a **literacy-rich setting** would engage all students in various literacy activities, some working individually and others in groups. Students would explore different *genres* of books, not only during reading periods or in the library, but during math, social studies, and science periods or lessons. The teacher might read aloud to students from a book about math during math period, and lead class discussions of the book's content, and have students explore eyewitness science books during science time to learn about scientific concepts. These activities help students experience literacy across all curriculum subject content areas. Students also use books on tapes and CD-ROMs. The classroom includes adapted materials to motivate disabled students to read and help them interact with text. Students write in notebooks and journals, write reports in all subjects, and compose books. A literacy-rich classroom environment features *information resources* for students including dictionaries, encyclopedias, books in varied genres, word walls, and computers, as well as teachers and peers.

Copyright © Mometrix Media. You have been licensed one copy of this document for personal use only. Any other reproduction or redistribution is strictly prohibited. All rights reserved.

Vocabulary Instruction

There are a number of factors to consider when developing **vocabulary**, academic language, and background knowledge. To begin with, not all words should be given equal emphasis. Some words occur much more frequently and should therefore be of greater importance in instruction. This is yet another reason why the context of vocabulary and academic language is so important. It is a bad idea to find a list of difficult words and proceed through it alphabetically, because the students will have very little context for the words they are learning. Instead, teachers should approach vocabulary *thematically*. For instance, a teacher might spend one week teaching vocabulary words related to government, and the next teaching words related to legislation. It is a good idea to link new vocabulary to the lesson being covered in other content areas. The most important thing is to ensure that students have a context for new words, so that they will be able to incorporate them in their speaking and writing as soon as possible.

Word Analysis

Semantic and Syntactic Approaches

Word analysis instruction should be balanced and comprehensive. It is a good idea to let students approach unfamiliar words from both the semantic and syntactic perspectives. A **semantic approach** emphasizes the meaning of words. A child is using the semantic approach when he thinks about context and about what type of word would make sense in a given sentence. A teacher can guide the student towards an appreciation of semantics by asking questions about the meaning of the sentence and the likely meaning of an unfamiliar word. The **syntactic approach**, on the other hand, emphasizes the order of the words in a sentence. English has fairly regular syntax, so the reader can often predict what type of word (e.g., noun, verb) will appear next in a sentence. A teacher can stimulate students to think about syntax by asking the student to read a sentence and determine whether it makes sense. A teacher can ask the student whether the words in a sentence appear to be in the right order.

Differentiation of Word Analysis Instruction

Word analysis can be a challenge for many students, and so there is likely to be a great range of performance in the same class. Teachers must be able to address the strong and weak students in the class. In particular, teachers need to provide differentiated instruction for students who are struggling or have reading difficulties or disabilities. For instance, a teacher needs to be able to go back and focus on key skills and knowledge, like syllable patterns and morphemes that occur frequently. Some students need to have the same material approached from different perspectives before they fully master it. The teacher should be able to outline a number of real-world examples for an abstract concept. The use of songs and poems to illustrate syllabification is one helpful way to bring struggling students up to speed. Finally, a teacher should be able to provide differentiated practice situations for the skills that have been taught.

Review Video: Defining a Word
Visit mometrix.com/academy and enter code: 648080

Review Video: Denotation and Connotation
Visit mometrix.com/academy and enter code: 310092

Copyright © Mometrix Media. You have been licensed one copy of this document for personal use only. Any other reproduction or redistribution is strictly prohibited. All rights reserved.

Literal and Critical Comprehension

Literal comprehension refers to the skills a reader uses to deal with the actual words in a text. It involves skills such as identifying the topic sentence, main idea, important facts, and supporting details; using context clues to determine the meaning of a word; and sequencing events.

Critical comprehension involves prior knowledge and an understanding that written material, especially in nonfiction, is the author's version of the subject and not necessarily anybody else's. Critical comprehension involves analysis of meaning, evaluation, validation, questioning, and the reasoning skills a reader uses to recognize:

- Inferences and conclusions
- Purpose, tone, point of view, and themes
- The organizational pattern of a work
- Explicit and implicit relationships among words, phrases, and sentences
- Biased language, persuasive tactics, valid arguments, and the difference between fact and opinion

Review Video: Author's Main Point or Purpose
Visit mometrix.com/academy and enter code: 734339

Review Video: Author's Position
Visit mometrix.com/academy and enter code: 827954

Review Video: Inference
Visit mometrix.com/academy and enter code: 379203

Metacognition

Metacognition is thinking about thinking. For the student, this involves taking control of their own learning process, self-monitoring progress, evaluating the effectiveness of strategies, and making adjustments to strategies and learning behaviors as needed. Students who develop good metacognitive skills become more independent and confident about learning. They develop a sense of ownership about their education and realize that information is readily available to them.

Metacognitive skills can be grouped into three categories:

- **Awareness** – This involves identifying prior knowledge; defining learning goals; inventorying resources such as textbooks, libraries, computers, and study time; identifying task requirements and evaluation standards; and recognizing motivation and anxiety levels.
- **Planning** – This involves doing time estimates for tasks, prioritizing, scheduling study time, making checklists of tasks, gathering needed materials, and choosing strategies for problem solving or task comprehension.
- **Self-monitoring and reflection** – This involves identifying which strategies or techniques work best, questioning throughout the process, considering feedback, and maintaining focus and motivation.

Role of Metacognitive Skills in Literacy Development

In terms of literacy development, **metacognitive skills** include taking an active role in reading, recognizing reading behaviors and changing them to employ the behaviors that are most effective, relating information to prior knowledge, and being aware of text structures. For example, if there is

Copyright © Mometrix Media. You have been licensed one copy of this document for personal use only. Any other reproduction or redistribution is strictly prohibited. All rights reserved.

a problem with comprehension, the student can try to form a mental image of what is described, read the text again, adjust the rate of reading, or employ other reading strategies such as identifying unknown vocabulary and predicting meaning. Being aware of **text structures** is critical to being able to follow the author's ideas and relationships among ideas. Being aware of difficulties with text structure allows the student to employ strategies such as hierarchical summaries, thematic organizers, or concept maps to remedy the problem.

Critical Thinking Tools

It is important to teach students to use critical thinking skills when reading. Three of the **critical thinking tools** that engage the reader are:

- **Summarization** – The student reviews the main point(s) of the reading selection and identifies important details. For nonfiction, a good summary will briefly describe the main arguments and the examples that support those arguments. For fiction, a good summary will identify the main characters and events of the story.
- **Question generation** – A good reader will constantly ask questions while reading about comprehension, vocabulary, connections to personal knowledge or experience, predictions, etc.
- **Textual marking** – This skill engages the reader by having him or her interact with the text. The student should mark the text with questions or comments that are generated by the text using underlining, highlighting, or shorthand marks such as "?," "!," and "*" that indicate lack of understanding, importance, or key points, for example.

Context Clues

Context clues are words or phrases that help the reader figure out the meaning of an unknown word. They are built into a sentence or paragraph by the writer to help the reader develop a clear understanding of the writer's message. Context clues can be used to make **intelligent guesses** about the meaning of a word instead of relying on a dictionary. Context clues are the reason most vocabulary is learned through reading. There are four types of commonly used context clues:

- **Synonyms** – A word with the same meaning as the unknown word is placed close by for comparison.
- **Antonyms** – A word with the opposite meaning as the unknown word is placed close by for contrast.
- **Explanations** – An obvious explanation is given close to the unknown word.
- **Examples** – Examples of what the word means are given to help the reader define the term.

Review Video: Synonyms and Antonyms
Visit mometrix.com/academy and enter code: 105612

Review Video: Multiple Meaning Words
Visit mometrix.com/academy and enter code: 371666

Topic Sentence

The **topic sentence** of a paragraph states the paragraph's subject. It presents the **main idea**. The rest of the paragraph should be related to the topic sentence, which should be explained and supported with facts, details, proofs, and examples. The topic sentence is more general than the **body sentences**, and should cover all the ideas in the body of the paragraph. It may contain words

Copyright © Mometrix Media. You have been licensed one copy of this document for personal use only. Any other reproduction or redistribution is strictly prohibited. All rights reserved.

such as "many," "most," or "several." The topic sentence is usually the first sentence in a paragraph, but it can appear after an introductory or background sentence, can be the last sentence in a paragraph, or may simply be implied, meaning a topic sentence is not present. **Supporting sentences** can often be identified by their use of transition terms such as "for example" or "that is." Supporting sentences may also be presented in numbered sequence. The topic sentence provides **unity** to a paragraph because it ties together the supporting details into a coherent whole.

> **Review Video: Topics and Main Ideas**
> Visit mometrix.com/academy and enter code: 407801
>
> **Review Video: Supporting Details**
> Visit mometrix.com/academy and enter code: 396297

Theme

Theme is the central idea of a work. It is the thread that ties all the elements of a story together and gives them purpose. The theme is not the subject of a work, but what a work says about a subject. A theme must be **universal**, which means it must apply to everyone, not just the characters in a story. Therefore, a theme is a comment about the nature of humanity, society, the relationship of humankind to the world, or moral responsibility. There may be more than one theme in a work, and the determination of the theme is affected by the viewpoint of the reader. Therefore, there is not always necessarily a definite, irrefutable theme. The theme can be implied or stated directly.

> **Review Video: Theme**
> Visit mometrix.com/academy and enter code: 732074

Types of Definition Paragraphs or Essays

A **definition paragraph** or essay describes what a word or term means. There are three ways the explanation can be presented:

- **Definition by synonym** – The term is defined by comparing it to a more familiar term that the reader can more easily understand (A phantom is a ghost or spirit that appears and disappears mysteriously and creates dread).
- **Definition by class** – Most commonly used in exams, papers, and reports, the class definition first puts the term in a larger category or class (The Hereford is a breed of cattle), and then describes the distinguishing characteristics or details of the term that differentiate it from other members of the class (The Hereford is a breed of cattle distinguished by a white face, reddish-brown hide, and short horns).
- **Definition by negation** – The term is defined by stating what it is not and then saying what it is (Courage is not the absence of fear, but the willingness to act in spite of fear).

Types of Paragraphs and Essays

Illustrative — An illustrative paragraph or essay explains a general statement through the use of specific examples. The writer starts with a topic sentence that is followed by one or more examples that clearly relate to and support the topic.

Narrative — A narrative tells a story. Like a news report, it tells the who, what, when, where, why, and how of an event. A narrative is usually presented in chronological order.

Copyright © Mometrix Media. You have been licensed one copy of this document for personal use only. Any other reproduction or redistribution is strictly prohibited. All rights reserved.

Descriptive — This type of writing appeals to the five senses to describe a person, place, or thing so that the readers can see the subject in their imaginations. Space order is most often used in descriptive writing to indicate place or position.

Process — There are two kinds of process papers: the "how-to" that gives step-by-step directions on how to do something and the explanation paper that tells how an event occurred or how something works.

Review Video: Reading Essays
Visit mometrix.com/academy and enter code: 169166

Cause and Effect

Causes are reasons for actions or events. **Effects** are the results of a cause or causes. There may be multiple causes for one effect (evolutionary extinction, climate changes, and a massive comet caused the demise of the dinosaurs, for example) or multiple effects from one cause (the break-up of the Soviet Union has had multiple effects on the world stage, for instance). Sometimes, one thing leads to another and the effect of one action becomes the cause for another (breaking an arm leads to not driving, which leads to reading more while staying home, for example). The ability to identify causes and effects is part of critical thinking, and enables the reader to follow the course of events, make connections among events, and identify the instigators and receivers of actions. This ability improves comprehension.

Review Video: Cause and Effect
Visit mometrix.com/academy and enter code: 428037

Review Video: Rhetorical Strategy of Cause-and-Effect Analysis
Visit mometrix.com/academy and enter code: 725944

Distinguishing Between Facts and Opinions

Facts are statements that can be verified through research. Facts answer the questions of who, what, when, and where, and evidence can be provided to prove factual statements. For example, it is a fact that water turns into ice when the temperature drops below 32 degrees Fahrenheit. This fact has been proven repeatedly. Water never becomes ice at a higher temperature. **Opinions** are personal views, but facts may be used to support opinions. For example, it may be one person's opinion that Jack is a great athlete, but the fact that he has made many achievements related to sports supports that opinion. It is important for a reader to be able to distinguish between fact and opinion to determine the validity of an argument. Readers need to understand that some unethical writers will try to pass off an opinion as a fact. Readers with good critical thinking skills will not be deceived by this tactic.

Review Video: Fact or Opinion
Visit mometrix.com/academy and enter code: 870899

Review Video: Text Evidence
Visit mometrix.com/academy and enter code: 486236

Copyright © Mometrix Media. You have been licensed one copy of this document for personal use only. Any other reproduction or redistribution is strictly prohibited. All rights reserved.

Inductive and Deductive Reasoning

Inductive reasoning is using particulars to draw a general conclusion. The inductive reasoning process starts with **data**. For example, if every apple taken out of the top of a barrel is rotten, it can be inferred without investigating further that all the apples are probably rotten. Unless all data is examined, conclusions are based on probabilities. Inductive reasoning is also used to make inferences about the universe. The entire universe cannot be examined, but inferences can be made based on observations about what can be seen. These inferences may be proven false when more data is available, but they are valid at the time they are made if observable data is used. **Deductive reasoning** is the opposite of inductive reasoning. It involves using general facts or premises to come to a specific conclusion. For example, if Susan is a sophomore in high school, and all sophomores take geometry, it can be inferred that Susan takes geometry. The word "all" does not allow for exceptions. If all sophomores take geometry, assuming Susan does too is a logical conclusion. It is important for a reader to recognize inductive and deductive reasoning so he or she can follow the line of an argument and determine if the inference or conclusion is **valid**.

Style, Tone, and Point of View

Style is the manner in which a writer uses language in prose or poetry. Style is affected by:

- Diction or word choices
- Sentence structure and syntax
- Types and extent of use of figurative language
- Patterns of rhythm or sound
- Conventional or creative use of punctuation

Tone is the attitude of the writer or narrator towards the theme of, subject of, or characters in a work. Sometimes the attitude is stated, but it is most often implied through word choices. Examples of tone are serious, humorous, satiric, stoic, cynical, flippant, and surprised.

Point of view is the angle from which a story is told. It is the perspective of the narrator, established by the author. Common points of view are:

- *Third person* – Third person points of view include omniscient (knows everything) and limited (confined to what is known by a single character or a limited number of characters). When the third person is used, characters are referred to as he, she, or they.
- *First person* – When this point of view is used, the narrator refers to himself or herself as "I."

Review Video: Style, Tone, and Mood
Visit mometrix.com/academy and enter code: 416961

Review Video: Point of View
Visit mometrix.com/academy and enter code: 383336

Types of Figurative Language

A **simile** is a comparison between two unlike things using the words "like" or "as." Examples are Robert Burn's sentence "O my love's like a red, red, rose" or the common expression "as pretty as a picture."

Copyright © Mometrix Media. You have been licensed one copy of this document for personal use only. Any other reproduction or redistribution is strictly prohibited. All rights reserved.

A **metaphor** is a direct comparison between two unlike things without the use of "like" or "as." One thing is identified as the other instead of simply compared to it. An example is D. H. Lawrence's sentence "My soul is a dark forest."

Personification is the giving of human characteristics to a non-human thing or idea. An example is "The hurricane howled its frightful rage."

Synecdoche is the use of a part of something to signify the whole. For example, "boots on the ground" could be used to describe soldiers in a field.

Metonymy is the use of one term that is closely associated with another to mean the other. An example is referring to the "crown" to refer to the monarchy.

Alliteration, Assonance, and Onomatopoeia

Alliteration is the repetition of the first sounds or stressed syllables (usually consonants) in words in close proximity. An example is: "Chirp, chirp," said the chickadee.

Assonance is the repetition of identical or similar vowel sounds, particularly in stressed syllables, in words in close proximity. Assonance is considered to be a form of near rhyme. An example is: the quiet bride cried.

Onomatopoeia refers to words that imitate sounds. It is sometimes called echoism. Examples are hiss, buzz, burp, rattle, and pop. It may also refer to words that correspond symbolically to what they describe, with high tones suggesting light and low tones suggesting darkness. An example is the *gloom* of night versus the *gleam* of the stars.

Parallelism, Euphemism, Hyperbole, and Climax

Parallelism — Subjects, objects, verbs, modifiers, phrases, and clauses can be structured in sentences to balance one with another through a similar grammatical pattern. Parallelism helps to highlight ideas while showing their relationship and giving style to writing.

Examples are:

- **Parallel words** - The killer behaved coldly, cruelly, and inexplicably.
- **Parallel phrases** - Praised by comrades, honored by commanders, the soldier came home a hero.
- **Parallel clauses** - "We shall fight on the beaches, we shall fight on the landing grounds, we shall fight in the hills." (Winston Churchill)

Euphemism — This is a "cover-up" word that avoids the explicit meaning of an offensive or unpleasant term by substituting a vaguer image. An example is using "expired" instead of "dead."

Hyperbole — This is an example or phrase that exaggerates for effect. An example is the extravagant overstatement "I thought I would die!" Hyperbole is also used in tall tales, such as those describing Paul Bunyan's feats.

Climax — This refers to the process of building up to a dramatic highpoint through a series of phrases or sentences. It can also refer to the highpoint or most intense event in a story.

Copyright © Mometrix Media. You have been licensed one copy of this document for personal use only. Any other reproduction or redistribution is strictly prohibited. All rights reserved.

Bathos, Oxymoron, Irony, and Malapropism

Bathos — This is an attempt to evoke pity, sorrow, or nobility that goes overboard and becomes ridiculous. It is an insincere pathos and a letdown. It is also sometimes called an anticlimax, although an anticlimax might be intentionally included for comic or satiric effect.

Oxymoron — This refers to two terms that are used together for contradictory effect, usually in the form of an adjective that doesn't fit the noun. An example is: a "new classic."

Irony — This refers to a difference between what is and what ought to be, or between what is said and what is meant. Irony can be an unexpected result in literature, such as a twist of fate. For example, it is ironic that the tortoise beat the hare.

Malapropism — This is confusing one word with another, similar-sounding word. For example, saying a movie was a cliff dweller instead of a cliffhanger is a malapropism.

Invalid Arguments

There are a number of **invalid or false arguments** that are used unethically to gain an advantage, such as:

- The "**ad hominem**" or "against the person" argument – This type attacks the character or behavior of a person taking a stand on an issue rather than the issue itself. The statement "That fat slob wants higher taxes" is an example of this type of argument.
- **Hasty generalizations** – These are condemnations of a group based on the behavior of one person or part. An example of this type of argument is someone saying that all McDonald's restaurants are lousy because he or she had a bad experience at one location.
- **Faulty causation** – This is assigning the wrong cause to an event. An example is blaming a flat tire on losing a lucky penny rather than on driving over a bunch of nails.
- **Bandwagon effect** – This is the argument that if everybody else is doing something, it must be a good thing to do. The absurdity of this type of argument is highlighted by the question: "If everybody else is jumping off a cliff, should you jump, too?"

It is important for a reader to be able to identify various types of invalid arguments to prevent being deceived and making faulty conclusions.

Fiction and Nonfiction

Fiction is a literary work usually presented in prose form that is not true. It is the product of the writer's imagination. Examples of fiction are novels, short stories, television scripts, and screenplays. **Nonfiction** is a literary work that is based on facts. In other words, the material is true. The purposeful inclusion of false information is considered dishonest, but the expression of opinions or suppositions is acceptable. Libraries divide their collections into works of fiction and

Copyright © Mometrix Media. You have been licensed one copy of this document for personal use only. Any other reproduction or redistribution is strictly prohibited. All rights reserved.

nonfiction. Examples of nonfiction include historical materials, scientific reports, memoirs, biographies, most essays, journals, textbooks, documentaries, user manuals, and news reports.

Review Video: Reading Fiction
Visit mometrix.com/academy and enter code: 391411

Review Video: Historical Context
Visit mometrix.com/academy and enter code: 169770

Review Video: Interpretation of Expository or Literary Text
Visit mometrix.com/academy and enter code: 860442

Prose and Poetry

Prose is language as it is ordinarily spoken as opposed to verse or language with metric patterns. Prose is used for everyday communication, and is found in textbooks, memos, reports, articles, short stories, and novels. Distinguishing characteristics of prose include:

- It may have some sort of rhythm, but there is **no formal arrangement**.
- The common unit of organization is the **sentence**.
- It may include literary devices of repetition and balance.
- It must have more coherent relationships among sentences than a list would.

Poetry, or verse, is the manipulation of language with respect to meaning, meter, sound, and rhythm. A line of poetry can be any length and may or may not rhyme. Related groups of lines are called **stanzas**, and may also be any length. Some poems are as short as a few lines, and some are as long as a book. Poetry is a more ancient form of literature than prose.

Role of Emotions in Poetry

Poetry is designed to appeal to the physical and emotional senses. Using appeals to the **physical senses** through words that evoke sight, sound, taste, smell, and touch also causes the imagination to respond **emotionally**. Poetry appeals to the soul and memories with language that can be intriguingly novel and profoundly emotional in connotation. Poetry can focus on any topic, but the feelings associated with the topic are magnified by the ordered presentation found in poetry. Verse, however, is merely a matter of structure. The thing that turns words into poetry is the feeling packed into those words. People write poetry to express their feelings and people read poetry to try to experience those same feelings. Poetry interprets the human condition with understanding and insight. Children respond well to poetry because it has an inviting, entertaining sound that they are eager to mimic.

Short Story

A **short story** is prose fiction that has the same elements as a novel, such as plot, characters, and point of view. Edgar Allan Poe defined the short story as a **narrative** that can be read in **one sitting** (one-half to two hours), and is limited to a **single effect**. In a short story, there is no time for extensive character development, large numbers of characters, in-depth analysis, complicated plot lines, or detailed backgrounds. Historically, the short story is related to the fable, the exemplum, and the folktale. Short stories have become mainly an American art form. Famous short story writers include William Faulkner, Katherine Anne Porter, Eudora Welty, Flannery O'Connor, O. Henry, and J. D. Salinger.

Copyright © Mometrix Media. You have been licensed one copy of this document for personal use only. Any other reproduction or redistribution is strictly prohibited. All rights reserved.

Character Types

Readers need to be able to differentiate between **major and minor characters**. The difference can usually be determined based on whether the characters are round, flat, dynamic, or static. **Round characters** have complex personalities, just like real people. They are more commonly found in longer works such as novels or full-length plays. **Flat characters** display only a few personality traits and are based on stereotypes. Examples include the bigoted redneck, the lazy bum, or the absent-minded professor. **Dynamic characters** are those that change or grow during the course of the narrative. They may learn important lessons, fall in love, or take new paths. **Static characters** remain the same throughout a story. Usually, round characters are dynamic and flat characters are static, but this is not always the case. Falstaff, the loyal and comical character in Shakespeare's plays about Henry IV, is a round character in terms of his complexity. However, he never changes, which makes him a reliable figure in the story.

Line Structure in Poems

A **line of poetry** can be any length and can have any metrical pattern. A line is determined by the physical position of words on a page. A line is simply a group of words on a single line. Consider the following example:

> When I consider how my light is spent,
>
> E're half my days, in this dark world and wide,

These are two lines of poetry written by John Milton. Lines may or may not have punctuation at the end, depending, of course, on the need for punctuation. If these two lines were written out in a paragraph, they would be written with a **slash line** and a **space** in between the lines: "When I consider how my light is spent, / E're half my days, in this dark world and wide."

Blank Verse and Free Verse

Blank verse is unrhymed verse that consists of lines of iambic pentameter, which is five feet (sets) of unstressed and stressed syllables. The rhythm that results is the closest to natural human speech. It is the most commonly used type of verse because of its versatility. Well-known examples of blank verse are Shakespearean plays, Milton's epic poems, and T. S. Eliot's *The Waste Land*. **Free verse** lacks regular patterns of poetic feet, but has more controlled rhythm than prose in terms of pace and pauses. Free verse has no rhyme and is usually written in short lines of irregular length. Well-known examples of free verse are the King James translation of the Psalms, Walt Whitman's *Leaves of Grass*, and the poetry of Ezra Pound and William Carlos Williams.

Review Video: Forms of Poetry
Visit mometrix.com/academy and enter code: 451705

Stanza Structure in Poems

A **stanza** is a group of lines. The grouping denotes a relationship among the lines. A stanza can be any length, but the separation of lines into different stanzas indicates an intentional *pattern* created by the poet. The breaks between stanzas indicate a change of subject or thought. As a group of lines, the stanza is a melodic unit that can be analyzed for *metrical and rhyme patterns*. Various common rhyme patterns have been named. The Spenserian stanza, which has a rhyme pattern of a b a b b c b c c, is an example. Stanzas of a certain length also have names. Examples include the **couplet**, which has two lines; the **tercet**, which has three lines; and the **quatrain**, which has four lines.

Copyright © Mometrix Media. You have been licensed one copy of this document for personal use only. Any other reproduction or redistribution is strictly prohibited. All rights reserved.

Meter

A recurring pattern of stressed and unstressed syllables in language creates a rhythm when spoken. When the pattern is regular, it is called **meter**. When meter is used in a composition, it is called **verse**. The most common types of meter are:

- **Iambic** – An unstressed syllable followed by a stressed syllable
- **Anapestic** – Two unstressed syllables followed by a stressed syllable
- **Trochaic** – One stressed syllable followed by an unstressed syllable
- **Dactylic** – A stressed syllable followed by two unstressed syllables
- **Spondaic** – Two consecutive syllables that are stressed almost equally
- **Pyrrhic** – Two consecutive syllables that are equally unstressed

Types of Children's Literature

A **fairy tale** is a fictional story involving humans, magical events, and usually animals. Characters such as fairies, elves, giants, and talking animals are taken from folklore. The plot often involves impossible events (as in "Jack and the Beanstalk") and/or an enchantment (as in "Sleeping Beauty"). Other examples of fairy tales include "Cinderella," "Little Red Riding Hood," and "Rumpelstiltskin." A **fable** is a tale in which animals, plants, and forces of nature act like humans. A fable also teaches a moral lesson. Examples are "The Tortoise and the Hare," *The Lion King*, and *Animal Farm*. A **tall tale** exaggerates human abilities or describes unbelievable events as if the story were true. Often, the narrator seems to have witnessed the event described. Examples are fish stories, Paul Bunyan and Pecos Bill stories, and hyperboles about real people such as Davy Crockett, Mike Fink, and Calamity Jane.

Preadolescent and Adolescent Literature

Preadolescent literature is mostly concerned with the "tween" issues of changing lives, relationships, and bodies. **Adolescents** seeking escape from their sometimes difficult lives enjoy fantasy and science fiction. For both groups, books about modern, real people are more interesting than those about historical figures or legends. Boys especially enjoy nonfiction. Reading interests as well as reading levels for this group vary. Reading levels will usually range from 6.0 to 8.9. Examples of popular literature for this age group and reading level include:

- Series – Sweet Valley High, Bluford High, Nancy Drew, Hardy Boys, and Little House on the Prairie
- Juvenile fiction authors – Judy Blume and S. E. Hinton
- Fantasy and horror authors – Ursula LeGuin and Stephen King
- Science fiction authors – Isaac Asimov, Ray Bradbury, and H. G. Wells
- Classic books: Lilies of the Field, Charlie and the Chocolate Factory, Pippi Longstocking, National Velvet, Call of the Wild, Anne of Green Gables, The Hobbit, The Member of the Wedding, and Tom Sawyer

Grammatical Terms

The definitions for grammatical terms are as follows:

Adjective – This is a word that modifies or describes a noun or pronoun. Examples are a *green* apple or *every* computer.

Copyright © Mometrix Media. You have been licensed one copy of this document for personal use only. Any other reproduction or redistribution is strictly prohibited. All rights reserved.

Adverb – This is a word that modifies a verb (*instantly* reviewed), an adjective (*relatively* odd), or another adverb (*rather* suspiciously).

Conjunctions: There are three types of conjunctions:

- **Coordinating conjunctions** are used to link words, phrases, and clauses. Examples are and, or, nor, for, but, yet, and so.
- **Correlative conjunctions** are paired terms used to link clauses. Examples are either/or, neither/nor, and if/then.
- **Subordinating conjunctions** relate subordinate or dependent clauses to independent ones. Examples are although, because, if, since, before, after, when, even though, in order that, and while.

Gerund – This is a verb form used as a noun. Most end in "ing." An example is: *Walking* is good exercise.

Infinitive – This is a verbal form comprised of the word "to" followed by the root form of a verb. An infinitive may be used as a noun, adjective, adverb, or absolute. Examples include:

- *To hold* a baby is a joy. (noun)
- Jenna had many files *to reorganize*. (adjective)
- Andrew tried *to remember* the dates. (adverb)
- *To be honest*, your hair looks awful. (absolute)

Noun – This is a word that names a person, place, thing, idea, or quality. A noun can be used as a subject, object, complement, appositive, or modifier.

Object – This is a word or phrase that receives the action of a verb.

- A direct object states *to* whom/what an action was committed. It answers the question "to what?" An example is: Joan served *the meal*.
- An indirect object states *for* whom/what an action was committed. An example is: Joan served *us* the meal.

Preposition – This is a word that links a noun or pronoun to other parts of a sentence. Examples include above, by, for, in, out, through, and to.

Prepositional phrase – This is a combination of a preposition and a noun or pronoun. Examples include across the bridge, against the grain, below the horizon, and toward the sunset.

Pronoun – This is a word that represents a specific noun in a generic way. A pronoun functions like a noun in a sentence. Examples include I, she, he, it, myself, they, these, what, all, and anybody.

Sentence – This is a group of words that expresses a thought or conveys information as an independent unit of speech. A **complete sentence** must contain a noun and a verb (I ran). However, all the other parts of speech can also be represented in a sentence.

Verb – This is a word or phrase in a sentence that expresses action (Mary played) or a state of being (Mary is).

Review Video: Parts of Speech
Visit mometrix.com/academy and enter code: 899611

Copyright © Mometrix Media. You have been licensed one copy of this document for personal use only. Any other reproduction or redistribution is strictly prohibited. All rights reserved.

Capitalization and Punctuation

Capitalization refers to the use of capital letters. Capital letters should be placed at the beginning of:

- **Proper names** (Ralph Waldo Emerson, Australia)
- **Places** (Mount Rushmore, Chicago)
- Historical periods and holidays (Renaissance, Christmas)
- **Religious terms** (Bible, Koran)
- **Titles** (Empress Victoria, General Smith)
- All main words in **literary, art, or music titles** (Grapes of Wrath, Sonata in C Major)

Punctuation consists of:

Periods – A period is placed at the end of a sentence.

Commas – A comma is used to separate:

- Two adjectives modifying the same word (long, hot summer)
- Three or more words or phrases in a list (Winken, Blinken, and Nod; life, liberty, and the pursuit of happiness)
- Phrases that are not needed to complete a sentence (The teacher, not the students, will distribute the supplies.)

Colons and Semicolons

Colons – A colon is used to:

- Set up a **list** (We will need these items: a pencil, paper, and an eraser.)
- Direct readers to **examples or explanations** (We have one chore left: clean out the garage.)
- Introduce **quotations or dialogue** (The Labor Department reported on unemployment: "There was a 3.67% increase in unemployment in 2010."; Scarlett exclaimed: "What shall I do?")

Review Video: Colons
Visit mometrix.com/academy and enter code: 868673

Semicolons – A semicolon is used to:

- Join **related independent clauses** (There were five major hurricanes this year; two of them hit Florida.)
- Join **independent clauses connected by conjunctive adverbs** (Popular books are often made into movies; however, it is a rare screenplay that is as good as the book.)
- Separate items in a **series** if commas would be confusing (The characters include: Robin Hood, who robs from the rich to give to the poor; Maid Marian, his true love; and Little John, Robin Hood's comrade-in-arms.)

Review Video: Semicolon Usage
Visit mometrix.com/academy and enter code: 370605

Copyright © Mometrix Media. You have been licensed one copy of this document for personal use only. Any other reproduction or redistribution is strictly prohibited. All rights reserved.

Subject-Verb Agreement

A verb must **agree** in number with its subject. Therefore, a verb changes form depending on whether the subject is singular or plural. Examples include "I do," "he does," "the ball is," and "the balls are." If two subjects are joined by "and," the **plural** form of a verb is usually used. For example: *Jack and Jill want* to get some water (Jack wants, Jill wants, but together they want). If the compound subjects are preceded by each or every, they take the **singular** form of a verb. For example: *Each man and each woman brings* a special talent to the world (each brings, not bring). If one noun in a compound subject is plural and the other is singular, the verb takes the form of the subject **nearest** to it. For example: Neither the *students* nor their *teacher was* ready for the fire drill. **Collective nouns** that name a group are considered singular if they refer to the group acting as a unit. For example: The *choir is going* on a concert tour.

Review Video: Subject Verb Agreement
Visit mometrix.com/academy and enter code: 479190

Syntax

Syntax refers to the rules related to how to properly **structure** sentences and phrases. Syntax is not the same as grammar. For example, "I does" is syntactically correct because the subject and verb are in proper order, but it is grammatically incorrect because the subject and verb don't agree.

There are three types of sentence structures:

- **Simple** – This type is composed of a single independent clause with one subject and one predicate (verb or verb form).
- **Compound** – This type is composed of two independent clauses joined by a conjunction (Amy flew, but Brenda took the train), a correlative conjunction (Either Tom goes with me or I stay here), or a semicolon (My grandfather stays in shape; he plays tennis nearly every day).
- **Complex** – This type is composed of one independent clause and one or more dependent clauses joined by a subordinating conjunction (Before we set the table, we should replace the tablecloth).

Types of Paragraphs or Essays

A **comparison and contrast essay** examines the similarities and differences between two things. In a paragraph, the writer presents all the points about subject A and then all the points about subject B. In an essay, the writer might present one point at a time, comparing subject A and subject B side by side.

A **classification paper** sorts information. It opens with a topic sentence that identifies the group to be classified, and then breaks that group into categories. For example, a group might be baseball players, while a category might be positions they play.

A **cause and effect paper** discusses the causes or reasons for an event or the effects of a cause or causes. Topics discussed in this type of essay might include the causes of a war or the effects of global warming.

A **persuasive essay** is one in which the writer tries to convince the audience to agree with a certain opinion or point of view. The argument must be supported with facts, examples, anecdotes, expert

Copyright © Mometrix Media. You have been licensed one copy of this document for personal use only. Any other reproduction or redistribution is strictly prohibited. All rights reserved.

testimony, or statistics, and must anticipate and answer the questions of those who hold an opposing view. It may also predict consequences.

Role of Purpose and Audience in Writing a Paper

Early in the writing process, the writer needs to definitively determine the **purpose** of the paper and then keep that purpose in mind throughout the writing process. The writer needs to ask: "Is the purpose to explain something, to tell a story, to entertain, to inform, to argue a point, or some combination of these purposes?" Also at the beginning of the writing process, the writer needs to determine the **audience** of the paper by asking questions such as: "Who will read this paper?" "For whom is this paper intended?" "What does the audience already know about this topic?" "How much does the audience need to know?" and "Is the audience likely to agree or disagree with my point of view?" The answers to these questions will determine the content of the paper, the tone, and the style.

Writing Processes

Drafting is creating an early version of a paper. A draft is a prototype or sketch of the finished product. A draft is a rough version of the final paper, and it is expected that there will be multiple drafts.

Revising is the process of making major changes to a draft in regards to clarity of purpose, focus (thesis), audience, organization, and content.

Editing is the process of making changes in style, word choice, tone, examples, and arrangement. These are more minor than the changes made during revision. Editing can be thought of as fine tuning. The writer makes the language more precise, checks for varying paragraph lengths, and makes sure that the title, introduction, and conclusion fit well with the body of the paper.

Proofreading is performing a final check and correcting errors in punctuation, spelling, grammar, and usage. It also involves looking for parts of the paper that may be omitted.

Review Video: Recursive Writing Process
Visit mometrix.com/academy and enter code: 951611

Title and Conclusion of an Essay

The **title** is centered on the page and the main words are capitalized. The title is not surrounded by quotation marks, nor is it underlined or italicized. The title is rarely more than four or five words, and is very rarely a whole sentence. A good title suggests the subject of the paper and catches the reader's interest. The **conclusion** should flow logically from the body of the essay, should tie back to the introduction, and may provide a summary or a final thought on the subject. New material should never be introduced in the conclusion. The conclusion is a wrap-up that may contain a call to action, something the writer wants the audience to do in response to the paper. The conclusion might end with a question to give the reader something to think about.

Review Video: Drafting Conclusions
Visit mometrix.com/academy and enter code: 209408

Copyright © Mometrix Media. You have been licensed one copy of this document for personal use only. Any other reproduction or redistribution is strictly prohibited. All rights reserved.

Introduction of an Essay

The **introduction** contains the **thesis statement**, which is usually the first or last sentence of the opening paragraph. It needs to be interesting enough to make the reader want to continue reading.

- Possible openings for an introduction include:
- The thesis statement
- A general idea that gives background or sets the scene
- An illustration that will make the thesis more concrete and easy to picture
- A surprising fact or idea to arouse curiosity
- A contradiction to popular belief that attracts interest
- A quotation that leads into the thesis

Review Video: Introduction
Visit mometrix.com/academy and enter code: 961328

Review Video: Introduction II
Visit mometrix.com/academy and enter code: 254411

Sentence Types

A **declarative sentence** makes a statement and is punctuated by a period at the end. An example is: The new school will be built at the south end of Main Street.

An **interrogative sentence** asks a question and is punctuated by a question mark at the end. An example is: Why will the new school be built so far out?

An **exclamatory sentence** shows strong emotion and is punctuated by an exclamation mark at the end. An example is: The new school has the most amazing state-of-the-art technology!

An **imperative sentence** gives a direction or command and may be punctuated by an exclamation mark or a period. Sometimes, the subject of an imperative sentence is you, which is understood instead of directly stated. An example is: Come to the open house at the new school next Sunday.

Transitional Words and Phrases

Transitional words are used to signal a relationship. They are used to link thoughts and sentences. Some types of transitional words and phrases are:

- **Addition** – Also, in addition, furthermore, moreover, and then, another
- **Admitting a point** – Granted, although, while it is true that
- **Cause and effect** – Since, so, consequently, as a result, therefore, thus
- **Comparison** – Similarly, just as, in like manner, likewise
- **Contrast** – On the other hand, yet, nevertheless, despite, but, still
- **Emphasis** – Indeed, in fact, without a doubt, certainly, to be sure
- **Illustration** – For example, for instance, in particular, specifically
- **Purpose** – In order to, for this purpose, for this to occur
- **Spatial arrangement** – Beside, above, below, around, across, inside, near, far, to the left
- **Summary or clarification** – In summary, in conclusion, that is, in other words
- **Time sequence** – Before, after, later, soon, next, meanwhile, suddenly, finally

Copyright © Mometrix Media. You have been licensed one copy of this document for personal use only. Any other reproduction or redistribution is strictly prohibited. All rights reserved.

Pre-Writing Techniques

Pre-writing techniques that help a writer find, explore, and organize a topic include:

- **Brainstorming** – This involves letting thoughts make every connection to the topic possible, and then spinning off ideas and making notes of them as they are generated. This is a process of using imagination, uninhibited creativity, and instincts to discover a variety of possibilities.
- **Freewriting** – This involves choosing items from the brainstorming list and writing about them nonstop for a short period. This unedited, uncensored process allows one thing to lead to another and permits the writer to think of additional concepts and themes.
- **Clustering/mapping** – This involves writing a general word or phrase related to the topic in the middle of a paper and circling it, and then quickly jotting down related words or phrases. These are circled and lines are drawn to link words and phrases to others on the page. Clustering is a visual representation of brainstorming that reveals patterns and connections.
- **Listing** – Similar to brainstorming, listing is writing down as many descriptive words and phrases (not whole sentences) as possible that relate to the subject. Correct spelling and grouping of these descriptive terms can come later if needed. This list is merely intended to stimulate creativity and provide a vibrant vocabulary for the description of the subject once the actual writing process begins.
- **Charting** – This prewriting technique works well for comparison/contrast purposes or for the examination of advantages and disadvantages (pros and cons). Any kind of chart will work, even a simple two-column list. The purpose is to draw out points and examples that can be used in the paper.

Purpose of Writing

Writing always has a purpose. The five reasons to write are:

- **To tell a story** – The story does not necessarily need to be fictional. The purposes are to explain what happened, to narrate events, and to explain how things were accomplished. The story will need to make a point, and plenty of details will need to be provided to help the reader imagine the event or process.
- **To express oneself** – This type of writing is commonly found in journals, diaries, or blogs. This kind of writing is an exercise in reflection that allows writers to learn something about themselves and what they have observed, and to work out their thoughts and feelings on paper.
- **To convey information** – Reports are written for this purpose. Information needs to be as clearly organized and accurate as possible. Charts, graphs, tables, and other illustrations can help make the information more understandable.
- **To make an argument** – This type of writing also makes a point, but adds opinion to the facts presented. Argumentative, or persuasive, writing is one of the most common and important types of writing. It should follow rules of logic and ethics.
- **To explore ideas** – This is speculative writing that is quite similar to reflective writing. This type of writing explores possibilities and asks questions without necessarily expecting an answer. The purpose is to stimulate readers to further consider and reflect on the topic.

Review Video: Author's Main Point or Purpose
Visit mometrix.com/academy and enter code: 734339

Copyright © Mometrix Media. You have been licensed one copy of this document for personal use only. Any other reproduction or redistribution is strictly prohibited. All rights reserved.

Arranging Information Strategically

The order of the elements in a writing project can be organized in the following ways:

- **Logical order** – There is a coherent pattern in the presentation of information, such as inductive or deductive reasoning or a division of a topic into its parts.
- **Hierarchical order** – There is a ranking of material from most to least important or least to most important, depending on whether the writer needs a strong start or a sweeping finish. It can also involve breaking down a topic from a general form into specifics.
- **Chronological order** – This is an order that follows a sequence. In a narrative, the sequence will follow the time order of beginning to middle to end. In a "how to," the sequence will be step 1, step 2, step 3, and so on.
- **Order defined by genre** – This is a pre-determined order structured according to precedent or professional guidelines, such as the order required for a specific type of research or lab report, a resume, or an application form.
- **Order of importance** – This method of organization relies on a ranking determined by priorities. For example, in a persuasive paper, the writer usually puts the strongest argument in the last body paragraph so that readers will remember it. In a news report, the most important information comes first.
- **Order of interest** – This order is dependent on the level of interest the audience has in the subject. If the writer anticipates that reader knowledge and interest in the subject will be low, normal order choices need to be changed. The piece should begin with something very appealing. This will hook the reader and make for a strong opening.

Beginning Stages of Learning to Write

The following are the beginning stages of learning to write:

- **Drawing pictures** is the first written attempt to express thoughts and feelings. Even when the picture is unrecognizable to the adult, it means something to the child.
- The **scribble stage** begins when the child attempts to draw shapes. He or she may also try to imitate writing. The child may have a story or explanation to go with the shapes.
- Children have the most interest in learning to **write their own names**, so writing lessons usually start with that. Children will soon recognize that there are other letters too.
- Children are learning the **alphabet** and how to associate a **sound with each letter**. Reversing letters is still common, but instruction begins with teaching children to write from left to right.
- Written words may not be complete, but will likely have the correct **beginning and end sounds/letters**.
- Children will make some attempt to use **vowels** in writing.
- Children will write with more ease, although spelling will still be phonetic and only some punctuation will be used.

Journal Writing

Writing in a **journal** gives students practice in writing, which makes them more comfortable with the writing process. Journal writing also gives students the opportunity to sort out their thoughts, solve problems, examine relationships and values, and see their personal and academic growth when they revisit old entries. The advantages for the teacher are that the students become more experienced with and accustomed to writing. Through reading student journals, the teacher can also gain **insight** into the students' problems and attitudes, which can help the teacher tailor his or

Copyright © Mometrix Media. You have been licensed one copy of this document for personal use only. Any other reproduction or redistribution is strictly prohibited. All rights reserved.

her lesson plans. A journal can be kept in a **notebook** or in a **computer file**. It shouldn't be just a record of daily events, but an expression of thoughts and feelings about everything and anything. Grammar and punctuation don't matter since journaling is a form of private communication. Teachers who review journals need to keep in mind that they should not grade journals and that comments should be encouraging and polite.

Revising a Paper

Revising a paper involves rethinking the choices that were made while constructing the paper and then rewriting it, making any necessary changes or additions to word choices or arrangement of points. Questions to keep in mind include:

- Is the thesis clear?
- Do the body paragraphs logically flow and provide details to support the thesis?
- Is anything unnecessarily repeated?
- Is there anything not related to the topic?
- Is the language understandable?
- Does anything need to be defined?
- Is the material interesting?

Another consideration when revising is **peer feedback**. It is helpful during the revision process to have someone who is knowledgeable enough to be helpful and will be willing to give an honest critique read the paper.

Review Video: General Revision and Proofreading
Visit mometrix.com/academy and enter code: 385882

Paragraph Coherence

Paragraph coherence can be achieved by linking sentences by using the following strategies:

- **Repetition of key words** – It helps the reader follow the progression of thought from one sentence to another if key words (which should be defined) are repeated to assure the reader that the writer is still on topic and the discussion still relates to the key word.
- **Substitution of pronouns** – This doesn't just refer to using single word pronouns such as I, they, us, etc., but also alternate descriptions of the subject. For example, if someone was writing about Benjamin Franklin, it gets boring to keep saying Franklin or he. Other terms that describe him, such as that notable American statesman, this printer, the inventor, and so forth can also be used.
- **Substitution of synonyms** – This is similar to substitution of pronouns, but refers to using similar terms for any repeated noun or adjective, not just the subject. For example, instead of constantly using the word great, adjectives such as terrific, really cool, awesome, and so on can also be used.

Copyright © Mometrix Media. You have been licensed one copy of this document for personal use only. Any other reproduction or redistribution is strictly prohibited. All rights reserved.

Verbs

In order to understand the role of a verb and be able to identify the verb that is necessary to make a sentence, it helps to know the different types of verbs. These are:

- **Action verbs** – These are verbs that express an action being performed by the subject. An example is: The outfielder caught the ball (outfielder = subject and caught = action).
- **Linking verbs** – These are verbs that link the subject to words that describe or identify the subject. An example is: Mary is an excellent teacher (Mary = subject and "is" links Mary to her description as an excellent teacher). Common linking verbs are all forms of the verb "to be," appear, feel, look, become, and seem.
- **Helping verbs** – When a single verb cannot do the job by itself because of tense issues, a second, helping verb is added. Examples include: should have gone ("gone" is the main verb, while "should" and "have" are helping verbs), and was playing ("playing" is the main verb, while "was" is the helping verb).

Coordinating Conjunctions and Subordinating Conjunctions

There are different ways to connect two clauses and show their relationship:

- A **coordinating conjunction** is one that can join two independent clauses by placing a comma and a coordinating conjunction between them. The most common coordinating conjunctions are and, but, or, nor, yet, for, and so. Examples include: "It was warm, so I left my jacket at home" and "It was warm, and I left my jacket at home."
- A **subordinating conjunction** is one that joins a subordinate clause and an independent clause and establishes the relationship between them. An example is: "We can play a game after Steve finishes his homework." The dependent clause is "after Steve finishes his homework" because the reader immediately asks, "After Steve finishes, then what?" The independent clause is "We can play a game." The concern is not the ability to play a game, but "when?" The answer to this question is dependent on when Steve finishes his homework.

Review Video: Conjunctions
Visit mometrix.com/academy and enter code: 904603

Run-On Sentences and Comma Splices

A **run-on sentence** is one that tries to connect two independent clauses without the needed conjunction or punctuation and makes it hard for the reader to figure out where one sentence ends and the other starts. An example is: "Meagan is three years old she goes to pre-school." Two possible ways to fix the run-on would be: "Meagan is three years old, and she goes to pre-school" or "Meagan is three years old; however, she goes to pre-school." A **comma splice** occurs when a comma is used to join two independent clauses without a proper conjunction. The comma should be replaced by a period or one of the methods for coordination or subordination should be used. An example of a comma splice is: "Meagan is three years old, she goes to pre-school."

Copyright © Mometrix Media. You have been licensed one copy of this document for personal use only. Any other reproduction or redistribution is strictly prohibited. All rights reserved.

Fragments

A **fragment** is an incomplete sentence, which is one that does not have a subject to go with the verb, or vice versa. The following are types of fragments:

- **Dependent clause fragments** – These usually start with a subordinating conjunction. An example is: "Before you can graduate." "You can graduate" is a sentence, but the subordinating conjunction "before" makes the clause dependent, which means it needs an independent clause to go with it. An example is: "Before you can graduate, you have to meet all the course requirements."
- **Relative clause fragments** – These often start with who, whose, which, or that. An example is: "Who is always available to the students." This is a fragment because the "who" is not identified. A complete sentence would be: "Mr. Jones is a principal who is always available to the students."
- **The "-ing" fragment** lacks a subject. The "-ing" form of a verb has to have a helping verb. An example is: "Walking only three blocks to his job." A corrected sentence would be: "Walking only three blocks to his job, Taylor has no need for a car."
- **Prepositional phrase fragments** are ones that begin with a preposition and are only a phrase, not a complete thought. An example is: "By the time we arrived." "We arrived" by itself would be a complete sentence, but the "by" makes the clause dependent and the reader asks, "By the time you arrived, what happened?" A corrected sentence would be: "By the time we arrived, all the food was gone."
- **Infinitive phrase fragments** have the same problem as prepositional phrase ones. An example is: "To plant the seed." A corrected sentence would be: "To plant the seed, Isaac used a trowel."

Review Video: Fragments and Run-on Sentences
Visit mometrix.com/academy and enter code: 541989

Primary and Secondary Research Information

Primary research material is material that comes from the "horse's mouth." It is a document or object that was created by the person under study or during the time period under study. Examples of primary sources are original documents such as manuscripts, diaries, interviews, autobiographies, government records, letters, news videos, and artifacts (such as Native American pottery or wall writings in Egyptian tombs). **Secondary research material** is anything that is not primary. Secondary sources are those things that are written or otherwise recorded about the main subject. Examples include a critical analysis of a literary work (a poem by William Blake is primary, but the analysis of the poem by T. S. Eliot is secondary), a magazine article about a person (a direct quote would be primary, but the report is secondary), histories, commentaries, and encyclopedias.

Primary sources are the raw material of research. This can include results of experiments, notes, and surveys or interviews done by the researcher. Other primary sources are books, letters, diaries, eyewitness accounts, and performances attended by the researcher. **Secondary sources** consist of oral and written accounts prepared by others. This includes reports, summaries, critical reviews, and other sources not developed by the researcher. Most research writing uses both primary and secondary sources: primary sources from first-hand accounts and secondary sources for background and supporting documentation. The research process calls for active reading and writing throughout. As research yields information, it often calls for more reading and research, and the cycle continues.

Copyright © Mometrix Media. You have been licensed one copy of this document for personal use only. Any other reproduction or redistribution is strictly prohibited. All rights reserved.

Drafting Research Essays

Introduction

The **introduction** to a research essay is particularly important, as it sets the *context* for the essay. It needs to draw the reader into the subject and provide necessary background to understand the subject. It is sometimes helpful to open with the research question and explain how the question will be answered. The major points of the essay may be forecast or previewed to prepare readers for the coming arguments. In a research essay, it is a good idea to establish the writer's credibility by reviewing credentials and experience with the subject. Another useful opening involves quoting several sources that support the points of the essay, again to establish credibility. The tone should be appropriate to the audience and subject, maintaining a sense of careful authority while building the arguments. *Jargon* should be kept to a minimum, and language should be carefully chosen to reflect the appropriate tone.

Conclusion

The **conclusion** to a research essay helps readers summarize what they have learned. Conclusions are not meant to convince, as this has been done in the body of the essay. It can be useful to leave the reader with a memorable phrase or example that supports the argument. Conclusions should be both memorable and logical restatements of the arguments in the body of the essay. A *specific-to-general pattern* can be helpful, opening with the thesis statement and expanding to more general observations. A good idea is to restate the main points in the body of the essay, leading to the conclusion. An ending that evokes a vivid image or asks a provocative question makes the essay memorable. The same effect can be achieved by a call for action, or a warning. Conclusions may be tailored to the audience's background, in terms of language, tone, and style.

Reviewing the Draft

Checklist for Reviewing a Draft of a Research Essay

1. **Introduction**: Is the reader's attention gained and held by the introduction?
2. **Thesis**: Does the essay fulfill the promise of the thesis? Is it strong enough?
3. **Main points**: Are the main points listed and ranked in order of importance?
4. **Organization**: What is the organizing principle of the essay? Does it work?
5. **Supporting information**: Is the thesis adequately supported? Is the thesis convincing?
6. **Source material**: Are there adequate sources and are they smoothly integrated into the essay?
7. **Conclusion**: Does the conclusion have sufficient power? Does it summarize the essay well?
8. **Paragraphs, sentences, words**: Are these elements effective in promoting the thesis?
9. **Overall review**: Evaluate the essay's strengths and weaknesses. What revisions are needed?

Modern Language Association Style

The **Modern Language Association style** is widely used in literature and languages as well as other fields. The MLA style calls for noting brief references to sources in parentheses in the text of an essay and adding an alphabetical list of sources, called "Works Cited," at the end. Specific recommendations of the MLA include the following:

1. "**Works Cited**": Include in this section only works actually cited. List on a separate page the author's name, title, and publication information, which must include the location of the publisher, the publisher's name, and the date of publication.

Copyright © Mometrix Media. You have been licensed one copy of this document for personal use only. Any other reproduction or redistribution is strictly prohibited. All rights reserved.

2. **Parenthetical citations**: MLA style uses parenthetical citations following each quotation, reference, paraphrase, or summary to a source. Each citation is made up of the author's last name and page reference, keyed to a reference in Works Cited.
3. **Explanatory notes**: Explanatory notes are numbered consecutively and identified by superscript numbers in the text. The full notes may appear as endnotes or as footnotes at the bottom of the page.

Media Literacy

Media literacy is the ability to access, read, and interpret information from various parts of the media. Parts of the media can include the Internet, artifacts, printed materials, primary source documents, and visual media. A student who has achieved media literacy can effectively navigate the Internet (and other facets of media) without losing focus or accessing information deemed inappropriate or unsafe. Students with media literacy also develop the ability to question the validity of the information they are accessing by questioning the source and accuracy of the information being presented. In addition, students with media literacy can identify the key components of what they are accessing without becoming overwhelmed by the amount of information available.

Key Points Related to Speaking

The following are key points to remember about volume, pace, pronunciation, body language, word choice, and visual aids as they relate to speaking:

- **Volume** – Voice volume should be appropriate to the room and adjusted according to whether or not a microphone is used. The speaker should not shout at the audience, mumble, or speak so softly that his or her voice is inaudible.
- **Pace and pronunciation** – The speaker shouldn't talk so fast that his or her speech is unintelligible, nor should the speaker speak so slowly as to be boring. The speaker should enunciate words clearly.
- **Body language and gestures** – Body language can add to or distract from the message, so annoying, repetitive gestures such as waving hands about, flipping hair, or staring at one spot should be avoided. Good posture is critical.
- **Word choice** – The speaker should use a vocabulary level that fits the age and interest level of the audience. Vocabulary may be casual or formal depending on the audience.
- **Visual aids** – The speaker should use whatever aids will enhance the presentation, such as props, models, media, etc., but should not use anything that will be distracting or unmanageable.

Communicating Emotions

The majority of communications taking place in academic and business settings involve **factual information**. Unfortunately, individuals who are adept at communicating facts may struggle when attempting to communicate **personal feelings** in a relationship. Personal relationships, which are basic to happiness, can develop only when feelings are openly and honestly shared. In order to do this, people should work on asking straight-forward questions and honestly answering questions about themselves. Being a good listener, asking the right questions, and respecting the other person's answers are necessary parts of establishing good emotional communication. Sometimes, though, this may mean putting aside your own opinions so that you can fully engage with another person and come to understand the other's point of view.

Copyright © Mometrix Media. You have been licensed one copy of this document for personal use only. Any other reproduction or redistribution is strictly prohibited. All rights reserved.

Nonverbal Communication

Even though we normally think of communication as something we do through spoken or written language, we are constantly sending messages to one another with our **bodies** and **tone of voice**. Often, physical messages are sent and interpreted without either party being aware. Some of the signals that are used are consistent across cultures, whereas others are unique to a particular culture. For instance, slumped shoulders generally mean passivity and submission in every society. Alternatively, some cultures interpret eye contact as a sign of respect, and others see it as a sign of hostility. One should try to be aware of the messages one is sending with one's posture and gestures to avoid sending messages that are insulting or self-defeating.

Self-Concept in Interpersonal Communication

During **interpersonal communication**, all the participating parties filter information through their own **self-concept**. Everyone naturally applies new information to his or her own self-concept. Often, however, self-interested concerns can make it difficult for a listener to get a true sense of what the other person is saying. As much as possible, listeners should strive to understand and take into account their own self-image, so they can be as objective as possible when evaluating an incoming message. Although a slight degree of egotism or self-centeredness is natural, these traits can hinder accurate and insightful listening. Therefore, the goal of speech communication education is to mitigate these distorting factors.

Images of Self and Others Existing During Two-Person Conversations

When two individuals have a conversation, their **self-images** and the **images they hold of each other** exert a great influence on the course of the conversation. For instance, imagine you are talking to your teacher. You have a self-image and an image of the teacher. You also have an image of how you hope your teacher sees you. Finally, you have an image of how you think your teacher actually sees you. Similarly, your teacher holds his or her own set of four images in mind. Obviously, then, even carrying on a simple conversation becomes a complicated event. Speech communication theorists assert that conversations tend to go better when there is less discrepancy between these various images. For instance, if your self-image is similar to the image you imagine your teacher has of you, you are less likely to have trouble coming up with appropriate things to say. Similarly, if your impression of what the teacher thinks of you is similar to what you *hope* the teacher would think of you, you are less likely to make outlandish claims or try to justify yourself.

Self-Disclosure

According to speech communication theorists, conversations work best when both parties are as honest and forthcoming about themselves as possible. In other words, when engaged in conversation, a person should strive to be as accurate as possible in revealing his or her self-image. This process is known as **self-disclosure**. To the degree that we hide information about ourselves, we prevent others from truly understanding us. There are a number of reasons why a person might not engage in total self-disclosure. Propriety, pride, and fear are probably the most common reasons for hiding information about oneself. Difficulty can also arise when one individual in a conversation has information about the other without the other party being aware of it. This kind of asymmetrical knowledge can create underlying but unexpressed tension in a conversation. Ideally, people should attempt to continually increase their level of self-disclosure while encouraging their interlocutor to do the same.

Copyright © Mometrix Media. You have been licensed one copy of this document for personal use only. Any other reproduction or redistribution is strictly prohibited. All rights reserved.

Encoding Meaning

When one person speaks to another, he or she is "**encoding**" the verbal message with supplemental nonverbal forms of communication. The precise "**code**" the speaker uses is the particular set of words, with their agreed-upon meaning, as well as syntax and grammar. To the degree that the speaker has a command of vocabulary and a strong sense of meaning, he or she will be able to construct a subtle and effective code. The process of encoding meaning is also influenced by individual bias, desire, and perception. People encode meaning differently based on the personal "agenda" they bring to any conversation. Two people speaking to one another should be able to increase the complexity and accuracy of their message encoding as the conversation progresses because they will be acquiring more and better information about one another's intentions, knowledge, and character.

Interpreting Meaning

When we listen to another person speak in conversation, we are attempting to **decode** their meaning through the **filter** of our own prejudices and perceptions. Speech communication theorists assert that listeners tend to emphasize the components of a message that are associated with their own pre-existing knowledge or interests. In particular, we all tend to emphasize the importance of those aspects of a message that directly pertain to us. Starting out, we are more likely to make mistakes in the interpretation of what a speaker is saying. As we acquire more information and become more familiar with the other person's speaking style, however, we tend to make beneficial adjustments to our interpretation. The more time we spend with another person, the better we are able to correctly interpret the meanings of their communications.

Communication Appropriate to Cooperating on Tasks

For people to **cooperate** effectively on a task, they all need good **communication skills**. This is especially true in the adult professional world. Without effective communication among those involved, success will be more difficult to achieve, but many people do not learn to work effectively with others until late childhood. For the most part, any job-related task is most easily accomplished when all parties know enough about the task-related tools, ideas, and skills to communicate effectively among themselves. In some cases, two individuals working together on a task may have unequal power, such as in the case of an employer and employee collaborating on a work-related project. Such unequal distribution of power also has a strong effect on communication.

Classroom Materials That Support Literacy Across the Curriculum

In a classroom that supports literacy, the teacher should provide **labels** combining words and pictures on all objects. This continually stimulates students to associate written language with the objects and concepts it represents. Especially to support disabled students, teachers should use their particular interests and needs as a guide for labeling things. Printed directions, signs, calendars, and schedules are materials that students should use regularly in the classroom. These help students realize how language is used in everyday life. When the class is studying a certain topic, theme, or book, the teacher and students can work together to redesign the classroom using printed/written materials that reflect that topic, theme, or book. This enables students to experience fully and "live" the lesson rather than just observing it. All of the materials must be adapted for any students' special needs. For instance, in a class including blind/visually impaired students, labels, signs and other print materials can incorporate Braille words and textured surfaces.

Copyright © Mometrix Media. You have been licensed one copy of this document for personal use only. Any other reproduction or redistribution is strictly prohibited. All rights reserved.

Addressing Diverse Student Abilities and Needs

Teachers must consider the **diversity** among the skills and needs of their students as they design their classroom learning environments. The teachers should **individualize** the setting and their instruction so that these represent every student. Individualization and instructional differentiation should not only address disabled students' needs; they should also regularly provide suitable opportunities for these students to participate on an ongoing basis in activities that involve literacy and integrate it into all content areas. According to research, a salient need of students with diverse literacy backgrounds is that they often have trouble connecting new information to their existing knowledge. This ability is a critical component of learning. When teachers plan and organize their classrooms to offer literacy activities that are accessible to disabled students—and that immerse them in literacy experiences and give them opportunities to connect both new with old information, and spoken with printed language—these students can then access the general education curriculum.

Activities for Students with Disabilities to Develop Literacy Skills and Participate in General Curriculum

To participate in the general curriculum, students with disabilities need to understand the **alphabetic principle**, i.e. that printed language represents spoken language; connect print with speech; and be able to relate new information to their prior knowledge. Teachers can support these developments by designing classrooms as literacy-rich settings, immersing special-needs and other students in **accessible literacy activities** across all content areas. For example, students can interact with alphabet-letter magnets, cookie-cutters, and stamps: concrete manipulatives allow students not developmentally ready for exclusively abstract thought to understand concepts using real objects. Discussing daily schedules requires students to read and comprehend printed language, and then use spoken language to demonstrate and apply their understanding. Playing letter/word games like Bingo, Pictionary, Boggle, and Scrabble gives practice with creating and manipulating language, enhancing recognition and cognitive flexibility. Providing photos of peers, teachers, staff, and classroom activities and having students label them helps students connect written language with familiar, meaningful images. Daily communication notebooks help students further integrate literacy into their school days.

Implications of Cultural and Linguistic Differences Regarding Literacy Development

Educational research shows that the **cultural values** of families and/or communities influence children's literacy development, and also that culture is a significant factor to understanding children's home literacy environments. Researchers have also found that cultural purposes, perspectives, and contexts affect how students with disabilities in particular interact with the literacy environments they encounter. They say children's preparation levels entering formal education reflect their families'/communities' values and beliefs about literacy. Cultural attitudes about literacy then influence how schools deliver instruction and literacy experiences. Teachers must assess culturally diverse students' interactions with the environment, and design literacy-rich classrooms, with students' diverse backgrounds in mind. Students learning English (ELL/ESL) enter school either not knowing English or just learning it, lacking exposure to specific vocabulary and literature. Literacy-rich classrooms help them participate in regular curriculum. Teacher should read aloud often to these students; include print in their native language in classrooms; permit mistakes during student attempts to use English; encourage students to reread books repeatedly; and plan activities entailing language use.

Copyright © Mometrix Media. You have been licensed one copy of this document for personal use only. Any other reproduction or redistribution is strictly prohibited. All rights reserved.

Drawbacks of Whole-Class and Small-Group Reading, and Flexible Grouping Model

A major disadvantage of **whole-class reading** is that students who read above the average class level go unchallenged and can become bored, while students reading below average level are lost. Yet the **small-group method** intended to remedy this also has the drawback that, as traditionally implemented, most time is used for skill instruction, leaving far too little time for students actually to read the text. One solution is a **flexible grouping model**, e.g., Grouping Without Tracking (Paratore, 1990). This model uses a "sandwich" structure: teachers give students shared-reading processes at the beginning and end of the lesson, but provide differentiated instruction to two groups in the middle as they read the text. Teachers give indirect guidance to students who can read more independently, and more direct support to struggling readers. Teachers reunite the groups to lead them in a final discussion. Students with reading difficulties gain reading proficiency and comprehension from direct teacher support, enabling them to contribute better to the whole-class discussion, so all share this experience equally.

Jigsaw Approach to Shared Reading

Students reading below grade level may be able to access and comprehend some texts or portions of them, but have difficulty with harder parts/texts—for example, informational texts with more challenging subject matter and specialized vocabulary. When a text intended for the whole class contains such challenging material, one solution the teacher can use is a **jigsaw approach**. The teacher selects various portions of the text that are less difficult and assigns them to students reading below grade level. Whereas such texts overall might present struggles for these students, they find the easier portions more manageable when they tackle only these parts, as selected and assigned by the teacher, in small groups of students with comparable reading levels. The teacher makes each small student group responsible for comprehension of their assigned portion of text. Then the teacher brings the class back together, having each group report what they read, understood, and learned. The whole class then collaborates to help each other make connections among the learning each group reported.

Using Themes to Connect Texts

Any inclusive classroom will contain students who read at various age/grade levels. As a result, some books used as core texts are going to present difficulties for some of the students, who read below grade level and/or lack background knowledge and vocabulary of the subject. One way a teacher can facilitate all students' comprehension of such texts is to provide **supplementary texts** that allow readers at different levels easier access—texts on the same subject or theme as the more difficult core text. Teachers have students read these more accessible texts independently during small-group reading periods. This makes it easier for students with less reading proficiency to learn the core vocabulary and build their background knowledge. Thus, they are more prepared to tackle the more difficult core text during whole-class shared reading periods. With such preparation, less proficient readers are more likely to become engaged and active participants in the shared reading of a difficult text in the whole-group setting.

Assigning Students to Small Groups for Guided Reading Exercises

Expert educators and researchers recommend that when teachers divide classes into small student groups for **guided reading**, they should not be overly concerned with assigning students to exact reading levels. Rather, though they will want to group students whose literacy development is similar and who read around a similar level, they should give more attention to organizing groups according to the students' *areas of need*. For example, a teacher might identify students who share

Copyright © Mometrix Media. You have been licensed one copy of this document for personal use only. Any other reproduction or redistribution is strictly prohibited. All rights reserved.

in common a need for help with noticing changes in setting; other students who share difficulties with recognizing and differentiating characters; some students who demonstrate problems with following and/or reproducing events they read in a text in the correct chronological sequence; some students who have trouble identifying and/or articulating the main idea in a text portion, etc. The teacher can create a group of students sharing one of these challenges; announce to the class what this group's focus is; and then invite other students to join this group by choice if they experience the same need.

Helping Teachers Provide More Equitable Learning Opportunities Using Word Counts

Books designed for lower reading levels typically contain fewer words, both per page and overall. Yet students who are reading below their grade levels require not fewer reading opportunities, but more, to practice and improve their reading skills. For example, within one class of second-grade students, the teacher might have one group using a text with over 80 words on just the first page, while another group uses a text with a total of 80 words in the entire book. This difference shows that the teacher will need to use several texts within certain groups to give them equal amounts of reading material and practice as readers of denser/longer texts during group reading times. Teachers can look at the backs of the books they assign during guided reading sessions, and maintain simple logs of their **word counts**. Comparing these word counts among groups can help teachers to equalize the numbers of words that each student group actually works with during small-group guided reading periods.

Connecting Text Sets for Small-Group Guided Reading Across Different Reading Difficulty Levels

When teachers select textbooks to teach a unit/lesson on a certain topic, they often compile **text sets**—groups of books all related to the same topic/theme. Because classes usually include students reading at different levels, teachers also often gather books at different reading levels for text sets. When collecting books representing multiple reading levels, the teacher can also intentionally organize the text set so all books are connected. For example, the books might share similar content; similar language, style, and vocabulary words; or similar layouts. Selecting books sharing such a commonality at different reading levels makes it easier for students to draw useful connections between easier and harder texts. It also facilitates students' flexibility in working across multiple reading levels, which builds their skills and confidence for faster progress. Additionally, to prepare some students to read books that teachers felt would prove too difficult otherwise, they can use easier texts with similar themes/language/formats to establish contexts for the harder ones.

Enhancing Students' Independent Reading Through the Reading Material Provided

In addition to whole-class and small-group reading exercises, students need some time reading **texts of their own choice**, which they can easily read with little/no support, to attain comfort, fluency, and confidence. To ensure more opportunities for practice, with equal time for all students, teachers should provide text sets at multiple reading levels for each content area. Experts suggest 70% of books should be easily accessible; and, in addition to classroom libraries, using rolling carts lets book collections travel among classrooms. Multiple reading levels let more advanced readers peruse a harder text, while less advanced readers read several easier texts; this equalizes the time and words they have for practicing. Because critics find some leveled readers lack variety in gender/race/class/other sociocultural aspects of characters, teachers should build diverse book collections representing all students. Teachers can inform their selections via student interest

Copyright © Mometrix Media. You have been licensed one copy of this document for personal use only. Any other reproduction or redistribution is strictly prohibited. All rights reserved.

surveys; and familiarity with students' individual identities, personalities, and special interests. Knowing individual students can help match them to texts as effectively as leveled book lists.

Engaging Students in Reading

Experts find excessive attention to **leveling** as a way of matching texts to students can be restrictive, undermining high-quality instruction that balances the needs of the reader with the demands of the text. Teachers must consider that assigning certain texts will cause students to disengage from reading and avoid it rather than engage in it. In the real world, people read many different kinds of materials. Therefore, a teacher has better chances of finding texts that engage students, and that motivate them to read and allow them to perceive themselves as readers, by mindfully selecting **varied text genres** with **varied difficulty**. In classrooms incorporating various student reading levels, this can be the best method to procure classroom acceptability of accessible texts. Teachers can also use **individualized instructional formats**, such as Readers Workshop (Atwell, 1998), which balance issues of difficulty, choice, and engagement; develop reader communities affording more reading experiences with authenticity, meaning, and enjoyment; and stronger positive teacher-student relationships via individualized consultations. Teachers should also incorporate **accessible alternative texts** for independent activities.

Alternative Reading and Writing Forms to Help Students Attain Greater Progress in Reading

When students read and write outside of school, they choose many alternative forms of reading and writing. To engage these students while they are in school, teachers should think about adding such **alternative materials** to their own instructional programs. For example, teachers might incorporate such media as graphic novels, magazines, newspapers, plays, anthologies of poetry, e-books and other digital/online content, and text that students have written themselves. Educational experts advise that just because it can be harder to determine the reading levels of such alternative text formats, teachers should not shy away from using them. Because they represent examples of text that people (including students) read in real life, they provide not only excellent practice for students' present and future reading of real-world materials, but also motivation to read and meaningful experiences in reading. Another boon of using these authentic, alternative texts is that they frequently incorporate multiple reading levels, so that nearly every student can read some portions of them.

Viewing Skills

Viewing skills can be sharpened by having students look at a single image, such as a work of art or a cartoon, and simply asking students what they **see**. The teacher can ask what is happening in the image, and then elicit the details that clue the students in to what is happening. Of course, there may be more than one thing happening. The teacher should also question the students about the message of the image, its purpose, its point of view, and its intended audience. The teacher should ask for first impressions, and then provide some background or additional information to see if it changes the way students look at or interpret the image. The conclusion of the lesson should include questions about what students learned from the exercise about the topic, themselves, and others.

Benefits

Students are exposed to multiple **images** every day. It is important for them to be able to effectively **interpret** these images. They should be able to make sense of the images and the spoken and print language that often accompany them. Learning can be enhanced with images because they allow for quicker connections to prior knowledge than verbal information. Visuals in the classroom can also

Copyright © Mometrix Media. You have been licensed one copy of this document for personal use only. Any other reproduction or redistribution is strictly prohibited. All rights reserved.

be motivational, can support verbal information, and can express main points, sometimes resulting in instant recognition.

Some of the common types of images that students see every day include: bulletin boards, computer graphics, diagrams, drawings, illustrations, maps, photographs, posters, book covers, advertisements, Internet sites, multimedia presentations, puppet shows, television, videos, print cartoons, models, paintings, animation, drama or dance performances, films, and online newscasts and magazines.

Activities to Strengthen Skills

Activities at school that can be used to strengthen the **viewing skills** of students of varying ages include:

- **Picture book discussions** – Students can develop an appreciation of visual text and the language that goes with it through guided discussions of picture books that focus on the style and color of the images and other details that might capture a child's attention.
- **Gallery walks** – Students can walk around a room or hallway viewing the posted works of other students and hear presentations about the works. They can also view a display prepared by the teacher. Students are expected to take notes as they walk around, have discussions, and perhaps do a follow-up report.
- **Puppet theater and drama presentations** – Students can learn about plots, dialogue, situations, characters, and the craft of performance from viewing puppet or drama presentations, which also stimulate oral communication and strengthen listening skills. Discussions or written responses should follow performances to check for detail acquisition.

Classroom Viewing Center

A **classroom viewing center** should contain magazines, CD-ROMs, books, videos, and individual pictures (photographs or drawings). Students should have a **viewing guide** that explains expectations related to the viewing center (before, during, and after using the center). For younger students, the teacher can ask questions that guide them through the viewing rather than expecting them to read the guidelines and write responses.

- **Before** viewing, students should think about what they already know about the subject and what they want to learn from the viewing.
- **During** the viewing, students should make notes about whatever interests them or is new to them.
- **After** viewing, students could discuss or individually write down what they found to be the most interesting idea or striking image and explain why it caught their attention.

Types of Questions to Ask If Viewing Is a Narrative

A teacher should make students responsible for gaining information or insight from the **viewing**. Setting expectations increases student attention and critical thinking. As with any viewing, the students should consider what they already know about the topic and what they hope to gain by watching the narrative before viewing it. During the viewing, the students should take notes (perhaps to answer questions provided by the teacher).

Copyright © Mometrix Media. You have been licensed one copy of this document for personal use only. Any other reproduction or redistribution is strictly prohibited. All rights reserved.

After the viewing, students should be able to answer the following questions:

- What was the time period and setting of the story?
- Who were the main characters?
- How effective was the acting?
- What was the problem or goal in the story?
- How was the problem solved or the goal achieved?
- How would you summarize the story?
- What did you learn from the story?
- What did you like or dislike about the story or its presentation?
- Would you recommend this viewing to others?
- How would you rate it?

Difficulties Related to Learning by Listening

It is difficult to learn just by listening because the instruction is presented only in spoken form. Therefore, unless students take notes, there is nothing for them to review. However, an active listener will anticipate finding a **message** in an oral presentation and will listen for it, **interpreting** tone and gestures as the presentation progresses. In group discussions, students are often too busy figuring out what they will say when it is their turn to talk to concentrate on what others are saying. Therefore, they don't learn from others, but instead come away knowing only what they already knew. Students should be required to respond directly to the previous speaker before launching into their own comments. This practice will force students to listen to each other and learn that their own responses will be better because of what can be added by listening to others.

Graphic Organizers

The purpose of **graphic organizers** is to help students classify ideas and communicate more efficiently and effectively. Graphic organizers are visual outlines or templates that help students grasp key concepts and master subject matter by simplifying them down to basic points. They also help guide students through processes related to any subject area or task. Examples of processes include brainstorming, problem solving, decision making, research and project planning, and studying. Examples of graphic organizers include:

- **Reading** – These can include beginning, middle, and end graphs or event maps.
- **Science** – These can include charts that show what animals need or how to classify living things.
- **Math** – These can include horizontal bar graphs or time lines.
- **Language arts** – These can include alphabet organizers or charts showing the components of the five-paragraph essay.
- **General** – These can include KWL charts or weekly planners.

Speaking Skills Children in Elementary/Intermediate School Should Have

Children of elementary/intermediate school age should be able to:

- Speak at an appropriate volume, tone, and pace that is understandable and appropriate to the audience
- Pronounce most words accurately
- Use complete sentences
- Make eye contact

Copyright © Mometrix Media. You have been licensed one copy of this document for personal use only. Any other reproduction or redistribution is strictly prohibited. All rights reserved.

- Use appropriate gestures with speech
- Exhibit an awareness of audience and adjust content to fit the audience (adjust word choices and style to be appropriate for peers or adults)
- Ask relevant questions
- Respond appropriately when asked questions about information or an opinion, possibly also being able to provide reasons for opinions
- Speak in turn, not interrupt, and include others in conversations
- Provide a summary or report orally
- Participate in small and large group discussions and debates
- Read orally before an audience
- Conduct short interviews
- Provide directions and explanations orally, including explanations of class lessons

Viewing Skills Elementary/Intermediate School Children Should Have

Children of elementary school age should be developing or have attained the ability to understand the importance of **media** in people's lives. They should understand that television, radio, films, and the Internet have a role in everyday life. They should also be able to use media themselves (printing out material from the Internet or making an audio or video tape, for example). They should also be aware that the purpose of advertising is to sell. Children of intermediate school age should be developing or have attained the ability to **obtain and compare information** from newspapers, television, and the Internet. They should also be able to judge its **reliability and accuracy** to some extent. Children of this age should be able to tell the difference between fictional and non-fictional materials in media. They should also be able to use a variety of media, visuals, and sounds to make a presentation.

Listening Skills Children Should Develop Through Their Elementary/Intermediate School Years

Through the elementary/intermediate school years, children should develop the following listening skills:

- Follow oral instructions consistently
- Actively listen to peers and teachers
- Avoid creating distracting behavior or being distracted by the behavior of others most of the time
- Respond to listening activities and exhibit the ability to discuss, illustrate, or write about the activity and show knowledge of the content and quality of the listening activity
- Respond to listening activities and exhibit the ability to identify themes, similarities/differences, ideas, forms, and styles of activities
- Respond to a persuasive speaker and exhibit the ability to analyze and evaluate the credibility of the speaker and form an opinion describing whether they agree or disagree with the point made
- Demonstrate appropriate social behavior while part of an audience

Stages of Writing

The **three stages of writing** are drawing, dictating, and writing. During the **drawing stage**, young learners use scribbles or pictures to convey their message. When asked to "read" their drawing, children in the drawing stage will use their picture to tell a story, as if they were mimicking a book being read to them. In the **dictation stage**, learners will tell their thoughts to a literate person, who

Copyright © Mometrix Media. You have been licensed one copy of this document for personal use only. Any other reproduction or redistribution is strictly prohibited. All rights reserved.

will in turn write the words for the child. During this stage, the student is aware that the written words on the page represent their thoughts and can sometimes recognize the beginning sounds of the words they are saying, including some sight words. In the third and final stage, the **writing stage**, students are able to write their own thoughts in a way that can be recognized by others. Both beginning and ending sounds are represented in the words, along with some vowels. Students in this stage also understand spacing between words and the idea of creating complete sentences.

Norm-Referenced and Criterion-Referenced Assessments

Norm-referenced assessments are used to gauge a student success by comparing his or her score to a theoretical "average" score achieved by students of the same age or grade level. With a norm-referenced assessment, a student's achievement is decided based on how much better or worse that student scored in comparison to his or her peers. In contrast, **criterion-referenced assessments** are scored based on each student's individual ability to show mastery of specific learning standards. Students are deemed successful if they are able to achieve mastery of concepts that are appropriate for their age or grade level, regardless of how their peers perform.

IRI

The **Informal Reading Inventory (IRI)**, also known as the **Qualitative Reading Inventory (QRI)** is a survey used to assess the instructional needs of individual readers. The IRI is used to determine a reader's grade-level reading, fluency, comprehension, vocabulary, oral reading accuracy, word recognition, word meaning, and reading strategies. The IRI is an ongoing assessment that should be administered several times a year starting from first grade through twelfth grade. Teachers should use the outcomes of these assessments to determine appropriate reading material for individual students and to identify and implement specific needs and strategies for individual learners or groups of learners.

Universal Screening Assessments, Diagnostic Assessments, and Progress Monitoring

Universal screening assessments are brief surveys given to all students at the beginning of each school year, which are used to determine the mastery of critical skills and concepts. These screenings should be repeated approximately three times a year to ensure that students are performing at age-appropriate levels. **Diagnostic assessments** are used to help educators make sense of universal screening assessment scores. Based on diagnostics, teachers can identify the specific educational gaps of individual students and use that information to modify and differentiate instruction. **Progress monitoring** is used to determine if the educational interventions and strategies put in place (based on the diagnostic testing) are actually working. Struggling students are often monitored more closely to ensure that educational gaps are being filled at an appropriate and sufficient rate.

Formal and Informal Assessments

Formal assessments, which include norm-based assessments, criterion-based assessments, intelligence tests, and diagnostic assessments are data driven. These types of assessments are used to determine a student's overall achievement and can be used to compare each student's abilities to his or her peers. Formal assessments are often shared with students and stakeholders to determine whether or not a student is performing at an appropriate level for his or her age or grade level. **Informal assessments**, which include running records, cloze tests, reading inventories, portfolios, and so on are not data driven. Instead, informal assessments use performance-driven tasks to guide instruction and provide informal ratings about each student's individual progress. During these

Copyright © Mometrix Media. You have been licensed one copy of this document for personal use only. Any other reproduction or redistribution is strictly prohibited. All rights reserved.

assessments, each student's performance is used to monitor his or her progress and guide future instruction, often in preparation for a formal assessment.

Evaluating Appropriateness of Assessment Instrument or Practice

The two main factors that must be considered when evaluating the appropriateness of assessment instruction and practices are curriculum alignment and cultural bias. **Curriculum alignment** is the act of teaching students the concepts that they will eventually be tested on. To reach proficiency on the standards outlined by state or district mandates, teachers must continuously teach and assess the standards. Avoiding **cultural bias** ensures that all students are given access to all relevant lessons, instruction, and materials. Furthermore, avoiding cultural bias ensures that all students are given a fair opportunity to succeed on any given assessment. This includes accommodating students of certain subgroups with assessment modifications, such as additional testing time, taking the test in his or her native language, and creating types of assessments that are accessible and achievable for students of all backgrounds.

Example Evaluation of Scoring Method

A teacher is assessing a student's ability to identify the main idea of a text. The student correctly identifies the main idea but includes several spelling errors in her written response. The teacher lowers the student's grade, taking points off for misspellings. In this example, the teacher's scoring method is **inappropriate** for the concept being assessed. Although misspellings should be addressed and remedied, the question was designed to assess the student's ability to identify the main idea of the passage. It was not intended to assess the spelling abilities of the student. By lowering the student's score based on misspellings, the teacher is insinuating that the student is unable to correctly identify the main idea of a passage, which is not the case. When assessing a specific skill, it is important that teachers score students based on their ability to complete isolated skills for data to accurately drive future instruction.

Penmanship

Penmanship is a word used to describe a person's *handwriting*. The three main characteristics of penmanship are letter formation, size, and spacing. When teaching penmanship, teachers should start by helping students to correctly form each letter, using arrows to dictate the order and direction in which parts of each letter should be written. Once students have mastered each letter, teachers should focus on letter size or proportion. For example, smaller letters (like c, e, and n) should be half the size of larger letters (such as k, l, or t). Finally, proper spacing should be taught, both between letters and words. Once spacing between words has been mastered, students should begin to work on including punctuation and appropriate spacing between sentences.

Importance of Listening and Speaking Strategies

Both listening and speaking strategies are important skills for students in all areas of education. To achieve the highest success, students should be taught how to effectively **speak** and exchange dialogue in large- and small-group settings. In addition, students should be encouraged to question, retell, or reenact the words of others. Equally important, students must learn to actively **listen** and visualize the words of others so that they are able to understand the purpose of what someone else is saying. To check for listening, students should be encouraged to summarize what they have heard and complete graphic organizers outlining important concepts or facts. When given ample opportunity to both speak and listen, students are more likely to excel across all content areas.

Copyright © Mometrix Media. You have been licensed one copy of this document for personal use only. Any other reproduction or redistribution is strictly prohibited. All rights reserved.

Developing Listening and Speaking Skills with Dramatic Plays

Dramatic play is a type of play in which students are assigned specific roles and encouraged to act those roles out. In dramatic play, students are typically assigned a character but not a script. They are encouraged to take on the feelings and actions of the character they have been assigned and act as that character would act. Dramatic play is an excellent strategy for developing speaking skills as students must clearly identify and express the feelings of their characters. They must speak clearly and loud enough so that the other actors and audience can hear what they are saying. In addition, students must actively listen to what the other students in the play are saying to appropriately respond to the actions and words of the other characters in an effort to further develop the story line.

Copyright © Mometrix Media. You have been licensed one copy of this document for personal use only. Any other reproduction or redistribution is strictly prohibited. All rights reserved.

Mathematics

Numbers and Operations

Classifications of Numbers

- **Numbers** are the basic building blocks of mathematics. Specific features of numbers are identified by the following terms:
- **Integer** – any positive or negative whole number, including zero. Integers do not include fractions $\left(\frac{1}{3}\right)$, decimals (0.56), or mixed numbers $\left(7\frac{3}{4}\right)$.
- **Prime number** – any whole number greater than 1 that has only two factors, itself and 1; that is, a number that can be divided evenly only by 1 and itself.
- **Composite number** – any whole number greater than 1 that has more than two different factors; in other words, any whole number that is not a prime number. For example: The composite number 8 has the factors of 1, 2, 4, and 8.
- **Even number** – any integer that can be divided by 2 without leaving a remainder. For example: 2, 4, 6, 8, and so on.
- **Odd number** – any integer that cannot be divided evenly by 2. For example: 3, 5, 7, 9, and so on.
- **Decimal number** – any number that uses a decimal point to show the part of the number that is less than one. Example: 1.234.
- **Decimal point** – a symbol used to separate the ones place from the tenths place in decimals or dollars from cents in currency.
- **Decimal place** – the position of a number to the right of the decimal point. In the decimal 0.123, the 1 is in the first place to the right of the decimal point, indicating tenths; the 2 is in the second place, indicating hundredths; and the 3 is in the third place, indicating thousandths.
- The **decimal**, or base 10, system is a number system that uses ten different digits (0, 1, 2, 3, 4, 5, 6, 7, 8, 9). An example of a number system that uses something other than ten digits is the **binary**, or base 2, number system, used by computers, which uses only the numbers 0 and 1. It is thought that the decimal system originated because people had only their 10 fingers for counting.
- **Rational numbers** include all integers, decimals, and fractions. Any terminating or repeating decimal number is a rational number.
- **Irrational numbers** cannot be written as fractions or decimals because the number of decimal places is infinite and there is no recurring pattern of digits within the number. For example, pi (π) begins with 3.141592 and continues without terminating or repeating, so pi is an irrational number.
- **Real numbers** are the set of all rational and irrational numbers.

Review Video: Numbers and Their Classifications
Visit mometrix.com/academy and enter code: 461071

Place Value

Write the place value of each digit in the following number: 14,059.826

1: ten-thousands
4: thousands

Copyright © Mometrix Media. You have been licensed one copy of this document for personal use only. Any other reproduction or redistribution is strictly prohibited. All rights reserved.

0: hundreds
5: tens
9: ones
8: tenths
2: hundredths
6: thousandths

Review Video: Number Place Value
Visit mometrix.com/academy and enter code: 205433

Writing Numbers in Word Form

Example 1

Write each number in words.
29: twenty-nine

478: four hundred seventy-eight

9,435: nine thousand four hundred thirty-five

98,542: ninety-eight thousand five hundred forty-two

302, 876: three hundred two thousand eight hundred seventy-six

Example 2

Write each decimal in words.
0.06: six hundredths

0.6: six tenths

6.0: six

0.009: nine thousandths

0.113: one hundred thirteen thousandths

0.901: nine hundred one-thousandths

Rounding and Estimation

Rounding is reducing the digits in a number while still trying to keep the value similar. The result will be less accurate, but will be in a simpler form, and will be easier to use. Whole numbers can be rounded to the nearest ten, hundred or thousand.

Example 1

Round each number:
a. Round each number to the nearest ten: 11, 47, 118

b. Round each number to the nearest hundred: 78, 980, 248

Copyright © Mometrix Media. You have been licensed one copy of this document for personal use only. Any other reproduction or redistribution is strictly prohibited. All rights reserved.

c. Round each number to the nearest thousand: 302, 1274, 3756

Answer

a. Remember, when rounding to the nearest ten, anything ending in 5 or greater rounds up. So, 11 rounds to 10, 47 rounds to 50, and 118 rounds to 120

b. Remember, when rounding to the nearest hundred, anything ending in 50 or greater rounds up. So, 78 rounds to 100, 980 rounds to 1000, and 248 rounds to 200.

c. Remember, when rounding to the nearest thousand, anything ending in 500 or greater rounds up. So, 302 rounds to 0, 1274 rounds to 1000, and 3756 rounds to 4000.

When you are asked for the solution a problem, you may need to provide only an approximate figure or **estimation** for your answer. In this situation, you can round the numbers that will be calculated to a non-zero number. This means that the first digit in the number is not zero, and the following numbers are zeros.

Example 2

Estimate the solution to $345{,}932 + 96{,}369$.

Start by rounding each number to have only one digit as a non-zero number: 345,932 becomes 300,000 and 96,369 becomes 100,000.

Then, add the rounded numbers: $300{,}000 + 100{,}000 = 400{,}000$. So, the answer is approximately 400,000.

The exact answer would be $345{,}932 + 96{,}369 = 442{,}301$. So, the estimate of 400,000 is a similar value to the exact answer.

Example 3

A runner's heart beats 422 times over the course of six minutes. About how many times did the runner's heart beat during each minute?

"About how many" indicates that you need to estimate the solution. In this case, look at the numbers you are given. 422 can be rounded down to 420, which is easily divisible by 6. A good estimate is $420 \div 6 = 70$ beats per minute. More accurately, the patient's heart rate was just over 70 beats per minute since his heart actually beat a little more than 420 times in six minutes.

Review Video: Rounding and Estimation
Visit mometrix.com/academy and enter code: 126243

Measurement Conversion

When going from a larger unit to a smaller unit, multiply the number of the known amount by the **equivalent amount**. When going from a smaller unit to a larger unit, divide the number of the known amount by the equivalent amount.

Also, you can set up conversion fractions. In these fractions, one fraction is the **conversion factor**. The other fraction has the unknown amount in the numerator. So, the known value is placed in the denominator. Sometimes the second fraction has the known value from the problem in the numerator, and the unknown in the denominator. Multiply the two fractions to get the converted measurement.

Copyright © Mometrix Media. You have been licensed one copy of this document for personal use only. Any other reproduction or redistribution is strictly prohibited. All rights reserved.

Conversion Units

Metric Conversions

1000 mcg (microgram)	1 mg
1000 mg (milligram)	1 g
1000 g (gram)	1 kg
1000 kg (kilogram)	1 metric ton
1000 mL (milliliter)	1 L
1000 um (micrometer)	1 mm
1000 mm (millimeter)	1 m
100 cm (centimeter)	1 m
1000 m (meter)	1 km

U.S. and Metric Equivalents

Unit	U.S. equivalent	Metric equivalent
Inch	1 inch	2.54 centimeters
Foot	12 inches	0.305 meters
Yard	3 feet	0.914 meters
Mile	5280 feet	1.609 kilometers

Capacity Measurements

Unit	U.S. equivalent	Metric equivalent
Ounce	8 drams	29.573 milliliters
Cup	8 ounces	0.237 liter
Pint	16 ounces	0.473 liter
Quart	2 pints	0.946 liter
Gallon	4 quarts	3.785 liters

Weight Measurements

Unit	U.S. equivalent	Metric equivalent
Ounce	16 drams	28.35 grams
Pound	16 ounces	453.6 grams
Ton	2,000 pounds	907.2 kilograms

Fluid Measurements

Unit	English equivalent	Metric equivalent
1 tsp	1 fluid dram	5 milliliters
3 tsp	4 fluid drams	15 or 16 milliliters
2 tbsp	1 fluid ounce	30 milliliters
1 glass	8 fluid ounces	240 milliliters

Measurement Conversion Practice Problems

Example 1

a. Convert 1.4 meters to centimeters.

b. Convert 218 centimeters to meters.

Copyright © Mometrix Media. You have been licensed one copy of this document for personal use only. Any other reproduction or redistribution is strictly prohibited. All rights reserved.

Example 2

a. Convert 42 inches to feet.

b. Convert 15 feet to yards.

Example 3

a. How many pounds are in 15 kilograms?

b. How many pounds are in 80 ounces?

Example 4

a. How many kilometers are in 2 miles?

b. How many centimeters are in 5 feet?

Example 5

a. How many gallons are in 15.14 liters?

b. How many liters are in 8 quarts?

Example 6

a. How many grams are in 13.2 pounds?

b. How many pints are in 9 gallons?

Measurement Conversion Practice Solutions

Example 1

Write ratios with the conversion factor $\frac{100 \text{ cm}}{1 \text{ m}}$. Use proportions to convert the given units.

a. $\frac{100 \text{ cm}}{1 \text{ m}} = \frac{x \text{ cm}}{1.4 \text{ m}}$. Cross multiply to get $x = 140$. So, 1.4 m is the same as 140 cm.

b. $\frac{100 \text{ cm}}{1 \text{ m}} = \frac{218 \text{ cm}}{x \text{ m}}$. Cross multiply to get $100x = 218$, or $x = 2.18$. So, 218 cm is the same as 2.18 m.

Example 2

Write ratios with the conversion factors $\frac{12 \text{ in}}{1 \text{ ft}}$ and $\frac{3 \text{ ft}}{1 \text{ yd}}$. Use proportions to convert the given units.

a. $\frac{12 \text{ in}}{1 \text{ ft}} = \frac{42 \text{ in}}{x \text{ ft}}$. Cross multiply to get $12x = 42$, or $x = 3.5$. So, 42 inches is the same as 3.5 feet.

b. $\frac{3 \text{ ft}}{1 \text{ yd}} = \frac{15 \text{ ft}}{x \text{ yd}}$. Cross multiply to get $3x = 15$, or $x = 5$. So, 15 feet is the same as 5 yards.

Example 3

a. 15 kilograms $\times \frac{2.2 \text{ pounds}}{1 \text{ kilogram}} = 33$ pounds

b. 80 ounces $\times \frac{1 \text{ pound}}{16 \text{ ounces}} = 5$ pounds

Copyright © Mometrix Media. You have been licensed one copy of this document for personal use only. Any other reproduction or redistribution is strictly prohibited. All rights reserved.

Example 4

a. $2 \text{ miles } \times \frac{1.609 \text{ kilometers}}{1 \text{ mile}} = 3.218 \text{ kilometers}$

b. $5 \text{ feet } \times \frac{12 \text{ inches}}{1 \text{ foot}} \times \frac{2.54 \text{ centimeters}}{1 \text{ inch}} = 152.4 \text{ centimeters}$

Example 5

a. $15.14 \text{ liters } \times \frac{1 \text{ gallon}}{3.785 \text{ liters}} = 4 \text{ gallons}$

b. $8 \text{ quarts } \times \frac{1 \text{ gallon}}{4 \text{ quarts}} \times \frac{3.785 \text{ liters}}{1 \text{ gallon}} = 7.57 \text{ liters}$

Example 6

a. $13.2 \text{ pounds } \times \frac{1 \text{ kilogram}}{2.2 \text{ pounds}} \times \frac{1000 \text{ grams}}{1 \text{ kilogram}} = 6000 \text{ grams}$

b. $9 \text{ gallons } \times \frac{4 \text{ quarts}}{1 \text{ gallon}} \times \frac{2 \text{ pints}}{1 \text{ quarts}} = 72 \text{ pints}$

Operations

There are four basic mathematical operations:

Addition and Subtraction

Addition increases the value of one quantity by the value of another quantity. Example: $2 + 4 = 6$; $8 + 9 = 17$. The result is called the **sum**. With addition, the order does not matter. $4 + 2 = 2 + 4$.

Subtraction is the opposite operation to addition; it decreases the value of one quantity by the value of another quantity. Example: $6 - 4 = 2$; $17 - 8 = 9$. The result is called the **difference**. Note that with subtraction, the order does matter. $6 - 4 \neq 4 - 6$.

Review Video: Addition and Subtraction
Visit mometrix.com/academy and enter code: 521157

Multiplication and Division

Multiplication can be thought of as repeated addition. One number tells how many times to add the other number to itself. Example: 3×2 (three times two) $= 2 + 2 + 2 = 6$. With multiplication, the order does not matter. $2 \times 3 = 3 \times 2$ or $3 + 3 = 2 + 2 + 2$.

Division is the opposite operation to multiplication; one number tells us how many parts to divide the other number into. Example: $20 \div 4 = 5$; if 20 is split into 4 equal parts, each part is 5. With division, the order of the numbers does matter. $20 \div 4 \neq 4 \div 20$.

Review Video: Multiplication and Division
Visit mometrix.com/academy and enter code: 643326

Order of Operations

Order of operations is a set of rules that dictates the order in which we must perform each operation in an expression so that we will evaluate it accurately. If we have an expression that includes multiple different operations, order of operations tells us which operations to do first. The most common mnemonic for order of operations is **PEMDAS**, or "Please Excuse My Dear Aunt

Copyright © Mometrix Media. You have been licensed one copy of this document for personal use only. Any other reproduction or redistribution is strictly prohibited. All rights reserved.

Sally." PEMDAS stands for parentheses, exponents, multiplication, division, addition, and subtraction. It is important to understand that multiplication and division have equal precedence, as do addition and subtraction, so those pairs of operations are simply worked from left to right in order.

Example

Evaluate the expression $5 + 20 \div 4 \times (2 + 3) - 6$ using the correct order of operations.

P: Perform the operations inside the parentheses: $(2 + 3) = 5$

E: Simplify the exponents.

The equation now looks like this: $5 + 20 \div 4 \times 5 - 6$

MD: Perform multiplication and division from left to right: $20 \div 4 = 5$; then $5 \times 5 = 25$

The equation now looks like this: $5 + 25 - 6$

AS: Perform addition and subtraction from left to right: $5 + 25 = 30$; then $30 - 6 = 24$

Review Video: Order of Operations
Visit mometrix.com/academy and enter code: 259675

Subtraction with Regrouping

Example 1

Demonstrate how to subtract 189 from 525 using regrouping.

First, set up the subtraction problem:

$$\begin{array}{r} 525 \\ -\quad 189 \\ \hline \end{array}$$

Notice that the numbers in the ones and tens columns of 525 are smaller than the numbers in the ones and tens columns of 189. This means you will need to use regrouping to perform subtraction.

$$\begin{array}{cccc} & 5 & 2 & 5 \\ - & 1 & 8 & 9 \end{array}$$

To subtract 9 from 5 in the ones column you will need to borrow from the 2 in the tens columns:

$$\begin{array}{cccc} & 5 & 1 & 15 \\ - & 1 & 8 & 9 \\ \hline & & & 6 \end{array}$$

Next, to subtract 8 from 1 in the tens column you will need to borrow from the 5 in the hundreds column:

$$\begin{array}{cccc} & 4 & 11 & 15 \\ - & 1 & 8 & 9 \\ \hline & & 3 & 6 \end{array}$$

Copyright © Mometrix Media. You have been licensed one copy of this document for personal use only. Any other reproduction or redistribution is strictly prohibited. All rights reserved.

Last, subtract the 1 from the 4 in the hundreds column:

	4	11	15
–	1	8	9
	3	3	6

Example 2

Demonstrate how to subtract 477 from 620 using regrouping.

First, set up the subtraction problem:

	620
–	477

Notice that the numbers in the ones and tens columns of 620 are smaller than the numbers in the ones and tens columns of 477. This means you will need to use regrouping to perform subtraction.

	6	2	0
–	4	7	7

To subtract 7 from 0 in the ones column you will need to borrow from the 2 in the tens column.

	6	1	10
–	4	7	7
			3

Next, to subtract 7 from the 1 that's still in the tens column you will need to borrow from the 6 in the hundreds column.

	5	11	10
–	4	7	7
		4	3

Lastly, subtract 4 from the 5 remaining in the hundreds column to get:

	5	11	10
–	4	7	7
	1	4	3

Real World One or Multi-Step Problems with Rational Numbers

Example 1
A woman's age is thirteen more than half of 60. How old is the woman?

"More than" indicates addition, and "of" indicates multiplication. The expression can be written as $\frac{1}{2}(60) + 13$. So, the woman's age is equal to $\frac{1}{2}(60) + 13 = 30 + 13 = 43$. The woman is 43 years old.

Example 2
A patient was given pain medicine at a dosage of 0.22 grams. The patient's dosage was then increased to 0.80 grams. By how much was the patient's dosage increased?

Copyright © Mometrix Media. You have been licensed one copy of this document for personal use only. Any other reproduction or redistribution is strictly prohibited. All rights reserved.

The first step is to determine what operation (addition, subtraction, multiplication, or division) the problem requires. Notice the keywords and phrases "by how much" and "increased." "Increased" means that you go from a smaller amount to a larger amount. This change can be found by subtracting the smaller amount from the larger amount: 0.80 grams– 0.22 grams = 0.58 grams.

Remember to line up the decimal when subtracting.

$$\begin{array}{rr} & 0.80 \\ - & 0.22 \\ & 0.58 \end{array}$$

Example 3

At a hotel, $\frac{3}{4}$ of the 100 rooms are occupied today. Yesterday, $\frac{4}{5}$ of the 100 rooms were occupied. On which day were more of the rooms occupied and by how much more?

First, find the number of rooms occupied each day. To do so, multiply the fraction of rooms occupied by the number of rooms available:

$$\text{Number occupied} = \text{Fraction occupied} \times \text{Total number}$$

Today:

$$\text{Number of rooms occupied} = \frac{3}{4} \times 100 = 75$$

Today, 75 rooms are occupied.

Yesterday:

$$\text{Number of rooms occupied} = \frac{4}{5} \times 100 = 80$$

Yesterday, 80 rooms were occupied.

The difference in the number of rooms occupied is

$$80 - 75 = 5 \text{ rooms}$$

Therefore, five more rooms were occupied yesterday than today.

Review Video: Rational Numbers
Visit mometrix.com/academy and enter code: 280645

Example 4

At a school, 40% of the teachers teach English. If 20 teachers teach English, how many teachers work at the school?

To answer this problem, first think about the number of teachers that work at the school. Will it be more or less than the number of teachers who work in a specific department such as English? More teachers work at the school, so the number you find to answer this question will be greater than 20.

Copyright © Mometrix Media. You have been licensed one copy of this document for personal use only. Any other reproduction or redistribution is strictly prohibited. All rights reserved.

40% of the teachers are English teachers. "Of" indicates multiplication, and words like "is" and "are" indicate equivalence. Translating the problem into a mathematical sentence gives $40\% \times t = 20$, where t represents the total number of teachers. Solving for t gives $t = \frac{20}{40\%} = \frac{20}{0.40} = 50$. Fifty teachers work at the school.

Example 5

A patient was given blood pressure medicine at a dosage of 2 grams. The patient's dosage was then decreased to 0.45 grams. By how much was the patient's dosage decreased?

The decrease is represented by the difference between the two amounts:

$$2 \text{ grams} - 0.45 \text{ grams} = 1.55 \text{ grams}.$$

Remember to line up the decimal point before subtracting.

$$\begin{array}{r} 2.00 \\ -\ \ 0.45 \\ \hline 1.55 \end{array}$$

Example 6

Two weeks ago, $\frac{2}{3}$ of the 60 customers at a skate shop were male. Last week, $\frac{3}{6}$ of the 80 customers were male. During which week were there more male customers?

First, you need to find the number of male customers that were in the skate shop each week. You are given this amount in terms of fractions. To find the actual number of male customers, multiply the fraction of male customers by the number of customers in the store.

Actual number of male customers = fraction of male customers × total number of customers.

Two weeks ago: Actual number of male customers $= \frac{2}{3} \times 60$.

$$\frac{2}{3} \times \frac{60}{1} = \frac{2 \times 60}{3 \times 1} = \frac{120}{3} = 40$$

Two weeks ago, 40 of the customers were male.

Last week: Actual number of male customers $= \frac{3}{6} \times 80$.

$$\frac{3}{6} \times \frac{80}{1} = \frac{3 \times 80}{6 \times 1} = \frac{240}{6} = 40$$

Last week, 40 of the customers were male.

The number of male customers was the same both weeks.

Example 7

Jane ate lunch at a local restaurant. She ordered a \$4.99 appetizer, a \$12.50 entrée, and a \$1.25 soda. If she wants to tip her server 20%, how much money will she spend in all?

Copyright © Mometrix Media. You have been licensed one copy of this document for personal use only. Any other reproduction or redistribution is strictly prohibited. All rights reserved.

To find total amount, first find the sum of the items she ordered from the menu and then add 20% of this sum to the total.

In other words:

$$\$4.99 + \$12.50 + \$1.25 = \$18.74$$

Then 20% of \$18.74 is $(20\%)(\$18.74) = (0.20)(\$18.74) = \$3.75$.

So, the total she spends is cost of the meal plus the tip or $\$18.74 + \$3.75 = \$22.49$.

Another way to find this sum is to multiply 120% by the cost of the meal.

$$\$18.74(120\%) = \$18.74(1.20) = \$22.49.$$

Parentheses

Parentheses are used to designate which operations should be done first when there are multiple operations. Example: $4 - (2 + 1) = 1$; the parentheses tell us that we must add 2 and 1, and then subtract the sum from 4, rather than subtracting 2 from 4 and then adding 1 (this would give us an answer of 3).

Review Video: Mathematical Parentheses
Visit mometrix.com/academy and enter code: 978600

Exponents

An **exponent** is a superscript number placed next to another number at the top right. It indicates how many times the base number is to be multiplied by itself. Exponents provide a shorthand way to write what would be a longer mathematical expression. Example: $a^2 = a \times a$; $2^4 = 2 \times 2 \times 2 \times 2$. A number with an exponent of 2 is said to be "squared," while a number with an exponent of 3 is said to be "cubed." The value of a number raised to an exponent is called its power. So, 8^4 is read as "8 to the 4th power," or "8 raised to the power of 4." A negative exponent is the same as the **reciprocal** of a positive exponent. Example: $a^{-2} = \frac{1}{a^2}$.

Review Video: Exponents
Visit mometrix.com/academy and enter code: 600998

Roots

A **root**, such as a square root, is another way of writing a fractional exponent. Instead of using a superscript, roots use the radical symbol ($\sqrt{}$) to indicate the operation. A radical will have a number underneath the bar, and may sometimes have a number in the upper left: $\sqrt[n]{a}$, read as "the nth root of a." The relationship between radical notation and exponent notation can be described by this equation: $\sqrt[n]{a} = a^{\frac{1}{n}}$. The two special cases of $n = 2$ and $n = 3$ are called square roots and cube roots. If there is no number to the upper left, it is understood to be a square root ($n = 2$). Nearly all of the roots you encounter will be square roots. A square root is the same as a number raised to the

Copyright © Mometrix Media. You have been licensed one copy of this document for personal use only. Any other reproduction or redistribution is strictly prohibited. All rights reserved.

one-half power. When we say that a is the square root of b ($a = \sqrt{b}$), we mean that a multiplied by itself equals b: ($a \times a = b$).

Review Video: Roots
Visit mometrix.com/academy and enter code: 795655

Review Video: Square Root and Perfect Square
Visit mometrix.com/academy and enter code: 648063

A **perfect square** is a number that has an integer for its square root. There are 10 perfect squares from 1 to 100: 1, 4, 9, 16, 25, 36, 49, 64, 81, 100 (the squares of integers 1 through 10).

Parentheses are used to designate which operations should be done first when there are multiple operations. Example: $4-(2+1)=1$; the parentheses tell us that we must add 2 and 1, and then subtract the sum from 4, rather than subtracting 2 from 4 and then adding 1 (this would give us an answer of 3).

Absolute Value

A precursor to working with negative numbers is understanding what **absolute values** are. A number's absolute value is simply the distance away from zero a number is on the number line. The absolute value of a number is always positive and is written $|x|$.

Example
Show that $|3| = |-3|$.

The absolute value of 3, written as $|3|$, is 3 because the distance between 0 and 3 on a number line is three units. Likewise, the absolute value of –3, written as $|-3|$, is 3 because the distance between 0 and –3 on a number line is three units. So, $|3| = |-3|$.

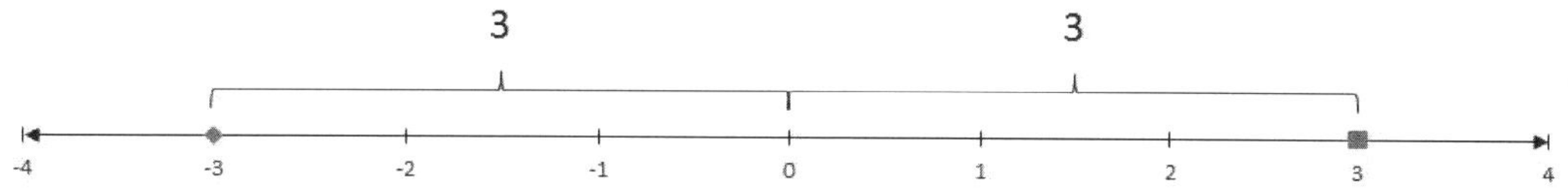

Review Video: Absolute Value
Visit mometrix.com/academy and enter code: 314669

Operations with Positive and Negative Numbers

Addition
When adding signed numbers, if the signs are the same simply add the absolute values of the addends and apply the original sign to the sum. For example, $(+4) + (+8) = +12$ and $(-4) + (-8) = -12$. When the original signs are different, take the absolute values of the addends and subtract the smaller value from the larger value, then apply the original sign of the larger value to the difference. For instance, $(+4) + (-8) = -4$ and $(-4) + (+8) = +4$.

Subtraction
For subtracting signed numbers, change the sign of the number after the minus symbol and then follow the same rules used for addition. For example, $(+4) - (+8) = (+4) + (-8) = -4$.

Copyright © Mometrix Media. You have been licensed one copy of this document for personal use only. Any other reproduction or redistribution is strictly prohibited. All rights reserved.

Multiplication

If the signs are the same the product is positive when multiplying signed numbers. For example, $(+4) \times (+8) = +32$ and $(-4) \times (-8) = +32$. If the signs are opposite, the product is negative. For example, $(+4) \times (-8) = -32$ and $(-4) \times (+8) = -32$. When more than two factors are multiplied together, the sign of the product is determined by how many negative factors are present. If there are an odd number of negative factors then the product is negative, whereas an even number of negative factors indicates a positive product. For instance, $(+4) \times (-8) \times (-2) = +64$ and $(-4) \times (-8) \times (-2) = -64$.

Division

The rules for dividing signed numbers are similar to multiplying signed numbers. If the dividend and divisor have the same sign, the quotient is positive. If the dividend and divisor have opposite signs, the quotient is negative. For example, $(-4) \div (+8) = -0.5$.

The Number Line

A number line is a graph to see the distance between numbers. Basically, this graph shows the relationship between numbers. So, a number line may have a point for zero and may show negative numbers on the left side of the line. Also, any positive numbers are placed on the right side of the line.

Example

Name each point on the number line below:

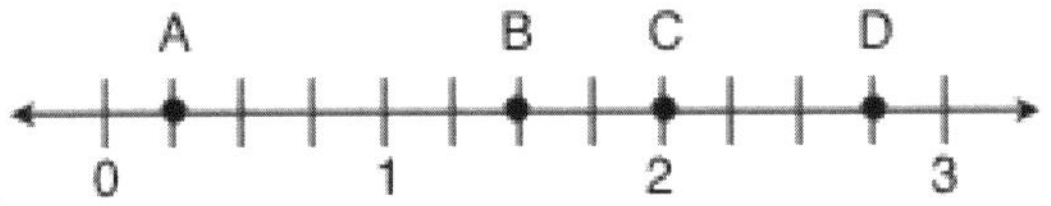

Use the dashed lines on the number line to identify each point. Each dashed line between two whole numbers is $\frac{1}{4}$. The line halfway between two numbers is $\frac{1}{2}$.

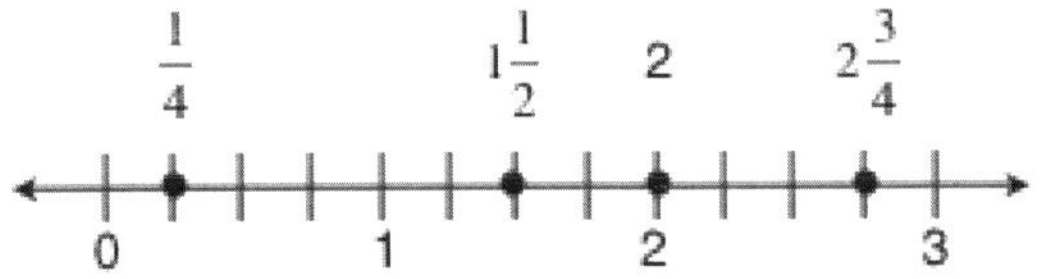

Review Video: Negative and Positive Number Line
Visit mometrix.com/academy and enter code: 816439

Fractions, Decimals, and Percentages

Fractions

A **fraction** is a number that is expressed as one integer written above another integer, with a dividing line between them $\left(\frac{x}{y}\right)$. It represents the **quotient** of the two numbers "x divided by y." It can also be thought of as x out of y equal parts.

Copyright © Mometrix Media. You have been licensed one copy of this document for personal use only. Any other reproduction or redistribution is strictly prohibited. All rights reserved.

The top number of a fraction is called the **numerator**, and it represents the number of parts under consideration. The 1 in $\frac{1}{4}$ means that 1 part out of the whole is being considered in the calculation. The bottom number of a fraction is called the **denominator**, and it represents the total number of equal parts. The 4 in $\frac{1}{4}$ means that the whole consists of 4 equal parts. A fraction cannot have a denominator of zero; this is referred to as "*undefined*."

Fractions can be manipulated, without changing the value of the fraction, by multiplying or dividing (but not adding or subtracting) both the numerator and denominator by the same number. If you divide both numbers by a common factor, you are **reducing** or simplifying the fraction. Two fractions that have the same value but are expressed differently are known as **equivalent fractions**. For example, $\frac{2}{10}, \frac{3}{15}, \frac{4}{20}$, and $\frac{5}{25}$ are all equivalent fractions. They can also all be reduced or simplified to $\frac{1}{5}$.

When two fractions are manipulated so that they have the same denominator, this is known as finding a **common denominator**. The number chosen to be that common denominator should be the least common multiple of the two original denominators. Example: $\frac{3}{4}$ and $\frac{5}{6}$; the least common multiple of 4 and 6 is 12. Manipulating to achieve the common denominator: $\frac{3}{4} = \frac{9}{12}; \frac{5}{6} = \frac{10}{12}$.

<u>Proper Fractions and Mixed Numbers</u>

A fraction whose denominator is greater than its numerator is known as a **proper fraction**, while a fraction whose numerator is greater than its denominator is known as an **improper fraction**. Proper fractions have values *less than one* and improper fractions have values *greater than one*.

A **mixed number** is a number that contains both an integer and a fraction. Any improper fraction can be rewritten as a mixed number. Example: $\frac{8}{3} = \frac{6}{3} + \frac{2}{3} = 2 + \frac{2}{3} = 2\frac{2}{3}$. Similarly, any mixed number can be rewritten as an improper fraction. Example: $1\frac{3}{5} = 1 + \frac{3}{5} = \frac{5}{5} + \frac{3}{5} = \frac{8}{5}$.

Review Video: <u>Proper and Improper Fractions and Mixed Numbers</u>
Visit mometrix.com/academy and enter code: 211077

Review Video: <u>Fractions</u>
Visit mometrix.com/academy and enter code: 262335

Decimals

<u>Decimal Illustration</u>

Use a model to represent the decimal: 0.24. Write 0.24 as a fraction.

The decimal 0.24 is twenty-four hundredths. One possible model to represent this fraction is to draw 100 pennies, since each penny is worth one-hundredth of a dollar. Draw one hundred circles

Copyright © Mometrix Media. You have been licensed one copy of this document for personal use only. Any other reproduction or redistribution is strictly prohibited. All rights reserved.

to represent one hundred pennies. Shade 24 of the pennies to represent the decimal twenty-four hundredths.

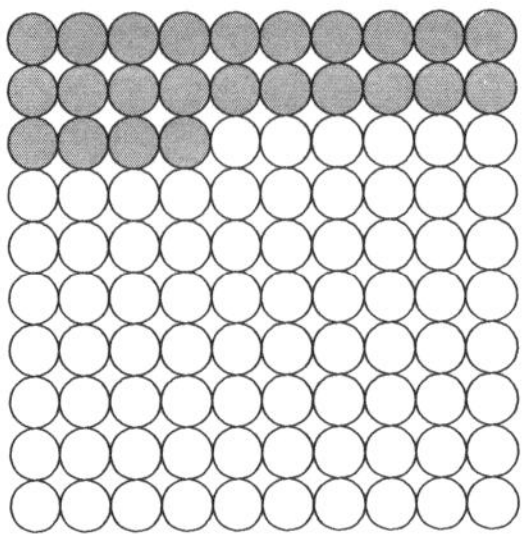

To write the decimal as a fraction, write a fraction: $\frac{\text{\# shaded spaces}}{\text{\# total spaces}}$. The number of shaded spaces is 24, and the total number of spaces is 100, so as a fraction 0.24 equals $\frac{24}{100}$. This fraction can then be reduced to $\frac{6}{25}$.

Review Video: Decimals
Visit mometrix.com/academy and enter code: 837268

Percentages

Percentages can be thought of as fractions that are based on a whole of 100; that is, one whole is equal to 100%. The word percent means "per hundred." Fractions can be expressed as a percentage by finding equivalent fractions with a denomination of 100. Example: $\frac{7}{10} = \frac{70}{100} = 70\%$; $\frac{1}{4} = \frac{25}{100} = 25\%$.

To express a *percentage as a fraction*, divide the percentage number by 100 and reduce the fraction to its simplest possible terms. Example: $60\% = \frac{60}{100} = \frac{3}{5}$; $96\% = \frac{96}{100} = \frac{24}{25}$.

Review Video: Percentages
Visit mometrix.com/academy and enter code: 141911

Real World Problems with Percentages

A percentage problem can be presented three main ways: (1) Find what percentage of some number another number is. Example: What percentage of 40 is 8? (2) Find what number is some percentage of a given number. Example: What number is 20% of 40? (3) Find what number another number is a given percentage of. Example: What number is 8 20% of?

The three components in all of these cases are the same: a **whole** (*W*), a **part** (*P*), and a **percentage** (%). These are related by the equation: $\boldsymbol{P} = \boldsymbol{W} \times \%$. This is the form of the equation you would use to solve problems of type (2). To solve types (1) and (3), you would use these two forms:

$$\% = \frac{P}{W} \text{ and } W = \frac{P}{\%}$$

The thing that frequently makes percentage problems difficult is that they are most often also word problems, so a large part of solving them is figuring out which quantities are what. Example: In a school cafeteria, 7 students choose pizza, 9 choose hamburgers, and 4 choose tacos. Find the

Copyright © Mometrix Media. You have been licensed one copy of this document for personal use only. Any other reproduction or redistribution is strictly prohibited. All rights reserved.

percentage that chooses tacos. To find the whole, you must first add all of the parts: $7 + 9 + 4 = 20$. The percentage can then be found by dividing the part by the whole $(\% = \frac{P}{W})$: $\frac{4}{20} = \frac{20}{100} = 20\%$.

Example 1

What is 30% of 120?

The word "of" indicates multiplication, so 30% of 120 is found by multiplying 30% by 120. First, change 30% to a fraction or decimal. Recall that "percent" means per hundred, so $30\% = \frac{30}{100} = 0.30$. 120 times 0.3 is 36.

Review Video: Finding Percentage of Number Given Whole
Visit mometrix.com/academy and enter code: 932623

Example 2

What is 150% of 20?

150% of 20 is found by multiplying 150% by 20. First, change 150% to a fraction or decimal. Recall that "percent" means per hundred, so $150\% = \frac{150}{100} = 1.50$. So, $(1.50)(20) = 30$. Notice that 30 is greater than the original number of 20. This makes sense because you are finding a number that is more than 100% of the original number.

Example 3

What is 14.5% of 96?

Change 14.5% to a decimal before multiplying. $0.145 \times 96 = 13.92$. Notice that 13.92 is much smaller than the original number of 96. This makes sense because you are finding a small percentage of the original number.

Example 4

According to a survey, about 82% of engineers were highly satisfied with their job. If 145 engineers were surveyed, how many reported that they were highly satisfied?

82% of $145 = 0.82 \times 145 = 118.9$. Because you can't have 0.9 of a person, we must round up to say that 119 engineers reported that they were highly satisfied with their jobs.

Example 5

On Monday, Lucy spent 5 hours observing sales, 3 hours working on advertising, and 4 hours doing paperwork. On Tuesday, she spent 4 hours observing sales, 6 hours working on advertising, and 2 hours doing paperwork. What was the percent change for time spent on each task between the two days?

The three tasks are observing sales, working on advertising, and doing paperwork. To find the amount of change, compare the first amount with the second amount for each task. Then, write this difference as a percentage compared to the initial amount.

Amount of change for observing sales:

$$5 \text{ hours} - 4 \text{ hours} = 1 \text{ hour}$$

The percent of change is

Copyright © Mometrix Media. You have been licensed one copy of this document for personal use only. Any other reproduction or redistribution is strictly prohibited. All rights reserved.

$$\frac{\text{amount of change}}{\text{original amount}} \times 100\%. \frac{1 \text{ hour}}{5 \text{ hours}} \times 100\% = 20\%.$$

Lucy spent 20% less time observing sales on Tuesday than she did on Monday.

Amount of change for working on advertising:

$$6 \text{ hours} - 3 \text{ hours} = 3 \text{ hours}$$

The percent of change is

$$\frac{\text{amount of change}}{\text{original amount}} \times 100\%. \frac{3 \text{ hours}}{3 \text{ hours}} \times 100\% = 100\%.$$

Lucy spent 100% more time (or twice as much time) working on advertising on Tuesday than she did on Monday.

Amount of change for doing paperwork:

$$4 \text{ hours} - 2 \text{ hours} = 2 \text{ hours}$$

The percent of change is

$$\frac{\text{amount of change}}{\text{original amount}} \times 100\%. \frac{2 \text{ hours}}{4 \text{ hours}} \times 100\% = 50\%.$$

Lucy spent 50% less time (or half as much time) working on paperwork on Tuesday than she did on Monday.

<u>Example 6</u>
A patient was given 40 mg of a certain medicine. Later, the patient's dosage was increased to 45 mg. What was the percent increase in his medication?

To find the percent increase, first compare the original and increased amounts. The original amount was 40 mg, and the increased amount is 45 mg, so the dosage of medication was increased by 5 mg $(45 - 40 = 5)$. Note, however, that the question asks not by how much the dosage increased but by what percentage it increased. Percent increase $= \frac{\text{new amount} - \text{original amount}}{\text{original amount}} \times 100\%$.

So, $\frac{45 \text{ mg} - 40 \text{ mg}}{40 \text{ mg}} \times 100\% = \frac{5}{40} \times 100\% = 0.125 \times 100\% = 12.5\%$

The percent increase is 12.5%.

<u>Example 7</u>
A patient was given 100 mg of a certain medicine. The patient's dosage was later decreased to 88 mg. What was the percent decrease?

The medication was decreased by 12 mg:

$$(100 \text{ mg} - 88 \text{ mg} = 12 \text{ mg})$$

To find by what percent the medication was decreased, this change must be written as a percentage when compared to the original amount.

Copyright © Mometrix Media. You have been licensed one copy of this document for personal use only. Any other reproduction or redistribution is strictly prohibited. All rights reserved.

In other words, $\frac{\text{new amount} - \text{original amount}}{\text{original amount}} \times 100\% = \text{percent change}$

So $\frac{12\text{ mg}}{100\text{ mg}} \times 100\% = 0.12 \times 100\% = 12\%$.

The percent decrease is 12%.

<u>Example 8</u>

A barista used 125 units of coffee grounds to make a liter of coffee. The barista later reduced the amount of coffee to 100 units. By what percentage was the amount of coffee grounds reduced?

In this problem you must determine which information is necessary to answer the question. The question asks by what percentage the coffee grounds were reduced. Find the two amounts and perform subtraction to find their difference. The first pot of coffee used 125 units. The second time, the barista used 100 units. Therefore, the difference is 125 units − 100 units = 25 units. The percentage reduction can then be calculated as:

$$\frac{\text{change}}{\text{original}} = \frac{25}{125} = \frac{1}{5} = 20\%$$

<u>Example 9</u>

In a performance review, an employee received a score of 70 for efficiency and 90 for meeting project deadlines. Six months later, the employee received a score of 65 for efficiency and 96 for meeting project deadlines. What was the percent change for each score on thc performance review?

To find the percent change, compare the first amount with the second amount for each score; then, write this difference as a percentage of the initial amount.

Percent change for efficiency score:

$$70 - 65 = 5; \ \frac{5}{70} \approx 7.1\%$$

The employee's efficiency decreased by about 7.1%.

Percent change for meeting project deadlines score:

$$96 - 90 = 6; \ \frac{6}{90} \approx 6.7\%$$

The employee increased his ability to meet project deadlines by about 6.7%.

Simplify

<u>Example 1</u>

How to simplify:

$$\frac{\frac{2}{5}}{\frac{4}{7}}$$

Copyright © Mometrix Media. You have been licensed one copy of this document for personal use only. Any other reproduction or redistribution is strictly prohibited. All rights reserved.

Dividing a fraction by a fraction may appear tricky, but it's not if you write out your steps carefully. Follow these steps to divide a fraction by a fraction.

Step 1: Rewrite the problem as a multiplication problem. Dividing by a fraction is the same as multiplying by its **reciprocal**, also known as its **multiplicative inverse**. The product of a number and its reciprocal is 1. Because $\frac{4}{7}$ times $\frac{7}{4}$ is 1, these numbers are reciprocals. Note that reciprocals can be found by simply interchanging the numerators and denominators. So, rewriting the problem as a multiplication problem gives $\frac{2}{5} \times \frac{7}{4}$.

Step 2: Perform multiplication of the fractions by multiplying the numerators by each other and the denominators by each other. In other words, multiply across the top and then multiply across the bottom.

$$\frac{2}{5} \times \frac{7}{4} = \frac{2 \times 7}{5 \times 4} = \frac{14}{20}$$

Step 3: Make sure the fraction is reduced to lowest terms. Both 14 and 20 can be divided by 2.

$$\frac{14}{20} = \frac{14 \div 2}{20 \div 2} = \frac{7}{10}$$

The answer is $\frac{7}{10}$.

<u>Example 2</u>

How to simplify:

$$\frac{1}{4} + \frac{3}{6}$$

Fractions with common denominators can be easily added or subtracted. Recall that the denominator is the bottom number in the fraction and that the numerator is the top number in the fraction.

The denominators of $\frac{1}{4}$ and $\frac{3}{6}$ are 4 and 6, respectively. The lowest common denominator of 4 and 6 is 12 because 12 is the least common multiple of 4 (multiples 4, 8, 12, 16, ...) and 6 (multiples 6, 12, 18, 24, ...). Convert each fraction to its equivalent with the newly found common denominator of 12.

$$\frac{1 \times 3}{4 \times 3} = \frac{3}{12}; \quad \frac{3 \times 2}{6 \times 2} = \frac{6}{12}$$

Now that the fractions have the same denominator, you can add them.

$$\frac{3}{12} + \frac{6}{12} = \frac{9}{12}$$

Be sure to write your answer in lowest terms. Both 9 and 12 can be divided by 3, so the answer is $\frac{3}{4}$.

Copyright © Mometrix Media. You have been licensed one copy of this document for personal use only. Any other reproduction or redistribution is strictly prohibited. All rights reserved.

Example 3

How to simplify:

$$\frac{7}{8}-\frac{8}{16}$$

Fractions with common denominators can be easily added or subtracted. Recall that the denominator is the bottom number in the fraction and that the numerator is the top number in the fraction.

The denominators of $\frac{7}{8}$ and $\frac{8}{16}$ are 8 and 16, respectively. The lowest common denominator of 8 and 16 is 16 because 16 is the least common multiple of 8 (multiples 8, 16, 24 ...) and 16 (multiples 16, 32, 48, ...). Convert each fraction to its equivalent with the newly found common denominator of 16.

$$\frac{7\times 2}{8\times 2}=\frac{14}{16};\ \frac{8\times 1}{16\times 1}=\frac{8}{16}$$

Now that the fractions have the same denominator, you can subtract them.

$$\frac{14}{16}-\frac{8}{16}=\frac{6}{16}$$

Be sure to write your answer in lowest terms. Both 6 and 16 can be divided by 2, so the answer is $\frac{3}{8}$.

Example 4

How to simplify:

$$\frac{1}{2}+\left(3\left(\frac{3}{4}\right)-2\right)+4$$

When simplifying expressions, first perform operations within groups. Within the set of parentheses are multiplication and subtraction operations. Perform the multiplication first to get $\frac{1}{2}+\left(\frac{9}{4}-2\right)+4$. Then, subtract two to obtain $\frac{1}{2}+\frac{1}{4}+4$. Finally, perform addition from left to right:

$$\frac{1}{2}+\frac{1}{4}+4=\frac{2}{4}+\frac{1}{4}+\frac{16}{4}=\frac{19}{4}$$

Example 5

How to simplify: $0.22+0.5-(5.5+3.3\div 3)$

First, evaluate the terms in the parentheses $(5.5+3.3\div 3)$ using order of operations. $3.3\div 3=1.1$, and $5.5+1.1=6.6$.

Next, rewrite the problem: $0.22+0.5-6.6$.

Finally, add and subtract from left to right: $0.22+0.5=0.72$; $0.72-6.6=-5.88$. The answer is -5.88.

Copyright © Mometrix Media. You have been licensed one copy of this document for personal use only. Any other reproduction or redistribution is strictly prohibited. All rights reserved.

Example 6

How to simplify:

$$\frac{3}{2} + (4(0.5) - 0.75) + 2$$

First, simplify within the parentheses:

$$\frac{3}{2} + (2 - 0.75) + 2 =$$

$$\frac{3}{2} + 1.25 + 2$$

Finally, change the fraction to a decimal and perform addition from left to right:

$$1.5 + 1.25 + 2 = 4.75$$

Example 7

How to simplify: $1.45 + 1.5 + (6 - 9 \div 2) + 45$

First, evaluate the terms in the parentheses using proper order of operations.

$$1.45 + 1.5 + (6 - 4.5) + 45$$

$$1.45 + 1.5 + 1.5 + 45$$

Finally, add from left to right.

$$1.45 + 1.5 + 1.5 + 45 = 49.45$$

Converting Percentages, Fractions, and Decimals

Converting decimals to percentages and percentages to decimals is as simple as moving the decimal point. To *convert from a decimal to a percentage*, move the decimal point **two places to the right**. To *convert from a percentage to a decimal*, move it **two places to the left**. Example: $0.23 = 23\%$; $5.34 = 534\%$; $0.007 = 0.7\%$; $700\%\ 7.00$; $86\% = 0.86$; $0.15\% = 0.0015$.

It may be helpful to remember that the percentage number will always be larger than the equivalent decimal number.

Review Video: Converting Decimals to Fractions and Percentages Visit mometrix.com/academy and enter code: 986765

Example 1

Convert 15% to both a fraction and a decimal.

First, write the percentage over 100 because percent means "per one hundred." So, 15% can be written as $\frac{15}{100}$. Fractions should be written in the simplest form, which means that the numbers in the numerator and denominator should be reduced if possible. Both 15 and 100 can be divided by 5:

Copyright © Mometrix Media. You have been licensed one copy of this document for personal use only. Any other reproduction or redistribution is strictly prohibited. All rights reserved.

$$\frac{15 \div 5}{100 \div 5} = \frac{3}{20}$$

As before, write the percentage over 100 because percent means "per one hundred." So, 15% can be written as $\frac{15}{100}$. Dividing a number by a power of ten (10, 100, 1000, etc.) is the same as moving the decimal point to the left by the same number of spaces that there are zeros in the divisor. Since 100 has 2 zeros, move the decimal point two places to the left:

$$15\% = 0.15$$

In other words, when converting from a percentage to a decimal, drop the percent sign and move the decimal point two places to the left.

Example 2

Write 24.36% as a fraction and then as a decimal. Explain how you made these conversions.

24.36% written as a fraction is $\frac{24.36}{100}$, or $\frac{2436}{10{,}000}$, which reduces to $\frac{609}{2500}$. 24.36% written as a decimal is 0.2436. Recall that dividing by 100 moves the decimal two places to the left.

> **Review Video: Converting Percentages to Decimals and Fractions**
> Visit mometrix.com/academy and enter code: 287297

Example 3

Convert $\frac{4}{5}$ to a decimal and to a percentage.

To convert a fraction to a decimal, simply divide the numerator by the denominator in the fraction. The numerator is the top number in the fraction and the denominator is the bottom number in a fraction. So $\frac{4}{5} = 4 \div 5 = 0.80 = 0.8$.

Percent means "per hundred." $\frac{4 \times 20}{5 \times 20} = \frac{80}{100} = 80\%$.

Example 4

Convert $3\frac{2}{5}$ to a decimal and to a percentage.

The mixed number $3\frac{2}{5}$ has a whole number and a fractional part. The fractional part $\frac{2}{5}$ can be written as a decimal by dividing 5 into 2, which gives 0.4. Adding the whole to the part gives 3.4. Alternatively, note that $3\frac{2}{5} = 3\frac{4}{10} = 3.4$

To change a decimal to a percentage, multiply it by 100.

$3.4(100) = 340\%$. Notice that this percentage is greater than 100%. This makes sense because the original mixed number $3\frac{2}{5}$ is greater than 1.

> **Review Video: Converting Fractions to Percentages and Decimals**
> Visit mometrix.com/academy and enter code: 306233

Copyright © Mometrix Media. You have been licensed one copy of this document for personal use only. Any other reproduction or redistribution is strictly prohibited. All rights reserved.

Scientific Notation

Scientific notation is a way of writing large numbers in a shorter form. The form $a \times 10^n$ is used in scientific notation, where a is greater than or equal to 1, but less than 10, and n is the number of places the decimal must move to get from the original number to a. Example: The number 230,400,000 is cumbersome to write. To write the value in scientific notation, place a decimal point between the first and second numbers, and include all digits through the last non-zero digit ($a = 2.304$). To find the appropriate power of 10, count the number of places the decimal point had to move ($n = 8$). The number is positive if the decimal moved to the left, and negative if it moved to the right. We can then write 230,400,000 as 2.304×10^8. If we look instead at the number 0.00002304, we have the same value for a, but this time the decimal moved 5 places to the right ($n = -5$). Thus, 0.00002304 can be written as 2.304×10^{-5}. Using this notation makes it simple to compare very large or very small numbers. By comparing exponents, it is easy to see that 3.28×10^4 is smaller than 1.51×10^5, because 4 is less than 5.

Review Video: Scientific Notation
Visit mometrix.com/academy and enter code: 976454

Operations with Decimals

Adding and Subtracting Decimals

When adding and subtracting decimals, the decimal points must always be aligned. Adding decimals is just like adding regular whole numbers. Example: $4.5 + 2 = 6.5$.

If the problem-solver does not properly align the decimal points, an incorrect answer of 4.7 may result. An easy way to add decimals is to align all of the decimal points in a vertical column visually. This will allow one to see exactly where the decimal should be placed in the final answer. Begin adding from right to left. Add each column in turn, making sure to carry the number to the left if a column adds up to more than 9. The same rules apply to the subtraction of decimals.

Review Video: Adding and Subtracting Decimals
Visit mometrix.com/academy and enter code: 381101

Multiplying Decimals

A simple multiplication problem has two components: a **multiplicand** and a **multiplier**. When multiplying decimals, work as though the numbers were whole rather than decimals. Once the final product is calculated, count the number of places to the right of the decimal in both the multiplicand and the multiplier. Then, count that number of places from the right of the product and place the decimal in that position.

For example, 12.3×2.56 has three places to the right of the respective decimals. Multiply 123×256 to get 31488. Now, beginning on the right, count three places to the left and insert the decimal. The final product will be 31.488.

Review Video: Multiplying Decimals
Visit mometrix.com/academy and enter code: 731574

Dividing Decimals

Every division problem has a **divisor** and a **dividend**. The dividend is the number that is being divided. In the problem $14 \div 7$, 14 is the dividend and 7 is the divisor. In a division problem with

Copyright © Mometrix Media. You have been licensed one copy of this document for personal use only. Any other reproduction or redistribution is strictly prohibited. All rights reserved.

decimals, the divisor must be converted into a whole number. Begin by moving the decimal in the divisor to the right until a whole number is created. Next, move the decimal in the dividend the same number of spaces to the right. For example, 4.9 into 24.5 would become 49 into 245. The decimal was moved one space to the right to create a whole number in the divisor, and then the same was done for the dividend. Once the whole numbers are created, the problem is carried out normally: $245 \div 49 = 5$.

> **Review Video: Dividing Decimals**
> Visit mometrix.com/academy and enter code: 560690

Operations with Fractions

Adding and Subtracting Fractions

If two fractions have a common denominator, they can be added or subtracted simply by adding or subtracting the two numerators and retaining the same denominator. Example: $\frac{1}{2}+\frac{1}{4}=\frac{2}{4}+\frac{1}{4}=\frac{3}{4}$. If the two fractions do not already have the same denominator, one or both of them must be manipulated to achieve a common denominator before they can be added or subtracted.

> **Review Video: Adding and Subtracting Fractions**
> Visit mometrix.com/academy and enter code: 378080

Multiplying Fractions

Two fractions can be multiplied by multiplying the two numerators to find the new numerator and the two denominators to find the new denominator. Example: $\frac{1}{3}\times\frac{2}{3}=\frac{1\times2}{3\times3}=\frac{2}{9}$.

> **Review Video: Multiplying Fractions**
> Visit mometrix.com/academy and enter code: 638849

Dividing Fractions

Two fractions can be divided by flipping the numerator and denominator of the second fraction and then proceeding as though it were a multiplication. Example: $\frac{2}{3}\div\frac{3}{4}=\frac{2}{3}\times\frac{4}{3}=\frac{8}{9}$.

> **Review Video: Dividing Fractions**
> Visit mometrix.com/academy and enter code: 300874

Rational Numbers from Least to Greatest

Example

Order the following rational numbers from least to greatest: 0.55, 17%, $\sqrt{25}$, $\frac{64}{4}$, $\frac{25}{50}$, 3.

Recall that the term **rational** simply means that the number can be expressed as a ratio or fraction. The set of rational numbers includes integers and decimals. Notice that each of the numbers in the problem can be written as a decimal or integer:

$$17\% = 0.1717$$
$$\sqrt{25} = 5$$
$$\frac{64}{4} = 16$$

Copyright © Mometrix Media. You have been licensed one copy of this document for personal use only. Any other reproduction or redistribution is strictly prohibited. All rights reserved.

$$\frac{25}{50} = \frac{1}{2} = 0.5$$

So, the answer is 17%, $\frac{25}{50}$, 0.55, 3, $\sqrt{25}$, $\frac{64}{4}$.

Rational Numbers from Greatest to Least

Example

Order the following rational numbers from greatest to least: 0.3, 27%, $\sqrt{100}$, $\frac{72}{9}$, $\frac{1}{9}$. 4.5

Recall that the term **rational** simply means that the number can be expressed as a ratio or fraction. The set of rational numbers includes integers and decimals. Notice that each of the numbers in the problem can be written as a decimal or integer:

$$27\% = 0.27$$
$$\sqrt{100} = 10$$
$$\frac{72}{9} = 8$$
$$\frac{1}{9} \approx 0.11$$

So, the answer is $\sqrt{100}$, $\frac{72}{9}$, 4.5, 0.3, 27%, $\frac{1}{9}$.

Review Video: Ordering Rational Numbers
Visit mometrix.com/academy and enter code: 419578

Common Denominators with Fractions

When two fractions are manipulated so that they have the same denominator, this is known as finding a **common denominator**. The number chosen to be that common denominator should be the **least common multiple** of the two original denominators. Example: $\frac{3}{4}$ and $\frac{5}{6}$; the least common multiple of 4 and 6 is 12. Manipulating to achieve the common denominator: $\frac{3}{4} = \frac{9}{12}$; $\frac{5}{6} = \frac{10}{12}$.

Factors and Greatest Common Factor

Factors are numbers that are multiplied together to obtain a **product**. For example, in the equation $2 \times 3 = 6$, the numbers 2 and 3 are factors. A **prime number** has only two factors (1 and itself), but other numbers can have many factors.

A **common factor** is a number that divides exactly into two or more other numbers. For example, the factors of 12 are 1, 2, 3, 4, 6, and 12, while the factors of 15 are 1, 3, 5, and 15. The common factors of 12 and 15 are 1 and 3.

A **prime factor** is also a prime number. Therefore, the prime factors of 12 are 2 and 3. For 15, the prime factors are 3 and 5.

Review Video: Factors
Visit mometrix.com/academy and enter code: 920086

Copyright © Mometrix Media. You have been licensed one copy of this document for personal use only. Any other reproduction or redistribution is strictly prohibited. All rights reserved.

The **greatest common factor** (**GCF**) is the largest number that is a factor of two or more numbers. For example, the factors of 15 are 1, 3, 5, and 15; the factors of 35 are 1, 5, 7, and 35. Therefore, the greatest common factor of 15 and 35 is 5.

> **Review Video: Greatest Common Factor (GCF)**
> Visit mometrix.com/academy and enter code: 838699

Multiples and Least Common Multiple

The least common multiple (**LCM**) is the smallest number that is a multiple of two or more numbers. For example, the multiples of 3 include 3, 6, 9, 12, 15, etc.; the multiples of 5 include 5, 10, 15, 20, etc. Therefore, the least common multiple of 3 and 5 is 15.

> **Review Video: Multiples**
> Visit mometrix.com/academy and enter code: 626738
>
> **Review Video: Multiples and Least Common Multiple (LCM)**
> Visit mometrix.com/academy and enter code: 520269

Pre-Algebra

Proportions and Ratios

Proportions

A proportion is a relationship between two quantities that dictates how one changes when the other changes. A **direct proportion** describes a relationship in which a quantity increases by a set amount for every increase in the other quantity, or decreases by that same amount for every decrease in the other quantity. Example: Assuming a constant driving speed, the time required for a car trip increases as the distance of the trip increases. The distance to be traveled and the time required to travel are directly proportional.

Inverse proportion is a relationship in which an increase in one quantity is accompanied by a decrease in the other, or vice versa. Example: the time required for a car trip decreases as the speed increases, and increases as the speed decreases, so the time required is inversely proportional to the speed of the car.

> **Review Video: Proportions**
> Visit mometrix.com/academy and enter code: 505355

Ratios

A **ratio** is a comparison of two quantities in a particular order. Example: If there are 14 computers in a lab, and the class has 20 students, there is a student to computer ratio of 20 to 14, commonly written as 20:14. Ratios are normally reduced to their smallest whole number representation, so 20:14 would be reduced to 10:7 by dividing both sides by 2.

> **Review Video: Ratios**
> Visit mometrix.com/academy and enter code: 996914

Copyright © Mometrix Media. You have been licensed one copy of this document for personal use only. Any other reproduction or redistribution is strictly prohibited. All rights reserved.

Real World Problems with Proportions and Ratios

Example 1

A child was given 100 mg of chocolate every two hours. How much chocolate will the child receive in five hours?

Using proportional reasoning, since five hours is two and a half times as long as two hours, the child will receive two and a half times as much chocolate, $2.5 \times 100 \text{ mg} = 250 \text{ mg}$, in five hours.

To compute the answer methodically, first write the amount of chocolate per 2 hours as a ratio.

$$\frac{100 \text{ mg}}{2 \text{ hours}}$$

Next create a proportion to relate the different time increments of 2 hours and 5 hours.

$\frac{100 \text{ mg}}{2 \text{ hours}} = \frac{x \text{ mg}}{5 \text{ hours}}$, where x is the amount of chocolate the child receives in five hours. Make sure to keep the same units in either the numerator or denominator. In this case the numerator units must be mg for both ratios and the denominator units must be hours for both ratios.

Use cross multiplication and division to solve for x:

$$\frac{100 \text{ mg}}{2 \text{ hours}} = \frac{x \text{ mg}}{5 \text{ hours}}$$
$$100(5) = 2(x)$$
$$500 = 2x$$
$$500 \div 2 = 2x \div 2$$
$$250 = x$$

Therefore, the child receives 250 mg every five hours.

Review Video: Proportions in the Real World
Visit mometrix.com/academy and enter code: 221143

Example 2

At a school, for every 20 female students there are 15 male students. This same student ratio happens to exist at another school. If there are 100 female students at the second school, how many male students are there?

One way to find the number of male students is to set up and solve a proportion.

$$\frac{\text{number of female students}}{\text{number of male students}} = \frac{20}{15} = \frac{100}{\text{number of male students}}$$

Represent the unknown number of male students as the variable x.

$$\frac{20}{15} = \frac{100}{x}$$

Follow these steps to solve for x:

1. Cross multiply. $20 \times x = 15 \times 100$.

Copyright © Mometrix Media. You have been licensed one copy of this document for personal use only. Any other reproduction or redistribution is strictly prohibited. All rights reserved.

$$20x = 1500$$

2. Divide each side of the equation by 20.

$$x = 75$$

Or, notice that: $\frac{20 \times 5}{15 \times 5} = \frac{100}{75}$, so $x = 75$.

Example 3

In a hospital emergency room, there are 4 nurses for every 12 patients. What is the ratio of nurses to patients? If the nurse-to-patient ratio remains constant, how many nurses must be present to care for 24 patients?

The ratio of nurses to patients can be written as 4 to 12, 4:12, or $\frac{4}{12}$. Because four and twelve have a common factor of four, the ratio should be reduced to 1:3, which means that there is one nurse present for every three patients. If this ratio remains constant, there must be eight nurses present to care for 24 patients.

Example 4

In a bank, the banker-to-customer ratio is 1:2. If seven bankers are on duty, how many customers are currently in the bank?

Use proportional reasoning or set up a proportion to solve. Because there are twice as many customers as bankers, there must be fourteen customers when seven bankers are on duty. Setting up and solving a proportion gives the same result:

$$\frac{\text{number of bankers}}{\text{number of customers}} = \frac{1}{2} = \frac{7}{\text{number of customers}}$$

Represent the unknown number of patients as the variable *x*.

$$\frac{1}{2} = \frac{7}{x}$$

To solve for *x*, cross multiply:

$1 \times x = 7 \times 2$, so $x = 14$.

Constant of Proportionality

When two quantities have a proportional relationship, there exists a **constant of proportionality** between the quantities; the product of this constant and one of the quantities is equal to the other quantity. For example, if one lemon costs \$0.25, two lemons cost \$0.50, and three lemons cost \$0.75, there is a proportional relationship between the total cost of lemons and the number of lemons purchased. The constant of proportionality is the **unit price**, namely \$0.25/lemon. Notice that the total price of lemons, *t*, can be found by multiplying the unit price of lemons, *p*, and the number of lemons, *n*: $t = pn$.

Slope

On a graph with two points, (x_1, y_1) and (x_2, y_2), the **slope** is found with the formula $m = \frac{y_2 - y_1}{x_2 - x_1}$; where $x_1 \neq x_2$ and m stands for slope. If the value of the slope is **positive**, the line has an *upward*

Copyright © Mometrix Media. You have been licensed one copy of this document for personal use only. Any other reproduction or redistribution is strictly prohibited. All rights reserved.

direction from left to right. If the value of the slope is **negative**, the line has a *downward direction* from left to right.

Unit Rate as the Slope

A new book goes on sale in bookstores and online stores. In the first month, 5,000 copies of the book are sold. Over time, the book continues to grow in popularity. The data for the number of copies sold is in the table below.

# of Months on Sale	1	2	3	4	5
# of Copies Sold (In Thousands)	5	10	15	20	25

So, the number of copies that are sold and the time that the book is on sale is a proportional relationship. In this example, an equation can be used to show the data: $y = 5x$, where x is the number of months that the book is on sale. Also, y is the number of copies sold. So, the slope is $\frac{\text{rise}}{\text{run}} = \frac{5}{1}$. This can be reduced to 5.

Review Video: Finding the Slope of a Line
Visit mometrix.com/academy and enter code: 766664

Work/Unit Rate

Unit rate expresses a quantity of one thing in terms of one unit of another. For example, if you travel 30 miles every two hours, a unit rate expresses this comparison in terms of one hour: in one hour you travel 15 miles, so your unit rate is 15 miles per hour. Other examples are how much one ounce of food costs (price per ounce) or figuring out how much one egg costs out of the dozen (price per 1 egg, instead of price per 12 eggs). The denominator of a unit rate is always 1. Unit rates are used to compare different situations to solve problems. For example, to make sure you get the best deal when deciding which kind of soda to buy, you can find the unit rate of each. If Soda #1 costs $1.50 for a 1-liter bottle, and soda #2 costs $2.75 for a 2-liter bottle, it would be a better deal to buy Soda #2, because its unit rate is only $1.375 per 1-liter, which is cheaper than Soda #1. Unit rates can also help determine the length of time a given event will take. For example, if you can paint 2 rooms in 4.5 hours, you can determine how long it will take you to paint 5 rooms by solving for the unit rate per room and then multiplying that by 5.

Review Video: Rates and Unit Rates
Visit mometrix.com/academy and enter code: 185363

Example 1

Janice made $40 during the first 5 hours she spent babysitting. She will continue to earn money at this rate until she finishes babysitting in 3 more hours. Find how much money Janice earned babysitting and how much she earns per hour.

Janice will earn $64 babysitting in her 8 total hours (adding the first 5 hours to the remaining 3 gives the 8 hour total). This can be found by setting up a proportion comparing money earned to babysitting hours. Since she earns $40 for 5 hours and since the rate is constant, she will earn a

Copyright © Mometrix Media. You have been licensed one copy of this document for personal use only. Any other reproduction or redistribution is strictly prohibited. All rights reserved.

proportional amount in 8 hours: $\frac{40}{5} = \frac{x}{8}$. Cross multiplying will yield $5x = 320$, and division by 5 shows that $x = 64$.

Janice earns \$8 per hour. This can be found by taking her total amount earned, \$64, and dividing it by the total number of hours worked, 8. Since $\frac{64}{8} = 8$, Janice makes \$8 in one hour. This can also be found by finding the unit rate, money earned per hour: $\frac{64}{8} = \frac{x}{1}$. Since cross multiplying yields $8x = 64$, and division by 8 shows that $x = 8$, Janice earns \$8 per hour.

<u>Example 2</u>

The McDonalds are taking a family road trip, driving 300 miles to their cabin. It took them 2 hours to drive the first 120 miles. They will drive at the same speed all the way to their cabin. Find the speed at which the McDonalds are driving and how much longer it will take them to get to their cabin.

The McDonalds are driving 60 miles per hour. This can be found by setting up a proportion to find the unit rate, the number of miles they drive per one hour: $\frac{120}{2} = \frac{x}{1}$. Cross multiplying yields $2x = 120$ and division by 2 shows that $x = 60$.

Since the McDonalds will drive this same speed, it will take them another 3 hours to get to their cabin. This can be found by first finding how many miles the McDonalds have left to drive, which is $300 - 120 = 180$. The McDonalds are driving at 60 miles per hour, so a proportion can be set up to determine how many hours it will take them to drive 180 miles: $\frac{180}{x} = \frac{60}{1}$. Cross multiplying yields $60x = 180$, and division by 60 shows that $x = 3$. This can also be found by using the formula $D = r \times t$ (or Distance = rate $\times$ time), where $180 = 60 \times t$, and division by 60 shows that $t = 3$.

<u>Example 3</u>

It takes Andy 10 minutes to read 6 pages of his book. He has already read 150 pages in his book that is 210 pages long. Find how long it takes Andy to read 1 page and also find how long it will take him to finish his book if he continues to read at the same speed.

It takes Andy 1 minute and 40 seconds to read one page in his book. This can be found by finding the unit rate per one page, by dividing the total time it takes him to read 6 pages by 6. Since it takes him 10 minutes to read 6 pages, $\frac{10}{6} = 1\frac{2}{3}$ minutes, which is 1 minute and 40 seconds.

It will take Andy another 100 minutes, or 1 hour and 40 minutes to finish his book. This can be found by first figuring out how many pages Andy has left to read, which is $210 - 150 = 60$. Since it is now known that it takes him $1\frac{2}{3}$ minutes to read each page, then that rate must be multiplied by however many pages he has left to read (60) to find the time he'll need: $60 \times 1\frac{2}{3} = 100$, so it will take him 100 minutes, or 1 hour and 40 minutes, to read the rest of his book.

Algebra

Function and Relation

When expressing functional relationships, the **variables** x and y are typically used. These values are often written as the **coordinates** (x, y). The x-value is the independent variable and the y-value is the dependent variable. A **relation** is a set of data in which there is not a unique y-value for each x-value in the dataset. This means that there can be two of the same x-values assigned to different y-

Copyright © Mometrix Media. You have been licensed one copy of this document for personal use only. Any other reproduction or redistribution is strictly prohibited. All rights reserved.

values. A relation is simply a relationship between the x and y-values in each coordinate but does not apply to the relationship between the values of x and y in the data set. A **function** is a relation where one quantity depends on the other. For example, the amount of money that you make depends on the number of hours that you work. In a function, each x-value in the data set has one unique y-value because the y-value depends on the x-value.

> **Review Video: Definition of a Function**
> Visit mometrix.com/academy and enter code: 784611

Determining a Function

You can determine whether an equation is a **function** by substituting different values into the equation for x. These values are called input values. All possible input values are referred to as the **domain**. The result of substituting these values into the equation is called the output, or **range**. You can display and organize these numbers in a data table. A **data table** contains the values for x and y, which you can also list as coordinates. In order for a function to exist, the table cannot contain any repeating x-values that correspond with different y-values. If each x-coordinate has a unique y-coordinate, the table contains a function. However, there can be repeating y-values that correspond with different x-values. An example of this is when the function contains an exponent. For example, if $x^2 = y$, $2^2 = 4$, and $(-2)^2 = 4$.

> **Review Video: Basics of Functions**
> Visit mometrix.com/academy and enter code: 822500

Equation Using Independent and Dependent Variables

To write an equation, you must first assign **variables** to the unknown values in the problem and then translate the words and phrases into expressions containing numbers and symbols. For example, if Ray earns $10 an hour, this can be represented by the expression $10x$, where x is equal to the number of hours that Ray works. The value of x represents the number of hours because it is the **independent variable**, or the amount that you can choose and can manipulate. To find out how much money he earns in y hours, you would write the equation $10x = y$. The variable y is the **dependent variable** because it depends on x and cannot be manipulated. Once you have the equation for the function, you can choose any number of hours to find the corresponding amount that he earns. For example, if you want to know how much he would earn working 36 hours, you would substitute 36 in for x and multiply to find that he would earn $360.

> **Review Video: Dependent and Independent Variables and Inverting Functions**
> Visit mometrix.com/academy and enter code: 704764

Writing a Function Rule Using a Table

If given a set of data, place the corresponding x and y-values into a table and analyze the relationship between them. Consider what you can do to each x-value to obtain the corresponding y-value. Try adding or subtracting different numbers to and from x and then try multiplying or dividing different numbers to and from x. If none of these **operations** give you the y-value, try combining the operations. Once you find a rule that works for one pair, make sure to try it with each additional set of ordered pairs in the table. If the same operation or combination of operations

Copyright © Mometrix Media. You have been licensed one copy of this document for personal use only. Any other reproduction or redistribution is strictly prohibited. All rights reserved.

satisfies each set of coordinates, then the table contains a function. The rule is then used to write the equation of the function in "y =" form.

Equations and Graphing

When algebraic functions and equations are shown graphically, they are usually shown on a *Cartesian coordinate plane*. The Cartesian coordinate plane consists of two number lines placed perpendicular to each other, and intersecting at the zero point, also known as the origin. The horizontal number line is known as the x-axis, with positive values to the right of the origin, and negative values to the left of the origin. The vertical number line is known as the y-axis, with positive values above the origin, and negative values below the origin. Any point on the plane can be identified by an ordered pair in the form (x,y), called coordinates. The x-value of the coordinate is called the abscissa, and the y-value of the coordinate is called the ordinate. The two number lines divide the plane into *four quadrants*: I, II, III, and IV.

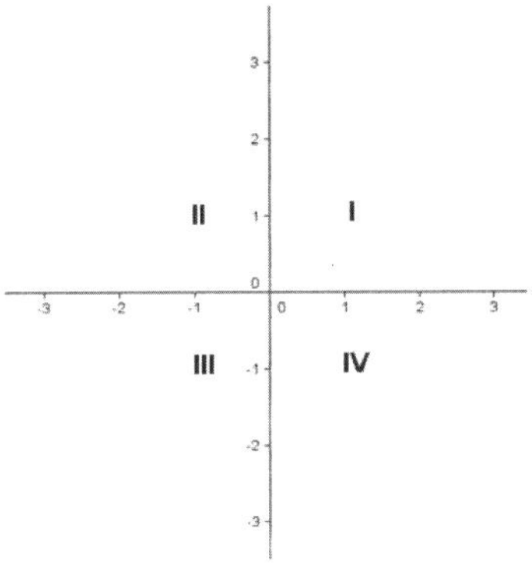

Before learning the different forms in which equations can be written, it is important to understand some terminology. A ratio of the change in the vertical distance to the change in horizontal distance is called the *slope*. On a graph with two points, (x_1, y_1) and (x_2, y_2), the slope is represented by the formula $s = \frac{y_2 - y_1}{x_2 - x_1}$; $x_1 \neq x_2$. If the value of the slope is positive, the line slopes upward from left to right. If the value of the slope is negative, the line slopes downward from left to right. If the y-coordinates are the same for both points, the slope is 0 and the line is a *horizontal line*. If the x-coordinates are the same for both points, there is no slope and the line is a *vertical line*. Two or more lines that have equal slopes are *parallel lines*. *perpendicular lines* have slopes that are negative reciprocals of each other, such as $\frac{a}{b}$ and $\frac{-b}{a}$.

Review Video: Graphs of Functions
Visit mometrix.com/academy and enter code: 492785

Equations are made up of monomials and polynomials. A *monomial* is a single variable or product of constants and variables, such as x, $2x$, or $\frac{2}{x}$. There will never be addition or subtraction symbols in a monomial. Like monomials have like variables, but they may have different coefficients. *Polynomials* are algebraic expressions which use addition and subtraction to combine two or more monomials. Two terms make a binomial; three terms make a trinomial; etc.. The d*egree of a monomial* is the sum of the exponents of the variables. The *degree of a polynomial* is the highest degree of any individual term.

Copyright © Mometrix Media. You have been licensed one copy of this document for personal use only. Any other reproduction or redistribution is strictly prohibited. All rights reserved.

As mentioned previously, equations can be written many ways. Below is a list of the many forms equations can take.

- Standard Form: $Ax + By = C$; the slope is $\frac{-A}{B}$ and the y-intercept is $\frac{C}{B}$
- *Slope Intercept Form*: $y = mx + b$, where m is the slope and b is the y-intercept
- Point-Slope Form: $y - y_1 = m(x - x_1)$, where m is the slope and (x_1, y_1) is a point on the line
- Two-Point Form: $\frac{y-y_1}{x-x_1} = \frac{y_2-y_1}{x_2-x_1}$, where (x_1, y_1) and (x_2, y_2) are two points on the given line
- *Intercept Form*: $\frac{x}{x_1} + \frac{y}{y_1} = 1$, where $(x_1, 0)$ is the point at which a line intersects the x-axis, and $(0, y_1)$ is the point at which the same line intersects the y-axis

Review Video: Slope-Intercept and Point-Slope Forms
Visit mometrix.com/academy and enter code: 113216

Equations can also be written as $ax + b = 0$, where $a \neq 0$. These are referred to as **one variable linear equations**. A solution to such an equation is called a **root**. In the case where we have the equation $5x + 10 = 0$, if we solve for x we get a solution of $x = -2$. In other words, the root of the equation is -2. This is found by first subtracting 10 from both sides, which gives $5x = -10$. Next, simply divide both sides by the coefficient of the variable, in this case 5, to get $x = -2$. This can be checked by plugging -2 back into the original equation $(5)(-2) + 10 = -10 + 10 = 0$.

The **solution set** is the set of all solutions of an equation. In our example, the solution set would simply be -2. If there were more solutions (there usually are in multivariable equations) then they would also be included in the solution set. When an equation has no true solutions, this is referred to as an **empty set**. Equations with identical solution sets are ***equivalent equations***. An **identity** is a term whose value or determinant is equal to 1.

Manipulation of Functions

Horizontal and vertical shift occur when values are added to or subtracted from the x or y values, respectively.

If a constant is added to the y portion of each point, the graph shifts up. If a constant is subtracted from the y portion of each point, the graph shifts down. This is represented by the expression $f(x) \pm k$, where k is a constant.

If a constant is added to the x portion of each point, the graph shifts left. If a constant is subtracted from the x portion of each point, the graph shifts right. This is represented by the expression $f(x \pm k)$, where k is a constant.

Stretch, compression, and reflection occur when different parts of a function are multiplied by different groups of constants. If the function as a whole is multiplied by a real number constant greater than 1, $(k \times f(x))$, the graph is stretched vertically. If k in the previous equation is greater than zero but less than 1, the graph is compressed vertically. If k is less than zero, the graph is reflected about the x-axis, in addition to being either stretched or compressed vertically if k is less than or greater than -1, respectively. If instead, just the x-term is multiplied by a constant greater than 1 $(f(k \times x))$, the graph is compressed horizontally. If k in the previous equation is greater than zero but less than 1, the graph is stretched horizontally. If k is less than zero, the graph is reflected about the y-axis, in addition to being either stretched or compressed horizontally if k is greater than or less than -1, respectively.

Copyright © Mometrix Media. You have been licensed one copy of this document for personal use only. Any other reproduction or redistribution is strictly prohibited. All rights reserved.

Classification of Functions

There are many different ways to classify functions based on their structure or behavior. Listed here are a few common classifications.

Constant functions are given by the equation *y*=b or $f(x) = b$, where *b* is a real number. There is no independent variable present in the equation, so the function has a constant value for all *x*. The graph of a constant function is a horizontal line of slope 0 that is positioned *b* units from the *x*-axis. If *b* is positive, the line is above the *x*-axis; if *b* is negative, the line is below the *x*-axis.

Identity functions are identified by the equation *y=x* or $f(x) = x$, where every value of *y* is equal to its corresponding value of *x*. The only zero is the point (0, 0). The graph is a diagonal line with slope 1.

In **linear functions**, the value of the function changes in direct proportion to *x*. The rate of change,represented by the slope on its graph, is constant throughout. The standard form of a linear equation is $ax + by = c$, where *a*, *b*, and *c* are real numbers. As a function, this equation is commonly written as $y = mx + b$ or $f(x) = mx + b$. This is known as the slope-intercept form, because the coefficients give the slope of the graphed function (m) and its *y*-intercept (b). Solve the equation $mx + b = 0$ for *x* to get $x = -\frac{b}{m}$, which is the only zero of the function. The domain and range are both the set of all real numbers.

A **polynomial function** is a function with multiple terms and multiple powers of *x*, such as:

$$f(x) = a_n x^n + a_{n-1} x^{n-1} + a_{n-2} x^{n-2} + \cdots + a_1 x + a_0$$

where *n* is a non-negative integer that is the highest exponent in the polynomial, and $a_n \neq 0$. The domain of a polynomial function is the set of all real numbers. If the greatest exponent in the polynomial is even, the polynomial is said to be of even degree and the range is the set of real numbers that satisfy the function. If the greatest exponent in the polynomial is odd, the polynomial is said to be odd and the range, like the domain, is the set of all real numbers.

Review Video: Simplifying Rational Polynomial Functions
Visit mometrix.com/academy and enter code: 351038

A **quadratic function** is a polynomial function that follows the equation pattern $y = ax^2 + bx + c$, or $f(x) = ax^2 + bx + c$, where *a*, *b*, and *c* are real numbers and $a \neq 0$. The domain of a quadratic function is the set of all real numbers. The range is also real numbers, but only those in the subset of the domain that satisfy the equation. The root(s) of any quadratic function can be found by plugging the values of *a*, *b*, and *c* into the **quadratic formula**:

$$x = \frac{-b \pm \sqrt{b^2 - 4ac}}{2a}$$

If the expression $b^2 - 4ac$ is negative, you will instead find complex roots.

A quadratic function has a parabola for its graph. In the equation $f(x) = ax^2 + bx + c$, if *a* is positive, the parabola will open upward. If *a* is negative, the parabola will open downward. The axis of symmetry is a vertical line that passes through the vertex. To determine whether or not the parabola will intersect the *x*-axis, check the number of real roots. An equation with two real roots

Copyright © Mometrix Media. You have been licensed one copy of this document for personal use only. Any other reproduction or redistribution is strictly prohibited. All rights reserved.

will cross the x-axis twice. An equation with one real root will have its vertex on the x-axis. An equation with no real roots will not contact the x-axis.

Review Video: Deriving the Quadratic Formula
Visit mometrix.com/academy and enter code: 317436

Review Video: Using the Quadratic Formula
Visit mometrix.com/academy and enter code: 163102

Review Video: Changing Constants in Graphs of Functions: Quadratic Equations
Visit mometrix.com/academy and enter code: 476276

A **rational function** is a function that can be constructed as a ratio of two polynomial expressions: $f(x) = \frac{p(x)}{q(x)}$, where $p(x)$ and $q(x)$ are both polynomial expressions and $q(x) \neq 0$. The domain is the set of all real numbers, except any values for which $q(x) = 0$. The range is the set of real numbers that satisfies the function when the domain is applied. When you graph a rational function, you will have vertical asymptotes wherever $q(x) = 0$. If the polynomial in the numerator is of lesser degree than the polynomial in the denominator, the x-axis will also be a horizontal asymptote. If the numerator and denominator have equal degrees, there will be a horizontal asymptote not on the x-axis. If the degree of the numerator is exactly one greater than the degree of the denominator, the graph will have an oblique, or diagonal, asymptote. The asymptote will be along the line $y = \frac{p_n}{q_{n-1}}x + \frac{p_{n-1}}{q_{n-1}}$, where p_n and q_{n-1} are the coefficients of the highest degree terms in their respective polynomials.

A **square root function** is a function that contains a radical and is in the format $f(x) = \sqrt{ax + b}$. The domain is the set of all real numbers that yields a positive radicand or a radicand equal to zero. Because square root values are assumed to be positive unless otherwise identified, the range is all real numbers from zero to infinity. To find the zero of a square root function, set the radicand equal to zero and solve for x. The graph of a square root function is always to the right of the zero and always above the x-axis.

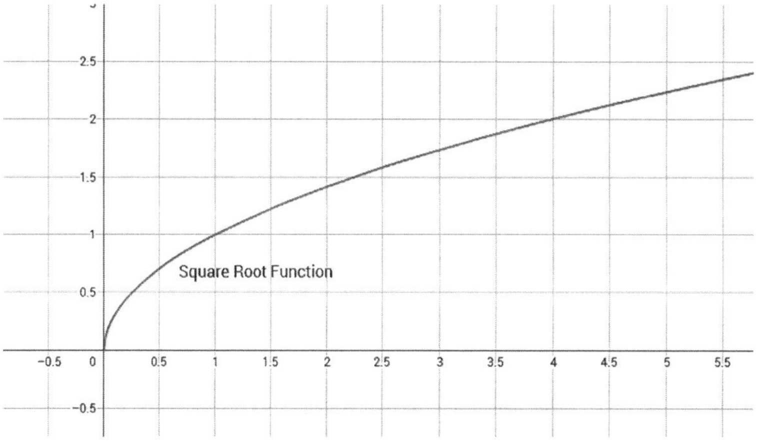

An **absolute value function** is in the format $f(x) = |ax + b|$. Like other functions, the domain is the set of all real numbers. However, because absolute value indicates positive numbers, the range is limited to positive real numbers. To find the zero of an absolute value function, set the portion inside the absolute value sign equal to zero and solve for x.

Copyright © Mometrix Media. You have been licensed one copy of this document for personal use only. Any other reproduction or redistribution is strictly prohibited. All rights reserved.

An absolute value function is also known as a piecewise function because it must be solved in pieces – one for if the value inside the absolute value sign is positive, and one for if the value is negative. The function can be expressed as

$$f(x) = \begin{cases} ax + b \text{ if } ax + b \geq 0 \\ -(ax + b) \text{ if } ax + b < 0 \end{cases}$$

This will allow for an accurate statement of the range.

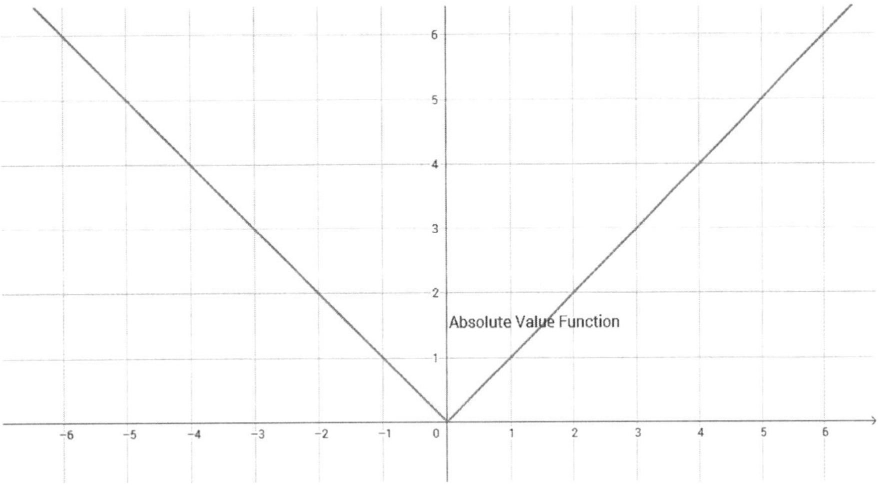

Exponential functions are equations that have the format $y = b^x$, where base $b > 0$ and $b \neq 1$. The exponential function can also be written $f(x) = b^x$.

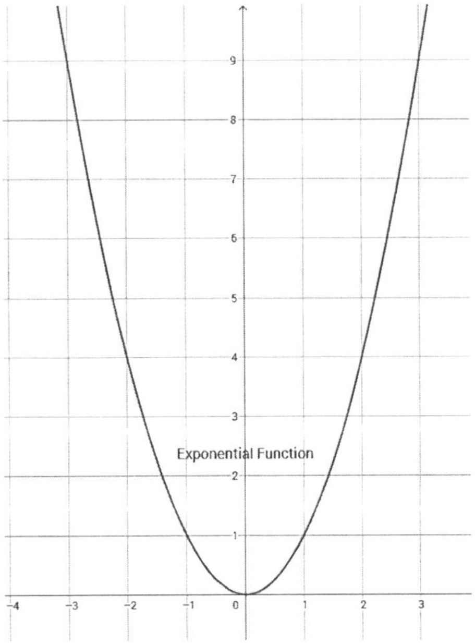

Logarithmic functions are equations that have the format $y = \log_b x$ or $f(x) = \log_b x$. The base b may be any number except one; however, the most common bases for logarithms are base 10 and base e. The log base e is known the natural logarithm, or *ln*, expressed by the function $f(x) = \ln x$.

Any logarithm that does not have an assigned value of b is assumed to be base 10: $\log x = \log_{10} x$. Exponential functions and logarithmic functions are related in that one is the inverse of the other. If

Copyright © Mometrix Media. You have been licensed one copy of this document for personal use only. Any other reproduction or redistribution is strictly prohibited. All rights reserved.

$f(x) = b^x$, then $f^{-1}(x) = \log_b x$. This can perhaps be expressed more clearly by the two equations: $y = b^x$ and $x = \log_b y$.

The following properties apply to logarithmic expressions:

$$\log_b 1 = 0$$
$$\log_b b = 1$$
$$\log_b b^p = p$$
$$\log_b MN = \log_b M + \log_b N$$
$$\log_b \frac{M}{N} = \log_b M - \log_b N$$
$$\log_b M^p = p \log_b M$$

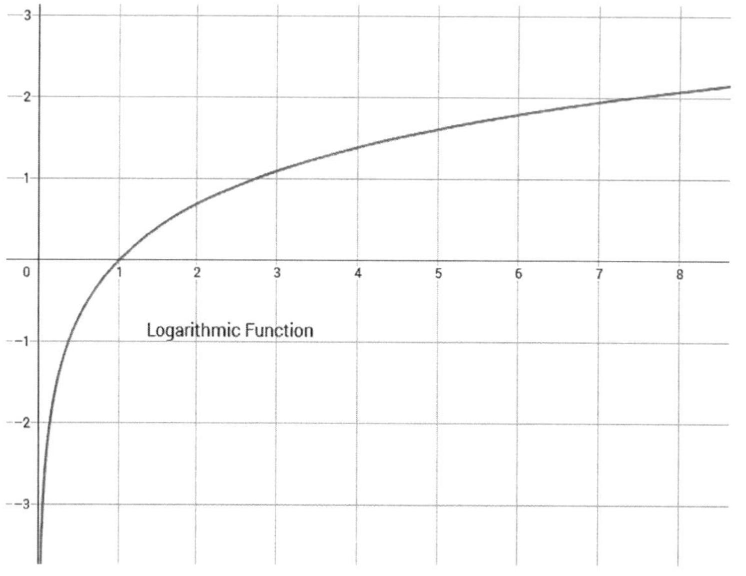

In a **one-to-one function**, each value of x has exactly one value for y (this is the definition of a function) *and* each value of y has exactly one value for x. While the vertical line test will determine if a graph is that of a function, the horizontal line test will determine if a function is a one-to-one function. If a horizontal line drawn at any value of y intersects the graph in more than one place, the graph is not that of a one-to-one function. Do not make the mistake of using the horizontal line test exclusively in determining if a graph is that of a one-to-one function. A one-to-one function must pass both the vertical line test and the horizontal line test. One-to-one functions are also **invertible functions**.

A **monotone function** is a function whose graph either constantly increases or constantly decreases. Examples include the functions $f(x) = x$, $f(x) = -x$, or $f(x) = x^3$.

An **even function** has a graph that is symmetric with respect to the y-axis and satisfies the equation $f(x) = f(-x)$. Examples include the functions $f(x) = x^2$ and $f(x) = ax^n$, where a is any real number and n is a positive even integer.

An **odd function** has a graph that is symmetric with respect to the origin and satisfies the equation $f(x) = -f(-x)$. Examples include the functions $f(x) = x^3$ and $f(x) = ax^n$, where a is any real number and n is a positive odd integer.

Copyright © Mometrix Media. You have been licensed one copy of this document for personal use only. Any other reproduction or redistribution is strictly prohibited. All rights reserved.

Algebraic functions are those that exclusively use polynomials and roots. These would include polynomial functions, rational functions, square root functions, and all combinations of these functions, such as polynomials as the radicand. These combinations may be joined by addition, subtraction, multiplication, or division, but may not include variables as exponents.

Transcendental functions are all functions that are non-algebraic. Any function that includes logarithms, trigonometric functions, variables as exponents, or any combination that includes any of these is not algebraic in nature, even if the function includes polynomials or roots.

Related Concepts

According to the **fundamental theorem of algebra**, every non-constant, single variable polynomial has exactly as many roots as the polynomial's highest exponent. For example, if x^4 is the largest exponent of a term, the polynomial will have exactly 4 roots. However, some of these roots may have multiplicity or be non-real numbers. For instance, in the polynomial function $f(x) = x^4 - 4x + 3$, the only real roots are 1 and -1. The root 1 has multiplicity of 2 and there is one non-real root $(-1 - \sqrt{2}i)$.

The **remainder theorem** is useful for determining the remainder when a polynomial is divided by a binomial. The Remainder Theorem states that if a polynomial function $f(x)$ is divided by a binomial $x - a$, where a is a real number, the remainder of the division will be the value of $f(a)$. If $f(a) = 0$, then a is a root of the polynomial.

The **factor theorem** is related to the Remainder Theorem and states that if $f(a) = 0$ then $(x - a)$ is a factor of the function.

According to the **rational root theorem,** any rational root of a polynomial function $f(x) = a_n x^n + a_{n-1}x^{n-1} + \cdots + a_1 x + a_0$ with integer coefficients will, when reduced to its lowest terms, be a positive or negative fraction such that the numerator is a factor of a_0 and the denominator is a factor of a_n. For instance, if the polynomial function $f(x) = x^3 + 3x^2 - 4$ has any rational roots, the numerators of those roots can only be factors of 4 (1, 2, 4), and the denominators can only be factors of 1 (1). The function in this example has roots of 1 $\left(\text{or } \frac{1}{1}\right)$ and -2 $\left(\text{or } -\frac{2}{1}\right)$.

Variables that vary directly are those that either both increase at the same rate or both decrease at the same rate. For example, in the functions $f(x) = kx$ or $f(x) = kx^n$, where k and n are positive, the value of $f(x)$ increases as the value of x increases and decreases as the value of x decreases.

Variables that vary inversely are those where one increases while the other decreases. For example, in the functions $f(x) = \frac{k}{x}$ or $f(x) = \frac{k}{x^n}$ where k is a positive constant, the value of y increases as the value of x decreases, and the value of y decreases as the value of x increases.

In both cases, k is the constant of variation.

Applying the Basic Operations to Functions

For each of the basic operations, we will use these functions as examples: $f(x) = x^2$ and $g(x) = x$.

To find the sum of two functions f and g, assuming the domains are compatible, simply add the two functions together: $(f + g)(x) = f(x) + g(x) = x^2 + x$

Copyright © Mometrix Media. You have been licensed one copy of this document for personal use only. Any other reproduction or redistribution is strictly prohibited. All rights reserved.

To find the difference of two functions *f* and *g*, assuming the domains are compatible, simply subtract the second function from the first: $(f - g)(x) = f(x) - g(x) = x^2 - x$.

To find the product of two functions *f* and *g*, assuming the domains are compatible, multiply the two functions together: $(f \cdot g)(x) = f(x) \cdot g(x) = x^2 \cdot x = x^3$.

To find the quotient of two functions *f* and *g*, assuming the domains are compatible, divide the first function by the second: $\frac{f}{g}(x) = \frac{f(x)}{g(x)} = \frac{x^2}{x} = x\,; x \neq 0$.

The example given in each case is fairly simple, but on a given problem, if you are looking only for the value of the sum, difference, product or quotient of two functions at a particular *x*-value, it may be simpler to solve the functions individually and then perform the given operation using those values.

The composite of two functions *f* and *g*, written as $(f \circ g)(x)$ simply means that the output of the second function is used as the input of the first. This can also be written as $f(g(x))$. In general, this can be solved by substituting $g(x)$ for all instances of *x* in $f(x)$ and simplifying. Using the example functions $f(x) = x^2 - x + 2$ and $g(x) = x + 1$, we can find that $(f \circ g)(x)$ or $f(g(x))$ is equal to $f(x + 1) = (x + 1)^2 - (x + 1) + 2$, which simplifies to $x^2 + x + 2$.

It is important to note that $(f \circ g)(x)$ is not necessarily the same as $(g \circ f)(x)$. The process is not commutative like addition or multiplication expressions. If $(f \circ g)(x)$ does equal $(g \circ f)(x)$, the two functions are inverses of each other.

Solve Equations in One Variable

Manipulating Equations

Sometimes you will have variables missing in equations. So, you need to find the missing variable. To do this, you need to remember one important thing: *whatever you do to one side of an equation, you need to do to the other side.* If you subtract 100 from one side of an equation, you need to subtract 100 from the other side of the equation. This will allow you to change the form of the equation to find missing values.

Example

Ray earns \$10 an hour at his job. Write an equation for his earnings as a function of time spent working. Determine how long Ray has to work in order to earn \$360.

The number of dollars that Ray earns is dependent on the number of hours he works, so earnings will be represented by the dependent variable *y* and hours worked will be represented by the independent variable *x*. He earns 10 dollars per hour worked, so his earning can be calculated as

$$y = 10x$$

To calculate the number of hours Ray must work in order to earn \$360, plug in 360 for *y* and solve for *x*:

$$360 = 10x$$

$$x = \frac{360}{10} = 36$$

Copyright © Mometrix Media. You have been licensed one copy of this document for personal use only. Any other reproduction or redistribution is strictly prohibited. All rights reserved.

So, Ray must work 36 hours in order to earn \$360.

Solving One Variable Linear Equations

Another way to write an equation is $ax + b = 0$ where $a \neq 0$. This is known as a **one-variable linear equation**. A solution to an equation is called a **root**. Consider the following equation:

$$5x + 10 = 0$$

If we solve for x, the solution is $x = -2$. In other words, the root of the equation is –2.

The first step is to subtract 10 from both sides. This gives $5x = -10$.

Next, divide both sides by the **coefficient** of the variable. For this example, that is 5. So, you should have $x = -2$. You can make sure that you have the correct answer by substituting –2 back into the original equation. So, the equation now looks like this: $(5)(-2) + 10 = -10 + 10 = 0$.

Example 1

$\frac{45\%}{12\%} = \frac{15\%}{x}$. Solve for x.

First, cross multiply; then, solve for x: $\frac{45\%}{12\%} = \frac{15\%}{x}$

$$\frac{0.45}{0.12} = \frac{0.15}{x}$$
$$0.45(x) = 0.12(0.15)$$
$$0.45x = 0.0180$$
$$0.45x \div 0.45 = 0.0180 \div 0.45$$
$$x = 0.04 = 4\%$$

Alternatively, notice that $\frac{45\% \div 3}{12\% \div 3} = \frac{15\%}{4\%}$. So, $x = 4\%$.

Example 2

How do you solve for x in the proportion $\frac{0.50}{2} = \frac{1.50}{x}$?

First, cross multiply; then, solve for x.

$$\frac{0.50}{2} = \frac{1.50}{x}$$
$$0.50(x) = 2(1.50)$$
$$0.50x = 3$$
$$0.50x \div 0.50 = 3 \div 0.50$$
$$x = 6$$

Or, notice that $\frac{0.50 \times 3}{2 \times 3} = \frac{1.50}{6}$, so $x = 6$.

Example 3

$\frac{40}{8} = \frac{x}{24}$. Find x.

One way to solve for x is to first cross multiply.

Copyright © Mometrix Media. You have been licensed one copy of this document for personal use only. Any other reproduction or redistribution is strictly prohibited. All rights reserved.

$$\frac{40}{8} = \frac{x}{24}$$
$$40(24) = 8(x)$$
$$960 = 8x$$
$$960 \div 8 = 8x \div 8$$
$$x = 120$$

Or, notice that:

$$\frac{40 \times 3}{8 \times 3} = \frac{120}{24}, \text{so } x = 120$$

Other Important Concepts

Commonly in algebra and other upper-level fields of math you find yourself working with mathematical expressions that do not equal each other. The statement comparing such expressions with symbols such as < (less than) or > (greater than) is called an *inequality*. An example of an inequality is $7x > 5$. To solve for x, simply divide both sides by 7 and the solution is shown to be $x > \frac{5}{7}$. Graphs of the solution set of inequalities are represented on a number line. Open circles are used to show that an expression approaches a number but is never quite equal to that number.

Review Video: Inequalities
Visit mometrix.com/academy and enter code: 347842

Conditional inequalities are those with certain values for the variable that will make the condition true and other values for the variable where the condition will be false. **Absolute inequalities** can have any real number as the value for the variable to make the condition true, while there is no real number value for the variable that will make the condition false. Solving inequalities is done by following the same rules as for solving equations with the exception that when multiplying or dividing by a negative number the direction of the inequality sign must be flipped or reversed. **double inequalities** are situations where two inequality statements apply to the same variable expression. An example of this is $-c < ax + b < c$.

A **weighted mean**, or weighted average, is a mean that uses "weighted" values. The formula is weighted mean $= \frac{w_1x_1+w_2x_2+w_3x_3...+w_nx_n}{w_1+w_2+w_3+\cdots+w_n}$. Weighted values, such as $w_1, w_2, w_3, \ldots w_n$ are assigned to each member of the set $x_1, x_2, x_3, \ldots x_n$. If calculating weighted mean, make sure a weight value for each member of the set is used.

Graphing Inequalities

Graph the inequality $10 > -2x + 4$.

In order to **graph the inequality** $10 > -2x + 4$, you must first solve for x. The opposite of addition is subtraction, so subtract 4 from both sides. This results in $6 > -2x$. Next, the opposite of multiplication is division, so divide both sides by -2. Don't forget to flip the inequality symbol since you are dividing by a negative number. This results in $-3 < x$. You can rewrite this as $x > -3$. To graph an inequality, you create a number line and put a circle around the value that is being compared to x. If you are graphing a greater than or less than inequality, as the one shown, the circle remains open. This represents all of the values excluding -3. If the inequality happens to be a greater than or equal to or less than or equal to, you draw a closed circle around the value. This would represent all of the values including the number. Finally, take a look at the values that the

Copyright © Mometrix Media. You have been licensed one copy of this document for personal use only. Any other reproduction or redistribution is strictly prohibited. All rights reserved.

solution represents and shade the number line in the appropriate direction. You are graphing all of the values greater than -3 and since this is all of the numbers to the right of -3, shade this region on the number line.

Determining Solutions to Inequalities

Determine whether $(-2, 4)$ is a solution of the inequality $y \geq -2x + 3$.

To determine whether a coordinate is a **solution of an inequality**, you can either use the inequality or its graph. Using $(-2, 4)$ as (x, y), substitute the values into the inequality to see if it makes a true statement. This results in $4 \geq -2(-2) + 3$. Using the integer rules, simplify the right side of the inequality by multiplying and then adding. The result is $4 \geq 7$, which is a false statement. Therefore, the coordinate is not a solution of the inequality. You can also use the **graph** of an inequality to see if a coordinate is a part of the solution. The graph of an inequality is shaded over the section of the coordinate grid that is included in the solution. The graph of $y \geq -2x + 3$ includes the solid line $y = -2x + 3$ and is shaded to the right of the line, representing all of the points greater than and including the points on the line. This excludes the point $(-2, 4)$, so it is not a solution of the inequality.

Calculations Using Points

Sometimes you need to perform calculations using only points on a graph as input data. Using points, you can determine what the **midpoint** and **distance** are. If you know the equation for a line you can calculate the distance between the line and the point.

To find the **midpoint** of two points (x_1, y_1) and (x_2, y_2), average the x-coordinates to get the x-coordinate of the midpoint, and average the y-coordinates to get the y-coordinate of the midpoint. The formula is Midpoint $= \left(\frac{x_1+x_2}{2}, \frac{y_1+y_2}{2}\right)$.

The **distance** between two points is the same as the length of the hypotenuse of a right triangle with the two given points as endpoints, and the two sides of the right triangle parallel to the x-axis and y-axis, respectively. The length of the segment parallel to the x-axis is the difference between the x-coordinates of the two points. The length of the segment parallel to the y-axis is the difference between the y-coordinates of the two points. Use the Pythagorean theorem $a^2 + b^2 = c^2$ or $c = \sqrt{a^2 + b^2}$ to find the distance. The formula is distance $= \sqrt{(x_2 - x_1)^2 + (y_2 - y_1)^2}$.

When a line is in the format $Ax + By + C = 0$, where A, B, and C are coefficients, you can use a point (x_1, y_1) not on the line and apply the formula $d = \frac{|Ax_1+By_1+C|}{\sqrt{A^2+B^2}}$ to find the distance between the line and the point (x_1, y_1).

<u>Example</u>
Find the distance and midpoint between points (2, 4) and (8,6).

Midpoint

$$\text{Midpoint} = \left(\frac{x_1 + x_2}{2}, \frac{y_1 + y_2}{2}\right)$$
$$\text{Midpoint} = \left(\frac{2 + 8}{2}, \frac{4 + 6}{2}\right)$$
$$\text{Midpoint} = \left(\frac{10}{2}, \frac{10}{2}\right)$$

Copyright © Mometrix Media. You have been licensed one copy of this document for personal use only. Any other reproduction or redistribution is strictly prohibited. All rights reserved.

$$\text{Midpoint} = (5,5)$$

Distance

$$\text{Distance} = \sqrt{(x_2 - x_1)^2 + (y_2 - y_1)^2}$$
$$\text{Distance} = \sqrt{(8-2)^2 + (6-4)^2}$$
$$\text{Distance} = \sqrt{(6)^2 + (2)^2}$$
$$\text{Distance} = \sqrt{36+4}$$
$$\text{Distance} = \sqrt{40} \text{ or } 2\sqrt{10}$$

Systems of Equations

Systems of equations are a set of simultaneous equations that all use the same variables. A solution to a system of equations must be true for each equation in the system. *Consistent systems* are those with at least one solution. *Inconsistent systems* are systems of equations that have no solution.

Review Video: Systems of Equations
Visit mometrix.com/academy and enter code: 658153

Substitution

To solve a system of linear equations by *substitution*, start with the easier equation and solve for one of the variables. Express this variable in terms of the other variable. Substitute this expression in the other equation and solve for the other variable. The solution should be expressed in the form (x, y). Substitute the values into both of the original equations to check your answer. Consider the following problem.

Solve the system using substitution:

$$x + 6y = 15$$

$$3x - 12y = 18$$

Solve the first equation for x:

$$x = 15 - 6y$$

Substitute this value in place of x in the second equation, and solve for y:

$$3(15 - 6y) - 12y = 18$$

$$45 - 18y - 12y = 18$$

$$30y = 27$$

$$y = \frac{27}{30} = \frac{9}{10} = 0.9$$

Plug this value for y back into the first equation to solve for x:

$$x = 15 - 6(0.9) = 15 - 5.4 = 9.6$$

Copyright © Mometrix Media. You have been licensed one copy of this document for personal use only. Any other reproduction or redistribution is strictly prohibited. All rights reserved.

Check both equations if you have time:

$$9.6 + 6(0.9) = 9.6 + 5.4 = 15$$

$$3(9.6) - 12(0.9) = 28.8 - 10.8 = 18$$

Therefore, the solution is (9.6, 0.9).

Elimination

To solve a system of equations using *elimination*, begin by rewriting both equations in standard form $Ax + By = C$. Check to see if the coefficients of one pair of like variables add to zero. If not, multiply one or both of the equations by a non-zero number to make one set of like variables add to zero. Add the two equations to solve for one of the variables. Substitute this value into one of the original equations to solve for the other variable. Check your work by substituting into the other equation. Next, we will solve the same problem as above, but using the addition method.

Solve the system using elimination:

$$x + 6y = 15$$

$$3x - 12y = 18$$

If we multiply the first equation by 2, we can eliminate the y terms:

$$2x + 12y = 30$$

$$3x - 12y = 18$$

Add the equations together and solve for x:

$$5x = 48$$

$$x = \frac{48}{5} = 9.6$$

Plug the value for x back into either of the original equations and solve for y:

$$9.6 + 6y = 15$$

$$y = \frac{15 - 9.6}{6} = 0.9$$

Check both equations if you have time:

$$9.6 + 6(0.9) = 9.6 + 5.4 = 15$$

$$3(9.6) - 12(0.9) = 28.8 - 10.8 = 18$$

Therefore, the solution is (9.6, 0.9).

Graphically

To solve a system of linear equations **graphically**, plot both equations on the same graph. The solution of the equations is the point where both lines cross. If the lines do not cross (are parallel), then there is **no solution**.

Copyright © Mometrix Media. You have been licensed one copy of this document for personal use only. Any other reproduction or redistribution is strictly prohibited. All rights reserved.

For example, consider the following system of equations:

$$y = 2x + 7$$
$$y = -x + 1$$

Since these equations are given in slope-intercept form, they are easy to graph; the y intercepts of the lines are $(0, 7)$ and $(0, 1)$. The respective slopes are 2 and –1, thus the graphs look like this:

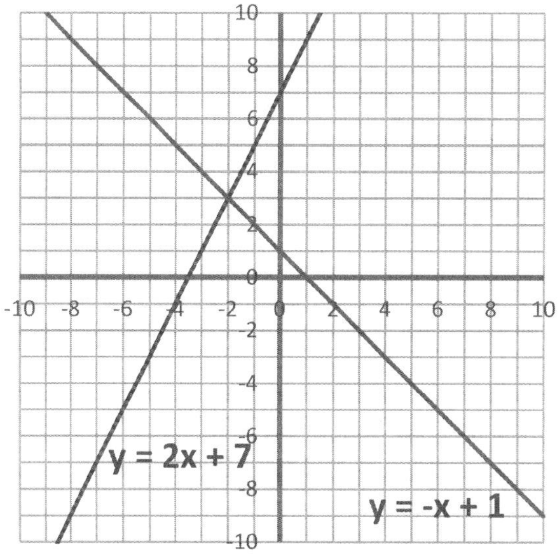

The two lines intersect at the point $(-2, 3)$, thus this is the solution to the system of equations.

Solving a system graphically is generally only practical if both coordinates of the solution are integers; otherwise the intersection will lie between gridlines on the graph and the coordinates will be difficult or impossible to determine exactly. It also helps if, as in this example, the equations are in slope-intercept form or some other form that makes them easy to graph. Otherwise, another method of solution (by substitution or elimination) is likely to be more useful.

Solving A System of Equations Consisting of a Linear Equation and a Quadratic Equation

Algebraically

Generally, the simplest way to solve a system of equations consisting of a linear equation and a quadratic equation algebraically is through the method of **substitution**. One possible strategy is to solve the linear equation for y and then substitute that expression into the quadratic equation. After expansion and combining like terms, this will result in a new quadratic equation for x which, like all quadratic equations, may have zero, one, or two solutions. Plugging each solution for x back into one of the original equations will then produce the corresponding value of y.

For example, consider the following system of equations:

$$x + y = 1$$
$$y = (x + 3)^2 - 2$$

We can solve the linear equation for y to yield $y = -x + 1$.

Substituting this expression into the quadratic equation produces $-x + 1 = (x + 3)^2 - 2$

Copyright © Mometrix Media. You have been licensed one copy of this document for personal use only. Any other reproduction or redistribution is strictly prohibited. All rights reserved.

We can simplify this equation:

$$-x + 1 = (x + 3)^2 - 2$$

$$-x + 1 = x^2 + 6x + 9 - 2$$

$$-x + 1 = x^2 + 6x + 7$$

$$x^2 + 7x + 6 = 0$$

This quadratic equation can be factored as $(x + 1)(x + 6) = 0$. It therefore has two solutions: $x_1 = -1$ and $x_2 = -6$. Plugging each of these back into the original linear equation yields $y_1 = -x_1 + 1 = -(-1) + 1 = 2$ and $y_2 = -x_2 + 1 = -(-6) + 1 = 7$. Thus this system of equations has two solutions, $(-1, 2)$ and $(-6, 7)$.

It may help to check your work by putting each x and y value back into the original equations and verifying that they do provide a solution.

Graphically

To solve a system of equations consisting of a linear equation and a quadratic equation **graphically**, plot both equations on the same graph. The linear equation will of course produce a straight line, while the quadratic equation will produce a parabola. These two graphs will intersect at zero, one, or two points; each point of intersection is a solution of the system.

For example, consider the following system of equations:

$$y = -2x + 2$$
$$y = -2x^2 + 4x + 2$$

The linear equation describes a line with a y-intercept of $(0, 2)$ and a slope of -2.

To graph the quadratic equation, we can first find the vertex of the parabola: the x-coordinate of the vertex is $h = -\frac{b}{2a} = -\frac{4}{2(-2)} = 1$, and the y coordinate is $k = -2(1)^2 + 4(1) + 2 = 4$. Thus, the vertex lies at $(1, 4)$. To get a feel for the rest of the parabola, we can plug in a few more values of x to find more points; by putting in $x = 2$ and $x = 3$ in the quadratic equation, we find that

Copyright © Mometrix Media. You have been licensed one copy of this document for personal use only. Any other reproduction or redistribution is strictly prohibited. All rights reserved.

the points $(2, 2)$ and $(3, -4)$ lie on the parabola; by symmetry thus do $(0, 2)$ and $(-1, -4)$. We can now plot both equations:

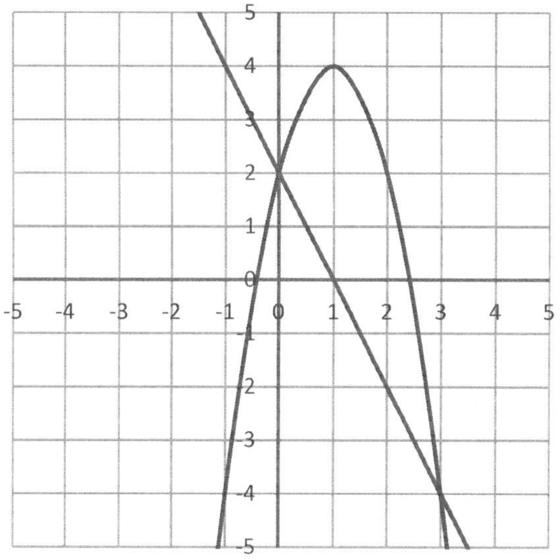

These two curves intersect at the points $(0, 2)$ and $(3, -4)$, thus these are the solutions of the equation.

Polynomial Algebra

To multiply two binomials, follow the **FOIL** method. FOIL stands for:

- First: Multiply the first term of each binomial
- Outer: Multiply the outer terms of each binomial
- Inner: Multiply the inner terms of each binomial
- Last: Multiply the last term of each binomial

Using FOIL $(Ax + By)(Cx + Dy) = ACx^2 + ADxy + BCxy + BDy^2$.

Example

Use the FOIL method on binomials $(x + 2)$ and $(x - 3)$.

$$\text{First: } (x + 2)(x - 3) = (x)(x) = x^2$$

$$\text{Outer: } (x + 2)\ (x - 3) = (x)(-3) = -3x$$

$$\text{Inner: } (x + 2)\ (x - 3) = (2)(x) = 2x$$

$$\text{Last: } (\mathrm{x} + 2)(\mathrm{x} - 3) = (2)(-3) = -6$$

Combine like Terms:

$$(x^2) + (-3x) + (2x) + (-6) = x^2 - x - 6$$

Review Video: Multiplying Terms Using the FOIL Method
Visit mometrix.com/academy and enter code: 854792

Copyright © Mometrix Media. You have been licensed one copy of this document for personal use only. Any other reproduction or redistribution is strictly prohibited. All rights reserved.

To divide polynomials, begin by arranging the terms of each polynomial in order of one variable. You may arrange in ascending or descending order, but make sure to be consistent with both polynomials. To get the first term of the quotient, divide the first term of the dividend by the first term of the divisor. Multiply the first term of the quotient by the entire divisor and subtract that product from the dividend. Repeat for the second and successive terms until you either get a remainder of zero or a remainder whose degree is less than the degree of the divisor. If the quotient has a remainder, write the answer as a mixed expression in the form: $\text{quotient} + \frac{\text{remainder}}{\text{divisor}}$.

Rational expressions are fractions with polynomials in both the numerator and the denominator; the value of the polynomial in the denominator cannot be equal to zero. To add or subtract rational expressions, first find the common denominator, then rewrite each fraction as an equivalent fraction with the common denominator. Finally, add or subtract the numerators to get the numerator of the answer, and keep the common denominator as the denominator of the answer. When multiplying rational expressions factor each polynomial and cancel like factors (a factor which appears in both the numerator and the denominator). Then, multiply all remaining factors in the numerator to get the numerator of the product, and multiply the remaining factors in the denominator to get the denominator of the product. Remember – cancel entire factors, not individual terms. To divide rational expressions, take the reciprocal of the divisor (the rational expression you are dividing by) and multiply by the dividend.

Review Video: Simplifying Rational Polynomial Functions
Visit mometrix.com/academy and enter code: 351038

Below are patterns of some special products to remember: *perfect trinomial squares*, the *difference between two squares*, the *sum and difference of two cubes*, and *perfect cubes*.

- Perfect trinomial squares: $x^2 + 2xy + y^2 = (x + y)^2$ or $x^2 - 2xy + y^2 = (x - y)^2$
- Difference between two squares: $x^2 - y^2 = (x + y)(x - y)$
- Sum of two cubes: $x^3 + y^3 = (x + y)(x^2 - xy + y^2)$
- Note: the second factor is *not* the same as a perfect trinomial square, so do not try to factor it further.
- Difference between two cubes: $x^3 - y^3 = (x - y)(x^2 + xy + y^2)$
- Again, the second factor is *not* the same as a perfect trinomial square.
- Perfect cubes: $x^3 + 3x^2y + 3xy^2 + y^3 = (x + y)^3$ and $x^3 - 3x^2y + 3xy^2 - y^3 = (x - y)^3$

In order to **factor a polynomial**, first check for a common monomial factor. When the greatest common monomial factor has been factored out, look for patterns of special products: differences of two squares, the sum or difference of two cubes for binomial factors, or perfect trinomial squares for trinomial factors. If the factor is a trinomial but not a perfect trinomial square, look for a factorable form, such as $x^2 + (a + b)x + ab = (x + a)(x + b)$ or$(ac)x^2 + (ad + bc)x + bd = (ax + b)(cx + d)$. For factors with four terms, look for groups to factor. Once you have found the factors, write the original polynomial as the product of all the factors. Make sure all of the polynomial factors are prime. Monomial factors may be prime or composite. Check your work by multiplying the factors to make sure you get the original polynomial.

Solving Quadratic Equations

The **quadratic formula** is used to solve quadratic equations when other methods are more difficult. To use the quadratic formula to solve a quadratic equation, begin by rewriting the equation in standard form $ax^2 + bx + c = 0$, where a, b, and c are coefficients. Once you have

Copyright © Mometrix Media. You have been licensed one copy of this document for personal use only. Any other reproduction or redistribution is strictly prohibited. All rights reserved.

identified the values of the coefficients, substitute those values into the quadratic formula $x = \frac{-b\pm\sqrt{b^2-4ac}}{2a}$. Evaluate the equation and simplify the expression. Again, check each root by substituting into the original equation. In the quadratic formula, the portion of the formula under the radical $(b^2 - 4ac)$ is called the **discriminant**. If the discriminant is zero, there is only one root: $-\frac{b}{2a}$. If the discriminant is positive, there are two different real roots. If the discriminant is negative, there are no real roots.

To solve a quadratic equation by factoring, begin by rewriting the equation in standard form, if necessary. Factor the side with the variable then set each of the factors equal to zero and solve the resulting linear equations. Check your answers by substituting the roots you found into the original equation. If, when writing the equation in standard form, you have an equation in the form $x^2 + c = 0$ or $x^2 - c = 0$, set $x^2 = -c$ or $x^2 = c$ and take the square root of c. If $c = 0$, the only real root is zero. If c is positive, there are two real roots—the positive and negative square root values. If c is negative, there are no real roots because you cannot take the square root of a negative number.

Review Video: Factoring Quadratic Equations
Visit mometrix.com/academy and enter code: 336566

To solve a quadratic equation by **completing the square**, rewrite the equation so that all terms containing the variable are on the left side of the equal sign, and all the constants are on the right side of the equal sign. Make sure the coefficient of the squared term is 1. If there is a coefficient with the squared term, divide each term on both sides of the equal side by that number. Next, work with the coefficient of the single-variable term. Square half of this coefficient and add that value to both sides. Now you can factor the left side (the side containing the variable) as the square of a binomial. $x^2 + 2ax + a^2 = C \Rightarrow (x + a)^2 = C$, where x is the variable, and a and C are constants. Take the square root of both sides and solve for the variable. Substitute the value of the variable in the original problem to check your work.

Quadratic Function

A *quadratic function* is a function in the form $y = ax^2 + bx + c$, where a does not equal 0. While a linear function forms a line, a quadratic function forms a **parabola**, which is a u-shaped figure that either opens upward or downward. A parabola that opens upward is said to be a **positive quadratic function** and a parabola that opens downward is said to be a **negative quadratic function**. The shape of a parabola can differ, depending on the values of a, b, and c. All parabolas contain a **vertex**, which is the highest possible point, the **maximum**, or the lowest possible point, the **minimum**. This is the point where the graph begins moving in the opposite direction. A quadratic function can have zero, one, or two solutions, and therefore, zero, one, or two x-intercepts. Recall that the x-intercepts are referred to as the zeros, or roots, of a function. A quadratic function will have only one y-intercept. Understanding the basic components of a quadratic function can give you an idea of the shape of its graph.

Copyright © Mometrix Media. You have been licensed one copy of this document for personal use only. Any other reproduction or redistribution is strictly prohibited. All rights reserved.

Example graph of a positive quadratic function:

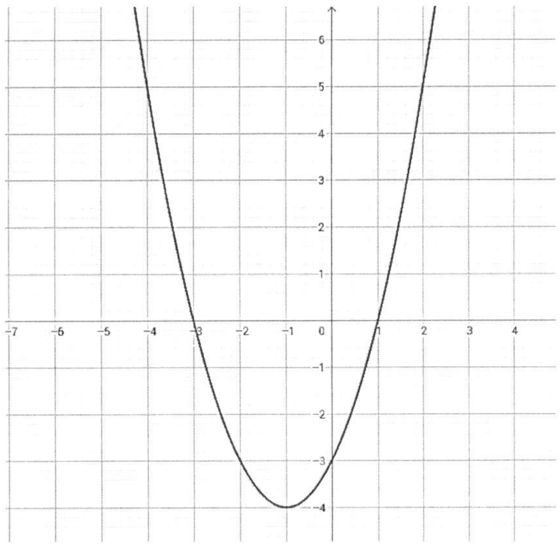

Simplifying Polynomial Expressions

A polynomial is a group of monomials added or subtracted together. Simplifying polynomials requires combining like terms. The like terms in a polynomial expression are those that have the same variable raised to the same power. It is often helpful to connect the like terms with arrows or lines in order to separate them from the other monomials. Once you have determined the like terms, you can rearrange the polynomial by placing them together. Remember to include the sign that is in front of each term. Once the like terms are placed together, you can apply each operation and simplify. When adding and subtracting polynomials, only add and subtract the **coefficient**, or the number part; the variable and exponent stay the same.

Position of Parabola

A **quadratic function** is written in the form $y = ax^2 + bx + c$. Changing the leading coefficient, a, in the equation changes the direction of the parabola. If the value of a is **positive**, the graph opens upward. The vertex of this parabola is the **minimum** value of the graph. If the value of a is **negative**, the graph opens downward. The vertex of this parabola is the **maximum** value of the graph. The leading coefficient, a, also affects the width of the parabola. The closer a is to 0, the wider the parabola will be. The values of b and c both affect the position of the parabola on the graph. The effect from changing b depends on the sign of a. If a is negative, increasing the value of b moves the parabola to the right and decreasing the value of b moves it to the left. If a is positive, changes to b have the opposite effect. The value of c in the quadratic equation represents the y-intercept and therefore, moves the parabola up and down the y-axis. The larger the c-value, the higher the parabola is on the graph.

Finding Roots

Find the roots of $y = x^2 + 6x - 16$ and explain why these values are important.

The **roots** of a quadratic equation are the solutions when $ax^2 + bx + c = 0$. To find the roots of a quadratic equation, first replace y with 0. If $0 = x^2 + 6x - 16$, then to find the values of x, you can factor the equation if possible. When factoring a quadratic equation where $a = 1$, find the factors of c that add up to b. That is the factors of -16 that add up to 6. The factors of -16 include, -4 and 4,

Copyright © Mometrix Media. You have been licensed one copy of this document for personal use only. Any other reproduction or redistribution is strictly prohibited. All rights reserved.

-8 and 2 and -2 and 8. The factors that add up to equal 6 are -2 and 8. Write these factors as the product of two binomials, $0 = (x - 2)(x + 8)$. You can verify that these are the correct factors by using FOIL to multiply them together. Finally, since these binomials multiply together to equal zero, set them each equal to zero and solve for x. This results in $x - 2 = 0$, which simplifies to $x = 2$ and $x + 8 = 0$, which simplifies to $x = -8$. Therefore, the roots of the equation are 2 and -8. These values are important because they tell you where the graph of the equation crosses the x-axis. The points of intersection are $(2, 0)$ and $(-8, 0)$.

Review Video: Finding the Missing Roots
Visit mometrix.com/academy and enter code: 198376

Solving Quadratic Equations

Methods

One way to find the solution or solutions of a quadratic equation is to use its **graph**. The solution(s) of a quadratic equation are the values of x when $y = 0$. On the graph, $y = 0$ is where the parabola crosses the x-axis, or the x-intercepts. This is also referred to as the **roots**, or zeros of a function. Given a graph, you can locate the x-intercepts to find the solutions. If there are no x-intercepts, the function has no solution. If the parabola crosses the x-axis at one point, there is one solution and if it crosses at two points, there are two solutions. Since the solutions exist where $y = 0$, you can also solve the equation by substituting 0 in for y. Then, try factoring the equation by finding the factors of ac that add up to equal b. You can use the guess and check method, the box method, or grouping. Once you find a pair that works, write them as the product of two binomials and set them equal to zero. Finally, solve for x to find the solutions. The last way to solve a quadratic equation is to use the **quadratic formula**. The quadratic formula is $x = \frac{-b \pm \sqrt{b^2 - 4ac}}{2a}$. Substitute the values of a, b, and c into the formula and solve for x. Remember that $\pm$ refers to two different solutions. Always check your solutions with the original equation to make sure they are valid.

Example

List the steps used in solving $y = 2x^2 + 8x + 4$.

First, substitute 0 in for y in the quadratic equation:

$$0 = 2x^2 + 8x + 4$$

Next, try to factor the quadratic equation. If $a \neq 1$, list the factors of ac, or 8:

$$(1, 8), (-1, -8), (2, 4), (-2, -4)$$

Look for the factors of ac that add up to b, or 8. Since none do, the equation cannot be factored with whole numbers. Substitute the values of a, b, and c into the quadratic formula, $x = \frac{-b \pm \sqrt{b^2 - 4ac}}{2a}$:

$$x = \frac{-8 \pm \sqrt{8^2 - 4(2)(4)}}{2(2)}$$

Copyright © Mometrix Media. You have been licensed one copy of this document for personal use only. Any other reproduction or redistribution is strictly prohibited. All rights reserved.

Use the order of operations to simplify:

$$x = \frac{-8 \pm \sqrt{64 - 32}}{4}$$

$$x = \frac{-8 \pm \sqrt{32}}{4}$$

Reduce and simplify:

$$x = \frac{-8 \pm \sqrt{(16)(2)}}{4}$$

$$x = \frac{-8 \pm 4\sqrt{2}}{4}$$

$$x = -2 \pm \sqrt{2}$$

$$x = -2 + \sqrt{2} \text{ and } x = -2 - \sqrt{2}$$

Check both solutions with the original equation to make sure they are valid.

Simplify the square roots and round to two decimal places.

$$x = -3.41 \text{ and } x = -0.586$$

Laws of Exponents

Multiply $(2x^4)^2(xy)^4 \cdot 4y^3$ using the **laws of exponents**.

According the order of operations, the first step in simplifying expressions is to evaluate within the parentheses. Moving from left to right, the first set of parentheses contains a power raised to a power. The rules of exponents state that when a power is raised to a power, you *multiply* the exponents. Since $4 \times 2 = 8$, $(2x^4)^2$ can be written as $4x^8$. The second set of parentheses raises a product to a power. The **rules of exponents** state that you raise every value within the parentheses to the given power. Therefore, $(xy)^4$ can be written as x^4y^4. Combining these terms with the last term gives you, $4x^8 \cdot x^4y^4 \cdot 4y^3$. In this expression, there are powers with the same base. The rules of exponents state that you *add* powers with the same base, while multiplying the coefficients. You can group the expression as $(4x^8 \cdot x^4) \cdot (y^4 \cdot 4y^3)$ to organize the values with the same base. Then, using this rule add the exponents. The result is $4x^{12} \cdot 4y^7$, or $16x^{12}y^7$.

Review Video: Laws of Exponents
Visit mometrix.com/academy and enter code: 532558

Using Given Roots to Find Quadratic Equation

Example
Find a quadratic equation whose real roots are $x = 2$ and $x = -1$.

One way to find the roots of a quadratic equation is to factor the equation and use the **zero product property**, setting each factor of the equation equal to zero to find the corresponding root. We can

Copyright © Mometrix Media. You have been licensed one copy of this document for personal use only. Any other reproduction or redistribution is strictly prohibited. All rights reserved.

use this technique in reverse to find an equation given its roots. Each root corresponds to a linear equation which in turn corresponds to a factor of the quadratic equation.

For example, the root x=2 corresponds to the equation $x - 2 = 0$, and the root $x = -1$ corresponds to the equation $x + 1 = 0$.

These two equations correspond to the factors (x - 2) and (x+1), from which we can derive the equation $(x - 2)(x + 1) = 0$, or $x^2 - x - 2 = 0$.

Any integer multiple of this entire equation will also yield the same roots, as the integer will simply cancel out when the equation is factored. For example, $2x^2 - 2x - 4 = 0$ factors as

$2(x - 2)(x + 1) = 0$.

Simplifying Rational Expressions

To *simplify a rational expression*, factor the numerator and denominator completely. Factors that are the same and appear in the numerator and denominator have a ratio of 1. The denominator, $(1 - x^2)$, is a difference of squares. It can be factored as $(1 - x)(1 + x)$. The factor $1 - x$ and the numerator $x - 1$ are opposites and have a ratio of -1. Rewrite the numerator as $-1(1 - x)$. So, the rational expression can be simplified as follows:

$$\frac{x-1}{1-x^2} = \frac{-1(1-x)}{(1-x)(1+x)} = \frac{-1}{1+x}$$

(Note that since the original expression is defined for $x \neq \{-1,1\}$, the simplified expression has the same restrictions.)

Review Video: Reducing Rational Expressions
Visit mometrix.com/academy and enter code: 788868

Matrix Basics

A **matrix** (plural: matrices) is a rectangular array of numbers or variables, often called **elements**, which are arranged in columns and rows. A matrix is generally represented by a capital letter, with its elements represented by the corresponding lowercase letter with two subscripts indicating the row and column of the element. For example, n_{ab} represents the element in row a column b of matrix N.

$$N = \begin{bmatrix} n_{11} & n_{12} & n_{13} \\ n_{21} & n_{22} & n_{23} \end{bmatrix}$$

A matrix can be described in terms of the number of rows and columns it contains in the format $a \times b$, where a is the number of rows and b is the number of columns. The matrix shown above is a 2×3 matrix. Any $a \times b$ matrix where $a = b$ is a square matrix. A **vector** is a matrix that has exactly one column (**column vector**) or exactly one row (**row vector**).

The **main diagonal** of a matrix is the set of elements on the diagonal from the top left to the bottom right of a matrix. Because of the way it is defined, only square matrices will have a main diagonal. For the matrix shown below, the main diagonal consists of the elements $n_{11}, n_{22}, n_{33}, n_{44}$.

Copyright © Mometrix Media. You have been licensed one copy of this document for personal use only. Any other reproduction or redistribution is strictly prohibited. All rights reserved.

$$\begin{bmatrix} n_{11} & n_{12} & n_{13} & n_{14} \\ n_{21} & n_{22} & n_{23} & n_{24} \\ n_{31} & n_{32} & n_{33} & n_{34} \\ n_{41} & n_{42} & n_{43} & n_{44} \end{bmatrix}$$

A 3×4 matrix such as the one shown below would not have a main diagonal because there is no straight line of elements between the top left corner and the bottom right corner that joins the elements.

$$\begin{bmatrix} n_{11} & n_{12} & n_{13} & n_{14} \\ n_{21} & n_{22} & n_{23} & n_{24} \\ n_{31} & n_{32} & n_{33} & n_{34} \end{bmatrix}$$

A **diagonal matrix** is a square matrix that has a zero for every element in the matrix except the elements on the main diagonal. All the elements on the main diagonal must be nonzero numbers.

$$\begin{bmatrix} n_{11} & 0 & 0 & 0 \\ 0 & n_{22} & 0 & 0 \\ 0 & 0 & n_{33} & 0 \\ 0 & 0 & 0 & n_{44} \end{bmatrix}$$

If every element on the main diagonal of a diagonal matrix is equal to one, the matrix is called an **identity matrix**. The identity matrix is often represented by the letter *I*.

$$I = \begin{bmatrix} 1 & 0 & 0 & 0 \\ 0 & 1 & 0 & 0 \\ 0 & 0 & 1 & 0 \\ 0 & 0 & 0 & 1 \end{bmatrix}$$

A **zero matrix** is a matrix that has zero as the value for every element in the matrix.

$$\begin{bmatrix} 0 & 0 & 0 & 0 \\ 0 & 0 & 0 & 0 \\ 0 & 0 & 0 & 0 \\ 0 & 0 & 0 & 0 \end{bmatrix}$$

The zero matrix is the *identity for matrix addition*. Do not confuse the zero matrix with the identity matrix.

The **negative of a matrix** is also known as the additive inverse of a matrix. If matrix *N* is the given matrix, then matrix –*N* is its negative. This means that every element n_{ab} is equal to $-n_{ab}$ in the negative. To find the negative of a given matrix, change the sign of every element in the matrix and keep all elements in their original corresponding positions in the matrix.

If two matrices have the same order and all corresponding elements in the two matrices are the same, then the two matrices are **equal matrices**.

Copyright © Mometrix Media. You have been licensed one copy of this document for personal use only. Any other reproduction or redistribution is strictly prohibited. All rights reserved.

A matrix N may be **transposed** to matrix N^T by changing all rows into columns and changing all columns into rows. The easiest way to accomplish this is to swap the positions of the row and column notations for each element. For example, suppose the element in the second row of the third column of matrix N is $n_{23} = 6$. In the transposed matrix N^T, the transposed element would be $n_{32} = 6$, and it would be placed in the third row of the second column.

$$N = \begin{bmatrix} 1 & 2 & 3 \\ 4 & 5 & 6 \end{bmatrix}; \; N^T = \begin{bmatrix} 1 & 4 \\ 2 & 5 \\ 3 & 6 \end{bmatrix}$$

To quickly transpose a matrix by hand, begin with the first column and rewrite a new matrix with those same elements in the same order in the first row. Write the elements from the second column of the original matrix in the second row of the transposed matrix. Continue this process until all columns have been completed. If the original matrix is identical to the transposed matrix, the matrices are symmetric.

The **determinant** of a matrix is a scalar value that is calculated by taking into account all the elements of a square matrix. A determinant only exists for square matrices. Finding the determinant of a 2×2 matrix is as simple as remembering a simple equation. For a 2×2 matrix $M = \begin{bmatrix} m_{11} & m_{12} \\ m_{21} & m_{22} \end{bmatrix}$, the determinant is obtained by the equation $|M| = m_{11}m_{22} - m_{12}m_{21}$. Anything larger than 2×2 requires multiple steps. Take matrix $N = \begin{bmatrix} a & b & c \\ d & e & f \\ g & h & j \end{bmatrix}$. The determinant of N is calculated as $|N| = a\begin{vmatrix} e & f \\ h & j \end{vmatrix} - b\begin{vmatrix} d & f \\ g & j \end{vmatrix} + c\begin{vmatrix} d & e \\ g & h \end{vmatrix}$ or $|N| = a(ej - fh) - b(dj - fg) + c(dh - eg)$.

There is a shortcut for 3×3 matrices: add the products of each unique set of elements diagonally left-to-right and subtract the products of each unique set of elements diagonally right-to-left. In matrix N, the left-to-right diagonal elements are (a, e, j), (b, f, g), and (c, d, h). The right-to-left diagonal elements are (a, f, h), (b, d, j), and (c, e, g). $\det(N) = aej + bfg + cdh - afh - bdj - ceg$.

Calculating the determinants of matrices larger than 3×3 is rarely, if ever, done by hand.

The **inverse** of a matrix M is the matrix that, when multiplied by matrix M, yields a product that is the identity matrix. Multiplication of matrices will be explained in greater detail shortly. Not all matrices have inverses. Only a square matrix whose determinant is not zero has an inverse. If a matrix has an inverse, that inverse is unique to that matrix. For any matrix M that has an inverse, the inverse is represented by the symbol M^{-1}. To calculate the inverse of a 2×2 square matrix, use the following pattern:

$$M = \begin{bmatrix} m_{11} & m_{12} \\ m_{21} & m_{22} \end{bmatrix}; \; M^{-1} = \begin{bmatrix} \frac{m_{22}}{|M|} & \frac{-m_{12}}{|M|} \\ \frac{-m_{21}}{|M|} & \frac{m_{11}}{|M|} \end{bmatrix}$$

Another way to find the inverse of a matrix by hand is use an augmented matrix and elementary row operations. An **augmented matrix** is formed by appending the entries from one matrix onto the end of another. For example, given a 2×2 invertible matrix $N = \begin{bmatrix} a & b \\ c & d \end{bmatrix}$, you can find the inverse N^{-1} by creating an augmented matrix by appending a 2×2 identity matrix: $\left[\begin{array}{cc|cc} a & b & 1 & 0 \\ c & d & 0 & 1 \end{array}\right]$.

Copyright © Mometrix Media. You have been licensed one copy of this document for personal use only. Any other reproduction or redistribution is strictly prohibited. All rights reserved.

To find the inverse of the original 2×2 matrix, perform elementary row operations to convert the original matrix on the left to an identity matrix: $\left[\begin{matrix}1 & 0\\0 & 1\end{matrix}\middle|\begin{matrix}e & f\\g & h\end{matrix}\right]$.

Elementary row operations include multiplying a row by a non-zero scalar, adding scalar multiples of two rows, or some combination of these. For instance, the first step might be to multiply the second row by $\frac{b}{d}$ and then subtract it from the first row to make its second column a zero. The end result is that the 2×2 section on the right will become the inverse of the original matrix: $N^{-1} = \begin{bmatrix} e & f \\ g & h \end{bmatrix}$.

Calculating the inverse of any matrix larger than 2×2 is cumbersome and using a graphing calculator is recommended.

Basic Operations with Matrices

There are two categories of basic operations with regard to matrices: operations between a matrix and a scalar, and operations between two matrices.

Scalar Operations

A scalar being added to a matrix is treated as though it were being added to each element of the matrix:

$$M + 4 = \begin{bmatrix} m_{11} + 4 & m_{12} + 4 \\ m_{21} + 4 & m_{22} + 4 \end{bmatrix}$$

The same is true for the other three operations.

Subtraction:

$$M - 4 = \begin{bmatrix} m_{11} - 4 & m_{12} - 4 \\ m_{21} - 4 & m_{22} - 4 \end{bmatrix}$$

Multiplication:

$$M \times 4 = \begin{bmatrix} m_{11} \times 4 & m_{12} \times 4 \\ m_{21} \times 4 & m_{22} \times 4 \end{bmatrix}$$

Division:

$$M \div 4 = \begin{bmatrix} m_{11} \div 4 & m_{12} \div 4 \\ m_{21} \div 4 & m_{22} \div 4 \end{bmatrix}$$

Matrix Addition and Subtraction

All four of the basic operations can be used with operations between matrices (although division is usually discarded in favor of multiplication by the inverse), but there are restrictions on the situations in which they can be used. Matrices that meet all the qualifications for a given operation are called **conformable matrices**. However, conformability is specific to the operation; two matrices that are conformable for addition are not necessarily conformable for multiplication.

For two matrices to be conformable for addition or subtraction, they must be of the same dimension; otherwise the operation is not defined. If matrix M is a 3×2 matrix and matrix N is a

Copyright © Mometrix Media. You have been licensed one copy of this document for personal use only. Any other reproduction or redistribution is strictly prohibited. All rights reserved.

2×3 matrix, the operations $M + N$ and $M - N$ are meaningless. If matrices M and N are the same size, the operation is as simple as adding or subtracting all of the corresponding elements:

$$\begin{bmatrix} m_{11} & m_{12} \\ m_{21} & m_{22} \end{bmatrix} + \begin{bmatrix} n_{11} & n_{12} \\ n_{21} & n_{22} \end{bmatrix} = \begin{bmatrix} m_{11} + n_{11} & m_{12} + n_{12} \\ m_{21} + n_{21} & m_{22} + n_{22} \end{bmatrix}$$

$$\begin{bmatrix} m_{11} & m_{12} \\ m_{21} & m_{22} \end{bmatrix} - \begin{bmatrix} n_{11} & n_{12} \\ n_{21} & n_{22} \end{bmatrix} = \begin{bmatrix} m_{11} - n_{11} & m_{12} - n_{12} \\ m_{21} - n_{21} & m_{22} - n_{22} \end{bmatrix}$$

The result of addition or subtraction is a matrix of the same dimension as the two original matrices involved in the operation.

Matrix Multiplication

The first thing it is necessary to understand about matrix multiplication is that it is not commutative. In scalar multiplication, the operation is commutative, meaning that $a \times b = b \times a$. For matrix multiplication, this is not the case: $A \times B \neq B \times A$. The terminology must be specific when describing matrix multiplication. The operation $A \times B$ can be described as A multiplied (or **post-multiplied**) by B, or B **pre-multiplied** by A.

For two matrices to be conformable for multiplication, they need not be of the same dimension, but specific dimensions must correspond. Taking the example of two matrices M and N to be multiplied $M \times N$, matrix M must have the same number of columns as matrix N has rows. Put another way, if matrix M has the dimensions $a \times b$ and matrix N has the dimensions $c \times d$, b must equal c if the two matrices are to be conformable for this multiplication. The matrix that results from the multiplication will have the dimensions $a \times d$. If a and d are both equal to 1, the product is simply a scalar. Square matrices of the same dimensions are always conformable for multiplication, and their product is always a matrix of the same size.

The simplest type of matrix multiplication is a 1×2 matrix (a row vector) times a 2×1 matrix (a column vector). These will multiply in the following way:

$$\begin{bmatrix} m_{11} & m_{12} \end{bmatrix} \times \begin{bmatrix} n_{11} \\ n_{21} \end{bmatrix} = m_{11}n_{11} + m_{12}n_{21}$$

The two matrices are conformable for multiplication because matrix M has the same number of columns as matrix N has rows. Because the other dimensions are both 1, the result is a scalar. Expanding our matrices to 1×3 and 3×1, the process is the same:

$$\begin{bmatrix} m_{11} & m_{12} & m_{13} \end{bmatrix} \times \begin{bmatrix} n_{11} \\ n_{21} \\ n_{31} \end{bmatrix} = m_{11}n_{11} + m_{12}n_{21} + m_{13}n_{31}$$

Once again, the result is a scalar. This type of basic matrix multiplication is the building block for the multiplication of larger matrices.

To multiply larger matrices, treat each **row from the first matrix** and each **column from the second matrix** as individual vectors and follow the pattern for multiplying vectors. The scalar value found from multiplying the first-row vector by the first column vector is placed in the first row, first column of the new matrix. The scalar value found from multiplying the second-row vector by the first column vector is placed in the second row, first column of the new matrix. Continue this pattern until each row of the first matrix has been multiplied by each column of the second vector.

Copyright © Mometrix Media. You have been licensed one copy of this document for personal use only. Any other reproduction or redistribution is strictly prohibited. All rights reserved.

Below is an example of the multiplication of a 3×2 matrix and a 2×3 matrix.

$$\begin{bmatrix} m_{11} & m_{12} \\ m_{21} & m_{22} \\ m_{31} & m_{32} \end{bmatrix} \times \begin{bmatrix} n_{11} & n_{12} & n_{13} \\ n_{21} & n_{22} & n_{23} \end{bmatrix} = \begin{bmatrix} m_{11}n_{11} + m_{12}n_{21} & m_{11}n_{12} + m_{12}n_{22} & m_{11}n_{13} + m_{12}n_{23} \\ m_{21}n_{11} + m_{22}n_{21} & m_{21}n_{12} + m_{22}n_{22} & m_{21}n_{13} + m_{22}n_{23} \\ m_{31}n_{11} + m_{32}n_{21} & m_{31}n_{12} + m_{32}n_{22} & m_{31}n_{13} + m_{32}n_{23} \end{bmatrix}$$

This process starts by taking the first column of the second matrix and running it through each row of the first matrix. Removing all but the first M row and first N column, we would see only the following:

$$\begin{bmatrix} m_{11} & m_{12} \end{bmatrix} \times \begin{bmatrix} n_{11} \\ n_{21} \end{bmatrix}$$

The first product would then be $m_{11}n_{11} + m_{12}n_{21}$. This process will be continued for each column of the N matrix to find the first full row of the product matrix, as shown below.

$$\begin{bmatrix} m_{11} & m_{12} \end{bmatrix} \times \begin{bmatrix} n_{11} \\ n_{21} \end{bmatrix} = \begin{bmatrix} m_{11}n_{11} + m_{12}n_{21} & m_{11}n_{12} + m_{12}n_{22} & m_{11}n_{13} + m_{12}n_{23} \end{bmatrix}$$

After completing the first row, the next step would be to simply move to the second row of the M matrix and repeat the process until all of the rows have been finished. The result is a 3×3 matrix.

$$\begin{bmatrix} m_{11} & m_{12} \\ m_{21} & m_{22} \\ m_{31} & m_{32} \end{bmatrix} \times \begin{bmatrix} n_{11} & n_{12} & n_{13} \\ n_{21} & n_{22} & n_{23} \end{bmatrix} = \begin{bmatrix} m_{11}n_{11} + m_{12}n_{21} & m_{11}n_{12} + m_{12}n_{22} & m_{11}n_{13} + m_{12}n_{23} \\ m_{21}n_{11} + m_{22}n_{21} & m_{21}n_{12} + m_{22}n_{22} & m_{21}n_{13} + m_{22}n_{23} \\ m_{31}n_{11} + m_{32}n_{21} & m_{31}n_{12} + m_{32}n_{22} & m_{31}n_{13} + m_{32}n_{23} \end{bmatrix}$$

If the operation were done in reverse ($N \times M$), the result would be a 2×2 matrix.

$$\begin{bmatrix} n_{11} & n_{12} & n_{13} \\ n_{21} & n_{22} & n_{23} \end{bmatrix} \times \begin{bmatrix} m_{11} & m_{12} \\ m_{21} & m_{22} \\ m_{31} & m_{32} \end{bmatrix} = \begin{bmatrix} m_{11}n_{11} + m_{21}n_{12} + m_{31}n_{13} & m_{12}n_{11} + m_{22}n_{12} + m_{32}n_{13} \\ m_{11}n_{21} + m_{21}n_{22} + m_{31}n_{23} & m_{12}n_{21} + m_{22}n_{22} + m_{32}n_{23} \end{bmatrix}$$

<u>Example</u>

A sporting-goods store sells baseballs, volleyballs, and basketballs.

Baseballs	\$3 each
Volleyballs	\$8 each
Basketballs	\$15 each

Here are the same store's sales numbers for one weekend:

	Baseballs	Volleyballs	Basketballs
Friday	5	4	4
Saturday	7	3	10
Sunday	4	3	6

Find the total sales for each day by multiplying matrices.

The first table can be represented by the following column-vector:

$$\begin{bmatrix} 3 \\ 8 \\ 15 \end{bmatrix}$$

Copyright © Mometrix Media. You have been licensed one copy of this document for personal use only. Any other reproduction or redistribution is strictly prohibited. All rights reserved.

And the second table can be represented by this matrix:

$$\begin{bmatrix} 5 & 4 & 4 \\ 7 & 3 & 10 \\ 4 & 3 & 6 \end{bmatrix}$$

Multiplying the second matrix by the first will result in a column vector showing the total sales for each day:

$$\begin{bmatrix} 5 & 4 & 4 \\ 7 & 3 & 10 \\ 4 & 3 & 6 \end{bmatrix} \times \begin{bmatrix} 3 \\ 8 \\ 15 \end{bmatrix} = \begin{bmatrix} 3 \times 5 + 8 \times 4 + 15 \times 4 \\ 3 \times 7 + 8 \times 3 + 15 \times 10 \\ 3 \times 4 + 8 \times 3 + 15 \times 6 \end{bmatrix} = \begin{bmatrix} 15 + 32 + 60 \\ 21 + 24 + 150 \\ 12 + 24 + 90 \end{bmatrix} = \begin{bmatrix} 107 \\ 195 \\ 126 \end{bmatrix}$$

From this, we can see that Friday's sales were \$107, Saturday's sales were \$195, and Sunday's sales were \$126.

Solving Systems of Equations

Matrices can be used to represent the coefficients of a system of linear equations and can be very useful in solving those systems. Take for instance three equations with three variables:

$$a_1x + b_1y + c_1z = d_1$$

$$a_2x + b_2y + c_2z = d_2$$

$$a_3x + b_3y + c_3z = d_3$$

where all *a*, *b*, *c*, and *d* are known constants.

To solve this system, define three matrices:

$$A = \begin{bmatrix} a_1 & b_1 & c_1 \\ a_2 & b_2 & c_2 \\ a_3 & b_3 & c_3 \end{bmatrix}; \; D = \begin{bmatrix} d_1 \\ d_2 \\ d_3 \end{bmatrix}; \; X = \begin{bmatrix} x \\ y \\ z \end{bmatrix}$$

The three equations in our system can be fully represented by a single matrix equation:

$$AX = D$$

We know that the identity matrix times X is equal to X, and we know that any matrix multiplied by its inverse is equal to the identity matrix.

$$A^{-1}AX = IX = X; \text{thus } X = A^{-1}D$$

Our goal then is to find the inverse of A, or A^{-1}. Once we have that, we can pre-multiply matrix D by A^{-1} (post-multiplying here is an undefined operation) to find matrix X.

Copyright © Mometrix Media. You have been licensed one copy of this document for personal use only. Any other reproduction or redistribution is strictly prohibited. All rights reserved.

Systems of equations can also be solved using the transformation of an augmented matrix in a process similar to that for finding a matrix inverse. Begin by arranging each equation of the system in the following format:

$$a_1x + b_1y + c_1z = d_1$$

$$a_2x + b_2y + c_2z = d_2$$

$$a_3x + b_3y + c_3z = d_3$$

Define matrices A and D and combine them into augmented matrix A_a:

$$A = \begin{bmatrix} a_1 & b_1 & c_1 \\ a_2 & b_2 & c_2 \\ a_3 & b_3 & c_3 \end{bmatrix};\ D = \begin{bmatrix} d_1 \\ d_2 \\ d_3 \end{bmatrix}; A_a = \begin{bmatrix} a_1 & b_1 & c_1 & d_1 \\ a_2 & b_2 & c_2 & d_2 \\ a_3 & b_3 & c_3 & d_3 \end{bmatrix}$$

To solve the augmented matrix and the system of equations, use elementary row operations to form an identity matrix in the first 3×3 section. When this is complete, the values in the last column are the solutions to the system of equations:

$$\begin{bmatrix} 1 & 0 & 0 & x \\ 0 & 1 & 0 & y \\ 0 & 0 & 1 & z \end{bmatrix}$$

If an identity matrix is not possible, the system of equations has no unique solution. Sometimes only a partial solution will be possible. The following are partial solutions you may find:

$\begin{bmatrix} 1 & 0 & k_1 & x_0 \\ 0 & 1 & k_2 & y_0 \\ 0 & 0 & 0 & 0 \end{bmatrix}$ gives the non-unique solution $x = x_0 - k_1z;\ y = y_0 - k_2z$

$\begin{bmatrix} 1 & j_1 & k_1 & x_0 \\ 0 & 0 & 0 & 0 \\ 0 & 0 & 0 & 0 \end{bmatrix}$ gives the non-unique solution $x = x_0 - j_1y - k_1z$

This process can be used to solve systems of equations with any number of variables, but three is the upper limit for practical purposes. Anything more ought to be done with a graphing calculator.

Geometric Transformations

The four *geometric transformations* are **translations**, **reflections**, **rotations**, and **dilations**. When geometric transformations are expressed as matrices, the process of performing the transformations is simplified. For calculations of the geometric transformations of a planar figure, make a $2 \times n$ matrix, where n is the number of vertices in the planar figure. Each column represents the rectangular coordinates of one vertex of the figure, with the top row containing the values of the x-coordinates and the bottom row containing the values of the y-coordinates. For example, given a planar triangular figure with coordinates (x_1, y_1), (x_2, y_2), and (x_3, y_3), the corresponding matrix is $\begin{bmatrix} x_1 & x_2 & x_3 \\ y_1 & y_2 & y_3 \end{bmatrix}$. You can then perform the necessary transformations on this matrix to determine the coordinates of the resulting figure.

Copyright © Mometrix Media. You have been licensed one copy of this document for personal use only. Any other reproduction or redistribution is strictly prohibited. All rights reserved.

Translation

A **translation** moves a figure along the x-axis, the y-axis, or both axes without changing the size or shape of the figure. To calculate the new coordinates of a planar figure following a translation, set up a matrix of the coordinates and a matrix of the translation values and add the two matrices.

$$\begin{bmatrix} h & h & h \\ v & v & v \end{bmatrix} + \begin{bmatrix} x_1 & x_2 & x_3 \\ y_1 & y_2 & y_3 \end{bmatrix} = \begin{bmatrix} h+x_1 & h+x_2 & h+x_3 \\ v+y_1 & v+y_2 & v+y_3 \end{bmatrix}$$

where h is the number of units the figure is moved along the x-axis (horizontally) and v is the number of units the figure is moved along the y-axis (vertically).

Reflection

To find the **reflection** of a planar figure over the x-axis, set up a matrix of the coordinates of the vertices and pre-multiply the matrix by the 2×2 matrix $\begin{bmatrix} 1 & 0 \\ 0 & -1 \end{bmatrix}$ so that $\begin{bmatrix} 1 & 0 \\ 0 & -1 \end{bmatrix}\begin{bmatrix} x_1 & x_2 & x_3 \\ y_1 & y_2 & y_3 \end{bmatrix} = \begin{bmatrix} x_1 & x_2 & x_3 \\ -y_1 & -y_2 & -y_3 \end{bmatrix}$. To find the reflection of a planar figure over the y-axis, set up a matrix of the coordinates of the vertices and pre-multiply the matrix by the 2×2 matrix $\begin{bmatrix} -1 & 0 \\ 0 & 1 \end{bmatrix}$ so that $\begin{bmatrix} -1 & 0 \\ 0 & 1 \end{bmatrix}\begin{bmatrix} x_1 & x_2 & x_3 \\ y_1 & y_2 & y_3 \end{bmatrix} = \begin{bmatrix} -x_1 & -x_2 & -x_3 \\ y_1 & y_2 & y_3 \end{bmatrix}$. To find the reflection of a planar figure over the line $y = x$, set up a matrix of the coordinates of the vertices and pre-multiply the matrix by the 2×2 matrix $\begin{bmatrix} 0 & 1 \\ 1 & 0 \end{bmatrix}$ so that $\begin{bmatrix} 0 & 1 \\ 1 & 0 \end{bmatrix}\begin{bmatrix} x_1 & x_2 & x_3 \\ y_1 & y_2 & y_3 \end{bmatrix} = \begin{bmatrix} y_1 & y_2 & y_3 \\ x_1 & x_2 & x_3 \end{bmatrix}$. Remember that the order of multiplication is important when multiplying matrices. The commutative property does not apply.

Rotation

To find the coordinates of the figure formed by rotating a planar figure about the origin θ degrees in a counterclockwise direction, set up a matrix of the coordinates of the vertices and pre-multiply the matrix by the 2×2 matrix $\begin{bmatrix} \cos\theta & \sin\theta \\ -\sin\theta & \cos\theta \end{bmatrix}$. For example, if you want to rotate a figure 90° clockwise around the origin, you would have to convert the degree measure to 270° counterclockwise and solve the 2×2 matrix you have set as the pre-multiplier: $\begin{bmatrix} \cos 270° & \sin 270° \\ -\sin 270° & \cos 270° \end{bmatrix} = \begin{bmatrix} 0 & -1 \\ 1 & 0 \end{bmatrix}$. Use this as the pre-multiplier for the matrix $\begin{bmatrix} x_1 & x_2 & x_3 \\ y_1 & y_2 & y_3 \end{bmatrix}$ and solve to find the new coordinates.

Dilation

To find the **dilation** of a planar figure by a scale factor of k, set up a matrix of the coordinates of the vertices of the planar figure and pre-multiply the matrix by the 2×2 matrix $\begin{bmatrix} k & 0 \\ 0 & k \end{bmatrix}$ so that $\begin{bmatrix} k & 0 \\ 0 & k \end{bmatrix}\begin{bmatrix} x_1 & x_2 & x_3 \\ y_1 & y_2 & y_3 \end{bmatrix} = \begin{bmatrix} kx_1 & kx_2 & kx_3 \\ ky_1 & ky_2 & ky_3 \end{bmatrix}$. This is effectively the same as multiplying the matrix by the scalar k, but the matrix equation would still be necessary if the figure were being dilated by different factors in vertical and horizontal directions. The scale factor k will be greater than 1 if the figure is being enlarged, and between 0 and 1 if the figure is being shrunk. Again, remember that when multiplying matrices, the order of the matrices is important. The commutative property does not apply, and the matrix with the coordinates of the figure must be the second matrix.

Copyright © Mometrix Media. You have been licensed one copy of this document for personal use only. Any other reproduction or redistribution is strictly prohibited. All rights reserved.

Geometry and Measurement

Lines and Planes

A **point** is a fixed location in space; has no size or dimensions; commonly represented by a dot.

A **line** is a set of points that extends infinitely in two opposite directions. It has length, but no width or depth. A line can be defined by any two distinct points that it contains. A line segment is a portion of a line that has definite endpoints. A ray is a portion of a line that extends from a single point on that line in one direction along the line. It has a definite beginning, but no ending.

A **plane** is a two-dimensional flat surface defined by three non-collinear points. A plane extends an infinite distance in all directions in those two dimensions. It contains an infinite number of points, parallel lines and segments, intersecting lines and segments, as well as parallel or intersecting rays. A plane will never contain a three-dimensional figure or skew lines. Two given planes will either be parallel or they will intersect to form a line. A plane may intersect a circular conic surface, such as a cone, to form conic sections, such as the parabola, hyperbola, circle or ellipse.

Perpendicular lines are lines that intersect at right angles. They are represented by the symbol $\perp$. The shortest distance from a line to a point not on the line is a perpendicular segment from the point to the line.

Parallel lines are lines in the same plane that have no points in common and never meet. It is possible for lines to be in different planes, have no points in common, and never meet, but they are not parallel because they are in different planes.

A **bisector** is a line or line segment that divides another line segment into two equal lengths. A perpendicular bisector of a line segment is composed of points that are equidistant from the endpoints of the segment it is dividing.

Intersecting lines are lines that have exactly one point in common. Concurrent lines are multiple lines that intersect at a single point.

A **transversal** is a line that intersects at least two other lines, which may or may not be parallel to one another. A transversal that intersects parallel lines is a common occurrence in geometry.

Angles

An **angle** is formed when two lines or line segments meet at a common point. It may be a common starting point for a pair of segments or rays, or it may be the intersection of lines. Angles are represented by the symbol $\angle$.

The **vertex** is the point at which two segments or rays meet to form an angle. If the angle is formed by intersecting rays, lines, and/or line segments, the vertex is the point at which four angles are formed. The pairs of angles opposite one another are called vertical angles, and their measures are equal.

An *acute* angle is an angle with a degree measure less than 90°.

A *right* angle is an angle with a degree measure of exactly 90°.

An *obtuse* angle is an angle with a degree measure greater than 90° but less than 180°.

Copyright © Mometrix Media. You have been licensed one copy of this document for personal use only. Any other reproduction or redistribution is strictly prohibited. All rights reserved.

A *straight angle* is an angle with a degree measure of exactly 180°. This is also a semicircle.

A *reflex angle* is an angle with a degree measure greater than 180° but less than 360°.

A *full angle* is an angle with a degree measure of exactly 360°.

Review Video: Geometric Symbols: Angles
Visit mometrix.com/academy and enter code: 452738

Two angles whose sum is exactly 90° are said to be **complementary**. The two angles may or may not be adjacent. In a right triangle, the two acute angles are complementary.

Two angles whose sum is exactly 180° are said to be **supplementary**. The two angles may or may not be adjacent. Two intersecting lines always form two pairs of supplementary angles. Adjacent supplementary angles will always form a straight line.

Two angles that have the same vertex and share a side are said to be **adjacent**. Vertical angles are not adjacent because they share a vertex but no common side.

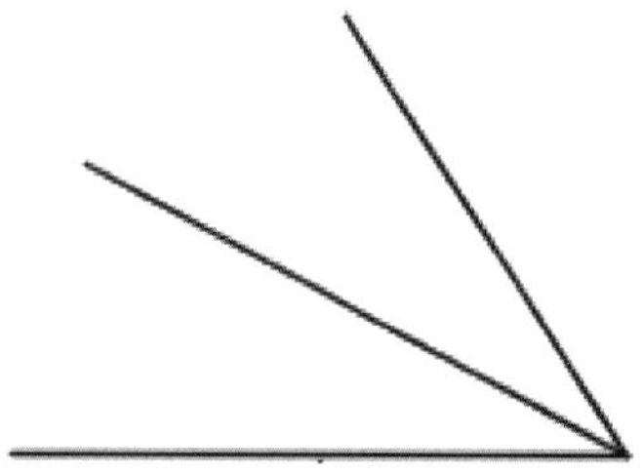

Adjacent
Share vertex and side

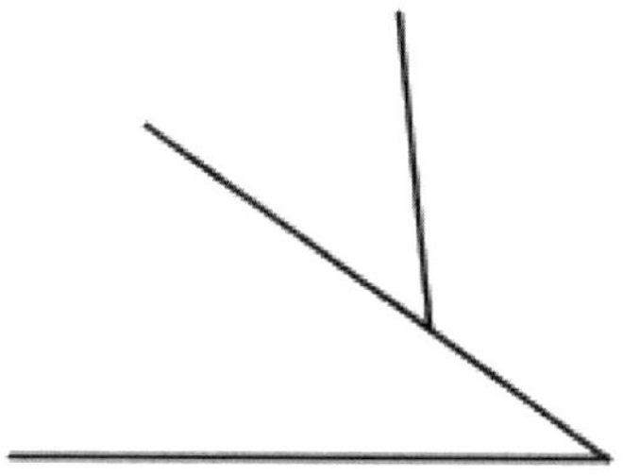

Not adjacent
Share part of side, but not vertex

When two parallel lines are cut by a transversal, the angles that are between the two parallel lines are **interior angles**. In the diagram below, angles 3, 4, 5, and 6 are interior angles.

When two parallel lines are cut by a transversal, the angles that are outside the parallel lines are **exterior angles**. In the diagram below, angles 1, 2, 7, and 8 are exterior angles.

When two parallel lines are cut by a transversal, the angles that are in the same position relative to the transversal and a parallel line are *corresponding angles*. The diagram below has four pairs of corresponding angles: angles 1 and 5; angles 2 and 6; angles 3 and 7; and angles 4 and 8. Corresponding angles formed by parallel lines are congruent.

When two parallel lines are cut by a transversal, the two interior angles that are on opposite sides of the transversal are called *alternate interior angles*. In the diagram below, there are two pairs of alternate interior angles: angles 3 and 6, and angles 4 and 5. Alternate interior angles formed by parallel lines are congruent.

When two parallel lines are cut by a transversal, the two exterior angles that are on opposite sides of the transversal are called *alternate exterior angles*.

Copyright © Mometrix Media. You have been licensed one copy of this document for personal use only. Any other reproduction or redistribution is strictly prohibited. All rights reserved.

In the diagram below, there are two pairs of alternate exterior angles: angles 1 and 8, and angles 2 and 7. Alternate exterior angles formed by parallel lines are congruent.

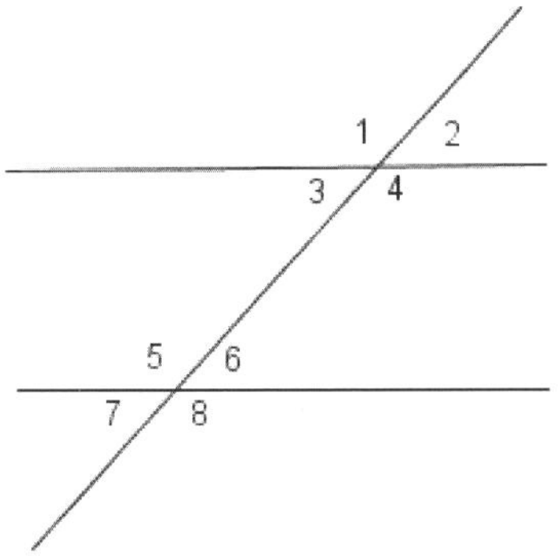

When two lines intersect, four angles are formed. The non-adjacent angles at this vertex are called vertical angles. Vertical angles are congruent. In the diagram, $\angle ABD \cong \angle CBE$ and $\angle ABC \cong \angle DBE$.

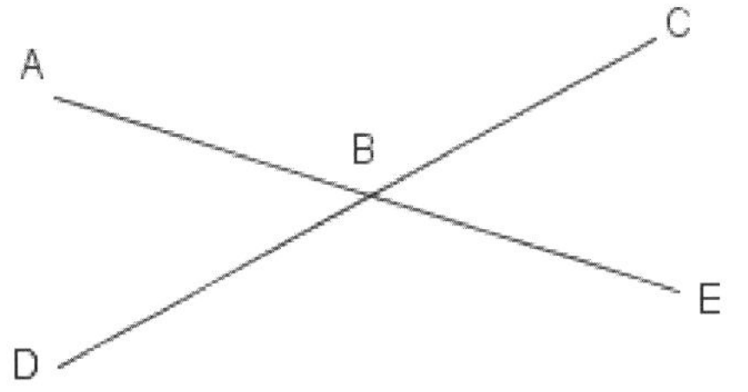

Polygons

Each straight line segment of a polygon is called a **side**.

The point at which two sides of a polygon intersect is called the **vertex**. In a polygon, the number of sides is always equal to the number of vertices.

A polygon with all sides congruent and all angles equal is called a **regular polygon**.

A line segment from the center of a polygon perpendicular to a side of the polygon is called the **apothem**. In a regular polygon, the apothem can be used to find the area of the polygon using the formula $A = \frac{1}{2}ap$, where a is the apothem and p is the perimeter.

A line segment from the center of a polygon to a vertex of the polygon is called a **radius**. The radius of a regular polygon is also the radius of a circle that can be circumscribed about the polygon.

Triangle – 3 sides

Quadrilateral – 4 sides

Pentagon – 5 sides

Hexagon – 6 sides

Heptagon – 7 sides

Octagon – 8 sides

Copyright © Mometrix Media. You have been licensed one copy of this document for personal use only. Any other reproduction or redistribution is strictly prohibited. All rights reserved.

Nonagon – 9 sides

Decagon – 10 sides

Dodecagon – 12 sides

More generally, an n-gon is a polygon that has n angles and n sides.

The sum of the interior angles of an n-sided polygon is $(n - 2)180°$. For example, in a triangle $n = 3$, so the sum of the interior angles is $(3-2)180° = 180°$. In a quadrilateral, $n = 4$, and the sum of the angles is $(4-2)180° = 360°$. The sum of the interior angles of a polygon is equal to the sum of the interior angles of any other polygon with the same number of sides.

A **diagonal** is a line segment that joins two non-adjacent vertices of a polygon.

A **convex polygon** is a polygon whose diagonals all lie within the interior of the polygon.

A **concave polygon** is a polygon with a least one diagonal that lies outside the polygon. In the diagram below, quadrilateral $ABCD$ is concave because diagonal $\overline{AC}$ lies outside the polygon.

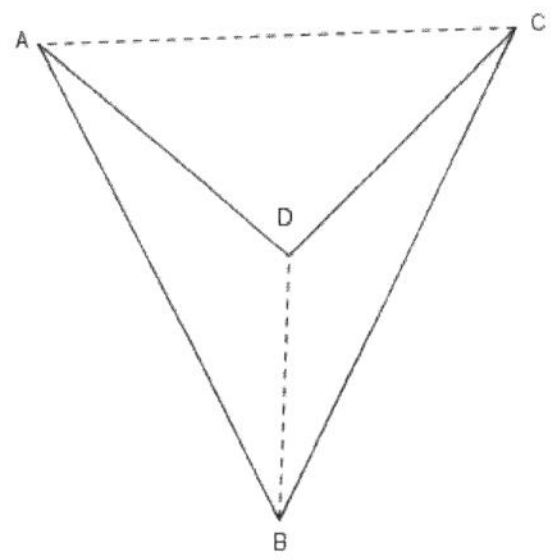

The number of diagonals a polygon has can be found by using the formula: number of diagonals $= \frac{n(n-3)}{2}$, where n is the number of sides in the polygon. This formula works for all polygons, not just regular polygons.

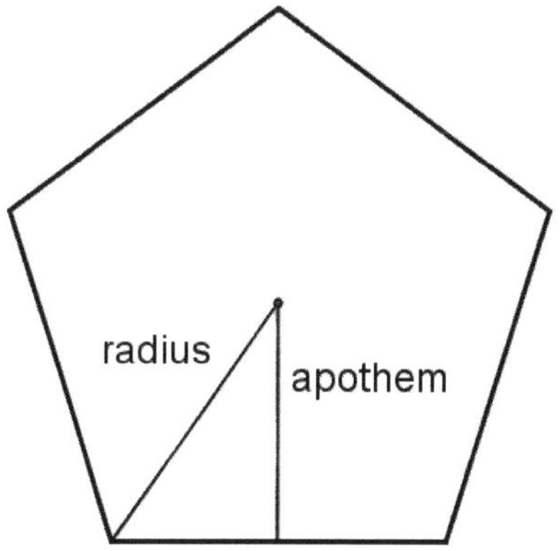

Copyright © Mometrix Media. You have been licensed one copy of this document for personal use only. Any other reproduction or redistribution is strictly prohibited. All rights reserved.

Congruent figures are geometric figures that have the same size and shape. All corresponding angles are equal, and all corresponding sides are equal. It is indicated by the symbol $\cong$.

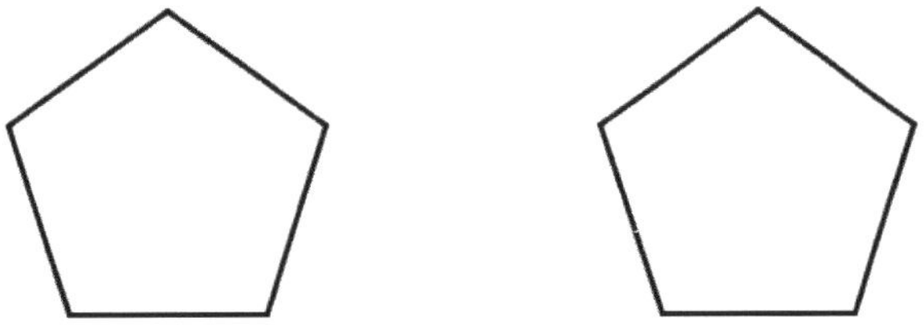

Congruent polygons

Similar figures are geometric figures that have the same shape, but do not necessarily have the same size. All corresponding angles are equal, and all corresponding sides are proportional, but they do not have to be equal. It is indicated by the symbol $\sim$.

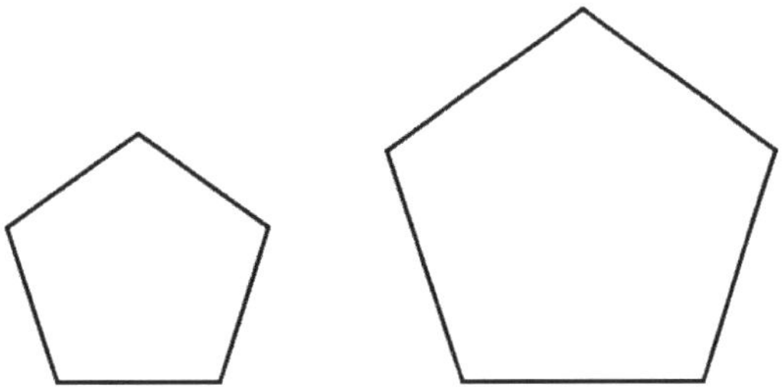

Similar polygons

Note that all congruent figures are also similar, but not all similar figures are congruent.

Review Video: Polygons, Similarity, and Congruence
Visit mometrix.com/academy and enter code: 686174

Line of Symmetry

A **line of symmetry** is a line that divides a figure or object into two symmetric parts. Each symmetric half is congruent to the other. An object may have no lines of symmetry, one line of symmetry, or more than one line of symmetry.

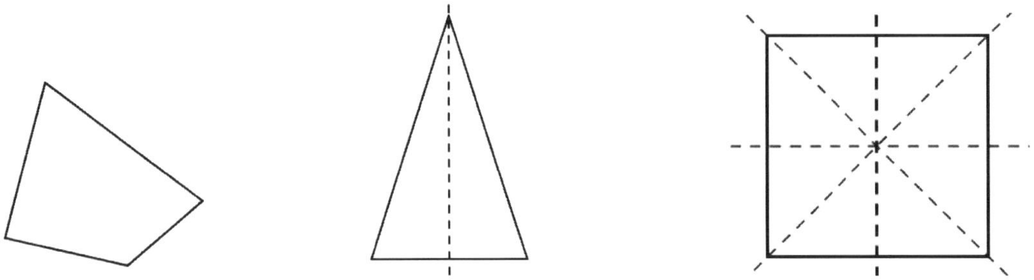

No lines of symmetry One line of symmetry Multiple lines of symmetry

Copyright © Mometrix Media. You have been licensed one copy of this document for personal use only. Any other reproduction or redistribution is strictly prohibited. All rights reserved.

Quadrilateral: A closed two-dimensional geometric figure composed of exactly four straight sides. The sum of the interior angles of any quadrilateral is 360°.

Review Video: Symmetry
Visit mometrix.com/academy and enter code: 528106

Parallelogram

A **parallelogram** is a quadrilateral that has exactly two pairs of opposite parallel sides. The sides that are parallel are also congruent. The opposite interior angles are always congruent, and the consecutive interior angles are supplementary. The diagonals of a parallelogram bisect each other. Each diagonal divides the parallelogram into two congruent triangles.

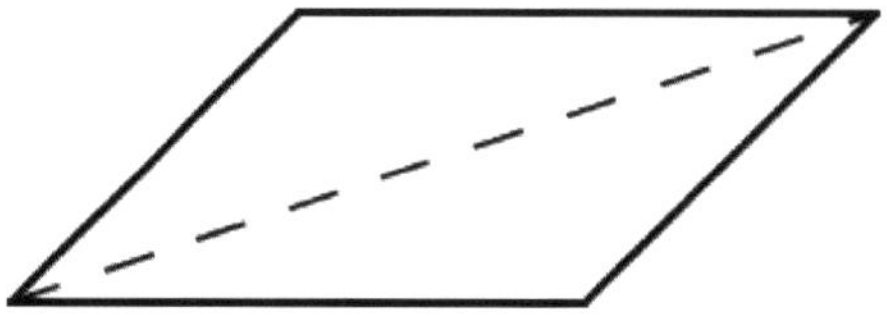

Review Video: Parallelogram
Visit mometrix.com/academy and enter code: 129981

Trapezoid

Traditionally, a **trapezoid** is a quadrilateral that has exactly one pair of parallel sides. Some math texts define trapezoid as a quadrilateral that has at least one pair of parallel sides. Because there are no rules governing the second pair of sides, there are no rules that apply to the properties of the diagonals of a trapezoid.

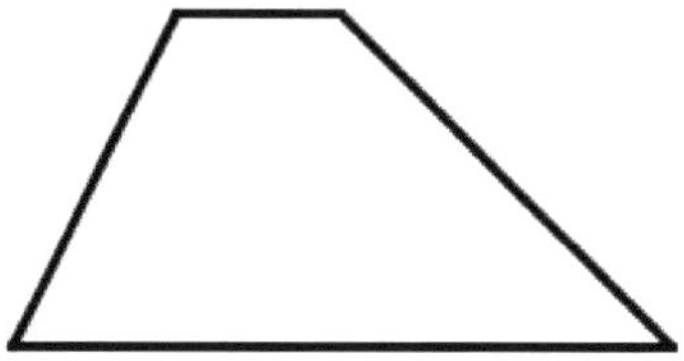

Rectangles, rhombuses, and squares are all special forms of parallelograms.

Rectangle

A **rectangle** is a parallelogram with four right angles. All rectangles are parallelograms, but not all parallelograms are rectangles. The diagonals of a rectangle are congruent.

Copyright © Mometrix Media. You have been licensed one copy of this document for personal use only. Any other reproduction or redistribution is strictly prohibited. All rights reserved.

Rhombus

A **rhombus** is a parallelogram with four congruent sides. All rhombuses are parallelograms, but not all parallelograms are rhombuses. The diagonals of a rhombus are perpendicular to each other.

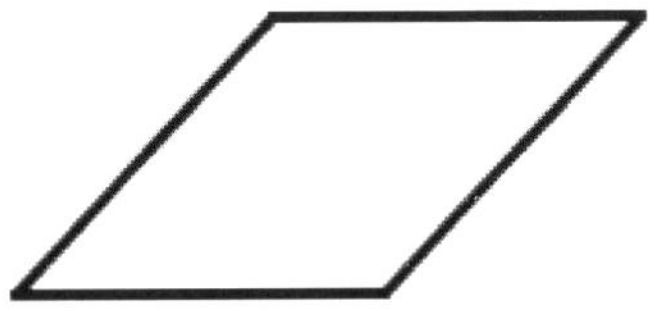

Review Video: Diagonals of Parallelograms, Rectangles, and Rhombi
Visit mometrix.com/academy and enter code: 320040

Square

A **square** is a parallelogram with four right angles and four congruent sides. All squares are also parallelograms, rhombuses, and rectangles. The diagonals of a square are congruent and perpendicular to each other.

A quadrilateral whose diagonals bisect each other is a **parallelogram**. A quadrilateral whose opposite sides are parallel (2 pairs of parallel sides) is a parallelogram.

A quadrilateral whose diagonals are perpendicular bisectors of each other is a **rhombus**. A quadrilateral whose opposite sides (both pairs) are parallel and congruent is a rhombus.

A parallelogram that has a right angle is a **rectangle**. (Consecutive angles of a parallelogram are supplementary. Therefore if there is one right angle in a parallelogram, there are four right angles in that parallelogram.)

A rhombus with one right angle is a **square**. Because the rhombus is a special form of a parallelogram, the rules about the angles of a parallelogram also apply to the rhombus.

Copyright © Mometrix Media. You have been licensed one copy of this document for personal use only. Any other reproduction or redistribution is strictly prohibited. All rights reserved.

Area and Perimeter Formulas

Triangle

The *perimeter of any triangle* is found by summing the three side lengths; $P = a + b + c$. For an equilateral triangle, this is the same as $P = 3s$, where *s* is any side length, since all three sides are the same length.

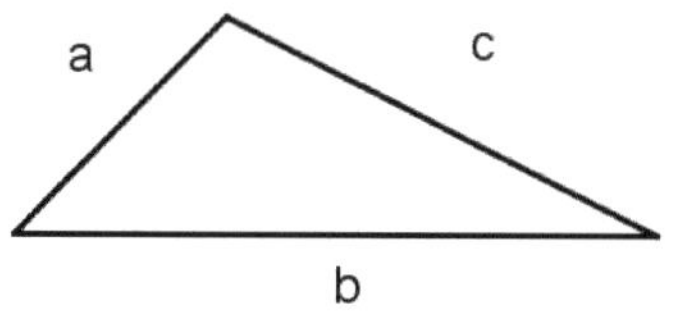

Square

The *area of a square* is found by using the formula $A = s^2$, where and *s* is the length of one side.

The *perimeter of a square* is found by using the formula $P = 4s$, where *s* is the length of one side. Because all four sides are equal in a square, it is faster to multiply the length of one side by 4 than to add the same number four times. You could use the formulas for rectangles and get the same answer.

> **Review Video:** Area and Perimeter of a Square
> Visit mometrix.com/academy and enter code: 620902

Rectangle

The *area of a rectangle* is found by the formula $A = lw$, where *A* is the area of the rectangle, *l* is the length (usually considered to be the longer side) and *w* is the width (usually considered to be the shorter side). The numbers for *l* and *w* are interchangeable.

The *perimeter of a rectangle* is found by the formula $P = 2l + 2w$ or $P = 2(l + w)$, where *l* is the length, and *w* is the width. It may be easier to add the length and width first and then double the result, as in the second formula.

> **Review Video:** Area and Perimeter of a Rectangle
> Visit mometrix.com/academy and enter code: 933707

Parallelogram

The *area of a parallelogram* is found by the formula $A = bh$, where *b* is the length of the base, and *h* is the height. Note that the base and height correspond to the length and width in a rectangle, so this formula would apply to rectangles as well. Do not confuse the height of a parallelogram with the length of the second side. The two are only the same measure in the case of a rectangle.

The *perimeter of a parallelogram* is found by the formula $P = 2a + 2b$ or $P = 2(a + b)$, where *a* and *b* are the lengths of the two sides.

> **Review Video:** Area and Perimeter of a Parallelogram
> Visit mometrix.com/academy and enter code: 718313

Copyright © Mometrix Media. You have been licensed one copy of this document for personal use only. Any other reproduction or redistribution is strictly prohibited. All rights reserved.

Trapezoid

The *area of a trapezoid* is found by the formula $A = \frac{1}{2}h(b_1 + b_2)$, where h is the height (segment joining and perpendicular to the parallel bases), and b_1 and b_2 are the two parallel sides (bases). Do not use one of the other two sides as the height unless that side is also perpendicular to the parallel bases.

The *perimeter of a trapezoid* is found by the formula $P = a + b_1 + c + b_2$, where a, b_1, c, and b_2 are the four sides of the trapezoid.

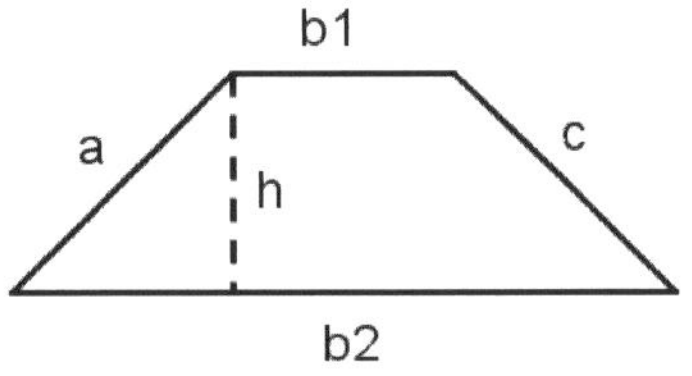

Review Video: Area and Perimeter of a Trapezoid
Visit mometrix.com/academy and enter code: 587523

Triangles

An **equilateral triangle** is a triangle with three congruent sides. An equilateral triangle will also have three congruent angles, each 60°. All equilateral triangles are also acute triangles.

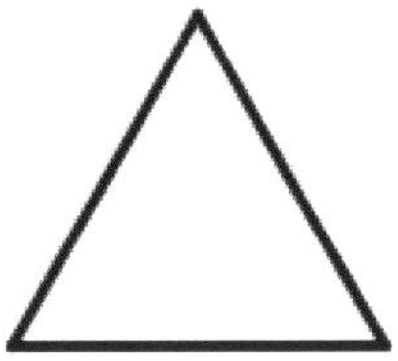

An **isosceles triangle** is a triangle with two congruent sides. An isosceles triangle will also have two congruent angles opposite the two congruent sides.

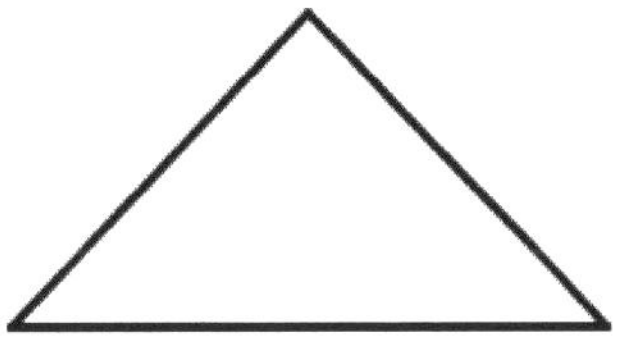

A **scalene triangle** is a triangle with no congruent sides. A scalene triangle will also have three angles of different measures. The angle with the largest measure is opposite the longest side, and the angle with the smallest measure is opposite the shortest side.

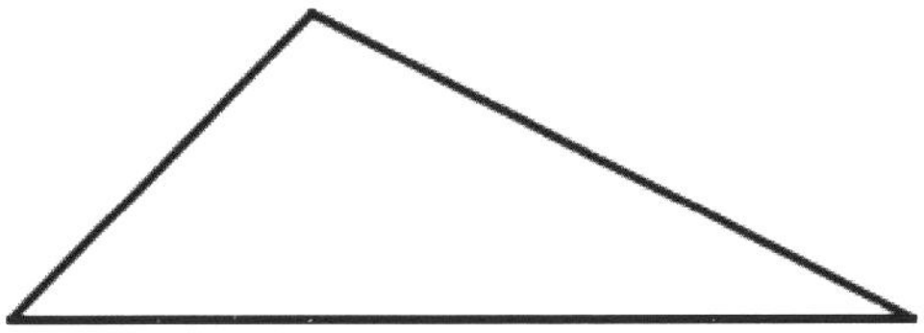

Copyright © Mometrix Media. You have been licensed one copy of this document for personal use only. Any other reproduction or redistribution is strictly prohibited. All rights reserved.

An **acute triangle** is a triangle whose three angles are all less than 90°. If two of the angles are equal, the acute triangle is also an isosceles triangle. If the three angles are all equal, the acute triangle is also an equilateral triangle.

A **right triangle** is a triangle with exactly one angle equal to 90°. All right triangles follow the Pythagorean theorem. A right triangle can never be acute or obtuse.

An **obtuse triangle** is a triangle with exactly one angle greater than 90°. The other two angles may or may not be equal. If the two remaining angles are equal, the obtuse triangle is also an isosceles triangle.

Review Video: Introduction to Types of Triangles
Visit mometrix.com/academy and enter code: 511711

Terminology

Altitude of a triangle

A line segment drawn from one vertex perpendicular to the opposite side. In the diagram below, $\overline{BE}$, $\overline{AD}$, and $\overline{CF}$ are altitudes. The three altitudes in a triangle are always concurrent.

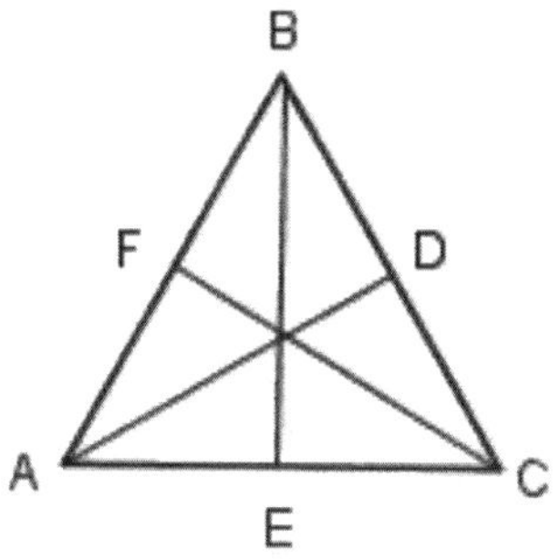

Height of a triangle

The length of the altitude, although the two terms are often used interchangeably.

Orthocenter of a triangle

The point of concurrency of the altitudes of a triangle. Note that in an obtuse triangle, the orthocenter will be outside the triangle, and in a right triangle, the orthocenter is the vertex of the right angle.

Median of a triangle

A line segment drawn from one vertex to the midpoint of the opposite side. This is not the same as the altitude, except the altitude to the base of an isosceles triangle and all three altitudes of an equilateral triangle.

Centroid of a triangle

The point of concurrency of the medians of a triangle. This is the same point as the orthocenter only in an equilateral triangle. Unlike the orthocenter, the centroid is always inside the triangle. The centroid can also be considered the exact center of the triangle. Any shape triangle can be perfectly balanced on a tip placed at the centroid. The centroid is also the point that is two-thirds the distance from the vertex to the opposite side.

Copyright © Mometrix Media. You have been licensed one copy of this document for personal use only. Any other reproduction or redistribution is strictly prohibited. All rights reserved.

Pythagorean Theorem

The side of a triangle opposite the right angle is called the **hypotenuse**. The other two sides are called the legs. The Pythagorean theorem states a relationship among the legs and hypotenuse of a right triangle: $a^2 + b^2 = c^2$, where a and b are the lengths of the legs of a right triangle, and c is the length of the hypotenuse. Note that this formula will only work with right triangles.

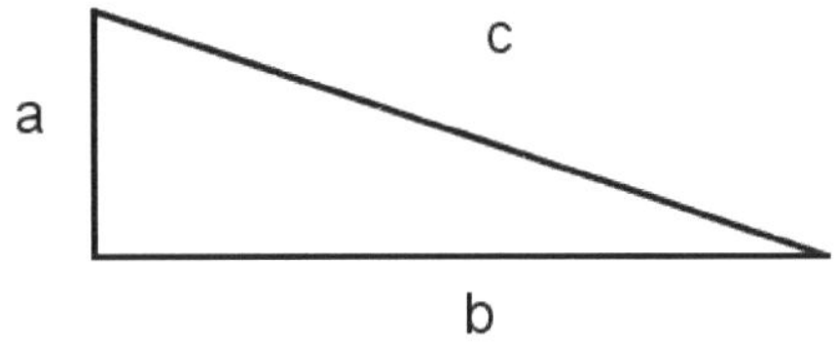

Review Video: Pythagorean Theorem
Visit mometrix.com/academy and enter code: 906576

General Rules

The *triangle inequality theorem* states that the sum of the measures of any two sides of a triangle is always greater than the measure of the third side. If the sum of the measures of two sides were equal to the third side, a triangle would be impossible because the two sides would lie flat across the third side and there would be no vertex. If the sum of the measures of two of the sides was less than the third side, a closed figure would be impossible because the two shortest sides would never meet.

The sum of the measures of the interior angles of a triangle is always 180°. Therefore, a triangle can never have more than one angle greater than or equal to 90°.

In any triangle, the angles opposite congruent sides are congruent, and the sides opposite congruent angles are congruent. The largest angle is always opposite the longest side, and the smallest angle is always opposite the shortest side.

The line segment that joins the midpoints of any two sides of a triangle is always parallel to the third side and exactly half the length of the third side.

Similarity and Congruence Rules

Similar triangles are triangles whose corresponding angles are equal and whose corresponding sides are proportional. Represented by AA. Similar triangles whose corresponding sides are congruent are also congruent triangles.

Review Video: Similar Triangles
Visit mometrix.com/academy and enter code: 398538

Three sides of one triangle are congruent to the three corresponding sides of the second triangle. Represented as SSS.

Two sides and the included angle (the angle formed by those two sides) of one triangle are congruent to the corresponding two sides and included angle of the second triangle. Represented by SAS.

Copyright © Mometrix Media. You have been licensed one copy of this document for personal use only. Any other reproduction or redistribution is strictly prohibited. All rights reserved.

Two angles and the included side (the side that joins the two angles) of one triangle are congruent to the corresponding two angles and included side of the second triangle. Represented by ASA.

Two angles and a non-included side of one triangle are congruent to the corresponding two angles and non-included side of the second triangle. Represented by AAS.

Note that AAA is not a form for congruent triangles. This would say that the three angles are congruent, but says nothing about the sides. This meets the requirements for similar triangles, but not congruent triangles.

Area and Perimeter Formulas

The *perimeter of any triangle* is found by summing the three side lengths; $P = a + b + c$. For an equilateral triangle, this is the same as $P = 3s$, where s is any side length, since all three sides are the same length.

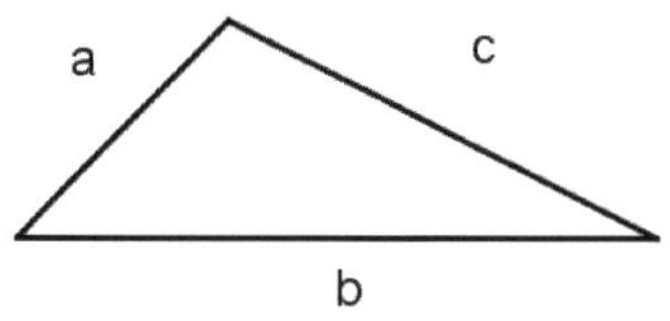

The area of any triangle can be found by taking half the product of one side length (base or b) and the perpendicular distance from that side to the opposite vertex (height or h). In equation form, $A = \frac{1}{2}bh$. For many triangles, it may be difficult to calculate h, so using one of the other formulas given here may be easier.

Another formula that works for any triangle is $A = \sqrt{s(s-a)(s-b)(s-c)}$, where A is the area, s is the semiperimeter $s = \frac{a+b+c}{2}$, and a, b, and c are the lengths of the three sides.

The area of an equilateral triangle can be found by the formula $A = \frac{\sqrt{3}}{4}s^2$, where A is the area and s is the length of a side. You could use the $30° - 60° - 90°$ ratios to find the height of the triangle and then use the standard triangle area formula, but this is faster.

The area of an isosceles triangle can be found by the formula, $A = \frac{1}{2}b\sqrt{a^2 - \frac{b^2}{4}}$, where A is the area, b is the base (the unique side), and a is the length of one of the two congruent sides. If you do not

Copyright © Mometrix Media. You have been licensed one copy of this document for personal use only. Any other reproduction or redistribution is strictly prohibited. All rights reserved.

remember this formula, you can use the Pythagorean theorem to find the height so you can use the standard formula for the area of a triangle.

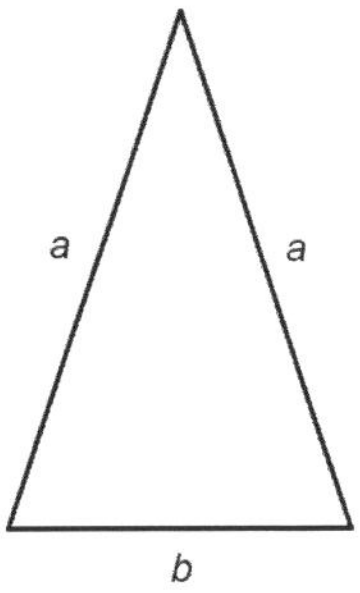

Review Video: Area and Perimeter of a Triangle
Visit mometrix.com/academy and enter code: 853779

Rotation, Center of Rotation, and Angle of Rotation

A *rotation* is a transformation that turns a figure around a point called the **center of rotation**, which can lie anywhere in the plane. If a line is drawn from a point on a figure to the center of rotation, and another line is drawn from the center to the rotated image of that point, the angle between the two lines is the **angle of rotation**. The vertex of the angle of rotation is the center of rotation.

Review Video: Rotation
Visit mometrix.com/academy and enter code: 602600

Reflection over a Line and Reflection in a Point

A reflection of a figure over a *line* (a "flip") creates a congruent image that is the same distance from the line as the original figure but on the opposite side. The **line of reflection** is the perpendicular bisector of any line segment drawn from a point on the original figure to its reflected image (unless the point and its reflected image happen to be the same point, which happens when a figure is reflected over one of its own sides).

A reflection of a figure in a *point* is the same as the rotation of the figure 180° about that point. The image of the figure is congruent to the original figure. The **point of reflection** is the midpoint of a line segment which connects a point in the figure to its image (unless the point and its reflected image happen to be the same point, which happens when a figure is reflected in one of its own points).

Review Video: Reflection
Visit mometrix.com/academy and enter code: 955068

Copyright © Mometrix Media. You have been licensed one copy of this document for personal use only. Any other reproduction or redistribution is strictly prohibited. All rights reserved.

Example

Use the coordinate plane of the given image below to reflect the image across the y-axis.

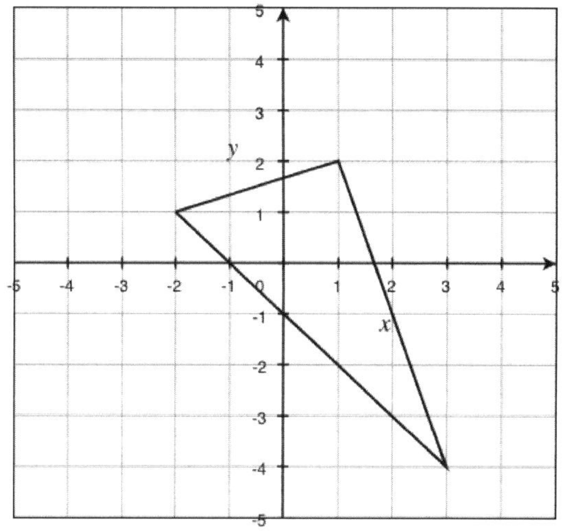

To reflect the image across the y-axis, replace each x-coordinate of the points that are the vertex of the triangle, x, with its negative, $-x$.

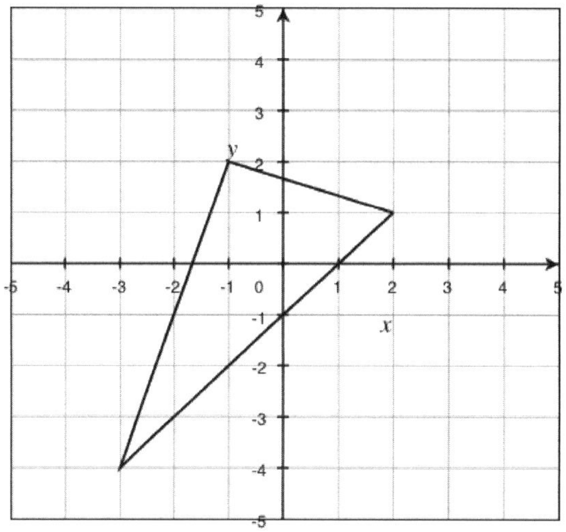

Translation

A *translation* is a transformation which slides a figure from one position in the plane to another position in the plane. The original figure and the translated figure have the same size, shape, and orientation.

Review Video: Translation
Visit mometrix.com/academy and enter code: 718628

Transforming a Given Figure Using Rotation, Reflection, and Translation

To **rotate** a given figure: 1. Identify the point of rotation. 2. Using tracing paper, geometry software, or by approximation, recreate the figure at a new location around the point of rotation.

Copyright © Mometrix Media. You have been licensed one copy of this document for personal use only. Any other reproduction or redistribution is strictly prohibited. All rights reserved.

To **reflect** a given figure: 1. Identify the line of reflection. 2. By folding the paper, using geometry software, or by approximation, recreate the image at a new location on the other side of the line of reflection.

To **translate** a given figure: 1. Identify the new location. 2. Using graph paper, geometry software, or by approximation, recreate the figure in the new location. If using graph paper, make a chart of the x- and y-values to keep track of the coordinates of all critical points.

Evidence of Transformation

To identify that a figure has been *rotated*, look for evidence that the figure is still face-up, but has changed its orientation.

To identify that a figure has been *reflected* across a line, look for evidence that the figure is now face-down.

To identify that a figure has been *translated*, look for evidence that a figure is still face-up and has not changed orientation; the only change is location.

To identify that a figure has been *dilated*, look for evidence that the figure has changed its size but not its orientation.

Dilation

A **dilation** is a transformation which proportionally stretches or shrinks a figure by a **scale factor**. The dilated image is the same shape and orientation as the original image but a different size. A polygon and its dilated image are similar.

<u>Example 1</u>

Use the coordinate plane to create a dilation of the given image below, where the dilation is the enlargement of the original image.

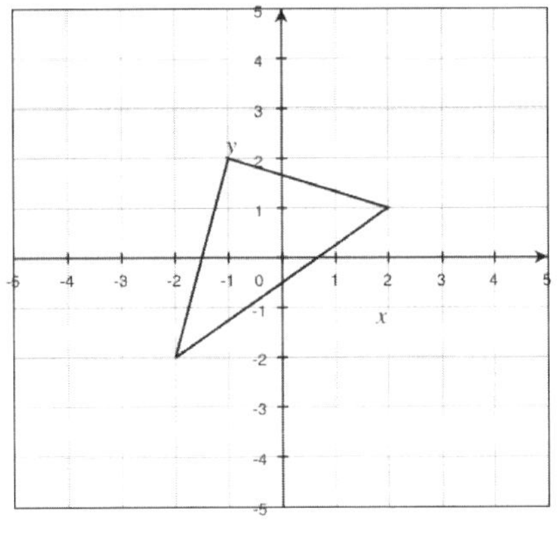

Copyright © Mometrix Media. You have been licensed one copy of this document for personal use only. Any other reproduction or redistribution is strictly prohibited. All rights reserved.

An enlargement can be found by multiplying each coordinate of the coordinate pairs located at the triangles vertices by a constant. If the figure is enlarged by a factor of 2, the new image would be:

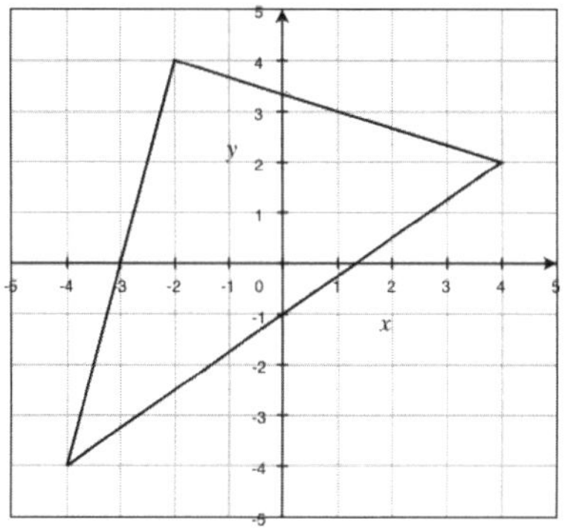

Review Video: Dilation
Visit mometrix.com/academy and enter code: 471630

Trigonometric Formulas

In the diagram below, angle *C* is the **right angle**, and side *c* is the **hypotenuse**. Side *a* is the side adjacent to angle *B* and side *b* is the side adjacent to angle *A*. These formulas will work for any acute angle in a right triangle. They will *not* work for any triangle that is not a right triangle. Also, they will not work for the right angle in a right triangle, since there are not distinct adjacent and opposite sides to differentiate from the hypotenuse.

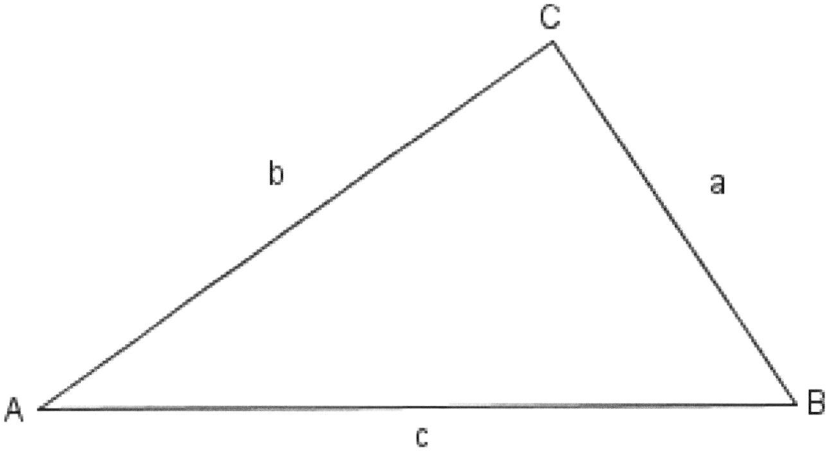

$$\sin A = \frac{\text{opposite side}}{\text{hypotenuse}} = \frac{a}{c}$$
$$\cos A = \frac{\text{adjacent side}}{\text{hypotenuse}} = \frac{b}{c}$$
$$\tan A = \frac{\text{opposite side}}{\text{adjacent side}} = \frac{a}{b}$$
$$\csc A = \frac{1}{\sin A} = \frac{\text{hypotenuse}}{\text{opposite side}} = \frac{c}{a}$$

Copyright © Mometrix Media. You have been licensed one copy of this document for personal use only. Any other reproduction or redistribution is strictly prohibited. All rights reserved.

$$\sec A = \frac{1}{\cos A} = \frac{\text{hypotenuse}}{\text{adjacent side}} = \frac{c}{b}$$
$$\cot A = \frac{1}{\tan A} = \frac{\text{adjacent side}}{\text{opposite side}} = \frac{b}{a}$$

Laws of Sines and Cosines

The **law of sines** states that $\frac{\sin A}{a} = \frac{\sin B}{b} = \frac{\sin C}{c}$, where A, B, and C are the angles of a triangle, and a, b, and c are the sides opposite their respective angles. This formula will work with all triangles, not just right triangles.

The **law of cosines** is given by the formula $c^2 = a^2 + b^2 - 2ab(\cos C)$, where a, b, and c are the sides of a triangle, and C is the angle opposite side c. This formula is similar to the *pythagorean theorem*, but unlike the pythagorean theorem, it can be used on any triangle.

Review Video: Cosine
Visit mometrix.com/academy and enter code: 361120

Circles

The **center** is the single point inside the circle that is **equidistant** from every point on the circle. (Point O in the diagram below.)

Review Video: Points of a Circle
Visit mometrix.com/academy and enter code: 420746

The **radius** is a line segment that joins the center of the circle and any one point on the circle. All radii of a circle are equal. (Segments OX, OY, and OZ in the diagram below.)

The **diameter** is a line segment that passes through the center of the circle and has both endpoints on the circle. The length of the diameter is exactly twice the length of the radius. (Segment XZ in the diagram below.)

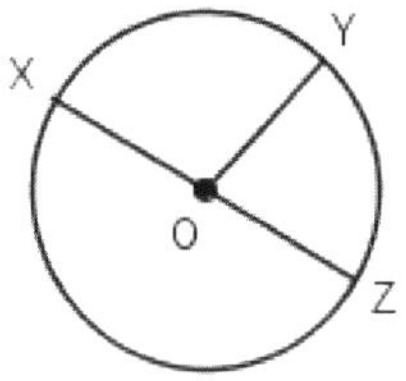

The **area of a circle** is found by the formula $A = \pi r^2$, where r is the length of the radius. If the diameter of the circle is given, remember to divide it in half to get the length of the radius before proceeding.

Review Video: The Diameter, Radius, and Circumference of Circles
Visit mometrix.com/academy and enter code: 448988

Copyright © Mometrix Media. You have been licensed one copy of this document for personal use only. Any other reproduction or redistribution is strictly prohibited. All rights reserved.

The **circumference** of a circle is found by the formula $C = 2\pi r$, where r is the radius. Again, remember to convert the diameter if you are given that measure rather than the radius.

Review Video: Area and Circumference of a Circle
Visit mometrix.com/academy and enter code: 243015

Concentric circles are circles that have the same center, but not the same length of radii. A bulls-eye target is an example of concentric circles.

An **arc** is a portion of a circle. Specifically, an arc is the set of points between and including two points on a circle. An arc does not contain any points inside the circle. When a segment is drawn from the endpoints of an arc to the center of the circle, a sector is formed.

A **central angle** is an angle whose vertex is the center of a circle and whose legs intercept an arc of the circle. Angle XOY in the diagram above is a central angle. A minor arc is an arc that has a measure less than 180°. The measure of a central angle is equal to the measure of the minor arc it intercepts. A major arc is an arc having a measure of at least 180°. The measure of the major arc can be found by subtracting the measure of the central angle from 360°.

A **semicircle** is an arc whose endpoints are the endpoints of the diameter of a circle. A semicircle is exactly half of a circle.

An **inscribed angle** is an angle whose vertex lies on a circle and whose legs contain chords of that circle. The portion of the circle intercepted by the legs of the angle is called the intercepted arc. The measure of the intercepted arc is exactly twice the measure of the inscribed angle. In the following diagram, angle ABC is an inscribed angle. $\widehat{AC} = 2(m\angle ABC)$

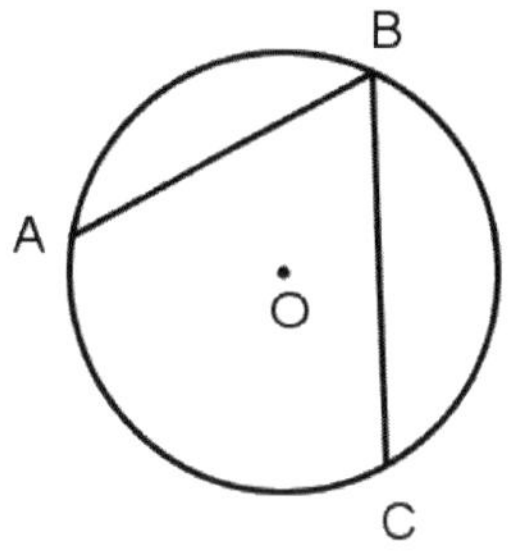

Any angle inscribed in a semicircle is a right angle. The intercepted arc is 180°, making the inscribed angle half that, or 90°. In the diagram below, angle ABC is inscribed in semicircle ABC, making angle ABC equal to 90°.

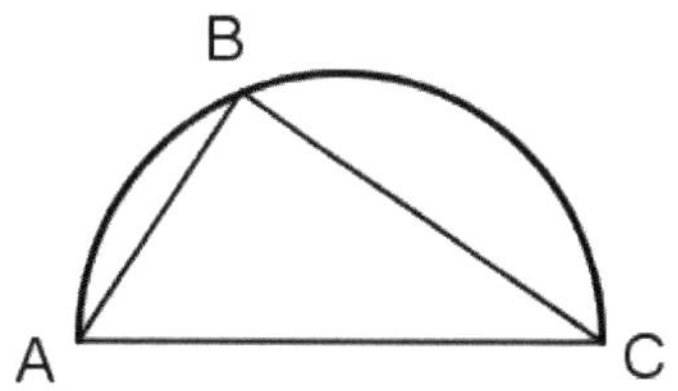

A **chord** is a line segment that has both endpoints on a circle. In the diagram below, $\overline{EB}$ is a chord.

Secant: A line that passes through a circle and contains a chord of that circle. In the diagram below, $\overleftrightarrow{EB}$ is a secant and contains chord $\overline{EB}$.

Copyright © Mometrix Media. You have been licensed one copy of this document for personal use only. Any other reproduction or redistribution is strictly prohibited. All rights reserved.

A **tangent** is a line in the same plane as a circle that touches the circle in exactly one point. While a line segment can be tangent to a circle as part of a line that is tangent, it is improper to say a tangent can be simply a line segment that touches the circle in exactly one point. In the diagram below, $\overleftrightarrow{CD}$ is tangent to circle A. Notice that $\overline{FB}$ is not tangent to the circle. $\overline{FB}$ is a line segment that touches the circle in exactly one point, but if the segment were extended, it would touch the circle in a second point. The point at which a tangent touches a circle is called the point of tangency. In the diagram below, point B is the point of tangency.

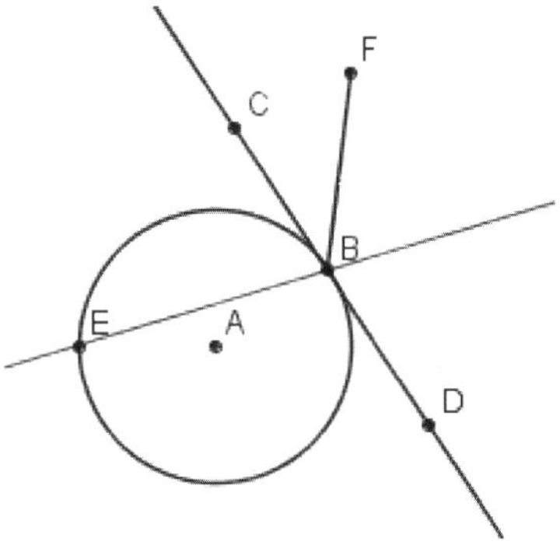

A **secant** is a line that intersects a circle in two points. Two secants may intersect inside the circle, on the circle, or outside the circle. When the two secants intersect on the circle, an inscribed angle is formed.

When two secants intersect inside a circle, the measure of each of two vertical angles is equal to half the sum of the two intercepted arcs. In the diagram below, $\text{m}\angle AEB = \frac{1}{2}(\widehat{AB} + \widehat{CD})$ and $\text{m}\angle BEC = \frac{1}{2}(\widehat{BC} + \widehat{AD})$.

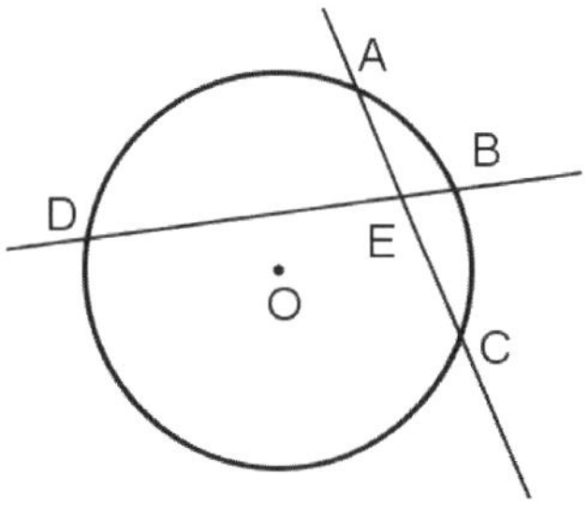

Copyright © Mometrix Media. You have been licensed one copy of this document for personal use only. Any other reproduction or redistribution is strictly prohibited. All rights reserved.

When two secants intersect outside a circle, the measure of the angle formed is equal to half the difference of the two arcs that lie between the two secants. In the diagram below, $m\angle AEB = \frac{1}{2}(\widehat{AB} - \widehat{CD})$.

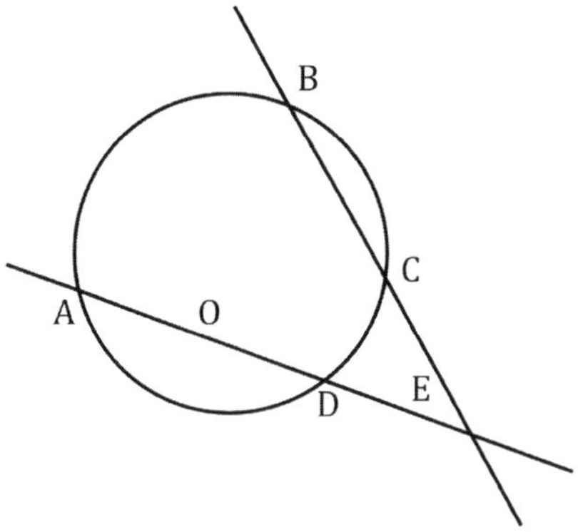

The **arc length** is the length of that portion of the circumference between two points on the circle. The formula for arc length is $s = \frac{\pi r \theta}{180°}$ where s is the arc length, r is the length of the radius, and θ is the angular measure of the arc in degrees, or $s = r\theta$, where θ is the angular measure of the arc in radians (2π radians $= 360$ degrees).

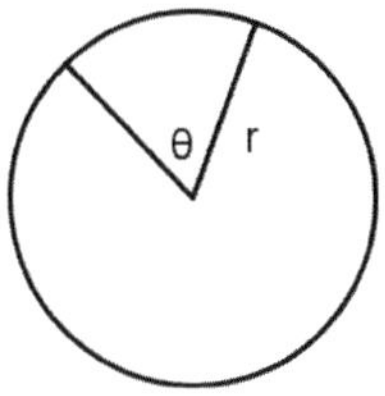

A **sector** is the portion of a circle formed by two radii and their intercepted arc. While the arc length is exclusively the points that are also on the circumference of the circle, the sector is the entire area bounded by the arc and the two radii.

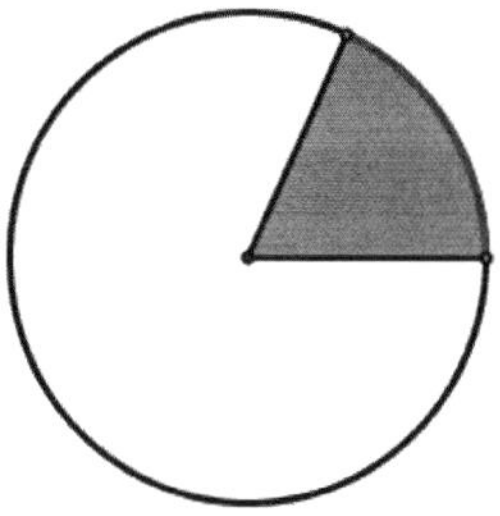

The **area of a sector** of a circle is found by the formula, $A = \frac{\theta r^2}{2}$, where A is the area, θ is the measure of the central angle in radians, and r is the radius. To find the area when the central angle is in degrees, use the formula, $A = \frac{\theta \pi r^2}{360}$, where θ is the measure of the central angle in degrees and r is the radius.

A circle is inscribed in a polygon if each of the sides of the polygon is tangent to the circle. A polygon is inscribed in a circle if each of the vertices of the polygon lies on the circle.

Copyright © Mometrix Media. You have been licensed one copy of this document for personal use only. Any other reproduction or redistribution is strictly prohibited. All rights reserved.

A circle is circumscribed about a polygon if each of the vertices of the polygon lies on the circle. A polygon is circumscribed about the circle if each of the sides of the polygon is tangent to the circle.

If one figure is inscribed in another, then the other figure is circumscribed about the first figure.

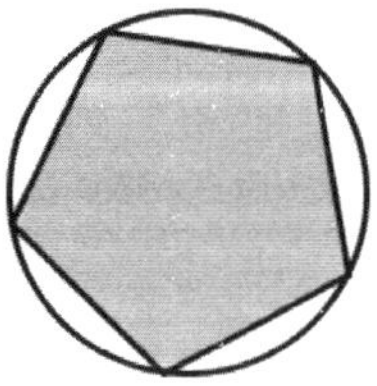

Circle circumscribed about a pentagon
Pentagon inscribed in a circle

Other Conic Sections

Ellipse
An **ellipse** is the set of all points in a plane, whose total distance from two fixed points called the foci (singular: focus) is constant, and whose center is the midpoint between the foci.

The standard equation of an ellipse that is taller than it is wide is $\frac{(y-k)^2}{a^2} + \frac{(x-h)^2}{b^2} = 1$, where a and b are coefficients. The center is the point (h, k) and the foci are the points $(h, k + c)$ and $(h, k - c)$, where $c^2 = a^2 - b^2$ and $a^2 > b^2$.

The major axis has length $2a$, and the minor axis has length $2b$.

Eccentricity (e) is a measure of how elongated an ellipse is, and is the ratio of the distance between the foci to the length of the major axis. Eccentricity will have a value between 0 and 1. The closer to 1 the eccentricity is, the closer the ellipse is to being a circle. The formula for eccentricity is $= \frac{c}{a}$.

Parabola
Parabola: The set of all points in a plane that are equidistant from a fixed line, called the **directrix**, and a fixed point not on the line, called the **focus**.

Axis: The line perpendicular to the directrix that passes through the focus.

For parabolas that open up or down, the standard equation is $(x - h)^2 = 4c(y - k)$, where h, c, and k are coefficients. If c is positive, the parabola opens up. If c is negative, the parabola opens down. The vertex is the point (h, k). The directrix is the line having the equation $y = -c + k$, and the focus is the point $(h, c + k)$.

For parabolas that open left or right, the standard equation is $(y - k)^2 = 4c(x - h)$, where k, c, and h are coefficients. If c is positive, the parabola opens to the right. If c is negative, the parabola opens to the left. The vertex is the point (h, k). The directrix is the line having the equation $x = -c + h$, and the focus is the point $(c + h, k)$.

Copyright © Mometrix Media. You have been licensed one copy of this document for personal use only. Any other reproduction or redistribution is strictly prohibited. All rights reserved.

Hyperbola

A **hyperbola** is the set of all points in a plane, whose distance from two fixed points, called foci, has a constant difference.

The standard equation of a horizontal hyperbola is $\frac{(x-h)^2}{a^2} - \frac{(y-k)^2}{b^2} = 1$, where a, b, h, and k are real numbers. The center is the point (h, k), the vertices are the points $(h + a, k)$ and $(h - a, k)$, and the foci are the points that every point on one of the parabolic curves is equidistant from and are found using the formulas $(h + c, k)$ and $(h - c, k)$, where $c^2 = a^2 + b^2$. The asymptotes are two lines the graph of the hyperbola approaches but never reaches, and are given by the equations $y = \left(\frac{b}{a}\right)(x - h) + k$ and $y = -\left(\frac{b}{a}\right)(x - h) + k$.

A **vertical hyperbola** is formed when a plane makes a vertical cut through two cones that are stacked vertex-to-vertex.

The standard equation of a vertical hyperbola is $\frac{(y-k)^2}{a^2} - \frac{(x-h)^2}{b^2} = 1$, where a, b, k, and h are real numbers. The center is the point (h, k), the vertices are the points $(h, k + a)$ and $(h, k - a)$, and the foci are the points that every point on one of the parabolic curves is equidistant from and are found using the formulas $(h, k + c)$ and $(h, k - c)$, where $c^2 = a^2 + b^2$. The asymptotes are two lines the graph of the hyperbola approaches but never reach, and are given by the equations $y = \left(\frac{a}{b}\right)(x - h) + k$ and $y = -\left(\frac{a}{b}\right)(x - h) + k$.

Solids

The **surface area of a solid object** is the area of all sides or exterior surfaces. For objects such as prisms and pyramids, a further distinction is made between base surface area (B) and lateral surface area (LA). For a prism, the total surface area (SA) is $SA = LA + 2B$. For a pyramid or cone, the total surface area is $SA = LA + B$.

Review Video: How to Calculate the Volume of 3D Objects
Visit mometrix.com/academy and enter code: 163343

The **surface area of a sphere** can be found by the formula $A = 4\pi r^2$, where r is the radius. The volume is given by the formula $V = \frac{4}{3}\pi r^3$, where r is the radius. Both quantities are generally given in terms of π.

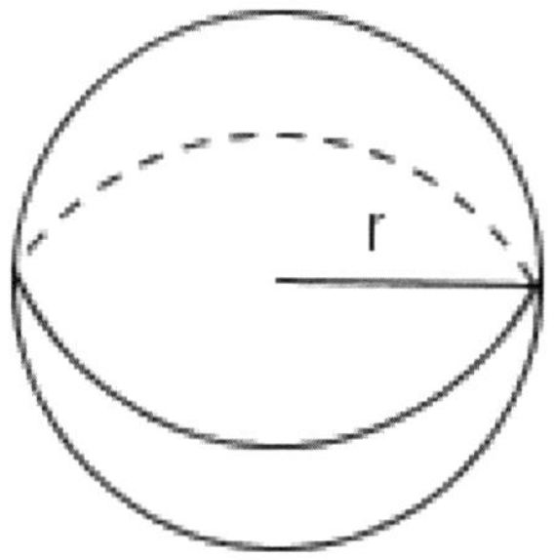

Review Video: Volume and Surface Area of a Sphere
Visit mometrix.com/academy and enter code: 786928

Copyright © Mometrix Media. You have been licensed one copy of this document for personal use only. Any other reproduction or redistribution is strictly prohibited. All rights reserved.

The **volume of any prism** is found by the formula $V = Bh$, where B is the area of the base, and h is the height (perpendicular distance between the bases). The surface area of any prism is the sum of the areas of both bases and all sides. It can be calculated as $SA = 2B + Ph$, where P is the perimeter of the base.

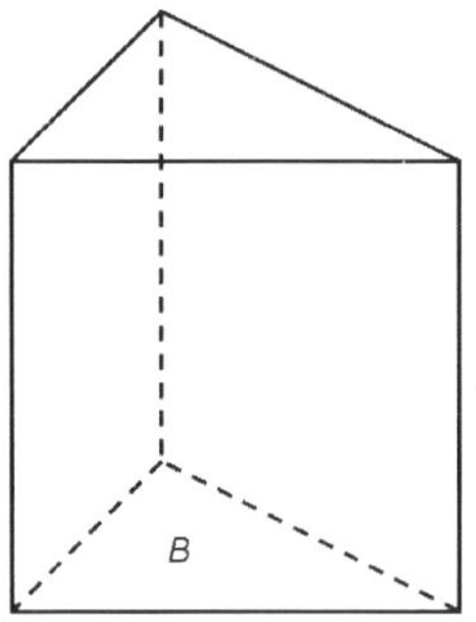

For a *rectangular prism*, the **volume** can be found by the formula $V = lwh$, where V is the volume, l is the length, w is the width, and h is the height. The surface area can be calculated as $SA = 2lw + 2hl + 2wh$ or $SA = 2(lw + hl + wh)$.

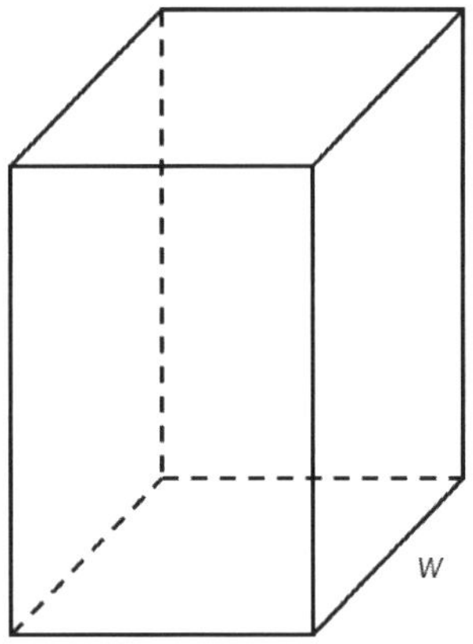

The **volume of a cube** can be found by the formula $V = s^3$, where s is the length of a side. The surface area of a cube is calculated as $SA = 6s^2$, where SA is the total surface area and s is the length of a side. These formulas are the same as the ones used for the volume and surface area of a rectangular prism, but simplified since all three quantities (length, width, and height) are the same.

Review Video: Volume and Surface Area of a Cube
Visit mometrix.com/academy and enter code: 664455

The **volume of a cylinder** can be calculated by the formula $V = \pi r^2 h$, where r is the radius, and h is the height. The surface area of a cylinder can be found by the formula $SA = 2\pi r^2 + 2\pi rh$. The first

Copyright © Mometrix Media. You have been licensed one copy of this document for personal use only. Any other reproduction or redistribution is strictly prohibited. All rights reserved.

term is the base area multiplied by two, and the second term is the perimeter of the base multiplied by the height.

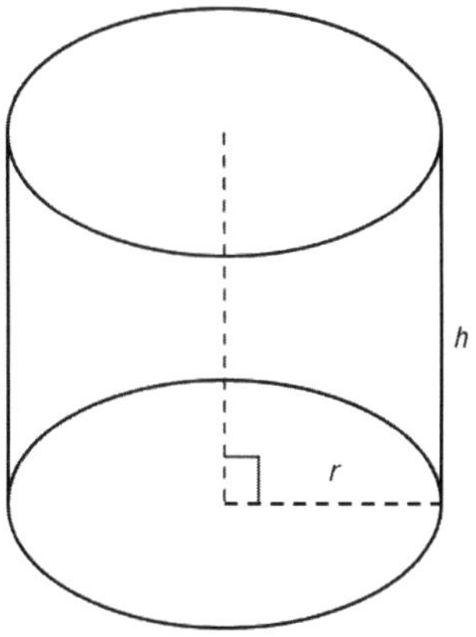

Review Video: Volume and Surface Area of a Right Circular Cylinder
Visit mometrix.com/academy and enter code: 226463

The **volume of a pyramid** is found by the formula $V = \frac{1}{3}Bh$, where B is the area of the base, and h is the height (perpendicular distance from the vertex to the base). Notice this formula is the same as $\frac{1}{3}$ times the volume of a prism. Like a prism, the base of a pyramid can be any shape.

Review Video: Volume and Surface Area of a Pyramid
Visit mometrix.com/academy and enter code: 621932

Finding the **surface area of a pyramid** is not as simple as the other shapes we've looked at thus far. If the pyramid is a right pyramid, meaning the base is a regular polygon and the vertex is directly over the center of that polygon, the surface area can be calculated as $SA = B + \frac{1}{2}Ph_s$, where P is the perimeter of the base, and h_s is the slant height (distance from the vertex to the midpoint of one side of the base). If the pyramid is irregular, the area of each triangle side must be calculated individually and then summed, along with the base.

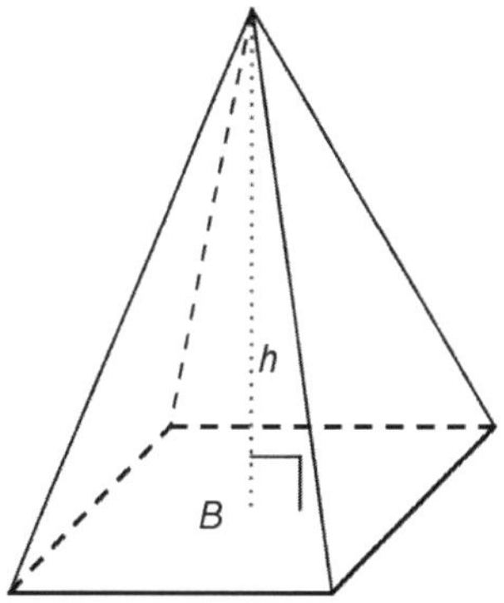

The **volume of a cone** is found by the formula $V = \frac{1}{3}\pi r^2 h$, where r is the radius, and h is the height. Notice this is the same as $\frac{1}{3}$ times the volume of a cylinder. The surface area can be calculated as

Copyright © Mometrix Media. You have been licensed one copy of this document for personal use only. Any other reproduction or redistribution is strictly prohibited. All rights reserved.

$SA = \pi r^2 + \pi rs$, where s is the slant height. The slant height can be calculated using the Pythagorean Thereom to be $\sqrt{r^2 + h^2}$, so the surface area formula can also be written as $SA = \pi r^2 + \pi r\sqrt{r^2 + h^2}$.

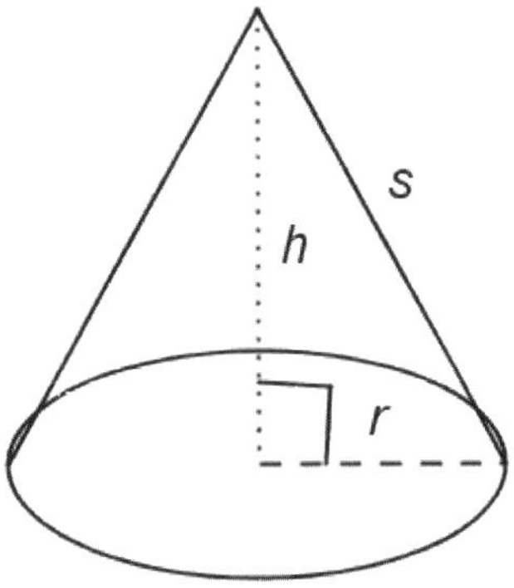

Review Video: Volume and Surface Area of a Right Circular Cone
Visit mometrix.com/academy and enter code: 573574

Probability

Probability Terminology

Probability is a branch of statistics that deals with the likelihood of something taking place. One classic example is a coin toss. There are only two possible results: heads or tails. The likelihood, or probability, that the coin will land as heads is 1 out of 2 ($\frac{1}{2}$, 0.5, 50%). Tails has the same probability. Another common example is a 6-sided die roll. There are six possible results from rolling a single die, each with an equal chance of happening, so the probability of any given number coming up is 1 out of 6.

Terms frequently used in probability

- **Event** – a situation that produces results of some sort (a coin toss)
- **Compound event** – event that involves two or more independent events (rolling a pair of dice; taking the sum)
- **Outcome** – a possible result in an experiment or event (heads, tails)
- **Desired outcome** (or success) – an outcome that meets a particular set of criteria (a roll of 1 or 2 if we are looking for numbers less than 3)
- **Independent events** – two or more events whose outcomes do not affect one another (two coins tossed at the same time)
- **Dependent events** – two or more events whose outcomes affect one another (two cards drawn consecutively from the same deck)
- **Certain outcome** – probability of outcome is 100% or 1
- **Impossible outcome** – probability of outcome is 0% or 0
- **Mutually exclusive outcomes** – two or more outcomes whose criteria cannot all be satisfied in a single event (a coin coming up heads and tails on the same toss)

Review Video: Intro to Probability
Visit mometrix.com/academy and enter code: 212374

Copyright © Mometrix Media. You have been licensed one copy of this document for personal use only. Any other reproduction or redistribution is strictly prohibited. All rights reserved.

Calculating Probability

Probability is the likelihood of a certain outcome occurring for a given event. The **theoretical probability** can usually be determined without actually performing the event. The likelihood of a outcome occurring, or the probability of an outcome occurring, is given by the formula

$$P(A) = \frac{\text{Number of acceptable outcomes}}{\text{Number of possible outcomes}}$$

where *P*(*A*) is the probability of an outcome *A* occurring, and each outcome is just as likely to occur as any other outcome. If each outcome has the same probability of occurring as every other possible outcome, the outcomes are said to be equally likely to occur. The total number of acceptable outcomes must be less than or equal to the total number of possible outcomes. If the two are equal, then the outcome is certain to occur and the probability is 1. If the number of acceptable outcomes is zero, then the outcome is impossible and the probability is 0.

Review Video: Theoretical and Experimental Probability
Visit mometrix.com/academy and enter code: 444349

Example:
There are 20 marbles in a bag and 5 are red. The theoretical probability of randomly selecting a red marble is 5 out of 20, ($\frac{5}{20} = \frac{1}{4}$, 0.25, or 25%).

Permutations and Combinations
When trying to calculate the probability of an event using the $\frac{\text{desired outcomes}}{\text{total outcomes}}$ formula, you may frequently find that there are too many outcomes to individually count them. **Permutation** and **combination formulas** offer a shortcut to counting outcomes. A permutation is an arrangement of a specific number of a set of objects in a specific order. The number of **permutations** of *r* items given a set of *n* items can be calculated as ${}_nP_r = \frac{n!}{(n-r)!}$. Combinations are similar to permutations, except there are no restrictions regarding the order of the elements. While ABC is considered a different permutation than BCA, ABC and BCA are considered the same combination. The number of **combinations** of *r* items given a set of *n* items can be calculated as ${}_nC_r = \frac{n!}{r!(n-r)!}$ or ${}_nC_r = \frac{{}_nP_r}{r!}$.

Example:
Suppose you want to calculate how many different 5-card hands can be drawn from a deck of 52 cards. This is a combination since the order of the cards in a hand does not matter. There are 52 cards available, and 5 to be selected. Thus, the number of different hands is ${}_{52}C_5 = \frac{52!}{5!\times 47!} =$ 2,598,960.

Complement of an Event
Sometimes it may be easier to calculate the possibility of something not happening, or the **complement of an event**. Represented by the symbol $\bar{A}$, the complement of *A* is the probability that event *A* does not happen. When you know the probability of event *A* occurring, you can use the formula $P(\bar{A}) = 1 - P(A)$, where $P(\bar{A})$ is the probability of event *A* not occurring, and $P(A)$ is the probability of event *A* occurring.

Copyright © Mometrix Media. You have been licensed one copy of this document for personal use only. Any other reproduction or redistribution is strictly prohibited. All rights reserved.

Addition Rule

The **addition rule** for probability is used for finding the probability of a compound event. Use the formula $P(A \text{ or } B) = P(A) + P(B) - P(A \text{ and } B)$, where $P(A \text{ and } B)$ is the probability of both events occurring to find the probability of a compound event. The probability of both events occurring at the same time must be subtracted to eliminate any overlap in the first two probabilities.

Conditional Probability

Conditional probability is the probability of an event occurring once another event has already occurred. Given event A and dependent event B, the probability of event B occurring when event A has already occurred is represented by the notation $P(A|B)$. To find the probability of event B occurring, take into account the fact that event A has already occurred and adjust the total number of possible outcomes. For example, suppose you have ten balls numbered 1–10 and you want ball number 7 to be pulled in two pulls. On the first pull, the probability of getting the 7 is $\frac{1}{10}$ because there is one ball with a 7 on it and 10 balls to choose from. Assuming the first pull did not yield a 7, the probability of pulling a 7 on the second pull is now $\frac{1}{9}$ because there are only 9 balls remaining for the second pull.

Multiplication Rule

The **multiplication rule** can be used to find the probability of two independent events occurring using the formula $P(A \text{ and } B) = P(A) \times P(B)$, where $P(A \text{ and } B)$ is the probability of two independent events occurring, $P(A)$ is the probability of the first event occurring, and $P(B)$ is the probability of the second event occurring.

The multiplication rule can also be used to find the probability of two dependent events occurring using the formula $P(A \text{ and } B) = P(A) \times P(B|A)$, where $P(A \text{ and } B)$ is the probability of two dependent events occurring and $P(B|A)$ is the probability of the second event occurring after the first event has already occurred.

Before using the multiplication rule, you MUST first determine whether the two events are *dependent* or *independent*.

Use a **combination of the multiplication** rule and the rule of complements to find the probability that at least one outcome of the element will occur. This given by the general formula $P(\text{at least one event occurring}) = 1 - P(\text{no outcomes occurring})$. For example, to find the probability that at least one even number will show when a pair of dice is rolled, find the probability that two odd numbers will be rolled (no even numbers) and subtract from one. You can always use a tree diagram or make a chart to list the possible outcomes when the sample space is small, such as in the dice-rolling example, but in most cases it will be much faster to use the multiplication and complement formulas.

Expected Value

Expected value is a method of determining expected outcome in a random situation. It is really a sum of the weighted probabilities of the possible outcomes. Multiply the probability of an event occurring by the weight assigned to that probability (such as the amount of money won or lost). A practical application of the expected value is to determine whether a game of chance is really fair. If the sum of the weighted probabilities is equal to zero, the game is generally considered fair because the player has a fair chance to at least to break even. If the expected value is less than zero, then players lose more than they win. For example, a lottery drawing might allow the player to choose any three-digit number, 000–999. The probability of choosing the winning number is 1:1000. If it

Copyright © Mometrix Media. You have been licensed one copy of this document for personal use only. Any other reproduction or redistribution is strictly prohibited. All rights reserved.

costs $1 to play, and a winning number receives $500, the expected value is $\left(-\$1 \cdot \frac{999}{1{,}000}\right) + \left(\$500 \cdot \frac{1}{1{,}000}\right) = -0.499$ or $-\$0.50$. You can expect to lose on average 50 cents for every dollar you spend.

Empirical Probability

Most of the time, when we talk about probability, we mean theoretical probability. **Empirical probability**, or experimental probability or relative frequency, is the number of times an outcome occurs in a particular experiment or a certain number of observed events. While theoretical probability is based on what *should* happen, experimental probability is based on what *has* happened. Experimental probability is calculated in the same way as theoretical, except that actual outcomes are used instead of possible outcomes.

Theoretical and experimental probability do not always line up with one another. Theoretical probability says that out of 20 coin-tosses, 10 should be heads. However, if we were actually to toss 20 coins, we might record just 5 heads. This doesn't mean that our theoretical probability is incorrect; it just means that this particular experiment had results that were different from what was predicted. A practical application of empirical probability is the insurance industry. There are no set functions that define lifespan, health, or safety. Insurance companies look at factors from hundreds of thousands of individuals to find patterns that they then use to set the formulas for insurance premiums.

Objective Probability

Objective probability is based on mathematical formulas and documented evidence. Examples of objective probability include raffles or lottery drawings where there is a pre-determined number of possible outcomes and a predetermined number of outcomes that correspond to an event. Other cases of objective probability include probabilities of rolling dice, flipping coins, or drawing cards. Most gambling games are based on objective probability.

Subjective Probability

Subjective probability is based on personal or professional feelings and judgments. Often, there is a lot of guesswork following extensive research. Areas where subjective probability is applicable include sales trends and business expenses. Attractions set admission prices based on subjective probabilities of attendance based on varying admission rates in an effort to maximize their profit.

Sample Space

The total set of all possible results of a test or experiment is called a **sample space**, or sometimes a universal sample space. The sample space, represented by one of the variables S, Ω, or U (for universal sample space) has individual elements called outcomes. Other terms for outcome that may be used interchangeably include elementary outcome, simple event, or sample point. The number of outcomes in a given sample space could be infinite or finite, and some tests may yield multiple unique sample sets. For example, tests conducted by drawing playing cards from a standard deck would have one sample space of the card values, another sample space of the card suits, and a third sample space of suit-denomination combinations. For most tests, the sample spaces considered will be finite.

An **event**, represented by the variable E, is a portion of a sample space. It may be one outcome or a group of outcomes from the same sample space. If an event occurs, then the test or experiment will generate an outcome that satisfies the requirement of that event. For example, given a standard deck of 52 playing cards as the sample space, and defining the event as the collection of face cards,

Copyright © Mometrix Media. You have been licensed one copy of this document for personal use only. Any other reproduction or redistribution is strictly prohibited. All rights reserved.

then the event will occur if the card drawn is a J, Q, or K. If any other card is drawn, the event is said to have not occurred.

For every sample space, each possible outcome has a specific likelihood, or probability, that it will occur. The probability measure, also called the **distribution**, is a function that assigns a real number probability, from zero to one, to each outcome. For a probability measure to be accurate, every outcome must have a real number probability measure that is greater than or equal to zero and less than or equal to one. Also, the probability measure of the sample space must equal one, and the probability measure of the union of multiple outcomes must equal the sum of the individual probability measures.

Probabilities of events are expressed as real numbers from zero to one. They give a numerical value to the chance that a particular event will occur. The probability of an event occurring is the sum of the probabilities of the individual elements of that event. For example, in a standard deck of 52 playing cards as the sample space and the collection of face cards as the event, the probability of drawing a specific face card is $\frac{1}{52} = 0.019$, but the probability of drawing any one of the twelve face cards is $12(0.019) = 0.228$. Note that rounding of numbers can generate different results. If you multiplied 12 by the fraction $\frac{1}{52}$ before converting to a decimal, you would get the answer $\frac{12}{52} = 0.231$.

Tree Diagram

For a simple sample space, possible outcomes may be determined by using a **tree diagram** or an organized chart. In either case, you can easily draw or list out the possible outcomes. For example, to determine all the possible ways three objects can be ordered, you can draw a tree diagram:

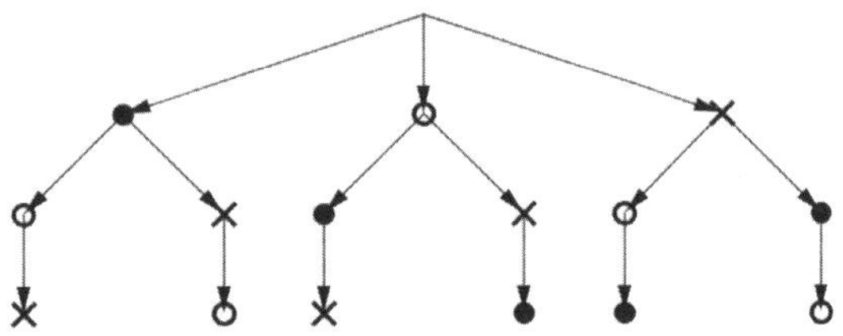

You can also make a chart to list all the possibilities:

First object	Second object	Third object
●	x	o
●	o	x
o	●	x
o	x	●
x	●	o
x	o	●

Either way, you can easily see there are six possible ways the three objects can be ordered.

If two events have no outcomes in common, they are said to be **mutually exclusive**. For example, in a standard deck of 52 playing cards, the event of all card suits is mutually exclusive to the event of all card values. If two events have no bearing on each other so that one event occurring has no influence on the probability of another event occurring, the two events are said to be independent. For example, rolling a standard six-sided die multiple times does not change that probability that a

Copyright © Mometrix Media. You have been licensed one copy of this document for personal use only. Any other reproduction or redistribution is strictly prohibited. All rights reserved.

particular number will be rolled from one roll to the next. If the outcome of one event does affect the probability of the second event, the two events are said to be dependent. For example, if cards are drawn from a deck, the probability of drawing an ace after an ace has been drawn is different than the probability of drawing an ace if no ace (or no other card, for that matter) has been drawn.

In probability, the **odds in favor of an event** are the number of times the event will occur compared to the number of times the event will not occur. To calculate the odds in favor of an event, use the formula $\frac{P(A)}{1-P(A)}$, where $P(A)$ is the probability that the event will occur. Many times, odds in favor is given as a ratio in the form $\frac{a}{b}$ or $a{:}b$, where a is the probability of the event occurring and b is the complement of the event, the probability of the event not occurring. If the odds in favor are given as 2:5, that means that you can expect the event to occur two times for every 5 times that it does not occur. In other words, the probability that the event will occur is $\frac{2}{2+5} = \frac{2}{7}$.

In probability, the **odds against an event** are the number of times the event will not occur compared to the number of times the event will occur. To calculate the odds against an event, use the formula $\frac{1-P(A)}{P(A)}$, where $P(A)$ is the probability that the event will occur. Many times, odds against is given as a ratio in the form $\frac{b}{a}$ or $b{:}a$, where b is the probability the event will not occur (the complement of the event) and a is the probability the event will occur. If the odds against an event are given as 3:1, that means that you can expect the event to not occur 3 times for every one time it does occur. In other words, 3 out of every 4 trials will fail.

Experimental and Theoretical Probability

Probability, P(A), is the likelihood that event A will occur. Probability is often expressed as the ratio of ways an event can occur to the total number of **outcomes**, also called the **sample space**. For example, the probability of flipping heads on a two-sided coin can be written as $\frac{1}{2}$ since there is one side with heads and a total of two sides, which means that there are two possible outcomes. Probabilities can also be expressed as decimals or percentages.

Tree diagrams are used to list all possible outcomes. Suppose you are packing for vacation and have set aside 4 shirts, 3 pairs of pants, and 2 hats. How many possible outfits are there? To construct a tree diagram, start with the first group of events, the shirts. You can use letters to label each of the articles (SA refers to the first shirt, SB refers to the second shirt, and so on). Then, from each shirt draw branches to each pair of pants that it could be paired with. Next, from each pair of pants, draw

Copyright © Mometrix Media. You have been licensed one copy of this document for personal use only. Any other reproduction or redistribution is strictly prohibited. All rights reserved.

a branch to each hat that it could be paired to and finally, repeat the process with the shoes. This method allows you to list all of the possible outcomes.

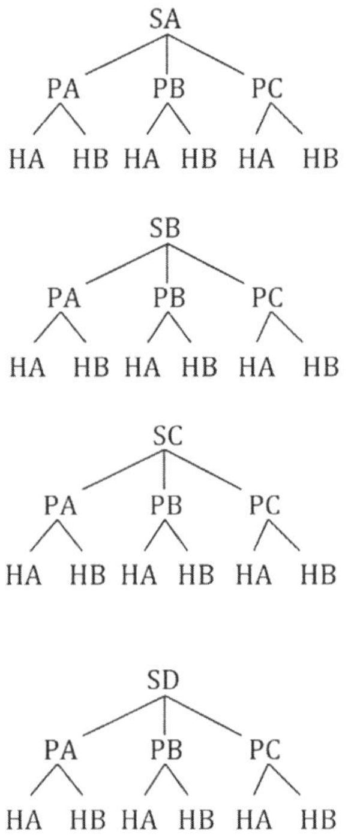

SA, PA, HA	SA, PB, HB
SA, PA, HB	SA, PC, HA
SB, PB, HA	SA, PC, HB
SB, PA, HA	SB, PB, HB
SB, PA, HB	SB, PC, HA
SB, PB, HA	SB, PC, HB
SC, PA, HA	SC, PB, HB
SC, PA, HB	SC, PC, HA
SC, PB, HA	SC, PC, HB
SD, PA, HA	SD, PB, HB
SD, PA, HB	SD, PC, HA
SD, PB, HA	SD, PC, HA

Altogether, there are 24 different combinations of shirts, pants, and hats.

A faster way to find the sample space without listing each individual outcome employs the **multiplication counting principle**. If one event can occur in a ways and a second event in b ways, then the two events can occur in $a \times b$ ways. In the previous example, there are 4 possible shirts, 3 possible pairs of pants, and 2 possible hats, so the possible number of combinations is $4 \times 3 \times 2$, or 24.

A similar principle is employed to determine the probability of two **independent events**. $P(A \text{ } and \text{ } B) = P(A) \times P(B)$, where A is the first event and B is the second such that the outcome of B does not depend on the outcome of A. For instance, suppose you choose a marble from a bag of 2 red marbles, 7 blue marbles, and 4 green marbles. The probability that you would choose a red marble, replace it, and then choose a green marble is found by multiplying the probabilities of each independent event:

$$\frac{2}{13} \times \frac{4}{13} = \frac{8}{169}, \text{or } 0.047, \text{or } 4.7\%$$

This method can also be used when finding the probability of more than 2 independent events.

When two events are dependent on one another, the likelihood of the second event is affected by the outcome of the first event. This formula for finding the probability of **dependent events** is $P(A \text{ then } B) = P(A) \times P(B \text{ after } A)$. The probability that you choose a 2 and then choose a 5 from a deck of 52 cards without replacement is

$$\frac{4}{52} \times \frac{4}{51} = \frac{1}{13} \times \frac{4}{51} = \frac{4}{663} \text{ or } 0.0060, \text{or } 0.60\%$$

Copyright © Mometrix Media. You have been licensed one copy of this document for personal use only. Any other reproduction or redistribution is strictly prohibited. All rights reserved.

Note that there are four of each number in a deck of cards, so the probability of choosing a 2 is $\frac{4}{52}$. Since you keep this card out of the deck, there are only 51 cards to choose from when selecting a 5.

Thus far, the discussion of probability has been limited to **theoretical probability, which is used to predict the likelihood of an event. Experimental probability** expresses the ratio of the number of times an event actually occurs to the number of **trials** performed in an experiment. Theoretically, the probability of rolling a one on an unloaded, six-sided die is $\frac{1}{6}$. Suppose you conduct an experiment to determine whether a dice is a fair one and obtain these results.

Trial #	1	2	3	4	5	6	7	8	9	10	11	12	13	14	15	16	17	18	19	20
Outcome	6	1	2	6	4	2	1	3	4	5	4	1	6	6	4	5	6	4	1	6

Out of the 20 trials, you rolled a 1 six times. $\frac{6}{20} = \frac{3}{10} = 0.30$, or 30%. This probability is different than the theoretical probability of $\frac{1}{6}$ or 16.6%. You might conclude that the die is loaded, but it would be advisable to conduct more trials to verify your conclusion: the larger the number of trials, the more accurate the experimental probability.

Statistics

Statistics Terminology

Statistics is the branch of mathematics that deals with collecting, recording, interpreting, illustrating, and analyzing large amounts of **data**. The following terms are often used in the discussion of data and **statistics**:

- **Data** – the collective name for pieces of *information* (singular is datum).
- **Quantitative data** – measurements (such as length, mass, and speed) that provide information about *quantities* in numbers
- **Qualitative data** – information (such as colors, scents, tastes, and shapes) that *cannot be measured* using numbers
- **Discrete data** – information that can be expressed only by a *specific value*, such as whole or half numbers. For example, since people can be counted only in whole numbers, a population count would be discrete data.
- **Continuous data** – information (such as time and temperature) that can be expressed by *any value within a given range*
- **Primary data** – information that has been *collected* directly from a survey, investigation, or experiment, such as a questionnaire or the recording of daily temperatures. Primary data that has not yet been organized or analyzed is called raw data.
- **Secondary data** – information that has been collected, sorted, and *processed* by the researcher
- **Ordinal data** – information that *can be placed in numerical order*, such as age or weight
- **Nominal data** – information that *cannot be placed in numerical order*, such as names or places.

Statistics

Population

In statistics, the **population** is the entire collection of people, plants, etc., that data can be collected from. For example, a study to determine how well students in the area schools perform on a

Copyright © Mometrix Media. You have been licensed one copy of this document for personal use only. Any other reproduction or redistribution is strictly prohibited. All rights reserved.

standardized test would have a population of all the students enrolled in those schools, although a study may include just a small sample of students from each school. A **parameter** is a numerical value that gives information about the population, such as the mean, median, mode, or standard deviation. Remember that the symbol for the mean of a population is μ and the symbol for the standard deviation of a population is σ.

Sample

A **sample** is a portion of the entire population. Whereas a parameter helped describe the population, a **statistic** is a numerical value that gives information about the sample, such as mean, median, mode, or standard deviation. Keep in mind that the symbols for mean and standard deviation are different when they are referring to a sample rather than the entire population. For a sample, the symbol for mean is $\bar{x}$ and the symbol for standard deviation is s. The mean and standard deviation of a sample may or may not be identical to that of the entire population due to a sample only being a subset of the population. However, if the sample is random and large enough, statistically significant values can be attained. Samples are generally used when the population is too large to justify including every element or when acquiring data for the entire population is impossible.

Inferential Statistics

Inferential statistics is the branch of statistics that uses samples to make predictions about an entire population. This type of statistics is often seen in political polls, where a sample of the population is questioned about a particular topic or politician to gain an understanding about the attitudes of the entire population of the country. Often, exit polls are conducted on election days using this method. Inferential statistics can have a large margin of error if you do not have a valid sample.

Sampling Distribution

Statistical values calculated from various samples of the same size make up the **sampling distribution**. For example, if several samples of identical size are randomly selected from a large population and then the mean of each sample is calculated, the distribution of values of the means would be a sampling distribution.

The **sampling distribution of the mean** is the distribution of the sample mean, $\bar{x}$, derived from random samples of a given size. It has three important characteristics. First, the mean of the sampling distribution of the mean is equal to the mean of the population that was sampled. Second, assuming the standard deviation is non-zero, the standard deviation of the sampling distribution of the mean equals the standard deviation of the sampled population divided by the square root of the sample size. This is sometimes called the standard error. Finally, as the sample size gets larger, the sampling distribution of the mean gets closer to a normal distribution via the Central Limit Theorem.

Survey Study

A **survey study** is a method of gathering information from a small group in an attempt to gain enough information to make accurate general assumptions about the population. Once a survey study is completed, the results are then put into a summary report.

Survey studies are generally in the format of surveys, interviews, or questionnaires as part of an effort to find opinions of a particular group or to find facts about a group.

Copyright © Mometrix Media. You have been licensed one copy of this document for personal use only. Any other reproduction or redistribution is strictly prohibited. All rights reserved.

It is important to note that the findings from a survey study are only as accurate as the sample chosen from the population.

Correlational Studies

Correlational studies seek to determine how much one variable is affected by changes in a second variable. For example, correlational studies may look for a relationship between the amount of time a student spends studying for a test and the grade that student earned on the test or between student scores on college admissions tests and student grades in college.

It is important to note that correlational studies cannot show a cause and effect, but rather can show only that two variables are or are not potentially correlated.

Experimental Studies

Experimental studies take correlational studies one step farther, in that they attempt to prove or disprove a cause-and-effect relationship. These studies are performed by conducting a series of experiments to test the hypothesis. For a study to be scientifically accurate, it must have both an experimental group that receives the specified treatment and a control group that does not get the treatment. This is the type of study pharmaceutical companies do as part of drug trials for new medications. Experimental studies are only valid when proper scientific method has been followed. In other words, the experiment must be well-planned and executed without bias in the testing process, all subjects must be selected at random, and the process of determining which subject is in which of the two groups must also be completely random.

Observational Studies

Observational studies are the opposite of experimental studies. In observational studies, the tester cannot change or in any way control all of the variables in the test. For example, a study to determine which gender does better in math classes in school is strictly observational. You cannot change a person's gender, and you cannot change the subject being studied. The big downfall of observational studies is that you have no way of proving a cause-and-effect relationship because you cannot control outside influences. Events outside of school can influence a student's performance in school, and observational studies cannot take that into consideration.

Random Samples

For most studies, a **random sample** is necessary to produce valid results. Random samples should not have any particular influence to cause sampled subjects to behave one way or another. The goal is for the random sample to be a **representative sample**, or a sample whose characteristics give an accurate picture of the characteristics of the entire population. To accomplish this, you must make sure you have a proper **sample size**, or an appropriate number of elements in the sample.

Biases

In statistical studies, biases must be avoided. **Bias** is an error that causes the study to favor one set of results over another. For example, if a survey to determine how the country views the president's job performance only speaks to registered voters in the president's party, the results will be skewed because a disproportionately large number of responders would tend to show approval, while a disproportionately large number of people in the opposite party would tend to express disapproval.

Extraneous Variables

Extraneous variables are, as the name implies, outside influences that can affect the outcome of a study. They are not always avoidable, but could trigger bias in the result.

Copyright © Mometrix Media. You have been licensed one copy of this document for personal use only. Any other reproduction or redistribution is strictly prohibited. All rights reserved.

Data Organization

Example

A nurse found the heart rates of ten different patients to be 76, 80, 90, 86, 70, 76, 72, 88, 88, and 68 beats per minute. Organize this information in a table.

There are several ways to organize data in a table. The table below is an example.

Patient Number	1	2	3	4	5	6	7	8	9	10
Heart Rate (bpm)	76	80	90	86	70	76	72	88	88	68

When making a table, be sure to label the columns and rows appropriately.

Data Analysis

Measures of Central Tendency

The **measure of central tendency** is a statistical value that gives a general tendency for the center of a group of data. There are several different ways of describing the measure of central tendency. Each one has a unique way it is calculated, and each one gives a slightly different perspective on the data set. Whenever you give a measure of central tendency, always make sure the units are the same. If the data has different units, such as hours, minutes, and seconds, convert all the data to the same unit, and use the same unit in the measure of central tendency. If no units are given in the data, do not give units for the measure of central tendency.

Mean

The **statistical mean** of a group of data is the same as the arithmetic average of that group. To find the mean of a set of data, first convert each value to the same units, if necessary. Then find the sum of all the values, and count the total number of data values, making sure you take into consideration each individual value. If a value appears more than once, count it more than once. Divide the sum of the values by the total number of values and apply the units, if any. Note that the mean does not have to be one of the data values in the set, and may not divide evenly.

$$\text{mean} = \frac{\text{sum of the data values}}{\text{quantity of data values}}$$

The mean of the data set {88, 72, 61, 90, 97, 68, 88, 79, 86, 93, 97, 71, 80, 84, 89, 72, 91, 95, 89, 83, 94, 90, 63, 69, 89} would be the sum of the twenty-five numbers divided by 25:

$$\frac{88 + 72 + 61 + 90 + 97 + \cdots + 94 + 90 + 63 + 69 + 89}{25}$$

$$= \frac{2078}{25}$$

$$= 83.12$$

While the mean is relatively easy to calculate and averages are understood by most people, the mean can be very misleading if used as the sole measure of central tendency. If the data set has outliers (data values that are unusually high or unusually low compared to the rest of the data values), the mean can be very distorted, especially if the data set has a small number of values. If unusually high values are countered with unusually low values, the mean is not affected as much. For example, if five of twenty students in a class get a 100 on a test, but the other 15 students have

Copyright © Mometrix Media. You have been licensed one copy of this document for personal use only. Any other reproduction or redistribution is strictly prohibited. All rights reserved.

an average of 60 on the same test, the class average would appear as 70. Whenever the mean is skewed by outliers, it is always a good idea to include the median as an alternate measure of central tendency.

Review Video: Mean, Median, and Mode
Visit mometrix.com/academy and enter code: 286207

Median

The **statistical median** is the value in the middle of the set of data. To find the median, list all data values in order from smallest to largest or from largest to smallest. Any value that is repeated in the set must be listed the number of times it appears. If there are an odd number of data values, the median is the value in the middle of the list. If there is an even number of data values, the median is the arithmetic mean of the two middle values.

Mode

The **statistical mode** is the data value that occurs the most number of times in the data set. It is possible to have exactly one mode, more than one mode, or no mode. To find the mode of a set of data, arrange the data like you do to find the median (all values in order, listing all multiples of data values). Count the number of times each value appears in the data set. If all values appear an equal number of times, there is no mode. If one value appears more than any other value, that value is the mode. If two or more values appear the same number of times, but there are other values that appear fewer times and no values that appear more times, all of those values are the modes.

The big disadvantage of using the median as a measure of central tendency is that is relies solely on a value's relative size as compared to the other values in the set. When the individual values in a set of data are evenly dispersed, the median can be an accurate tool. However, if there is a group of rather large values or a group of rather small values that are not offset by a different group of values, the information that can be inferred from the median may not be accurate because the distribution of values is skewed.

The main disadvantage of the mode is that the values of the other data in the set have no bearing on the mode. The mode may be the largest value, the smallest value, or a value anywhere in between in the set. The mode only tells which value or values, if any, occurred the most number of times. It does not give any suggestions about the remaining values in the set.

Dispersion

The **measure of dispersion** is a single value that helps to "interpret" the measure of central tendency by providing more information about how the data values in the set are distributed about the measure of central tendency. The measure of dispersion helps to eliminate or reduce the disadvantages of using the mean, median, or mode as a single measure of central tendency, and give a more accurate picture of the dataset as a whole. To have a measure of dispersion, you must know or calculate the range, standard deviation, or variance of the data set.

Range

The **range** of a set of data is the difference between the greatest and lowest values of the data in the set. To calculate the range, you must first make sure the units for all data values are the same, and then identify the greatest and lowest values. Use the formula $range = highest\ value - lowest\ value$. If there are multiple data values that are equal for the highest or lowest, just use one of the values in the formula. Write the answer with the same units as the data values you used to do the calculations.

Copyright © Mometrix Media. You have been licensed one copy of this document for personal use only. Any other reproduction or redistribution is strictly prohibited. All rights reserved.

Standard Deviation

Standard deviation is a measure of dispersion that compares all the data values in the set to the mean of the set to give a more accurate picture. To find the standard deviation of a population, use the formula

$$\sigma = \sqrt{\frac{\sum_{i=1}^{n}(x_i - \bar{x})^2}{n}}$$

where σ is the standard deviation of a population, x represents the individual values in the data set, $\bar{x}$ is the mean of the data values in the set, and n is the number of data values in the set. The higher the value of the standard deviation is, the greater the variance of the data values from the mean. The units associated with the standard deviation are the same as the units of the data values.

Variance

The **variance** of a population, or just variance, is the square of the standard deviation of that population. While the mean of a set of data gives the average of the set and gives information about where a specific data value lies in relation to the average, the variance of the population gives information about the degree to which the data values are spread out and tell you how close an individual value is to the average compared to the other values. The units associated with variance are the same as the units of the data values squared.

Percentile

Percentiles and **quartiles** are other methods of describing data within a set. *Percentiles* tell what percentage of the data in the set fall below a specific point. For example, achievement test scores are often given in percentiles. A score at the 80th percentile is one which is equal to or higher than 80 percent of the scores in the set. In other words, 80 percent of the scores were lower than that score.

Quartile

Quartiles are percentile groups that make up quarter sections of the data set. The first quartile is the 25th percentile. The second quartile is the 50th percentile; this is also the median of the dataset. The third quartile is the 75th percentile.

Skewness

Skewness is a way to describe the symmetry or asymmetry of the distribution of values in a dataset. If the distribution of values is symmetrical, there is no skew. In general the closer the mean of a data set is to the median of the data set, the less skew there is. Generally, if the mean is to the right of the median, the data set is *positively skewed*, or right-skewed, and if the mean is to the left of the median, the data set is *negatively skewed*, or left-skewed. However, this rule of thumb is not infallible. When the data values are graphed on a curve, a set with no skew will be a perfect bell curve. To estimate skew, use the formula

$$\text{skew} = \frac{\sqrt{n(n-1)}}{n-2}\left(\frac{\frac{1}{n}\sum_{i=1}^{n}(x_i - \bar{x})^3}{\left(\frac{1}{n}\sum_{i=1}^{n}(x_i - \bar{x})^2\right)^{\frac{3}{2}}}\right)$$

where n is the number of values is the set, x_i is the ith value in the set, and $\bar{x}$ is the mean of the set.

Copyright © Mometrix Media. You have been licensed one copy of this document for personal use only. Any other reproduction or redistribution is strictly prohibited. All rights reserved.

Simple Regression

In statistics, **simple regression** is using an equation to represent a relation between an independent and dependent variables. The independent variable is also referred to as the explanatory variable or the predictor, and is generally represented by the variable x in the equation. The dependent variable, usually represented by the variable y, is also referred to as the response variable. The equation may be any type of function – linear, quadratic, exponential, etc. The best way to handle this task is to use the regression feature of your graphing calculator. This will easily give you the curve of best fit and provide you with the coefficients and other information you need to derive an equation.

Line of Best Fit

In a scatter plot, the **line of best fit** is the line that best shows the trends of the data. The line of best fit is given by the equation $\hat{y} = ax + b$, where a and b are the regression coefficients. The regression coefficient a is also the slope of the line of best fit, and b is also the y-coordinate of the point at which the line of best fit crosses the x-axis. Not every point on the scatter plot will be on the line of best fit. The differences between the y-values of the points in the scatter plot and the corresponding y-values according to the equation of the line of best fit are the residuals. The line of best fit is also called the least-squares regression line because it is also the line that has the lowest sum of the squares of the residuals.

Correlation Coefficient

The **correlation coefficient** is the numerical value that indicates how strong the relationship is between the two variables of a linear regression equation. A correlation coefficient of −1 is a perfect negative correlation. A correlation coefficient of +1 is a perfect positive correlation. Correlation coefficients close to −1 or +1 are very strong correlations. A correlation coefficient equal to zero indicates there is no correlation between the two variables. This test is a good indicator of whether or not the equation for the line of best fit is accurate. The formula for the correlation coefficient is

$$r = \frac{\sum_{i=1}^{n}(x_i - \bar{x})(y_i - \bar{y})}{\sqrt{\sum_{i=1}^{n}(x_i - \bar{x})^2}\sqrt{\sum_{i=1}^{n}(y_i - \bar{y})^2}}$$

where r is the correlation coefficient, n is the number of data values in the set, (x_i, y_i) is a point in the set, and $\bar{x}$ and $\bar{y}$ are the means.

Z-Score

A **z-score** is an indication of how many standard deviations a given value falls from the mean. To calculate a z-score, use the formula $= \frac{x-\mu}{\sigma}$, where x is the data value, μ is the mean of the data set, and σ is the standard deviation of the population. If the z-score is positive, the data value lies above the mean. If the z-score is negative, the data value falls below the mean. These scores are useful in interpreting data such as standardized test scores, where every piece of data in the set has been counted, rather than just a small random sample. In cases where standard deviations are calculated from a random sample of the set, the z-scores will not be as accurate.

Central Limit Theorem

According to the ***central limit theorem***, regardless of what the original distribution of a sample is, the distribution of the means tends to get closer and closer to a normal distribution as the sample size gets larger and larger (this is necessary because the sample is becoming more all-encompassing of the elements of the population). As the sample size gets larger, the distribution of

Copyright © Mometrix Media. You have been licensed one copy of this document for personal use only. Any other reproduction or redistribution is strictly prohibited. All rights reserved.

the sample mean will approach a normal distribution with a mean of the population mean and a variance of the population variance divided by the sample size.

Shape of Data Distribution

Symmetry and Skewness

Symmetry is a characteristic of the shape of the plotted data. Specifically, it refers to how well the data on one side of the median *mirrors* the data on the other side.

A **skewed data** set is one that has a distinctly longer or fatter tail on one side of the peak or the other. A data set that is *skewed left* has more of its values to the left of the peak, while a set that is *skewed right* has more of its values to the right of the peak. When actually looking at the graph, these names may seem counterintuitive since, in a left-skewed data set, the bulk of the values seem to be on the right side of the graph, and vice versa. However, if the graph is viewed strictly in relation to the peak, the direction of skewness makes more sense.

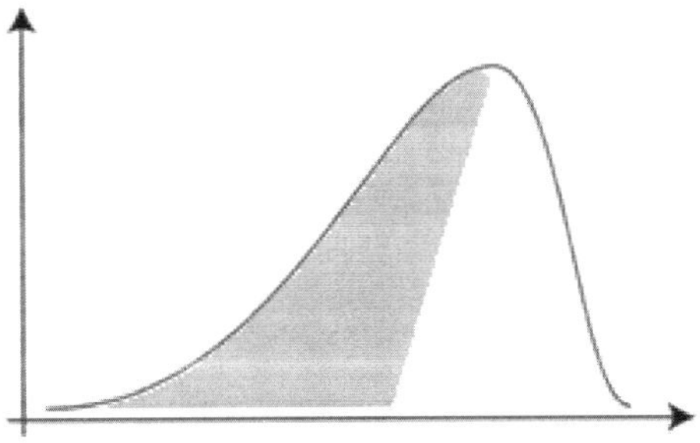

Left-skewed

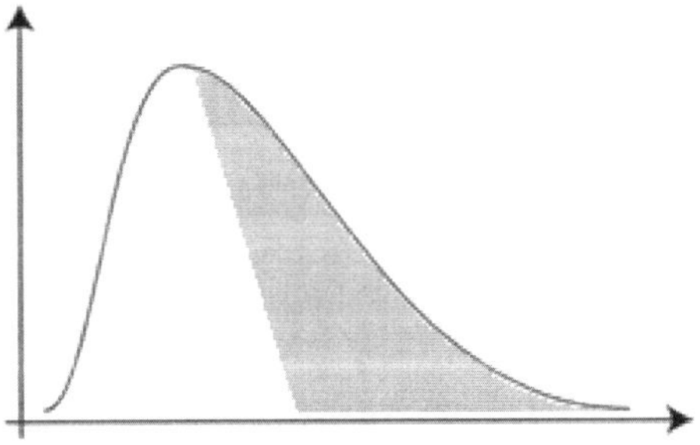

Right-skewed

Unimodal vs. Bimodal

If a distribution has a single peak, it would be considered **unimodal**. If it has two discernible peaks it would be considered **bimodal**. Bimodal distributions may be an indication that the set of data being considered is actually the combination of two sets of data with significant differences.

Uniformity

A uniform distribution is a distribution in which there is *no distinct peak or variation* in the data. No values or ranges are particularly more common than any other values or ranges.

Displaying Information

Charts and Tables

Charts and tables are ways of organizing information into separate rows and columns that are labeled to identify and explain the data contained in them. Some charts and tables are organized horizontally, with row lengths giving the details about the labeled information. Other charts and tables are organized vertically, with column heights giving the details about the labeled information.

Frequency Tables

Frequency tables show how frequently each unique value appears in the set. A r*elative frequency table* is one that shows the proportions of each unique value compared to the entire set. Relative frequencies are given as percents; however, the total percent for a relative frequency table will not

Copyright © Mometrix Media. You have been licensed one copy of this document for personal use only. Any other reproduction or redistribution is strictly prohibited. All rights reserved.

necessarily equal 100 percent due to rounding. An example of a frequency table with relative frequencies is below.

Favorite Color	Frequency	Relative Frequency
Blue	4	13%
Red	7	22%
Purple	3	9%
Green	6	19%
Cyan	12	38%

Pictographs

A **pictograph** is a graph, generally in the horizontal orientation, that uses pictures or symbols to represent the data. Each pictograph must have a key that defines the picture or symbol and gives the quantity each picture or symbol represents. Pictures or symbols on a pictograph are not always shown as whole elements. In this case, the fraction of the picture or symbol shown represents the same fraction of the quantity a whole picture or symbol stands for. For example, a row with $3\frac{1}{2}$ ears of corn, where each ear of corn represents 100 stalks of corn in a field, would equal $3\frac{1}{2} \cdot 100 = 350$ stalks of corn in the field.

Circle Graphs

Circle graphs, also known as *pie charts*, provide a visual depiction of the relationship of each type of data compared to the whole set of data. The circle graph is divided into sections by drawing radii to create central angles whose percentage of the circle is equal to the individual data's percentage of the whole set. Each 1% of data is equal to 3.6° in the circle graph. Therefore, data represented by a 90° section of the circle graph makes up 25% of the whole. When complete, a circle graph often looks like a pie cut into uneven wedges. The pie chart below shows the data from the frequency table referenced earlier where people were asked their favorite color.

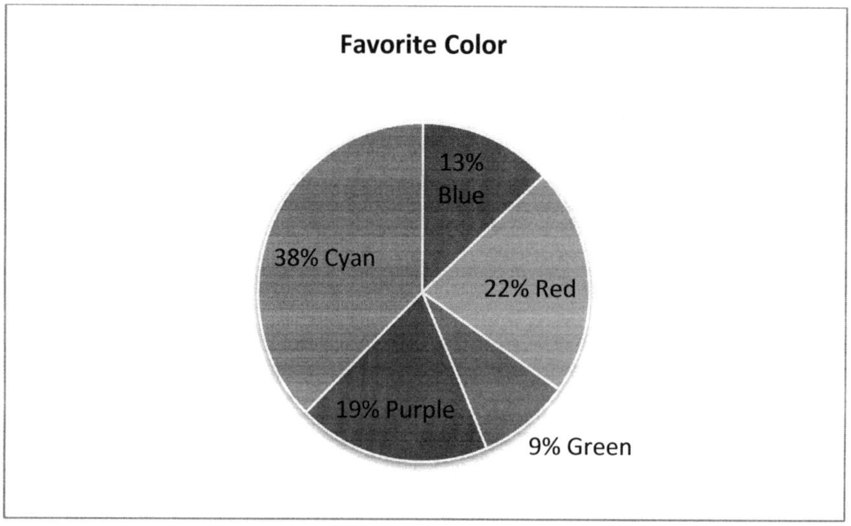

Review Video: Pie Chart
Visit mometrix.com/academy and enter code: 895285

Copyright © Mometrix Media. You have been licensed one copy of this document for personal use only. Any other reproduction or redistribution is strictly prohibited. All rights reserved.

Line Graphs

Line graphs have one or more lines of varying styles (solid or broken) to show the different values for a set of data. The individual data are represented as ordered pairs, much like on a Cartesian plane. In this case, the *x*- and *y*-axes are defined in terms of their units, such as dollars or time. The individual plotted points are joined by line segments to show whether the value of the data is increasing (line sloping upward), decreasing (line sloping downward) or staying the same (horizontal line). Multiple sets of data can be graphed on the same line graph to give an easy visual comparison. An example of this would be graphing achievement test scores for different groups of students over the same time period to see which group had the greatest increase or decrease in performance from year-to-year (as shown below).

Review Video: Line Graphs
Visit mometrix.com/academy and enter code: 480147

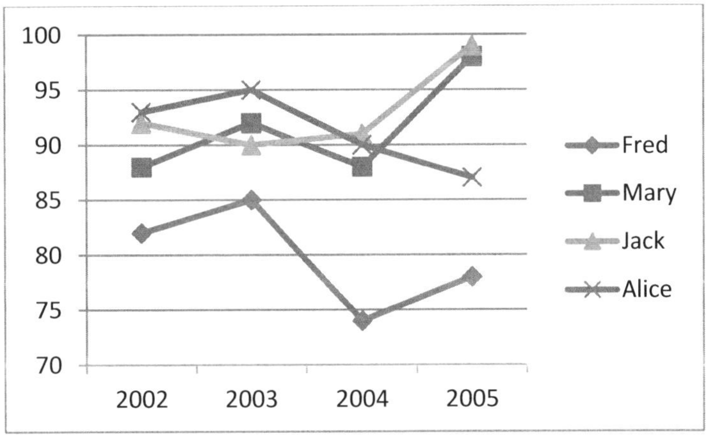

Line Plots

A **line plot**, also known as a *dot plot*, has plotted points that are not connected by line segments. In this graph, the horizontal axis lists the different possible values for the data, and the vertical axis lists the number of times the individual value occurs. A single dot is graphed for each value to show the number of times it occurs. This graph is more closely related to a bar graph than a line graph. Do not connect the dots in a line plot or it will misrepresent the data.

Review Video: Line Plot
Visit mometrix.com/academy and enter code: 754610

Stem and Leaf Plots

A **stem and leaf plot** is useful for depicting groups of data that fall into a range of values. Each piece of data is separated into two parts: the first, or left, part is called the stem; the second, or right, part is called the leaf. Each stem is listed in a column from smallest to largest. Each leaf that has the common stem is listed in that stem's row from smallest to largest. For example, in a set of two-digit numbers, the digit in the tens place is the stem, and the digit in the ones place is the leaf. With a stem and leaf plot, you can easily see which subset of numbers (10s, 20s, 30s, etc.) is the largest. This information is also readily available by looking at a histogram, but a stem and leaf plot also allows you to look closer and see exactly which values fall in that range. Using all of the test scores from above, we can assemble a stem and leaf plot like the one below.

Test Scores

Copyright © Mometrix Media. You have been licensed one copy of this document for personal use only. Any other reproduction or redistribution is strictly prohibited. All rights reserved.

7	4	8							
8	2	5	7	8	8				
9	0	0	1	2	2	3	5	8	9

Bar Graphs

A **bar graph** is one of the few graphs that can be drawn correctly in two different configurations – both horizontally and vertically. A bar graph is similar to a line plot in the way the data is organized on the graph. Both axes must have their categories defined for the graph to be useful. Rather than placing a single dot to mark the point of the data's value, a bar, or thick line, is drawn from zero to the exact value of the data, whether it is a number, percentage, or other numerical value. Longer bar lengths correspond to greater data values. To read a bar graph, read the labels for the axes to find the units being reported. Then look where the bars end in relation to the scale given on the corresponding axis and determine the associated value.

The bar chart below represents the responses from our favorite color survey.

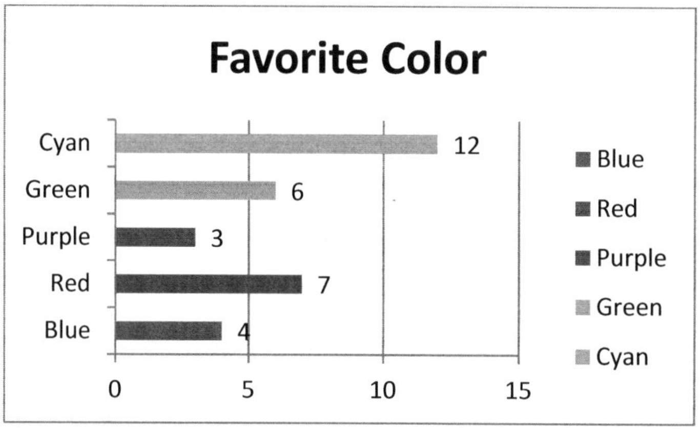

Review Video: Bar Graph
Visit mometrix.com/academy and enter code: 226729

Histograms

At first glance, a **histogram** looks like a vertical bar graph. The difference is that a bar graph has a separate bar for each piece of data and a histogram has one continuous bar for each r*ange* of data. For example, a histogram may have one bar for the range 0–9, one bar for 10–19, etc. While a bar graph has numerical values on one axis, a histogram has numerical values on both axes. Each range is of equal size, and they are ordered left to right from lowest to highest. The height of each column on a histogram represents the number of data values within that range. Like a stem and leaf plot, a

Copyright © Mometrix Media. You have been licensed one copy of this document for personal use only. Any other reproduction or redistribution is strictly prohibited. All rights reserved.

histogram makes it easy to glance at the graph and quickly determine which range has the greatest quantity of values. A simple example of a histogram is below.

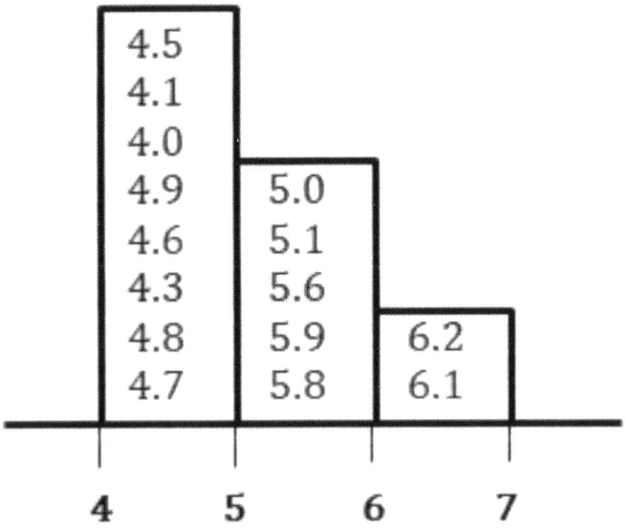

Review Video: Histogram
Visit mometrix.com/academy and enter code: 735897

Bivariate Data

Bivariate data is simply data from two different variables. (The prefix *bi-* means *two.*) In a *scatter plot,* each value in the set of data is plotted on a grid similar to a Cartesian plane, where each axis represents one of the two variables. By looking at the pattern formed by the points on the grid, you can often determine whether or not there is a relationship between the two variables, and what that relationship is, if it exists. The variables may be directly proportionate, inversely proportionate, or show no proportion at all. It may also be possible to determine if the data is linear, and if so, to find an equation to relate the two variables. The following scatter plot shows the relationship between preference for brand "A" and the age of the consumers surveyed.

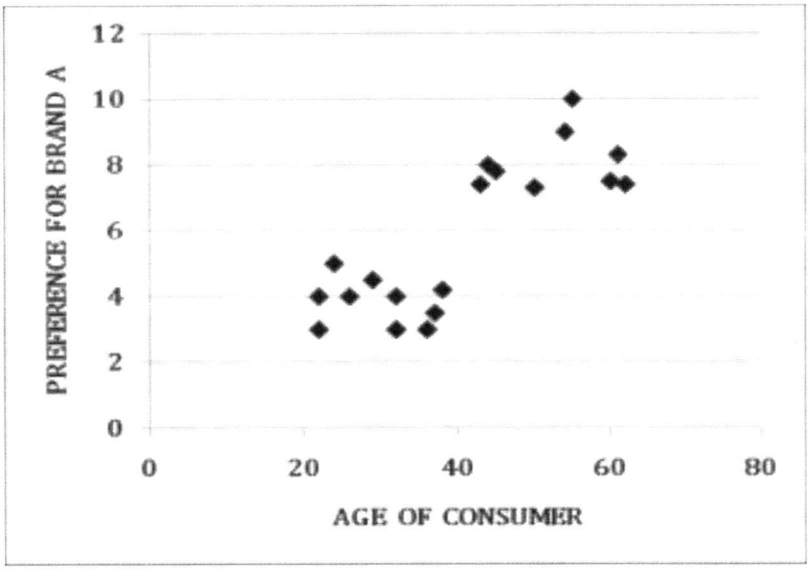

Copyright © Mometrix Media. You have been licensed one copy of this document for personal use only. Any other reproduction or redistribution is strictly prohibited. All rights reserved.

Scatter Plots

Scatter plots are also useful in determining the type of function represented by the data and finding the simple regression. Linear scatter plots may be positive or negative. Nonlinear scatter plots are generally exponential or quadratic. Below are some common types of scatter plots:

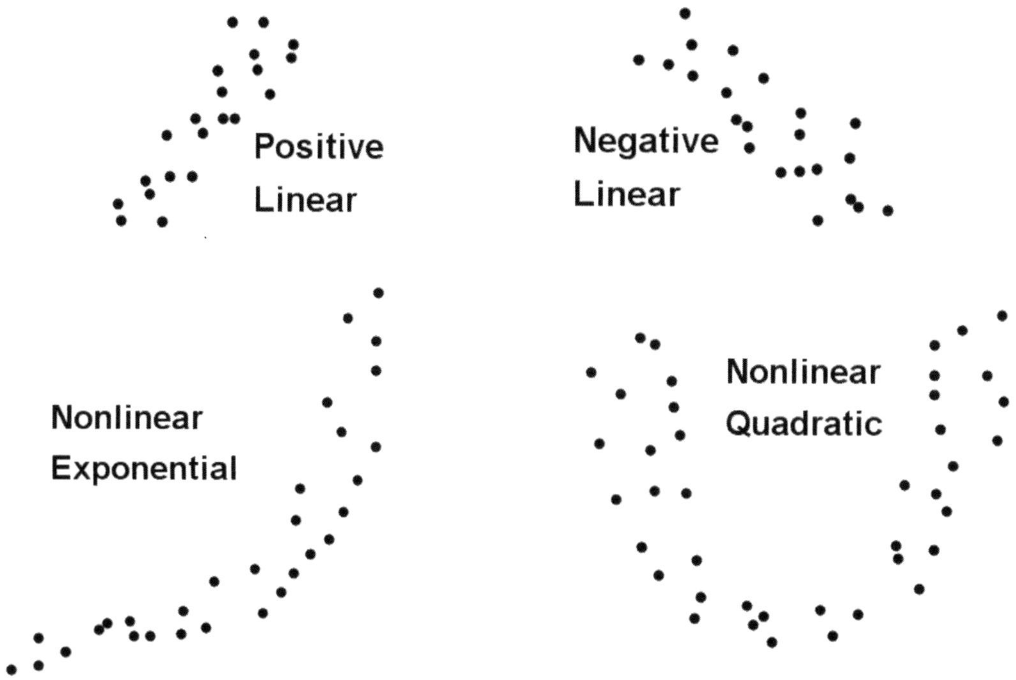

Review Video: Scatter Plot
Visit mometrix.com/academy and enter code: 596526

5-Number Summary

The **5-number summary** of a set of data gives a very informative picture of the set. The five numbers in the summary include the minimum value, maximum value, and the three quartiles. This information gives the reader the range and median of the set, as well as an indication of how the data is spread about the median.

Box and Whisker Plots

A **box-and-whisker plot** is a graphical representation of the 5-number summary. To draw a box-and-whiskers plot, plot the points of the 5-number summary on a number line. Draw a box whose ends are through the points for the first and third quartiles. Draw a vertical line in the box through the median to divide the box in half. Draw a line segment from the first quartile point to the minimum value, and from the third quartile point to the maximum value.

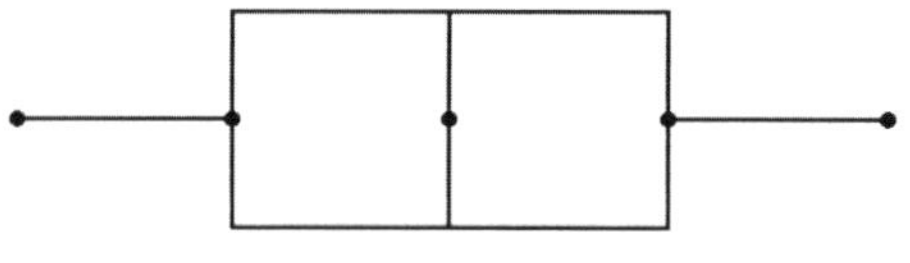

Copyright © Mometrix Media. You have been licensed one copy of this document for personal use only. Any other reproduction or redistribution is strictly prohibited. All rights reserved.

68-95-99.7 Rule

The **68–95–99.7 rule** describes how a normal distribution of data should appear when compared to the mean. This is also a description of a normal bell curve. According to this rule, 68 percent of the data values in a normally distributed set should fall within one standard deviation of the mean (34 percent above and 34 percent below the mean), 95 percent of the data values should fall within two standard deviations of the mean (47.5 percent above and 47.5 percent below the mean), and 99.7 percent of the data values should fall within three standard deviations of the mean, again, equally distributed on either side of the mean. This means that only 0.3 percent of all data values should fall more than three standard deviations from the mean. On the graph below, the normal curve is centered on the y-axis. The x-axis labels are how many standard deviations away from the center you are.

Therefore, it is easy to see how the 68-95-99.7 rule can apply.

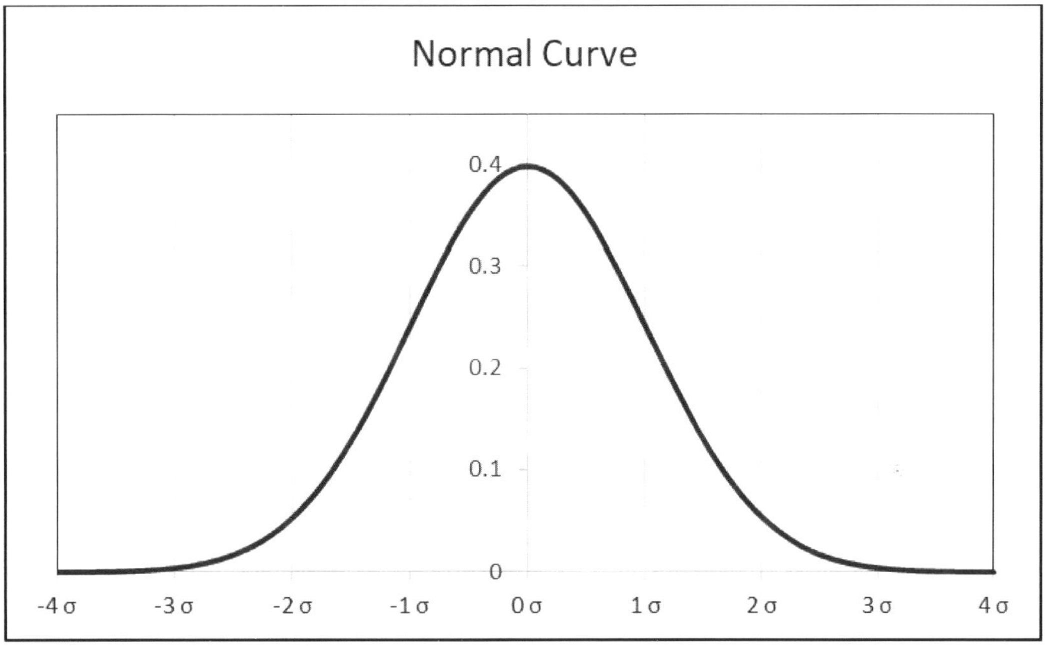

Shapes of Frequency Curves

The five general **shapes of frequency curves** are *symmetrical*, u-*shaped*, *skewed*, j-*shaped*, and *multimodal*. Symmetrical curves are also known as bell curves or normal curves. Values equidistant from the median have equal frequencies. U-shaped curves have two maxima – one at each end. Skewed curves have the maximum point off-center. Curves that are negative skewed, or left skewed, have the maximum on the right side of the graph so there is longer tail and lower slope on the left side. The opposite is true for curves that are positive-skewed, or right-skewed. J-shaped curves have a maximum at one end and a minimum at the other end. Multimodal curves have multiple maxima. For example, if the curve has exactly two maxima, it is called a bimodal curve.

Copyright © Mometrix Media. You have been licensed one copy of this document for personal use only. Any other reproduction or redistribution is strictly prohibited. All rights reserved.

Interpretation of Graphs

Example

The following graph shows the ages of five patients being cared for in a hospital:

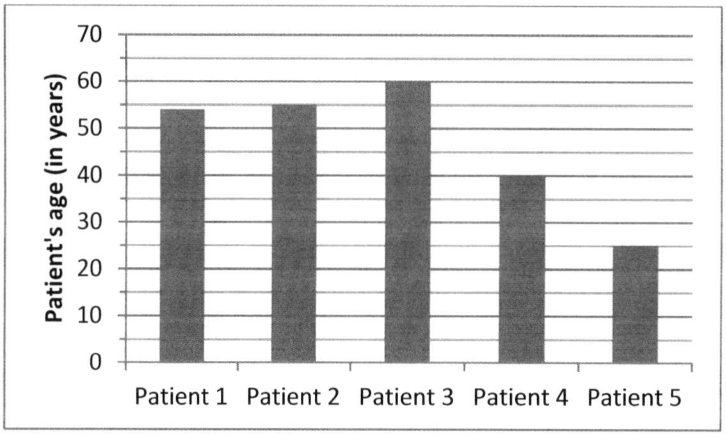

Determine the range of patient ages.

Patient 1 is 54 years old; Patient 2 is 55 years old; Patient 3 is 60 years old; Patient 4 is 40 years old; and Patient 5 is 25 years old. The range of patient ages is the age of the oldest patient minus the age of the youngest patient. In other words, $60 - 25 = 35$. The range of ages is 35 years.

Copyright © Mometrix Media. You have been licensed one copy of this document for personal use only. Any other reproduction or redistribution is strictly prohibited. All rights reserved.

Praxis II

Elementary Education: Content Knowledge for Teaching (7801) Exam Part 2 of 2

SECRETS

Study Guide

Your Key to Exam Success

Praxis II Test Review for the
Praxis II: Subject Assessments

Dear Future Exam Success Story:

First of all, **THANK YOU** for purchasing Mometrix study materials!

Second, congratulations! You are one of the few determined test-takers who are committed to doing whatever it takes to excel on your exam. **You have come to the right place.** We developed these study materials with one goal in mind: to deliver you the information you need in a format that's concise and easy to use.

In addition to optimizing your guide for the content of the test, we've outlined our recommended steps for breaking down the preparation process into small, attainable goals so you can make sure you stay on track.

We've also analyzed the entire test-taking process, identifying the most common pitfalls and showing how you can overcome them and be ready for any curveball the test throws you.

Standardized testing is one of the biggest obstacles on your road to success, which only increases the importance of doing well in the high-pressure, high-stakes environment of test day. Your results on this test could have a significant impact on your future, and this guide provides the information and practical advice to help you achieve your full potential on test day.

Your success is our success

We would love to hear from you! If you would like to share the story of your exam success or if you have any questions or comments in regard to our products, please contact us at **800-673-8175** or **support@mometrix.com**.

Thanks again for your business and we wish you continued success!

Sincerely,
The Mometrix Test Preparation Team

Need more help? Check out our flashcards at: http://MometrixFlashcards.com/PraxisII

Copyright © 2019 by Mometrix Media LLC. All rights reserved.
Written and edited by the Mometrix Exam Secrets Test Prep Team
Printed in the United States of America

TABLE OF CONTENTS

Science

Earth and Space Science

Earth System Science

The complex and interconnected dynamics of the continents, atmosphere, oceans, ice, and life forms are the subject of **earth system science**. These interconnected dynamics require an interdisciplinary approach that includes chemistry, physics, biology, mathematics, and applied sciences in order to study the Earth as an integrated system and determine (while considering human impact and interaction) the past, present, and future states of the earth. Scientific inquiry in this field includes exploration of:

- Extreme weather events as they pertain to a changing climate
- Earthquakes and volcanic eruptions as they pertain to tectonic shifts
- Losses in biodiversity in relation to the changes in the earth's ecosystems
- Causes and effects in the environment
- The sun's solar variability in relation to the earth's climate
- The atmosphere's increasing concentrations of carbon dioxide and aerosols
- Trends in the earth's systems in terms of changes and their consequences

Traditional Earth Science Disciplines

Modern science is approaching the study of the earth in an integrated fashion that sees the earth as an interconnected system that is impacted by humankind and, therefore, must include social dimensions. Traditionally, though, the following were the earth science disciplines:

- **Geology** – This is the study of the origin and structure of the earth and of the changes it has undergone and is in the process of undergoing. Geologists work from the crust inward.
- **Meteorology** – This is the study of the atmosphere, including atmospheric pressure, temperature, clouds, winds, precipitation, etc. It is also concerned with describing and explaining weather.
- **Oceanography** – This is the study of the oceans, which includes studying their extent and depth, the physics and chemistry of ocean waters, and the exploitation of their resources.
- **Ecology** – This is the study of living organisms in relation to their environment and to other living things. It is the study of the interrelations between the different components of the ecosystem.

Geological Eras

Geologists divide the history of the earth into units of time called **eons**, which are divided into **eras**, then into **periods**, then into **epochs** and finally into **ages**. Dates are approximate of course, and there may be variations of a few million years. (Million years ago is abbreviated as Ma.) Some of the most commonly known periods are:

- **Hadean Period** – About 4.5 to 3.8 billion years ago
- **Archaean Period** – 3.8 to 2.5 billion years ago
- **Proterozoic Period** – 2.5 billion to 542 Ma
- **Cambrian Period** – 542 to 488 Ma
- Ordovician Period – 488 to 443 Ma

Copyright © Mometrix Media. You have been licensed one copy of this document for personal use only. Any other reproduction or redistribution is strictly prohibited. All rights reserved.

- **Silurian Period** – 443 to 416 Ma
- **Devonian Period** – 416 to 359 Ma
- Carboniferous Period – 359 to 290 Ma
- **Permian Period** – 290 to 248 Ma
- **Triassic Period** – 251 to 200 Ma
- **Jurassic Period** – 200 to 150 Ma
- Cretaceous Period – 150 to 65 Ma
- Paleogene Period – 65 to 28 Ma
- Neogene Period – 28 to 2 Ma
- **Quaternary Period** – about 2 Ma to the present

Development of Life on Earth According to Time Periods

The **evolution** of life on earth is believed to have occurred as follows:

- Igneous rocks formed. (Hadean)
- The continents formed. (Archaean Eon)
- The first multi-cellular creatures such as hydras, jellyfish, and sponges appeared about 600 Ma.
- Flatworms, roundworms, and segmented worms appeared about 550 Ma.
- Moss, arthropods, octopus, and eels appeared. (Cambrian Period)
- Mushrooms, fungi, and other primitive plants appeared; sea animals began to use calcium to build bones and shells. (Ordovician Period)
- Fish with jaws appeared. (Silurian Period)
- Fish developed lungs and legs (frogs) and went on land; ferns appeared. (Devonian period)
- Reptiles developed the ability to lay eggs on land and pine trees appeared. (Carboniferous Period)
- Dinosaurs dominated the land during the Triassic and Jurassic Periods.
- Flying insects, birds, and the first flowering plants appeared; dinosaurs died out. (Cretaceous Period)
- Mammals evolved and dominated; grasses became widespread. (50 Ma)
- Hominids appeared more than 2 Ma.

Hydrosphere and Hydrologic Cycle

The **hydrosphere** is anything on earth that is related to water, whether it is in the air, on land, or in a plant or animal system. A water molecule consists of only two atoms of hydrogen and one of oxygen, yet it is what makes life possible. Unlike the other planets, earth is able to sustain life because its temperature allows water to be in its liquid state most of the time. Water vapor and ice are of no use to living organisms. The **hydrologic cycle** is the journey water takes as it assumes different forms. Liquid surface water evaporates to form the gaseous state of a cloud, and then becomes liquid again in the form of rain. This process takes about 10 days if water becomes a cloud. Water at the bottom of the ocean or in a glacier is not likely to change form, even over periods of thousands of years.

Review Video: Hydrologic Cycle
Visit mometrix.com/academy and enter code: 426578

Copyright © Mometrix Media. You have been licensed one copy of this document for personal use only. Any other reproduction or redistribution is strictly prohibited. All rights reserved.

Aquifers

An **aquifer** is an underground water reservoir formed from groundwater that has infiltrated from the surface by passing through the soil and permeable rock layers (the zone of aeration) to a zone of saturation where the rocks are impermeable. There are two types of aquifers. In one, the water is under pressure (**confined**) as the supply builds up between layers of impermeable rocks and has to move back towards the surface, resulting in a spring or artesian well. The second type of aquifer is called "**unconfined**" because it has room to expand and contract, and the water has to be pumped out. The highest level of the aquifer is called the water table. If water is pumped out of the aquifer such that the water table dips in a specific area, that area is called a cone of depression.

Biosphere

Biosphere is the term used by physical geographers to describe the living world of trees, bugs, and animals. It refers to any place where life exists on earth, and is the intersection of the hydrosphere, the atmosphere, the land, and the energy that comes from space. The biosphere includes the upper areas of the atmosphere where birds and insects can travel, areas deep inside caves, and hydrothermal vents at the bottom of the ocean.

Factors that affect the biosphere include:

- The **distance and tilt** between the earth and the sun – This produces temperatures that are conducive to life and causes the seasons.
- **Climate, daily weather, and erosion** – These change the land and the organisms on and in it.
- Earthquakes, tornadoes, volcanoes, tsunamis, and other **natural phenomena** – These all change the land.
- **Chemical erosion** – This changes the composition of rocks and organic materials, as well as how bacteria and single-celled organisms break down organic and inorganic materials.

Ecological System and Biome

An **ecological system**, or ecosystem, is the community of all the living organisms in a specific area interacting with non-living factors such as temperature, sunlight, atmospheric pressure, weather patterns, wind, types of nutrients, etc. An ecosystem's development depends on the energy that passes in and out of it. The boundaries of an ecosystem depend on the use of the term, whether it refers to an ecosystem under a rock or in a valley, pond, or ocean.

A **biome** is a general ecosystem type defined by the plants and animals that live there and the local climate patterns. Examples include tropical rainforests or savannas, deserts, grasslands, deciduous forests, tundra, woodlands, and ice caps. There can be more than one type of biome within a larger climate zone. The transition area between two biomes is an ecotone, which may have characteristics of both biomes.

Erosion

Erosion is the process that breaks down matter, whether it is a rock that is broken into pebbles or mountains that are rained on until they become hills. Erosion always happens in a downhill direction. The erosion of land by weather or breaking waves is called **denudation**. **Mass wasting** is the movement of masses of dirt and rock from one place to another. This can occur in two ways: **mechanical** (such as breaking a rock with a hammer) or **chemical** (such as pouring acid on a rock to dissolve it). If the material changes color, it indicates that a break down was chemical in nature.

Copyright © Mometrix Media. You have been licensed one copy of this document for personal use only. Any other reproduction or redistribution is strictly prohibited. All rights reserved.

Whatever is broken down must go somewhere, so erosion eventually builds something up. For example, an eroded mountain ends up in a river that carries the sediment towards the ocean, where it builds up and creates a wetland or delta at the mouth of the river.

Climates

Scientists have determined the following different types of **climates**:

- Polar (ice caps)
- Polar (tundra)
- Subtropical (dry summer)
- Subtropical (dry winter)
- Subtropical (humid)
- Subtropical (marine west coast)
- Subtropical (Mediterranean)
- Subtropical (wet)
- Tropical (monsoon)
- Tropical (savannah/grasslands)
- Tropical (wet)

Several factors make up and affect climates. These include:

- Temperature
- Atmospheric pressure
- The number of clouds and the amount of dust or smog
- Humidity
- Winds

The moistest and warmest of all the climates is that of the tropical rainforest. It has daily convection thunderstorms caused by the surface daytime heat and the high humidity, which combine to form thunderclouds.

Review Video: Climates
Visit mometrix.com/academy and enter code: 991320

Layers of the Earth

The earth has several distinct **layers**, each with its own properties:

- **Crust** – This is the outermost layer of the earth that is comprised of the continents and the ocean basins. It has a variable thickness (35-70 km in the continents and 5-10 km in the ocean basins) and is composed mostly of alumino-silicates.
- **Mantle** – This is about 2900 km thick, and is made up mostly of ferro-magnesium silicates. It is divided into an upper and lower mantle. Most of the internal heat of the earth is located in the mantle. Large convective cells circulate heat, and may cause plate tectonic movement.
- **Core** – This is separated into the liquid outer core and the solid inner core. The outer core is 2300 km thick (composed mostly of nickel-iron alloy), and the inner core (almost entirely iron) is 12 km thick. The earth's magnetic field is thought to be controlled by the liquid outer core.

Copyright © Mometrix Media. You have been licensed one copy of this document for personal use only. Any other reproduction or redistribution is strictly prohibited. All rights reserved.

Composition of Earth's Atmosphere

The earth's **atmosphere** is 79% nitrogen, 20% oxygen, and 1% other gases. The oxygen was originally produced almost entirely by algae-type plants. The atmosphere has four layers:

- **Troposphere** – This is the layer closest to the earth where all weather takes place. It is the region that contains rising and falling packets of air. Air pressure at sea level is 0.1 atmospheres, but the top of the troposphere is about 10% of that amount.
- **Stratosphere** – In this layer, air flow is mainly horizontal. The upper portion has a thin layer of concentrated ozone (a reactive form of oxygen) that is largely responsible for absorbing the sun's ultraviolet rays.
- **Mesosphere** – This is the coldest layer. Temperatures drop to -100°C at the top.
- **Thermosphere** – This is divided into the lower ionosphere and the higher exosphere. This layer is very thin and has many ionized atoms with a net electrical charge. The aurora and Van Allen Belts are here. This layer also absorbs the most energetic photons from the sun and reflects radio waves, enabling long distance radio communication.

Paleontology

Paleontology is the study of prehistoric plant and animal life through the analysis of **fossil remains**. These fossils reveal the ecologies of the past and the path of evolution for both extinct and living organisms. A historical science, paleontology seeks information about the identity, origin, environment, and evolution of past organisms and what they can reveal about the past of the earth as a whole. Paleontology explains causes as opposed to conducting experiments to observe effects. It is related to the fields of biology, geology, and archaeology, and is divided into several sub-disciplines concerned with the types of fossils studied, the process of fossilization, and the ecology and climate of the past. Paleontologists also help identify the composition of the earth's rock layers by the fossils that are found, thus identifying potential sites for oil, mineral, and water extraction.

Determining the Order in Which Geologic Events Occurred Using the Rock Record

The **Law of Superposition** logically assumes that the bottom layer of a series of sedimentary layers is the oldest, unless it has been overturned or older rock has been pushed over it. In addition, since **igneous intrusions** can cut through or flow above other rocks, these other rocks are older. For example, molten rock (lava) flows out over already present, older rocks. Another guideline for the rock record is that **rock layers** are older than the folds and faults in them because the rocks must exist before they can be folded or faulted. If a rock contains **atomic nuclei**, reference tables of the half-lives of commonly used radio isotopes can be used to match the decay rate of known substances to the nuclei in a rock, and thereby determine its age. Ages of rocks can also be determined from **contact metamorphism**, the re-crystallization of pre-existing rocks due to changes in physical and chemical conditions, such as heat, pressure, and chemically active fluids that might be present in lava or polluted waters.

Matching Rocks and Geologic Events in One Place with Those of Another

Geologists physically follow rock layers from one location to another by a process called "walking the outcrop." Geologists walk along the outcropping to see where it goes and what the differences and similarities of the neighboring locations they cross are. Similar rock **types** or **patterns** of rock layers that are similar in terms of thickness, color, composition, and fossil remains tell geologists that two locations have a similar geologic history. Fossils are found all over the earth, but are from a relatively **small time period** in earth's history. Therefore, fossil evidence helps date a rock layer,

Copyright © Mometrix Media. You have been licensed one copy of this document for personal use only. Any other reproduction or redistribution is strictly prohibited. All rights reserved.

regardless of where it occurs. **Volcanic ash** is a good time indicator since ash is deposited quickly over a widespread area. Matching the date of an eruption to the ash allows for a precise identification of time. Similarly, the **meteor impact** at the intersection of the Cretaceous and Tertiary Periods left a time marker. Wherever the meteor's iridium content is found, geologists are able to date rock layers.

Sequencing the Earth's Geologic History from the Fossil and Rock Record

Reference tables are used to match specimens and time periods. For example, the fossil record has been divided into time units of the earth's history. Rocks can therefore be dated by the fossils found with them. There are also reference tables for dating plate motions and mountain building events in geologic history. Since humans have been around for a relatively short period of time, **fossilized human remains** help to affix a date to a location. Some areas have missing **geologic layers** because of erosion or other factors, but reference tables specific to a region will list what is complete or missing. The theory of **uniformitarianism** assumes that geologic processes have been the same throughout history. Therefore, the way erosion or volcanic eruptions happen today is the same as the way these events happened millions of years ago because there is no reason for them to have changed. Therefore, knowledge about current events can be applied to the past to make judgments about events in the rock record.

Revealing Changes in Earth's History by the Fossil and Rock Records

Fossils can show how animal and plant life have changed or remained the same over time. For example, fossils have provided evidence of the existence of dinosaurs even though they no longer roam the earth, and have also been used to prove that certain insects have been around forever. Fossils have been used to identify four basic eras: **Proterozoic**, the age of primitive life; **Paleozoic**, the age of fishes; **Mesozoic**, the age of dinosaurs; and **Cenozoic**, the age of mammals. Most ancient forms of life have disappeared, and there are reference tables that list when this occurred. Fossil records also show the evolution of certain life forms, such as the horse from the eohippus. However, the majority of changes do not involve evolution from simple to complex forms, but rather an increase in the variety of forms.

Mountains

A **mountain** is a portion of the earth that has been raised above its surroundings by volcanic action or tectonic plate movement. Mountains are made up of igneous, metamorphic, and sedimentary rocks, and most lie along active plate boundaries. There are two major mountain systems. The **Circum-Pacific** encircles the entire Pacific Ocean, from New Guinea up across Japan and the Aleutians and down to southern South America. The **Alpine-Himalaya** stretches from northern Africa across the Alps and to the Himalayas and Indonesia. **Orogeny** is the term for the process of natural mountain formation. Therefore, physical mountains are orogens. **Folded mountains** are created through the folding of rock layers when two crustal plates come together. The Alps and Himalayas are folded mountains. The latter was formed by the collision of India with Asia. **Fault-block mountains** are created from the tension forces of plate movements. These produce faults that vertically displace one section to form a mountain. **Dome mountains** are created from magma pushing up through the earth's crust.

Volcanoes and Volcanic Mountains

Volcanoes are classified according to their activity level. An **active** volcano is in the process of erupting or building to an eruption; a dormant volcano has erupted before and may erupt again someday, but is not currently active; and an **extinct** volcano has died out volcanically and will not

Copyright © Mometrix Media. You have been licensed one copy of this document for personal use only. Any other reproduction or redistribution is strictly prohibited. All rights reserved.

erupt ever again. Active volcanoes endanger plant and animal life, but lava and ash add enriching minerals to the soil. There are three types of volcanic mountains:

- **Shield volcanoes** are the largest volcanic mountains because of a repeated, viscous lava flow from small eruptions over a long period of time that cause the mountain to grow.
- **Cinder cone volcanoes**, or linear volcanoes, are small in size, but have massive explosions through linear shafts that spread cinders and ash around the vent. This results in a cone-shaped hill.
- **Composite volcanoes** get their name from the mix of lava and ash layers that build the mountain.

Subdivisions of Rock

The three major subdivisions of rock are:

- **Igneous** (magmatites) – This type is formed from the cooling of liquid magma. In the process, minerals crystallize and amalgamate. If solidification occurs deep in the earth (plutonic rock), the cooling process is slow. This allows for the formation of large crystals, giving rock a coarse-grained texture (granite). Quickly cooled magma has a glassy texture (obsidian).
- **Metamorphic** – Under conditions of high temperature and pressure within the earth's crust, rock material melts and changes structure, transitioning or metamorphosing into a new type of rock with different minerals. If the minerals appear in bands, the rock is foliated. Examples include marble (unfoliated) and slate (foliated).
- **Sedimentary** – This is the most common type of rock on earth. It is formed by sedimentation, compaction, and then cementation of many small particles of mineral, animal, or plant material. There are three types of sedimentary rocks: clastic, clay, and sand that came from disintegrated rocks; chemical (rock salt and gypsum), formed by evaporation of aqueous solutions; and biogenic (coal), formed from animal or plant remnants.

Review Video: Igneous, Sedimentary, and Metamorphic Rocks
Visit mometrix.com/academy and enter code: 689294

Glaciers

Glaciers start high in the mountains, where snow and ice accumulate inside a cirque (a small semicircular depression). The snow becomes firmly packed into masses of coarse-grained ice that are slowly pulled down a slope by gravity. Glaciers grow with large amounts of snowfall and retreat (diminish) if warm weather melts more ice than can be replaced. Glaciers once covered large areas of both the northern and southern hemispheres with mile-thick ice that carved out valleys, fjords, and other land formations. They also moved plants, animals, and rocks from one area to another. There were two types of glaciers: **valley**, which produced U-shaped erosion and sharp-peaked mountains; and **continental**, which moved over and rounded mountain tops and ridges. These glaciers existed during the ice ages, the last of which occurred from 2.5 million years ago to 12,000 years ago.

Layers Above Surface of Earth Other Than Five Main Layers

The **ozone layer**, although contained within the stratosphere, is determined by ozone (O_3) concentrations. It absorbs the majority of ultraviolet light from the Sun. The ionosphere is part of

Copyright © Mometrix Media. You have been licensed one copy of this document for personal use only. Any other reproduction or redistribution is strictly prohibited. All rights reserved.

both the exosphere and the thermosphere. It is characterized by the fact that it is a plasma, a partially ionized gas in which free electrons and positive ions are attracted to each other, but are too energetic to remain fixed as a molecule. It starts at about 50 km above Earth's surface and goes to 1,000 km. It affects radio wave transmission and auroras. The ionosphere pushes against the inner edge of the Earth's magnetosphere, which is the highly magnetized, non-spherical region around the Earth. The homosphere encompasses the troposphere, stratosphere, and mesosphere. Gases in the homosphere are considered well mixed. In the heterosphere, the distance that particles can move without colliding is large. As a result, gases are stratified according to their molecular weights. Heavier gases such as oxygen and nitrogen occur near the bottom of the heterosphere, while hydrogen, the lightest element, is found at the top.

Tropospheric Circulation

Most weather takes place in the **troposphere**. Air circulates in the atmosphere by convection and in various types of "cells." Air near the equator is warmed by the Sun and rises. Cool air rushes under it, and the higher, warmer air flows toward Earth's poles. At the poles, it cools and descends to the surface. It is now under the hot air, and flows back to the equator. Air currents coupled with ocean currents move heat around the planet, creating winds, weather, and climate. Winds can change direction with the seasons. For example, in Southeast Asia and India, summer monsoons are caused by air being heated by the Sun. This air rises, draws moisture from the ocean, and causes daily rains. In winter, the air cools, sinks, pushes the moist air away, and creates dry weather.

Common Weather Phenomena and Equipment to Measure Them

Common **atmospheric conditions** that are frequently measured are temperature, precipitation, wind, and humidity. These weather conditions are often measured at permanently fixed **weather stations** so weather data can be collected and compared over time and by region. Measurements may also be taken by ships, buoys, and underwater instruments. Measurements may also be taken under special circumstances. The measurements taken include temperature, barometric pressure, humidity, wind speed, wind direction, and precipitation. Usually, the following instruments are used: A *thermometer* is used for measuring temperature; a *barometer* is used for measuring barometric/air pressure; a *hygrometer* is used for measuring humidity; an *anemometer* is used for measuring wind speed; a *weather vane* is used for measuring wind direction; and a *rain gauge* is used for measuring precipitation.

Weather, Climate, and Meteorology

Meteorology is the study of the atmosphere, particularly as it pertains to forecasting the weather and understanding its processes. **Weather** is the condition of the atmosphere at any given moment. Most weather occurs in the troposphere. Weather includes changing events such as clouds, storms, and temperature, as well as more extreme events such as tornadoes, hurricanes, and blizzards. **Climate** refers to the average weather for a particular area over time, typically at least 30 years. Latitude is an indicator of climate. Changes in climate occur over long time periods.

Review Video: Weather vs. Climate
Visit mometrix.com/academy and enter code: 237380

Winds and Global Wind Belts

Winds are the result of air moving by convection. Masses of warm air rise, and cold air sweeps into their place. The warm air also moves, cools, and sinks. The term "prevailing wind" refers to the

Copyright © Mometrix Media. You have been licensed one copy of this document for personal use only. Any other reproduction or redistribution is strictly prohibited. All rights reserved.

wind that usually blows in an area in a single direction. *Dominant winds* are the winds with the highest speeds. Belts or bands that run latitudinally and blow in a specific direction are associated with *convection cells*. *Hadley cells* are formed directly north and south of the equator. The *Farrell cells* occur at about 30° to 60°. The jet stream runs between the Farrell cells and the polar cells. At the higher and lower latitudes, the direction is easterly. At mid latitudes, the direction is westerly. From the North Pole to the south, the surface winds are Polar High Easterlies, Subpolar Low Westerlies, Subtropical High or Horse Latitudes, North-East Trade winds, Equatorial Low or Doldrums, South-East Trades, Subtropical High or Horse Latitudes, Subpolar Low Easterlies, and Polar High.

Relative Humidity, Absolute Humidity, and Dew Point Temperature

Humidity refers to water vapor contained in the air. The amount of moisture contained in air depends upon its temperature. The higher the air temperature, the more moisture it can hold. These higher levels of moisture are associated with higher humidity. **Absolute humidity** refers to the total amount of moisture air is capable of holding at a certain temperature. **Relative humidity** is the ratio of water vapor in the air compared to the amount the air is capable of holding at its current temperature. As temperature decreases, absolute humidity stays the same and relative humidity increases. A hygrometer is a device used to measure humidity. The **dew point** is the temperature at which water vapor condenses into water at a particular humidity.

Precipitation

After clouds reach the dew point, **precipitation** occurs. Precipitation can take the form of a liquid or a solid. It is known by many names, including rain, snow, ice, dew, and frost. **Liquid** forms of precipitation include rain and drizzle. Rain or drizzle that freezes on contact is known as freezing rain or freezing drizzle. **Solid or frozen** forms of precipitation include snow, ice needles or diamond dust, sleet or ice pellets, hail, and graupel or snow pellets. Virga is a form of precipitation that evaporates before reaching the ground. It usually looks like sheets or shafts falling from a cloud. The amount of rainfall is measured with a rain gauge. Intensity can be measured according to how fast precipitation is falling or by how severely it limits visibility. Precipitation plays a major role in the water cycle since it is responsible for depositing much of the Earth's fresh water.

Clouds

Clouds form when air cools and warm air is forced to give up some of its water vapor because it can no longer hold it. This vapor condenses and forms tiny droplets of water or ice crystals called clouds. Particles, or aerosols, are needed for water vapor to form water droplets. These are called **condensation nuclei**. Clouds are created by surface heating, mountains and terrain, rising air masses, and weather fronts. Clouds precipitate, returning the water they contain to Earth. Clouds can also create atmospheric optics. They can scatter light, creating colorful phenomena such as rainbows, colorful sunsets, and the green flash phenomenon.

Review Video: Clouds
Visit mometrix.com/academy and enter code: 803166

High, Middle, and Low Cloud Types

Most clouds can be classified according to the altitude of their base above Earth's surface. **High clouds** occur at altitudes between 5,000 and 13,000 meters. **Middle clouds** occur at altitudes between 2,000 and 7,000 meters. **Low clouds** occur from the Earth's surface to altitudes of 2,000

Copyright © Mometrix Media. You have been licensed one copy of this document for personal use only. Any other reproduction or redistribution is strictly prohibited. All rights reserved.

meters. Types of high clouds include cirrus (Ci), thin wispy mare's tails that consist of ice; cirrocumulus (Cc), small, pillow-like puffs that often appear in rows; and cirrostratus (Cs), thin, sheet-like clouds that often cover the entire sky. Types of middle clouds include altocumulus (Ac), gray-white clouds that consist of liquid water; and altostratus (As), grayish or blue-gray clouds that span the sky. Types of low clouds include stratus (St), gray and fog-like clouds consisting of water droplets that take up the whole sky; stratocumulus (Sc), low-lying, lumpy gray clouds; and nimbostratus (Ns), dark gray clouds with uneven bases that indicate rain or snow. Two types of clouds, cumulus (Cu) and cumulonimbus (Cb), are capable of great vertical growth. They can start at a wide range of altitudes, from the Earth's surface to altitudes of 13,000 meters.

Air Masses

Air masses are large volumes of air in the troposphere of the Earth. They are categorized by their temperature and by the amount of water vapor they contain. *Arctic* and *Antarctic* air masses are cold, polar air masses are cool, and tropical and equatorial air masses are hot. Other types of air masses include *maritime* and *monsoon*, both of which are moist and unstable. There are also *continental* and *superior* air masses, which are dry. A **weather front** separates two masses of air of different densities. It is the principal cause of meteorological phenomena. Air masses are quickly and easily affected by the land they are above. They can have certain characteristics, and then develop new ones when they get blown over a different area.

Weather Fronts and Weather Maps

A **weather front** is the area between two differing masses of air that affects weather. Frontal movements are influenced by the jet stream and other high winds. Movements are determined by the type of front. Cold fronts move up to twice as fast as warm ones. It is in the turbulent frontal area that commonplace and dramatic weather events take place. This area also creates temperature changes. Weather phenomena include rain, thunderstorms, high winds, tornadoes, cloudiness, clear skies, and hurricanes. Different fronts can be plotted on weather maps using a set of designated symbols. Surface weather maps can also include symbols representing clouds, rain, temperature, air pressure, and fair weather.

Astronomy

Astronomy is the scientific study of celestial objects and their positions, movements, and structures. *Celestial* does not refer to the Earth in particular, but does include its motions as it moves through space. Other objects include the Sun, the Moon, planets, satellites, asteroids, meteors, comets, stars, galaxies, the universe, and other space phenomena. The term astronomy has its roots in the Greek words "astro" and "nomos," which means "laws of the stars."

Review Video: Astronomy
Visit mometrix.com/academy and enter code: 640556

Universe

Origin

The **universe** can be said to consist of everything and nothing. The universe is the source of everything we know about space, matter, energy, and time. There are likely still phenomena that have yet to be discovered. The universe can also be thought of as nothing, since a vast portion of the known universe is empty space. It is believed that the universe is expanding. The *Big Bang theory*, which is widely accepted among astronomers, was developed to explain the origin of the universe.

Copyright © Mometrix Media. You have been licensed one copy of this document for personal use only. Any other reproduction or redistribution is strictly prohibited. All rights reserved.

There are other theories regarding the origin of the universe, such as the *Steady-State theory* and the *Creationist theory*. The Big Bang theory states that all the matter in the universe was once in one place. This matter underwent a huge explosion that spread the matter into space. Galaxies formed from this material and the universe is still expanding.

Structure

What can be seen of the universe is believed to be at least 93 billion light years across. To put this into perspective, the Milky Way galaxy is about 100,000 light years across. Our view of matter in the universe is that it forms into clumps. Matter is organized into stars, galaxies, clusters of galaxies, superclusters, and the Great Wall of galaxies. **Galaxies** consist of stars, some with planetary systems. Some estimates state that the universe is about 13 billion years old. It is not considered dense, and is believed to consist of 73 percent dark energy, 23 percent cold dark matter, and 4 percent regular matter. Cosmology is the study of the universe. Interstellar medium (ISM) is the gas and dust in the interstellar space between a galaxy's stars.

Galaxies

Galaxies consist of stars, stellar remnants, and dark matter. **Dwarf galaxies** contain as few as 10 million stars, while giant galaxies contain as many as 1 trillion stars. Galaxies are gravitationally bound, meaning the stars, star systems, other gases, and dust orbits the galaxy's center. The Earth exists in the **Milky Way galaxy** and the nearest galaxy to ours is the **Andromeda galaxy**. Galaxies can be classified by their visual shape into elliptical, spiral, irregular, and starburst galaxies. It is estimated that there are more than 100 billion galaxies in the universe ranging from 1,000 to 100,000 parsecs in diameter. Galaxies can be megaparsecs apart. Intergalactic space consists of a gas with an average density of less than one atom per cubic meter. Galaxies are organized into clusters which form superclusters. Dark matter may account for up to 90% of the mass of galaxies. Dark matter is still not well understood.

Review Video: Galaxies
Visit mometrix.com/academy and enter code: 226539

Planets

In order of their distance from the sun (closest to furthest away), the **planets** are: Mercury, Venus, Earth, Mars, Jupiter, Saturn, Uranus, and Neptune (Pluto is now considered to be a dwarf planet). All the planets revolve around the sun, which is an average-sized star in the spiral Milky Way galaxy. They revolve in the same direction in nearly circular orbits. If the planets were viewed by looking down from the sun, they would rotate in a counter-clockwise direction. All the planets are in or near the same plane, called the ecliptic, and the axis of rotation is nearly perpendicular to the ecliptic. The only exception is Uranus, which is tipped on its side.

Terrestrial Planets, Jovian Planets, and Mass of Planets

The **Terrestrial Planets** are: Mercury, Venus, Earth, and Mars. These are the four planets closest to the sun. They are called terrestrial because they all have a compact, rocky surface similar to the Earth's. Venus, Earth, and Mars have significant atmospheres, but Mercury has almost no atmosphere.

The **Jovian Planets** are: Jupiter (the largest planet), Saturn, Uranus, and Neptune. They are called Jovian (Jupiter-like) because of their huge sizes in relation to that of the Earth, and because they all have a gaseous nature like Jupiter. Although gas giants, some or all of the Jovian Planets may have small, solid cores.

Copyright © Mometrix Media. You have been licensed one copy of this document for personal use only. Any other reproduction or redistribution is strictly prohibited. All rights reserved.

Pluto does not have the characteristics necessary to fit into either the Terrestrial or the Jovian group, and is no longer considered to be a planet. The sun represents 99.85% of all the matter in our solar system. Combined, the planets make up only 0.135% of the mass of the solar system, with Jupiter having twice the mass of all the other planets combined. The remaining 0.015% of the mass comes from comets, planetary satellites, asteroids, meteoroids, and interplanetary medium.

Definition of Planet

On August 24, 2006, the International Astronomical Union redefined the criteria a body must meet to be classified as a planet, stating that the following conditions must be met:

- "A planet orbits around a star and is neither a star nor a moon."
- "Its shape is spherical due to its gravity."
- "It has 'cleared' the space of its orbit."

A **dwarf planet** such as Pluto does not meet the third condition. Small solar system bodies such as asteroids and comets meet only the first condition.

Solar System

The **solar system** developed about 4.6 billion years ago out of an enormous cloud of dust and gas circling around the sun. Four rocky planets orbit relatively close to the sun. Their inside orbit is separated from the outside orbit of the four, larger gaseous planets by an asteroid belt. Pluto, some comets, and several small objects circle in the Kuiper belt outside Neptune's orbit. The Oort cloud, composed of icy space objects, encloses the planetary system like a shell.

Review Video: Solar System
Visit mometrix.com/academy and enter code: 273231

Review Video: The Inner Planets of Our Solar System
Visit mometrix.com/academy and enter code: 103427

Review Video: The Outer Planets of Our Solar System
Visit mometrix.com/academy and enter code: 683995

Earth's Moon

Earth's **moon** is the closest celestial body to earth. Its proximity has allowed it to be studied since the invention of the telescope. As a result, its landforms have been named after astronomers, philosophers, and other scholars. Its surface has many craters created by asteroids since it has no protective atmosphere. These dark lowlands looked like seas to early astronomers, but there is virtually no water on the moon except possibly in its polar regions. These impact craters and depressions actually contain solidified lava flows. The bright highlands were thought to be continents, and were named terrae. The rocks of the moon have been pounded by asteroids so often that there is a layer of rubble and dust called the regolith. Also, because there is no protective atmosphere, temperatures on the moon vary widely, from 265°F to -255°F.

Earth's Sun and Other Stars

A **star** begins as a cloud of hydrogen and some heavier elements drawn together by their own mass. This matter then begins to rotate. The core heats up to several million degrees Fahrenheit, which causes the hydrogen atoms to lose their shells and their nuclei to fuse. This releases enormous amounts of energy. The star then becomes stable, a stage called the **main sequence**. This is the

Copyright © Mometrix Media. You have been licensed one copy of this document for personal use only. Any other reproduction or redistribution is strictly prohibited. All rights reserved.

stage our sun is in, and it will remain in this stage until its supply of hydrogen fuel runs out. Stars are not always alone like our sun, and may exist in pairs or groups. The hottest stars shine blue-white; medium-hot stars like our sun glow yellow; and cooler stars appear orange. The earth's sun is an **average star** in terms of mass, light production, and size. All stars, including our sun, have a **core** where fusion happens; a **photosphere** (surface) that produces sunspots (cool, dark areas); a red **chromosphere** that emits solar (bright) flares and shooting gases; and a **corona**, the transparent area only seen during an eclipse.

Review Video: The Sun
Visit mometrix.com/academy and enter code: 699233

Comets, Asteroids, and Meteoroids

Comets are celestial bodies composed of dust, rock, frozen gases, and ice. Invisible until they near the sun, the heat causes them to emit volatile components in jets of gas and dust. The **coma** is the comet's fog-like envelope that glows as it reflects sunlight and releases radiation. **Solar winds** blow a comet away from the sun and give it a tail of dust or electrically charged molecules. Each orbit of a comet causes it to lose matter until it breaks up or vaporizes into the sun.

Asteroids are irregularly-shaped boulders, usually less than 60 miles in diameter, that orbit the sun. Most are made of graphite; about 25% are silicates, or iron and nickel. Collisions or gravitational forces can cause them to fly off and possibly hit a planet.

Meteoroids are fragments of asteroids of various sizes. If they come through earth's atmosphere, they are called meteors or shooting stars. If they land on earth, they are called meteorites, and create craters on impact (the Barringer Crater in Arizona).

Review Video: Meteoroids, Meteors, and Meteorites
Visit mometrix.com/academy and enter code: 454866

Biology

Subfields of Biology

There are a number of subfields of biology:

- **Zoology** – The study of animals
- **Botany** – The study of plants
- **Biophysics** – The application of the laws of physics to the processes of organisms and the application of the facts about living things to human processes and inventions
- **Biochemistry** – The study of the chemistry of living organisms, including diseases and the pharmaceutical drugs used to cure them
- **Cytology** – The study of cells
- **Histology** – The study of the tissues of plants and animals
- **Organology** – The study of tissues organized into organs
- **Physiology** – The study of the way organisms function, including metabolism, the exchange of matter and energy in nutrition, the senses, reproduction and development, and the work of the nervous system and brain
- **Genetics** – The study of heredity as it relates to the transmission of genes

Copyright © Mometrix Media. You have been licensed one copy of this document for personal use only. Any other reproduction or redistribution is strictly prohibited. All rights reserved.

- **Ethology** – The study of animal behavior
- **Ecology** – The study of the relationship of living organisms to their environments

Kingdoms of Life Forms

All living creatures can be classified into one of these kingdoms:

- **The Moneran Kingdom** – This group contains the simplest known organisms (prokaryotes). Members have just one chromosome, reproduce asexually, may have flagella, and are very simple in form. Members are either bacteria or blue-green algae.
- **The Protist Kingdom** – This group contains the simplest eukaryotes. They have a true nucleus surrounded by a membrane that separates it from the cytoplasm. Most are one-celled and have no complex tissues like plants. Members include protozoa and algae.
- **The Fungi Kingdom** – Members have no chlorophyll, so they don't make their own food like plants. They reproduce using spores. Fungi are made up of filaments called hyphae that, in larger fungi, can interlace to form a tissue called mycelium. Fungi include mushrooms and microscopic organisms that may be parasitic.
- **The Plant Kingdom** – This group consists of all multi-celled organisms that have chlorophyll and make their own food. Plants have differentiated tissues and reproduce either sexually or asexually.
- **The Animal Kingdom** – This group consists of all multi-celled organisms that have no chlorophyll and have to feed on existing organic material. Animals have the most complex tissues and can move about.

Review Video: Kingdom Animalia
Visit mometrix.com/academy and enter code: 558413

Review Video: Kingdom Fungi
Visit mometrix.com/academy and enter code: 315081

Review Video: Kingdom Plantae
Visit mometrix.com/academy and enter code: 710084

Characteristics of Invertebrates

Invertebrates are animals with no internal skeletons. They can be divided into three groups:

1. **Marine Invertebrates** – Members of this group live in oceans and seas. Marine invertebrates include sponges, corals, jellyfish, snails, clams, octopuses, squids, and crustaceans, none of which live on the surface.
2. **Freshwater Invertebrates** – Members of this group live in lakes and rivers. Freshwater invertebrates include worms on the bottom, microscopic crustaceans, and terrestrial insect larvae that live in the water column, but only where there is no strong current. Some live on the surface of the water.
3. **Terrestrial Invertebrates** – Members of this group live on dry ground. Terrestrial invertebrates include insects, mollusks (snails, slugs), arachnids, and myriapods (centipedes and millipedes). Terrestrial invertebrates breathe through a series of tubes that penetrate into the body (trachea) and deliver oxygen into tissues. Underground terrestrial invertebrates are generally light-colored with atrophied eyes and no cuticle to protect them from desiccation. They include worms that live underground and in caves and rock crevices. This group also includes insects such as ants that create colonies underground.

Copyright © Mometrix Media. You have been licensed one copy of this document for personal use only. Any other reproduction or redistribution is strictly prohibited. All rights reserved.

Characteristics of Vertebrate Groups

The **vertebrates**, animals with an internal skeleton, are divided into four groups:

1. **Fish** – This group is the most primitive, but is also the group from which all other groups evolved. Fish live in water, breathe with gills, are cold-blooded, have fins and scales, and are typically oviparous. Fish typically have either cartilaginous skeletons (such as rays and sharks) or bony skeletons.
2. **Amphibians** – The skin of animals in this group is delicate and permeable, so they need water to keep it moist. Amphibians are oviparous. The young start out in water with gills, but the adults use lungs.
3. **Reptiles and birds** – The skin of animals in this group has very hard, horn-like scales. Birds have exchanged scales for feathers. Reptiles and birds are oviparous, although birds care for their eggs and reptiles do not. Members have a cloaca, an excretory and reproductive cavity that opens to the outside. Reptiles are cold-blooded, but birds are warm-blooded.
4. **Mammals** – These are the most highly evolved vertebrates. Mammals have bodies covered with fur; are warm-blooded; are viviparous, meaning they give birth to live young which are fed with milk from female mammary glands; and are tetrapods (four-legged). Most live on the ground (except whales and dolphins) and a few fly (bats).

Hunters and Prey Animals

The interaction between **predators** and their **prey** is important to controlling the balance of an ecosystem. **Hunters** are **carnivorous** animals at the top of the ecological pyramid that eat other animals. Hunters tend to be territorial, leaving signs to warn others to stay out or risk a fight. Hunters are equipped to capture with claws, curved beaks, spurs, fangs, etc. They try to use a minimum amount of energy for each capture, so they prey upon the more vulnerable (the old, ill, or very young) when given a choice. Predators never kill more than they can eat. Some hunters have great speed, some stalk, and some hunt in groups. **Prey** animals are those that are captured by predators for food. They are usually **herbivores** further down the ecological pyramid. Prey animals have special characteristics to help them flee from predators. They may hide in nests or caves, become totally immobile to escape detection, have protective coloration or camouflage, have warning coloration to indicate being poisonous, or have shells or quills for protection.

Life Processes That All Living Things Have in Common

Living things share many **processes** that are necessary to survival, but the ways these processes and interactions occur is highly diverse. Processes include those related to:

- **Nutrition** – the process of obtaining, ingesting, and digesting foods; excreting unused or excess substances; and extracting energy from the foods to maintain structure.
- **Transport** (circulation) – the process of circulating essential materials such as nutrients, cells, hormones, and gases (oxygen and hydrogen) to the places they are needed by moving them through veins, arteries, and capillaries. Needed materials do not travel alone, but are "piggybacked" on transporting molecules.
- **Respiration** – the process of breathing, which is exchanging gases between the interior and exterior using gills, trachea (insects), or lungs.
- **Regulation** – the process of coordinating life activities through the nervous and endocrine systems.

Copyright © Mometrix Media. You have been licensed one copy of this document for personal use only. Any other reproduction or redistribution is strictly prohibited. All rights reserved.

- **Reproduction and growth** – the process of producing more of one's own kind and growing from birth to adulthood. The more highly evolved an animal is, the longer its growth time is.
- **Locomotion** (in animals) – the process of moving from place to place in the environment by using legs, flight, or body motions.

Organisms That Interfere with Cell Activity

Viruses, bacteria, fungi, and other parasites may infect plants and animals and interfere with normal life functions, create imbalances, or disrupt the operations of cells.

- **Viruses** – These enter the body by inhalation (airborne) or through contact with contaminated food, water, or infected tissues. They affect the body by taking over the cell's protein synthesis mechanism to make more viruses. They kill the host cell and impact tissue and organ operations. Examples of viruses include measles, rabies, pneumonia, and AIDS.
- **Bacteria** – These enter the body through breaks in the skin or contaminated food or water, or by inhalation. They reproduce rapidly and produce toxins that kill healthy host tissues. Examples include diphtheria, bubonic plague, tuberculosis, and syphilis.
- **Fungi** – These feed on healthy tissues of the body by sending rootlike tendrils into the tissues to digest them extracellularly. Examples include athlete's foot and ringworm.
- **Parasites** – These enter the body through the skin, via insect bites, or through contaminated food or water. Examples include tapeworms, malaria, or typhus.

Hydrocarbons and Carbohydrates

Carbon is an element found in all living things. Two types of carbon molecules that are essential to life are hydrocarbons and carbohydrates. **Hydrocarbons**, composed only of hydrogen and carbon, are the simplest organic molecules. The simplest of these is methane, which has one carbon atom and four hydrogen atoms. Methane is produced by the decomposition of animal or vegetable matter, and is part of petroleum and natural gas. **Carbohydrates** are compounds made of hydrogen, carbon, and oxygen. There are three types of these macromolecules (large molecules):

1. **Sugars** are soluble in water and, although they have less energy than fats, provide energy more quickly.
2. **Starches**, insoluble in water, are long chains of glucose that act as reserve substances. Potatoes and cereals are valuable foods because they are rich in starch. Animals retain glucose in their cells as glucogen, a special type of starch.
3. **Cellulose**, composed of glucose chains, makes up the cells and tissues of plants. It is one of the most common organic materials.

Review Video: Basics of Hydrocarbons
Visit mometrix.com/academy and enter code: 824749

Lipids, Proteins, and Nucleic Acids

Besides hydrocarbons and carbohydrates, there are three other types of carbon molecules that are essential to life: lipids, proteins, and nucleic acids. **Lipids** are compounds that are insoluble or only partially soluble in water. There are three main types: fats, which act as an energy reserve for organisms; phospholipids, which are one of the essential components of cell membranes; and steroids such as cholesterol and estrogen, which are very important to metabolism. **Proteins** are complex substances that make up almost half the dry weight of animal bodies. These molecules contain hydrogen, carbon, oxygen, and other elements, chiefly nitrogen and sulfur. Proteins make

Copyright © Mometrix Media. You have been licensed one copy of this document for personal use only. Any other reproduction or redistribution is strictly prohibited. All rights reserved.

up muscle fibers and, as enzymes, act as catalysts. **Nucleic acids** are large molecules (polymers) composed of a large number of simpler molecules (nucleotides). Each one has a sugar containing five carbons (pentose), a phosphorous compound (phosphate group), and a nitrogen compound (nitrogenated base). Nucleic acids facilitate perpetuation of the species because they carry genetic information as DNA and RNA.

Cell

The **cell** is the basic organizational unit of all living things. Each piece within a cell has a function that helps organisms grow and survive. There are many different types of cells, but cells are unique to each type of organism. The one thing that all cells have in common is a **membrane**, which is comparable to a semi-permeable plastic bag. The membrane is composed of phospholipids. There are also some **transport holes**, which are proteins that help certain molecules and ions move in and out of the cell. The cell is filled with a fluid called **cytoplasm** or cytosol. Within the cell are a variety of **organelles**, groups of complex molecules that help a cell survive, each with its own unique membrane that has a different chemical makeup from the cell membrane. The larger the cell, the more organelles it will need to live.

Review Video: Plant and Animal Cells
Visit mometrix.com/academy and enter code: 115568

Nucleus and Mitochondria in Eukaryotic Cells

Eukaryotic cells have a nucleus, a big dark spot floating somewhere in the center that acts like the brain of the cell by controlling eating, movement, and reproduction. A **nuclear envelope** surrounds the nucleus and its contents, but allows RNA and proteins to pass through. **Chromatin**, made up of DNA, RNA, and nuclear proteins, is present in the nucleus. The nucleus also contains a nucleolus made of RNA and protein. **Mitochondria** are very small organelles that take in nutrients, break them down, and create energy for the cell through a process called cellular respiration. There might be thousands of mitochondria depending on the cell's purpose. A muscle cell needs more energy for movement than a cell that transmits nerve impulses, for example. Mitochondria have two membranes: a **cover** and the **inner cristae** that folds over many times to increase the surface work area. The fluid inside the mitochondria, the matrix, is filled with water and enzymes that take food molecules and combine them with oxygen so they can be digested.

Review Video: Mitochondria
Visit mometrix.com/academy and enter code: 444287

Chloroplasts of Plant Cells

Chloroplasts, which make plants green, are the food producers of a plant cell. They differ from an animal cell's mitochondria, which break down sugars and nutrients. **Photosynthesis** occurs when the energy from the sun hits a chloroplast and the chlorophyll uses that energy to combine carbon dioxide and water to make sugars and oxygen. The nutrition and oxygen obtained from plants makes them the basis of all life on earth. A chloroplast has two membranes to contain and protect the inner parts. The **stroma** is an area inside the chloroplast where reactions occur and starches are created. A **thylakoid** has chlorophyll molecules on its surface, and a stack of thylakoids is called a granum. The stacks of sacs are connected by **stromal lamellae**, which act like the skeleton of the chloroplast, keeping all the sacs a safe distance from each other and maximizing the efficiency of the organelle.

Copyright © Mometrix Media. You have been licensed one copy of this document for personal use only. Any other reproduction or redistribution is strictly prohibited. All rights reserved.

Passive and Active Transport

Passive transport within a cell does not require energy and work. For example, when there is a large concentration difference between the outside and the inside of a cell, the pressure of the greater concentration, not energy, will move molecules across the lipid bilayer into the cell. Another example of passive transport is osmosis, which is the movement of water across a membrane. Too much water in a cell can cause it to burst, so the cell moves ions in and out to help equalize the amount of water. **Active transport** is when a cell uses energy to move individual molecules across the cell membrane to maintain a proper balance. **Proteins** embedded in the lipid bilayer do most of the transport work. There are hundreds of different types of proteins because they are specific. For instance, a protein that moves glucose will not move calcium. The activity of these proteins can be stopped by inhibitors or poisons, which can destroy or plug up a protein.

Mitotic Cell Replication

Mitosis is the duplication of a cell and all its parts, including the DNA, into two identical daughter cells. There are five phases in the life cycle of a cell:

1. **Prophase** – This is the process of duplicating everything in preparation for division.
2. **Metaphase** – The cell's different pieces align themselves for the split. The DNA lines up along a central axis and the centrioles send out specialized tubules that connect to the centromere. The centromere has two strands of a chromosome (condensed DNA) attached to it.
3. **Anaphase** – Half of the chromosomes go one way and half go another.
4. **Telophase** – When the chromosomes get to the side of the cell, the cell membrane closes in and splits the cell into two pieces. This results in two separate cells, each with half of the original DNA.
5. **Interphase** – This is the normal state of the cell, or the resting stage between divisions. During this stage, the cell duplicates nucleic acids in preparation for the next division.

Microbes

Microbes are the smallest, simplest, and most abundant organisms on earth. Their numbers are incalculable, and a microscope is required to see them. There is a huge variety of microbes, including bacteria, fungi, some algae, and protozoa. Microbes can be harmful or helpful.

Microbes can be **heterotrophic** (eat other things) or **autotrophic** (make food for themselves). They can be solitary or colonial, sexual or asexual. Examples include mold, a multi-cellular type of fungus, and yeasts, which are single-celled (but may live in colonies). A **mushroom** is a fungus that lives as a group of strands underground called hyphae that decompose leaves or bark on the ground. When it reproduces, it develops a mushroom whose cap contains spores. **Mold** is a type of zygote fungi that reproduces with a stalk, but releases zygospores. **Good bacteria** can be those that help plants absorb the nitrogen needed for growth or help grazing animals break down the cellulose in plants. Some **bad bacteria** are killed by the penicillin developed from a fungus.

Roots, Stems, and Leaves

Roots are structures designed to pull water and minerals from soil or water. In large plants such as trees, the roots usually go deep into the ground to not only reach the water, but also to support and stabilize the tree. There are some plant species that have roots above ground, and there are also plants called epiphytes that live in trees with their roots clinging to the branches. Some roots, like carrots and turnips, serve as food. Roots are classified as **primary** and **lateral** (like a trunk and

Copyright © Mometrix Media. You have been licensed one copy of this document for personal use only. Any other reproduction or redistribution is strictly prohibited. All rights reserved.

branches). The **apical meristem** is the tip of a root or shoot that helps the plant increase in length. **Root hairs** are fuzzy root extensions that help with the absorption of water and nutrients. The majority of the plant above ground is made up of the stems (trunk and branches) and leaves. **Stems** transport food and water and act as support structures. **Leaves** are the site for photosynthesis, and are connected to the rest of the plant by a vascular system.

Gymnosperms, Cycads, and Conifers

Gymnosperms are plants with vascular systems and seeds but no flowers (flowers are an evolutionary advancement). The function of the seed is to ensure offspring can be produced by the plant by providing a protective coating that lets the plant survive for long periods until it germinates. It also stores food for the new plant to use until it can make its own. Seeds can be spread over a wide area. **Cycads** are sturdy plants with big, waxy fronds that make them look like ferns or palms. They can survive in harsh conditions if there is warm weather. For reproduction, they have big cones located in the center of the plant. The female plant grows a fruit in the middle of the stem. **Conifers** are trees that thrive in northern latitudes and have cones. Examples of conifers are pine, cedar, redwood, and spruce. Conifers are evergreens because they have needles that take full advantage of the sun year-round. They are also very tall and strong because of the chemical substance xylem in their systems.

Angiosperms

Angiosperms are plants that have flowers. This is advantageous because the plant's seeds and pollen can be spread not only by gravity and wind, but also by insects and animals. Flowers are able to attract organisms that can help pollinate the plant and distribute seeds. Some flowering plants also produce fruit. When an animal eats the fruit, the plant seeds within will be spread far and wide in the animal's excrement. There are two kinds of angiosperm seeds: monocotyledons (monocots) and dicotyledons (dicots). A **cotyledon** is the seed leaf or food package for the developing plant. **Monocots** are the simple flowering plants such as grasses, corn, palm trees, and lilies. They always have three petals on their flowers, and their leaves are long strands (like a palm frond). A **dicot** has seeds with two cotyledons, or two seed leaves of food. Most everyday flowers are dicots with four or five petals and extremely complex leaves with veins. Examples include roses, sunflowers, cacti, and cherry trees.

Arthropods

Arthropods have a number of unique characteristics:

- They have an **exoskeleton** (outside instead of inside).
- They **molt**. As the arthropod grows, it must shed its old shell and grow a new one.
- They have several **legs**, which are jointed.
- Their advanced **nervous systems** allow for hunting, moving around, finding a mate, and learning new behaviors for adaptation.
- They develop through **metamorphosis**. As arthropods develop, they change body shape. There are two types of metamorphosis:
- *Complete* – The entire body shape changes. An example is butterflies, which change from worm-like larvae to insects with wings.
- *Gradual* – The arthropod starts off small with no wings, and then molts and grows wings. Example: Grasshoppers.

Copyright © Mometrix Media. You have been licensed one copy of this document for personal use only. Any other reproduction or redistribution is strictly prohibited. All rights reserved.

Arthropods include spiders, crustaceans, and the enormous insect species (26 orders) called uniramians. Ranging from fleas to mosquitoes, beetles, dragonflies, aphids, bees, flies, and many more, uniramians have exoskeletons made of chitin, compound eyes, complex digestive systems, and usually six legs. This group is extremely diverse. Some can fly, some have toxins or antennae, and some can make wax, silk, or honey.

Review Video: Arthropoda
Visit mometrix.com/academy and enter code: 523466

Reptiles

One group of vertebrates is the **reptile**. This group includes:

- **Crocodilia** – This is a group of reptiles that can grow quite large, and includes alligators and crocodiles. Normally found near the water in warmer climates, Crocodilia might be more closely related to birds than other reptiles.
- **Squamata** – This is the order of reptiles that includes snakes and lizards. Snakes are special because they have no legs and no ears. They feel vibrations, smell with their tongues, have specialized scales, and can unhinge their jaws to swallow prey that is larger than they are. Like snakes, lizards have scales, but they differ in that they have legs, can dig, can climb trees, and can grab things.
- **Chelonia** – This is the order of reptiles that includes turtles and tortoises. It is a special group because its members have shells. Different varieties live in forests, water, and deserts, or anywhere the climate is warm enough. They also live a long time, even hundreds of years. Turtles are typically found near water and tortoises on land, even dry areas.

Reproduction in Mammals

When classified according to how they reproduce, there are three types of mammals:

1. **Monotremes** are rare mammals that lay eggs. These were the first mammals, and are more closely related to reptiles than other mammals. Examples include the duck-billed platypus and the spiny anteater.
2. **Marsupials** are special mammals. They give birth to live young, but the babies mature in pouches, where they are carried and can feed on milk. Many are found in Australia. The isolation of this island continent prevented placental mammals from taking hold. Examples of marsupials include kangaroos, possums, and koalas.
3. **Placental mammals** give birth from the females' placenta to live young. The young may be able to walk immediately, or they may need to be carried. They are still dependent on parental care for at least a short time. Placental mammals are the dominant form of mammals. Members of this group include cetaceans such as whales and dolphins, which are mammals that evolved but returned to the ocean.

Respiratory System

The **respiratory system** exchanges gases with the environment. Amphibians exchange gases through their moist skin and fish use gills, but mammals, birds, and reptiles have lungs. The human respiratory system is made up of the nose, mouth, pharynx, trachea, and two lungs. The purpose of the respiratory system is to bring oxygen into the body and expel carbon dioxide. The respiratory system can inhale viruses, bacteria, and dangerous chemicals, so it is vulnerable to toxins and diseases such as pneumonia, which causes the lungs to fill with fluid until they cannot take in

Copyright © Mometrix Media. You have been licensed one copy of this document for personal use only. Any other reproduction or redistribution is strictly prohibited. All rights reserved.

enough oxygen to support the body. **Emphysema**, often caused by smoking tobacco, destroys the tissues in the lungs, which cannot be regenerated. The respiratory system interacts with the **digestive system** in that the mouth and pharynx are used to swallow food and drink, as well as to breathe. It interacts with the circulatory system in that it provides fresh oxygen through blood vessels that pass through the lungs. This oxygen is then carried by the circulatory system throughout the body.

Skeletal System

The human body has an **endoskeleton**, meaning it is inside the body. It is made up of bones instead of the hard plate of exoskeletons or fluids in tubes, which comprise the hydrostatic system of the starfish. The purpose of the skeleton is to support the body, provide a framework to which the muscles and organs can connect, and protect the inner organs. The skull protects the all-important brain and the ribs protect the internal organs from impact. The skeletal system interacts with the muscular system to help the body move, and softer cartilage works with the calcified bone to allow smooth movement of the body. The skeletal system also interacts with the circulatory system in that the marrow inside the bones helps produce both white and red blood cells.

Nervous System

The **nervous system** is divided into two parts: the **central nervous system** (brain and spinal cord) and the **peripheral nervous system** (a network of billions of neurons of different types throughout the entire body). The neurons are connected end to end, and transmit electrical impulses to each other. **Efferent neurons** send impulses from the central system to the limbs and organs. **Afferent neurons** receive sensory information and transmit it back to the central system. The nervous system is concerned with **senses and action**. In other words, it senses something and then acts upon it. An example is a predator sensing prey and attacking it. The nervous system also automatically senses activity inside the body and reacts to stimuli. For example, the first bite of a meal sets the whole digestive system into motion. The nervous system **interacts** with every other system in the body because all the tissues and organs need instruction, even when individuals are not aware of any activity occurring. For instance, the endocrine system is constantly working to produce hormones or adrenalin as needed.

Genetics, Genes, and Chromosomes

Genetics is the science devoted to the study of how characteristics are transmitted from one generation to another. In the 1800s, Gregor Mendel discovered the three laws of heredity that explain how genetics works. Genes are the hereditary units of material that are transmitted from one generation to the next. They are capable of undergoing mutations, can be recombined with other genes, and can determine the nature of an organism, including its color, shape, and size. **Genotype** is the genetic makeup of an individual based on one or more characteristics, while phenotype is the external manifestation of the genotype. For example, genotype can determine hair color, and phenotype is the actual color of the hair. **Chromosomes** are the structures inside the nucleus of a cell made up primarily of deoxyribonucleic acid (DNA) and proteins. The chromosomes

Copyright © Mometrix Media. You have been licensed one copy of this document for personal use only. Any other reproduction or redistribution is strictly prohibited. All rights reserved.

carry the genes. The numbers vary according to the species, but they are always the same for each species. For example, the human has 46 chromosomes, and the water lily has 112.

Review Video: Gene & Alleles
Visit mometrix.com/academy and enter code: 363997

Review Video: Genetic vs. Environmental Traits
Visit mometrix.com/academy and enter code: 750684

Mendel's Contributions to Genetics

Johann Gregor Mendel is known as the father of **genetics**. Mendel was an Austrian monk who performed thousands of experiments involving the breeding of the common pea plant in the monastery garden. Mendel kept detailed records including seed color, pod color, seed type, flower color, and plant height for eight years and published his work in 1865. Unfortunately, his work was largely ignored until the early 1900s. Mendel's work showed that genes come in pairs and that dominant and recessive traits are inherited independently of each other. His work established the law of segregation, the law of independent assortment, and the law of dominance.

Darwin's Contributions to the Theory of Evolution

Charles Darwin's theory of evolution is the unifying concept in biology today. From 1831 to 1836, Darwin traveled as a naturalist on a five-year voyage on the *H.M.S. Beagle* around the tip of South America and to the Galápagos Islands. He studied finches, took copious amounts of meticulous notes, and collected thousands of plant and animal specimens. He collected 13 species of finches each with a unique bill for a distinct food source, which led him to believe that due to similarities between the finches, that the finches shared a common ancestor. The similarities and differences of fossils of extinct rodents and modern mammal fossils led him to believe that the mammals had changed over time. Darwin believed that these changes were the result of random genetic changes called mutations. He believed that mutations could be beneficial and eventually result in a different organism over time. In 1859, in his first book, *On the Origin of Species*, Darwin proposed that natural selection was the means by which adaptations would arise over time. He coined the term "natural selection" and said that natural selection is the mechanism of evolution. Because variety exists among individuals of a species, he stated that those individuals must compete for the same limited resources. Some would die, and others would survive. According to Darwin, evolution is a slow, gradual process. In 1871, Darwin published his second book, *Descent of Man, and Selection in Relation to Sex*, in which he discussed the evolution of man.

Contribution to Genetics Made by Alfred Hershey and Martha Chase

Alfred Hershey and Martha Chase did a series of experiments in 1952 known as the **Hershey-Chase experiments**. These experiments showed that deoxyribonucleic acid (DNA), not protein, is the genetic material that transfers information for inheritance. The Hershey-Chase experiments used a bacteriophage, a virus that infects bacteria, to infect the bacteria *Escherichia coli.* The bacteriophage T2 is basically a small piece of DNA enclosed in a protein coating. The DNA contains phosphorus, and the protein coating contains sulfur. In the first set of experiments, the T2 was marked with radioactive phosphorus-32. In the second set of experiments, the T2 was marked with radioactive sulfur-35. For both sets of experiments, after the *E. coli* was infected by the T2, the *E. coli* was isolated using a centrifuge. In the first set of experiments, the radioactive isotope (P-32) was found in the *E. coli*, showing that the genetic information was transferred by the DNA. In the second set of experiments, the radioactive isotope (S-35) was not found in the *E. coli*, showing that the genetic

Copyright © Mometrix Media. You have been licensed one copy of this document for personal use only. Any other reproduction or redistribution is strictly prohibited. All rights reserved.

information was not transferred by the protein as was previously thought. Hershey and Chase conducted further experiments allowing the bacteria from the first set of experiments to reproduce, and the offspring was also found to contain the radioactive isotope (P-32) further confirming that the DNA transferred the genetic material.

Autotrophs, Producers, Herbivores, Carnivores, Omnivores, and Decomposers

Energy flows in one direction: from the sun, through photosynthetic organisms such as green plants (producers) and algae (autotrophs), and then to herbivores, carnivores, and decomposers. **Autotrophs** are organisms capable of producing their own food. The organic molecules they produce are food for all other organisms (heterotrophs). **Producers** are green plants that manufacture food by photosynthesis. **Herbivores** are animals that eat only plants (deer, rabbits, etc.). Since they are the first animals to receive the energy captured by producers, herbivores are called primary consumers. **Carnivores**, or secondary consumers, are animals that eat the bodies of other animals for food. Predators (wolves, lions, etc.) kill other animals, while scavengers consume animals that are already dead from predation or natural causes (buzzards). **Omnivores** are animals that eat both plants and other animals (humans). **Decomposers** include saprophytic fungi and bacteria that break down the complex structures of the bodies of living things into simpler forms that can be used by other living things. This recycling process releases energy from organic molecules.

Abiotic Factors and Biotic Factors

Abiotic factors are the physical and chemical factors in the environment that are nonliving, but upon which the growth and survival of living organisms depends. These factors can determine the types of plants and animals that will establish themselves and thrive in a particular area. Abiotic factors include:

- Light intensity available for photosynthesis
- Temperature range
- Available moisture
- Type of rock substratum
- Type of minerals
- Type of atmospheric gases
- Relative acidity (pH) of the system

Biotic factors are the living components of the environment that affect, directly or indirectly, the ecology of an area, possibly limiting the type and number of resident species. The relationships of predator/prey, producer/consumer, and parasite/host can define a community. Biotic factors include:

- Population levels of each species
- The food requirements of each species
- The interactions between species
- The wastes produced

How Plants Manufacture Food

Plants are the only organisms capable of transforming **inorganic material** from the environment into **organic matter** by using water and solar energy. This transformation is made possible by chloroplasts, flat structures inside plant cells. **Chloroplasts**, located primarily in the leaves, contain

Copyright © Mometrix Media. You have been licensed one copy of this document for personal use only. Any other reproduction or redistribution is strictly prohibited. All rights reserved.

chlorophyll (the pigment capable of absorbing light and storing it in chemical compounds), DNA, ribosomes, and numerous enzymes. Chloroplasts are surrounded by a membrane. The leaves of plants are the main producers of oxygen, which helps purify the air. The **chlorophyll** in chloroplasts is responsible for the light, or luminous, phase of photosynthesis. The energy it absorbs breaks down water absorbed through the roots into hydrogen and oxygen to form ATP molecules that store energy. In the dark phase, when the plant has no light, the energy molecules are used to attach carbon dioxide to water and form glucose, a sugar.

Producers, Consumers, and Decomposers

The **food chain**, or food web, is a series of events that happens when one organism consumes another to survive. Every organism is involved in dozens of connections with others, so what happens to one affects the environment of the others. In the food chain, there are three main categories:

- **Producers** – Plants and vegetables are at the beginning of the food chain because they take energy from the sun and make food for themselves through photosynthesis. They are food sources for other organisms.
- **Consumers** – There are three levels of consumers: the organisms that eat plants (primary consumers, or herbivores); the organisms that eat the primary consumers (secondary consumers, or carnivores); and, in some ecosystems, the organisms that eat both plants and animals (tertiary consumers, or omnivores).
- **Decomposers** – These are the organisms that eat dead things or waste matter and return the nutrients to the soil, thus returning essential molecules to the producers and completing the cycle.

System of Classification for Living Organisms

The main characteristic by which living organisms are classified is the degree to which they are **related**, not the degree to which they resemble each other. The science of classification is called **taxonomy**, a difficult science since the division lines between groups is not always clear. Some animals have characteristics of two separate groups. The basic system of taxonomy involves placing an organism into a major **kingdom** (Moneran, Protist, Fungi, Plants, and Animals), and then dividing those kingdoms into phyla, then classes, then orders, then families, and finally genuses. For example, the family cat is in the kingdom of animals, the phylum of chordates, the class of mammals, the order of carnivores, the family of felidae, and the genus of felis. All species of living beings can be identified with Latin scientific names that are assigned by the worldwide binomial system. The genus name comes first, and is followed by the name of the species. The family cat is *felis domesticus*. Although not part of taxonomy, **behavior** is also considered in identifying living beings. For example, birds are identified according to their songs or means of flight.

Properties That Contribute to Earth's Life-Sustaining System

Life on earth is dependent on:

- All three states of **water** – gas (water vapor), liquid, and solid (ice)
- A variety of forms of **carbon**, the basis of life (carbon-based units)
- In the atmosphere, carbon dioxide in the forms of methane and black carbon soot produce the **greenhouse effect** that provides a habitable atmosphere.
- The earth's **atmosphere and electromagnetic field**, which shield the surface from harmful radiation and allow useful radiation to go through

Copyright © Mometrix Media. You have been licensed one copy of this document for personal use only. Any other reproduction or redistribution is strictly prohibited. All rights reserved.

- The **earth's relationship to the sun and the moon**, which creates the four seasons and the cycles of plant and animal life
- The combination of **water, carbon, and nutrients**, which provides sustenance for life and regulates the climate system in a habitable temperature range with non-toxic air.

Chemistry

Atomic Number, Neutrons, Nucleon, and Element

- **Atomic number** (proton number) — The atomic number of an element refers to the number of protons in the nucleus of an atom. It is a unique identifier. It can be represented as Z. Atoms with a neutral charge have an atomic number that is equal to the number of electrons.
- **Neutrons** — Neutrons are the uncharged atomic particles contained within the nucleus. The number of neutrons in a nucleus can be represented as "N."
- **Nucleon** — This refers collectively to the neutrons and protons.
- **Element** — An element is matter with one particular type of atom. It can be identified by its atomic number, or the number of protons in its nucleus. There are approximately 117 elements currently known, 94 of which occur naturally on Earth. Elements from the periodic table include hydrogen, carbon, iron, helium, mercury, and oxygen.

Past Atomic Models and Theories

There have been many revisions to theories regarding the structure of **atoms** and their **particles**. Part of the challenge in developing an understanding of matter is that atoms and their particles are too small to be seen. It is believed that the first conceptualization of the atom was developed by **Democritus** in 400 B.C. Some of the more notable models are the solid sphere or billiard ball model postulated by John Dalton, the plum pudding or raisin bun model by J.J. Thomson, the planetary or nuclear model by Ernest Rutherford, the Bohr or orbit model by Niels Bohr, and the electron cloud or quantum mechanical model by Louis de Broglie and Erwin Schrodinger. Rutherford directed the alpha scattering experiment that discounted the plum pudding model. The shortcoming of the Bohr model was the belief that electrons orbited in fixed rather than changing ecliptic orbits.

Review Video: Atomic Models
Visit mometrix.com/academy and enter code: 434851

Structure of Atoms

All matter consists of **atoms**. Atoms consist of a nucleus and electrons. The **nucleus** consists of protons and neutrons. The properties of these are measurable; they have mass and an electrical charge. The nucleus is positively charged due to the presence of protons. **Electrons** are negatively charged and orbit the nucleus. The nucleus has considerably more mass than the surrounding electrons. Atoms can bond together to make **molecules**. Atoms that have an equal number of protons and electrons are electrically neutral. If the number of protons and electrons in an atom is not equal, the atom has a positive or negative charge and is an ion.

Models of Atoms

Atoms are extremely small. A hydrogen atom is about 5×10^{-8} mm in diameter. According to some estimates, five trillion hydrogen atoms could fit on the head of a pin. **Atomic radius** refers to the average distance between the nucleus and the outermost electron. Models of atoms that include the

Copyright © Mometrix Media. You have been licensed one copy of this document for personal use only. Any other reproduction or redistribution is strictly prohibited. All rights reserved.

proton, nucleus, and electrons typically show the electrons very close to the nucleus and revolving around it, similar to how the Earth orbits the sun. However, another model relates the Earth as the nucleus and its atmosphere as electrons, which is the basis of the term "**electron cloud**." Another description is that electrons swarm around the nucleus. It should be noted that these atomic models are not to scale. A more accurate representation would be a nucleus with a diameter of about 2 cm in a stadium. The electrons would be in the bleachers. This model is similar to the not-to-scale solar system model.

Atom, Nucleus, Electrons, and Protons

- **Atom** — The atom is one of the most basic units of matter. An atom consists of a central nucleus surrounded by electrons.
- **Nucleus** — The nucleus of an atom consists of protons and neutrons. It is positively charged, dense, and heavier than the surrounding electrons. The plural form of nucleus is nuclei.
- **Electrons** — These are atomic particles that are negatively charged and orbit the nucleus of an atom.
- **Protons** — Along with neutrons, protons make up the nucleus of an atom. The number of protons in the nucleus determines the atomic number of an element. Carbon atoms, for example, have six protons. The atomic number of carbon is 6. The number of protons also indicates the charge of an atom. The number of protons minus the number of electrons indicates the charge of an atom.

Molecules

Electrons in an atom can orbit different levels around the nucleus. They can absorb or release energy, which can change the location of their orbit or even allow them to break free from the atom. The outermost layer is the **valence layer**, which contains the valence electrons. The valence layer tends to have or share eight electrons. **Molecules** are formed by a chemical bond between atoms, a bond which occurs at the valence level. Two basic types of bonds are covalent and ionic. A **covalent bond** is formed when atoms share electrons. An **ionic bond** is formed when an atom transfers an electron to another atom. A **hydrogen bond** is a weak bond between a hydrogen atom of one molecule and an electronegative atom (such as nitrogen, oxygen, or fluorine) of another molecule. The **Van der Waals force** is a weak force between molecules. This type of force is much weaker than actual chemical bonds between atoms.

Interaction of Atoms to Form Compounds

Atoms interact by **transferring** or sharing the electrons furthest from the nucleus. Known as the outer or **valence electrons**, they are responsible for the chemical properties of an element. **Bonds** between atoms are created when electrons are paired up by being transferred or shared. If electrons are transferred from one atom to another, the bond is ionic. If electrons are shared, the bond is covalent. Atoms of the same element may bond together to form molecules or crystalline solids. When two or more different types of atoms bind together chemically, a compound is made. The physical properties of compounds reflect the nature of the interactions among their molecules. These interactions are determined by the structure of the molecule, including the atoms they consist of and the distances and angles between them.

Copyright © Mometrix Media. You have been licensed one copy of this document for personal use only. Any other reproduction or redistribution is strictly prohibited. All rights reserved.

Matter

Matter refers to substances that have mass and occupy space (or volume). The traditional definition of matter describes it as having three states: solid, liquid, and gas. These different states are caused by differences in the distances and angles between molecules or atoms, which result in differences in the energy that binds them. **Solid** structures are rigid or nearly rigid and have strong bonds. Molecules or atoms of **liquids** move around and have weak bonds, although they are not weak enough to readily break. Molecules or atoms of **gases** move almost independently of each other, are typically far apart, and do not form bonds. The current definition of matter describes it as having four states. The fourth is **plasma**, which is an ionized gas that has some electrons that are described as free because they are not bound to an atom or molecule.

Most Abundant Elements in the Universe and on Earth

Aside from dark energy and dark matter, which are thought to account for all but four percent of the universe, the two most abundant elements in the universe are **hydrogen** (H) and **helium** (He). After hydrogen and helium, the most abundant elements are oxygen, neon, nitrogen, carbon, silicon, and magnesium. The most abundant isotopes in the solar system are hydrogen-1 and helium-4. Measurements of the masses of elements in the Earth's crust indicate that oxygen (O), silicon (Si), and aluminum (Al) are the most abundant on Earth. Hydrogen in its plasma state is the most abundant chemical element in stars in their main sequences, but is relatively rare on planet Earth.

Energy Transformations

The following are some examples of energy transformations:

- Electric to mechanical: Ceiling fan
- **Chemical to heat**: A familiar example of a chemical to heat energy transformation is the internal combustion engine, which transforms the chemical energy (a type of potential energy) of gas and oxygen into heat. This heat is transformed into propulsive energy, which is kinetic. Lighting a match and burning coal are also examples of chemical to heat energy transformations.
- **Chemical to light**: Phosphorescence and luminescence (which allow objects to glow in the dark) occur because energy is absorbed by a substance (charged) and light is re-emitted comparatively slowly. This process is different from the one involved with glow sticks. They glow due to chemiluminescence, in which an excited state is created by a chemical reaction and transferred to another molecule.
- **Heat to electricity**: Examples include thermoelectric, geothermal, and ocean thermal.
- **Nuclear to heat**: Examples include nuclear reactors and power plants.
- **Mechanical to sound**: Playing a violin or almost any instrument
- Sound to electric: Microphone
- Light to electric: Solar panels
- Electric to light: Light bulbs

Relationship Between Conservation of Matter and Atomic Theory

Atomic theory is concerned with the characteristics and properties of atoms that make up matter. It deals with matter on a *microscopic level* as opposed to a *macroscopic level*. Atomic theory, for instance, discusses the kinetic motion of atoms in order to explain the properties of macroscopic quantities of matter. John Dalton (1766-1844) is credited with making many contributions to the field of atomic theory that are still considered valid. This includes the notion that all matter consists

Copyright © Mometrix Media. You have been licensed one copy of this document for personal use only. Any other reproduction or redistribution is strictly prohibited. All rights reserved.

of atoms and that atoms are indestructible. In other words, atoms can be neither created nor destroyed. This is also the theory behind the conservation of matter, which explains why chemical reactions do not result in any detectable gains or losses in matter. This holds true for chemical reactions and smaller scale processes. When dealing with large amounts of energy, however, atoms can be destroyed by nuclear reactions. This can happen in particle colliders or atom smashers.

Review Video: Chemical Reactions
Visit mometrix.com/academy and enter code: 579876

Review Video: John Dalton
Visit mometrix.com/academy and enter code: 565627

Review Video: Nuclear and Chemical Reactions
Visit mometrix.com/academy and enter code: 572819

Difference Between Atoms and Molecules

Elements from the periodic table such as hydrogen, carbon, iron, helium, mercury, and oxygen are **atoms**. Atoms combine to form molecules. For example, two atoms of hydrogen (H) and one atom of oxygen (O) combine to form one molecule of water (H_2O).

Chemical and Physical Properties

Matter has both physical and chemical properties. **Physical properties** can be seen or observed without changing the identity or composition of matter. For example, the mass, volume, and density of a substance can be determined without permanently changing the sample. Other physical properties include color, boiling point, freezing point, solubility, odor, hardness, electrical conductivity, thermal conductivity, ductility, and malleability. **Chemical properties** cannot be measured without changing the identity or composition of matter. Chemical properties describe how a substance reacts or changes to form a new substance. Examples of chemical properties include flammability, corrosivity, oxidation states, enthalpy of formation, and reactivity with other chemicals.

Chemical and Physical Changes

Physical changes do not produce new substances. The atoms or molecules may be rearranged, but no new substances are formed. Phase changes or changes of state such as melting, freezing, and sublimation are physical changes. For example, physical changes include the melting of ice, the boiling of water, sugar dissolving into water, and the crushing of a piece of chalk into a fine powder. **Chemical changes** involve a chemical reaction and do produce new substances. When iron rusts, iron oxide is formed, indicating a chemical change. Other examples of chemical changes include baking a cake, burning wood, digesting a cracker, and mixing an acid and a base.

Physical and Chemical Properties and Changes

Both physical changes and chemical reactions are everyday occurrences. **Physical changes** do not result in different substances. For example, when water becomes ice it has undergone a physical change, but not a chemical change. It has changed its form, but not its composition. It is still H_2O. **Chemical properties** are concerned with the constituent particles that make up the physicality of a substance. Chemical properties are apparent when **chemical changes** occur. The chemical properties of a substance are influenced by its electron configuration, which is determined in part by the number of protons in the nucleus (the atomic number). Carbon, for example, has 6 protons

Copyright © Mometrix Media. You have been licensed one copy of this document for personal use only. Any other reproduction or redistribution is strictly prohibited. All rights reserved.

and 6 electrons. It is an element's outermost valence electrons that mainly determine its chemical properties. Chemical reactions may release or consume energy.

Elements, Compounds, Solutions, and Mixtures

- **Elements** — These are substances that consist of only one type of atom.
- **Compounds** — These are substances containing two or more elements. Compounds are formed by chemical reactions and frequently have different properties than the original elements. Compounds are decomposed by a chemical reaction rather than separated by a physical one.
- **Solutions** — These are homogeneous mixtures composed of two or more substances that have become one.
- **Mixtures** — Mixtures contain two or more substances that are combined but have not reacted chemically with each other. Mixtures can be separated using physical methods, while compounds cannot.

Heat, Energy, Work, and Thermal Energy

- **Heat** — Heat is the transfer of energy from a body or system as a result of thermal contact. Heat consists of random motion and the vibration of atoms, molecules, and ions. The higher the temperature is, the greater the atomic or molecular motion will be.
- **Energy** — Energy is the capacity to do work.
- **Work** — Work is the quantity of energy transferred by one system to another due to changes in a system that is the result of external forces, or macroscopic variables. Another way to put this is that work is the amount of energy that must be transferred to overcome a force. Lifting an object in the air is an example of work. The opposing force that must be overcome is gravity. Work is measured in joules (J). The rate at which work is performed is known as power.
- **Thermal energy** — Thermal energy is the energy present in a system due to temperature.

Types of Energy

Some discussions of energy consider only two types of energy: **kinetic energy** (the energy of motion) and **potential energy** (which depends on relative position or orientation). There are, however, other types of energy. **Electromagnetic waves**, for example, are a type of energy contained by a field. Another type of potential energy is electrical energy, which is the energy it takes to pull apart positive and negative electrical charges. **Chemical energy** refers to the manner in which atoms form into molecules, and this energy can be released or absorbed when molecules regroup. **Solar energy** comes in the form of visible light and non-visible light, such as infrared and ultraviolet rays. **Sound energy** refers to the energy in sound waves.

Chemical Reactions

Chemical reactions measured in human time can take place quickly or slowly. They can take fractions of a second or billions of years. The rates of chemical reactions are determined by how frequently reacting atoms and molecules interact. Rates are also influenced by the temperature and various properties (such as shape) of the reacting materials. **Catalysts** accelerate chemical reactions, while inhibitors decrease reaction rates. Some types of reactions release energy in the form of heat and light. Some types of reactions involve the transfer of either electrons or hydrogen ions between reacting ions, molecules, or atoms. In other reactions, chemical bonds are broken down by heat or light to form reactive radicals with electrons that will readily form new bonds.

Copyright © Mometrix Media. You have been licensed one copy of this document for personal use only. Any other reproduction or redistribution is strictly prohibited. All rights reserved.

Processes such as the formation of ozone and greenhouse gases in the atmosphere and the burning and processing of fossil fuels are controlled by radical reactions.

Review Video: Catalysts
Visit mometrix.com/academy and enter code: 288189

Reading Chemical Equations

Chemical equations describe chemical reactions. The **reactants** are on the left side before the arrow and the **products** are on the right side after the arrow. The arrow indicates the reaction or change. The **coefficient**, or stoichiometric coefficient, is the number before the element, and indicates the ratio of reactants to products in terms of moles. The equation for the formation of water from hydrogen and oxygen, for example, is $2H_2\ (g) + O_2\ (g) \rightarrow 2H_2O\ (l)$. The 2 preceding hydrogen and water is the coefficient, which means there are 2 moles of hydrogen and 2 of water. There is 1 mole of oxygen, which does not have to be indicated with the number 1. In parentheses, g stands for gas, l stands for liquid, s stands for solid, and aq stands for aqueous solution (a substance dissolved in water). Charges are shown in superscript for individual ions, but not for ionic compounds. Polyatomic ions are separated by parentheses so the ion will not be confused with the number of ions.

Review Video: Ionic Compounds
Visit mometrix.com/academy and enter code: 255084

Balancing Equations

An **unbalanced equation** is one that does not follow the **law of conservation of mass**, which states that matter can only be changed, not created. If an equation is unbalanced, the numbers of atoms indicated by the stoichiometric coefficients on each side of the arrow will not be equal. Start by writing the formulas for each species in the reaction. Count the atoms on each side and determine if the number is equal. Coefficients must be whole numbers. Fractional amounts, such as half a molecule, are not possible. Equations can be balanced by multiplying the coefficients by a constant that will produce the smallest possible whole number coefficient. $H_2 + O_2 \rightarrow H_2O$ is an example of an unbalanced equation. The balanced equation is $2H_2 + O_2 \rightarrow 2H_2O$, which indicates that it takes two moles of hydrogen and one of oxygen to produce two moles of water.

Review Video: Balancing Equations
Visit mometrix.com/academy and enter code: 490221

Periodic Table

The **periodic table** groups elements with similar chemical properties together. The grouping of elements is based on **atomic structure**. It shows periodic trends of physical and chemical properties and identifies families of elements with similar properties. It is a common model for organizing and understanding elements. In the periodic table, each element has its own cell that includes varying amounts of information presented in symbol form about the properties of the element. Cells in the table are arranged in **rows** (periods) and **columns** (groups or families). At minimum, a cell includes the symbol for the element and its atomic number. The cell for hydrogen, for example, which appears first in the upper left corner, includes an "H" and a "1" above the letter. Elements are ordered by atomic number, left to right, top to bottom.

Copyright © Mometrix Media. You have been licensed one copy of this document for personal use only. Any other reproduction or redistribution is strictly prohibited. All rights reserved.

Solutions

A **solution** is a homogeneous mixture. A **mixture** is two or more different substances that are mixed together, but not combined chemically. Homogeneous mixtures are those that are uniform in their composition. Solutions consist of a solute (the substance that is dissolved) and a solvent (the substance that does the dissolving). An example is sugar water. The solvent is the water and the solute is the sugar. The intermolecular attraction between the solvent and the solute is called solvation. **Hydration** refers to solutions in which water is the solvent. Solutions are formed when the forces of the molecules of the solute and the solvent are as strong as the individual molecular forces of the solute and the solvent. An example is that salt (NaCl) dissolves in water to create a solution. The Na^+ and the Cl^- ions in salt interact with the molecules of water and vice versa to overcome the individual molecular forces of the solute and the solvent.

Mixtures, Suspensions, Colloids, Emulsions, and Foams

A **mixture** is a combination of two or more substances that are not bonded. **Suspensions** are mixtures of heterogeneous materials. Particles are usually larger than those found in true solutions. Dirt mixed vigorously with water is an example of a suspension. The dirt is temporarily suspended in water, but the two separate once the mixing is ceased. A mixture of large (1 nm to 500 nm) particles is called a **colloidal suspension**. The particles are termed dispersants and the dispersing medium is similar to the solvent in a solution. Sol refers to a liquid or a solid that also has solids dispersed through it, such as milk or gelatin. An aerosol spray is a colloid suspension of gas and the solid or liquid being dispersed. An **emulsion** refers to a liquid or a solid that has a liquid dispersed through it. A **foam** is a liquid that has gas dispersed through it.

Properties of Bases

When they are dissolved in aqueous solutions, some properties of **bases** are that they conduct electricity, change red litmus paper to blue, feel slippery, and react with acids to neutralize their properties. A **weak base** is one that does not completely ionize in an aqueous solution, and usually has a low pH. **Strong bases** can free protons in very weak acids. Examples of strong bases are hydroxide compounds such as potassium, barium, and lithium hydroxides. Most are in the first and second groups of the periodic table. A **superbase** is extremely strong compared to sodium hydroxide and cannot be kept in an aqueous solution. Superbases are organized into organic, organometallic, and inorganic classes. Bases are used as insoluble catalysts in heterogeneous reactions and as catalysts in hydrogenation.

Properties of Salts

Some properties of **salts** are that they are formed from acid base reactions, are ionic compounds consisting of metallic and nonmetallic ions, dissociate in water, and are comprised of tightly bonded ions. Some common salts are sodium chloride (NaCl), sodium bisulfate, potassium dichromate ($K_2Cr_2O_7$), and calcium chloride ($CaCl_2$). Calcium chloride is used as a drying agent, and may be used to absorb moisture when freezing mixtures. Potassium nitrate (KNO_3) is used to make fertilizer and in the manufacture of explosives. Sodium nitrate ($NaNO_3$) is also used in the making of fertilizer. Baking soda (sodium bicarbonate) is a salt, as are Epsom salts [magnesium sulfate ($MgSO_4$)]. Salt and water can react to form a base and an acid. This is called a **hydrolysis reaction.**

Unique Properties of Water

The important properties of **water** (H_2O) are high polarity, hydrogen bonding, cohesiveness, adhesiveness, high specific heat, high latent heat, and high heat of vaporization. It is essential to life

Copyright © Mometrix Media. You have been licensed one copy of this document for personal use only. Any other reproduction or redistribution is strictly prohibited. All rights reserved.

as we know it, as water is one of the main if not the main constituent of many living things. Water is a liquid at room temperature. The high **specific heat** of water means it resists the breaking of its hydrogen bonds and resists heat and motion, which is why it has a relatively high boiling point and high vaporization point. It also resists temperature change. Water is peculiar in that its solid state floats in its liquid state. Most substances are denser in their solid forms. Water is *cohesive*, which means it is attracted to itself. It is also *adhesive*, which means it readily attracts other molecules. If water tends to adhere to another substance, the substance is said to be *hydrophilic*. Water makes a good solvent. Substances, particularly those with polar ions and molecules, readily dissolve in water.

Review Video: Properties of Water
Visit mometrix.com/academy and enter code: 279526

Properties of Acids

When they are dissolved in aqueous solutions, some properties of **acids** are that they conduct electricity, change blue litmus paper to red, have a sour taste, react with bases to neutralize them, and react with active metals to free hydrogen. A **weak acid** is one that does not donate all of its protons or disassociate completely. **Strong acids** include hydrochloric, hydriodic, hydrobromic, perchloric, nitric, and sulfuric. They ionize completely. **Superacids** are those that are stronger than 100 percent sulfuric acid. They include fluoroantimonic, magic, and perchloric acids. Acids can be used in pickling, a process used to remove rust and corrosion from metals. They are also used as catalysts in the processing of minerals and the production of salts and fertilizers. Phosphoric acid (H_3PO_4) is added to sodas and other acids are added to foods as preservatives or to add taste.

Review Video: Properties of Acids
Visit mometrix.com/academy and enter code: 645283

pH

The **potential of hydrogen** (pH) is a measurement of the concentration of hydrogen ions in a substance in terms of the number of moles of H^+ per liter of solution. A lower pH indicates a higher H^+ concentration, while a higher pH indicates a lower H^+ concentration. Pure water has a **neutral** pH, which is 7. Anything with a pH lower than water (less than 7) is considered **acidic**. Anything with a pH higher than water (greater than 7) is a **base**. Drain cleaner, soap, baking soda, ammonia, egg whites, and sea water are common bases. Urine, stomach acid, citric acid, vinegar, hydrochloric acid, and battery acid are acids. A pH indicator is a substance that acts as a detector of hydrogen or hydronium ions. It is halochromic, meaning it changes color to indicate that hydrogen or hydronium ions have been detected.

Review Video: pH
Visit mometrix.com/academy and enter code: 187395

Kinetic Theory of Gases

The **kinetic theory of gases** assumes that gas molecules are small compared to the distances between them and that they are in constant random motion. The attractive and repulsive forces between gas molecules are negligible. Their kinetic energy does not change with time as long as the temperature remains the same. The higher the temperature is, the greater the motion will be. As the temperature of a gas increases, so does the kinetic energy of the molecules. In other words, gas will

Copyright © Mometrix Media. You have been licensed one copy of this document for personal use only. Any other reproduction or redistribution is strictly prohibited. All rights reserved.

occupy a greater volume as the temperature is increased and a lesser volume as the temperature is decreased. In addition, the same amount of gas will occupy a greater volume as the temperature increases, but pressure remains constant. At any given temperature, gas molecules have the same average kinetic energy. The **ideal gas law** is derived from the kinetic theory of gases.

Review Video: Ideal Gas Law
Visit mometrix.com/academy and enter code: 381353

Inorganic Compounds

The main trait of **inorganic compounds** is that they **lack carbon**. Inorganic compounds include mineral salts, metals and alloys, non-metallic compounds such as phosphorus, and metal complexes. A metal complex has a central atom (or ion) bonded to surrounding ligands (molecules or anions). The ligands sacrifice the donor atoms (in the form of at least one pair of electrons) to the central atom. Many inorganic compounds are **ionic**, meaning they form ionic bonds rather than share electrons. They may have high melting points because of this. They may also be colorful, but this is not an absolute identifier of an inorganic compound. Salts, which are inorganic compounds, are an example of inorganic bonding of cations and anions. Some examples of salts are magnesium chloride ($MgCl_2$) and sodium oxide (Na_2O). Oxides, carbonates, sulfates, and halides are classes of inorganic compounds. They are typically poor conductors, are very water soluble, and crystallize easily. Minerals and silicates are also inorganic compounds.

Review Video: Phosphorus Halides
Visit mometrix.com/academy and enter code: 590810

Hydrogen Bonds

Hydrogen bonds are weaker than covalent and ionic bonds, and refer to the type of attraction in an electronegative atom such as oxygen, fluorine, or nitrogen. Hydrogen bonds can form within a single molecule or between molecules. A water molecule is **polar**, meaning it is partially positively charged on one end (the hydrogen end) and partially negatively charged on the other (the oxygen end). This is because the hydrogen atoms are arranged around the oxygen atom in a close tetrahedron. Hydrogen is **oxidized** (its number of electrons is reduced) when it bonds with oxygen to form water. Hydrogen bonds tend not only to be weak, but also short-lived. They also tend to be numerous. Hydrogen bonds give water many of its important properties, including its high specific heat and high heat of vaporization, its solvent qualities, its adhesiveness and cohesiveness, its hydrophobic qualities, and its ability to float in its solid form. Hydrogen bonds are also an important component of proteins, nucleic acids, and DNA.

Organic Compounds

Two of the main characteristics of **organic compounds** are that they **include carbon** and are formed by **covalent bonds**. Carbon can form long chains, double and triple bonds, and rings. While inorganic compounds tend to have high melting points, organic compounds tend to melt at temperatures below 300° C. They also tend to boil, sublimate, and decompose below this temperature. Unlike inorganic compounds, they are not very water soluble. Organic molecules are organized into functional groups based on their specific atoms, which helps determine how they will react chemically. A few groups are alkanes, nitro, alkenes, sulfides, amines, and carbolic acids.

Copyright © Mometrix Media. You have been licensed one copy of this document for personal use only. Any other reproduction or redistribution is strictly prohibited. All rights reserved.

The hydroxyl group (-OH) consists of alcohols. These molecules are polar, which increases their solubility. By some estimates, there are more than 16 million organic compounds.

Review Video: Basics of Alcohols
Visit mometrix.com/academy and enter code: 105795

Review Video: Functional Groups
Visit mometrix.com/academy and enter code: 390575

Review Video: Organic Compound Functional Groups
Visit mometrix.com/academy and enter code: 897644

Review Video: Organic Compounds
Visit mometrix.com/academy and enter code: 264922

Physics

Laws of Thermodynamics

The **laws of thermodynamics** are generalized principles dealing with energy and heat.

- The **zeroth law** of thermodynamics states that two objects in thermodynamic equilibrium with a third object are also in equilibrium with each other. Being in thermodynamic equilibrium basically means that different objects are at the same temperature.
- The **first law** deals with conservation of energy. It states that neither mass nor energy can be destroyed; only converted from one form to another.
- The **second law** states that the entropy (the amount of energy in a system that is no longer available for work or the amount of disorder in a system) of an isolated system can only increase. The second law also states that heat is not transferred from a lower-temperature system to a higher-temperature one unless additional work is done.
- The **third law** of thermodynamics states that as temperature approaches absolute zero, entropy approaches a constant minimum. It also states that a system cannot be cooled to absolute zero.

Review Video: Absolute Zero
Visit mometrix.com/academy and enter code: 666130

Review Video: The Second Law of Thermodynamics
Visit mometrix.com/academy and enter code: 251848

Review Video: Laws of Thermodynamics
Visit mometrix.com/academy and enter code: 253607

Heat and Temperature

Heat is energy transfer (other than direct work) from one body or system to another due to thermal contact. Everything tends to become less organized and less orderly over time (**entropy**). In all energy transfers, therefore, the overall result is that the energy is spread out uniformly. This transfer of heat energy from hotter to cooler objects is accomplished by conduction, radiation, or convection. **Temperature** is a measurement of an object's stored heat energy. More specifically, temperature is the average kinetic energy of an object's particles. When the temperature of an

Copyright © Mometrix Media. You have been licensed one copy of this document for personal use only. Any other reproduction or redistribution is strictly prohibited. All rights reserved.

object increases and its atoms move faster, kinetic energy also increases. Temperature is not energy since it changes and is not conserved. Thermometers are used to measure temperature.

Mass, Weight, Volume, Density, and Specific Gravity

Mass — Mass is a measure of the amount of substance in an object.

Weight — Weight is a measure of the gravitational pull of Earth on an object.

Volume — Volume is a measure of the amount of space occupied. There are many formulas to determine volume. For example, the volume of a cube is the length of one side cubed (a^3) and the volume of a rectangular prism is length times width times height ($l \cdot w \cdot h$). The volume of an irregular shape can be determined by how much water it displaces.

Density — Density is a measure of the amount of mass per unit volume. The formula to find density is mass divided by volume ($D=m/V$). It is expressed in terms of mass per cubic unit, such as grams per cubic centimeter (g/cm^3).

Specific gravity — This is a measure of the ratio of a substance's density compared to the density of water.

Thermal Contact

Thermal contact refers to energy transferred to a body by a means other than work. A system in thermal contact with another can exchange energy with it through the process of heat transfer. Thermal contact does not necessarily involve direct physical contact. **Heat** is energy that can be transferred from one body or system to another without work being done. Everything tends to become less organized and less useful over time (entropy). In all energy transfers, therefore, the overall result is that the heat is spread out so that objects are in thermodynamic equilibrium and the heat can no longer be transferred without additional work.

Models for Flow of Electric Charge

Models that can be used to explain the **flow of electric current, potential, and circuits** include water, gravity, and roller coasters. For example, just as gravity is a force and a mass can have a potential for energy based on its location, so can a charge within an electrical field. Just as a force is required to move an object uphill, a force is also required to move a charge from a low to high potential. Another example is water. Water does not flow when it is level. If it is lifted to a point and then placed on a downward path, it will flow. A roller coaster car requires work to be performed to transport it to a point where it has potential energy (the top of a hill). Once there, gravity provides the force for it to flow (move) downward. If either path is broken, the flow or movement stops or is not completed.

Atomic Structures

<u>Magnetic Fields</u>

The motions of subatomic structures (nuclei and electrons) produce a **magnetic field**. It is the direction of the spin and orbit that indicate the direction of the field. The strength of a magnetic field is known as the **magnetic moment**. As electrons spin and orbit a nucleus, they produce a magnetic field. Pairs of electrons that spin and orbit in opposite directions cancel each other out, creating a net magnetic field of zero. Materials that have an unpaired electron are magnetic. Those with a weak attractive force are referred to as paramagnetic materials, while ferromagnetic

Copyright © Mometrix Media. You have been licensed one copy of this document for personal use only. Any other reproduction or redistribution is strictly prohibited. All rights reserved.

materials have a strong attractive force. A diamagnetic material has electrons that are paired, and therefore does not typically have a magnetic moment. There are, however, some diamagnetic materials that have a weak magnetic field.

Electric Charges

The attractive force between the electrons and the nucleus is called the **electric force**. A positive (+) charge or a negative (-) charge creates a field of sorts in the empty space around it, which is known as an **electric field**. The direction of a positive charge is away from it and the direction of a negative charge is towards it. An electron within the force of the field is pulled towards a positive charge because an electron has a negative charge. A particle with a positive charge is pushed away, or repelled, by another positive charge. Like charges repel each other and opposite charges attract. Lines of force show the paths of charges. **Electric force** between two objects is directly proportional to the product of the charge magnitudes and inversely proportional to the square of the distance between the two objects. **Electric charge** is measured with the unit Coulomb (C). It is the amount of charge moved in one second by a steady current of one ampere (1C = 1A × 1s).

Review Video: Electric Charge
Visit mometrix.com/academy and enter code: 323587

Electric Current Movement Through Circuits

Electric current is the sustained flow of electrons that are part of an electric charge moving along a path in a circuit. This differs from a static electric charge, which is a constant non-moving charge rather than a continuous flow. The **rate of flow of electric charge** is expressed using the ampere (amp or A) and can be measured using an ammeter. A current of 1 ampere means that 1 coulomb of charge passes through a given area every second. Electric charges typically only move from areas of high electric potential to areas of low electric potential. To get charges to flow into a high potential area, you must to connect it to an area of higher potential, by introducing a battery or other voltage source.

Simple Circuits

Movement of electric charge along a path between areas of high electric potential and low electric potential, with a resistor or load device between them, is the definition of a **simple circuit**. It is a closed conducting path between the high and low potential points, such as the positive and negative terminals on a battery. One example of a circuit is the flow from one terminal of a car battery to the other. The electrolyte solution of water and sulfuric acid provides work in chemical form to start the flow. A frequently used classroom example of circuits involves using a D cell (1.5 V) battery, a small light bulb, and a piece of copper wire to create a circuit to light the bulb.

Magnets

A **magnet** is a piece of metal, such as iron, steel, or magnetite (lodestone) that can affect another substance within its **field of force** that has like characteristics. Magnets can either attract or repel other substances. Magnets have two **poles**: north and south. Like poles repel and opposite poles (pairs of north and south) attract. The magnetic field is a set of invisible lines representing the paths of attraction and repulsion. Magnetism can occur naturally, or ferromagnetic materials can be magnetized. Certain matter that is magnetized can retain its magnetic properties indefinitely and become a permanent magnet. Other matter can lose its magnetic properties. For example, an iron nail can be temporarily magnetized by stroking it repeatedly in the same direction using one pole of

Copyright © Mometrix Media. You have been licensed one copy of this document for personal use only. Any other reproduction or redistribution is strictly prohibited. All rights reserved.

another magnet. Once magnetized, it can attract or repel other magnetically inclined materials, such as paper clips. Dropping the nail repeatedly will cause it to lose its charge.

Review Video: Magnets
Visit mometrix.com/academy and enter code: 570803

Magnetic Fields, Current, and Magnetic Domains

A **magnetic field** can be formed not only by a magnetic material, but also by electric current flowing through a wire. When a coiled wire is attached to the two ends of a battery, for example, an electromagnet can be formed by inserting a ferromagnetic material such as an iron bar within the coil. When electric current flows through the wire, the bar becomes a magnet. If there is no current, the magnetism is lost. A **magnetic domain** occurs when the magnetic fields of atoms are grouped and aligned. These groups form what can be thought of as miniature magnets within a material. This is what happens when an object like an iron nail is temporarily magnetized. Prior to magnetization, the organization of atoms and their various polarities are somewhat random with respect to where the north and south poles are pointing. After magnetization, a significant percentage of the poles are lined up in one direction, which is what causes the magnetic force exerted by the material.

Motion and Displacement

Motion is a change in the location of an object, and is the result of an unbalanced net force acting on the object. Understanding motion requires the understanding of three basic quantities: displacement, velocity, and acceleration.

When something moves from one place to another, it has undergone **displacement**. Displacement along a straight line is a very simple example of a vector quantity. If an object travels from position $x = -5$ cm to $x = 5$ cm, it has undergone a displacement of 10 cm. If it traverses the same path in the opposite direction, its displacement is -10 cm. A vector that spans the object's displacement in the direction of travel is known as a displacement vector.

Gravitational Force

Gravitational force is a universal force that causes every object to exert a force on every other object. The gravitational force between two objects can be described by the formula, $F = Gm_1m_2/r^2$, where m_1 and m_2 are the masses of two objects, r is the distance between them, and G is the gravitational constant, $G = 6.672 \times 10^{-11}$ N-m^2/kg^2. In order for this force to have a noticeable effect, one or both of the objects must be extremely large, so the equation is generally only used in problems involving planetary bodies. For problems involving objects on the earth being affected by earth's gravitational pull, the force of gravity is simply calculated as $F = mg$, where g is 9.81 m/s^2 toward the ground.

Newton's First Two Laws of Motion

Newton's First Law

An object at rest or in motion will remain at rest or in motion unless acted upon by an external force.

This phenomenon is commonly referred to as **inertia**, the tendency of a body to remain in its present state of motion. In order for the body's state of motion to change, it must be acted on by an unbalanced force.

Copyright © Mometrix Media. You have been licensed one copy of this document for personal use only. Any other reproduction or redistribution is strictly prohibited. All rights reserved.

Newton's Second Law

An object's acceleration is **directly proportional** to the net force acting on the object, and **inversely proportional** to the object's mass.

It is generally written in equation form $F = ma$, where F is the net force acting on a body, m is the mass of the body, and a is its acceleration. Note that since the mass is always a positive quantity, the acceleration is always in the same direction as the force.

Simple Machines

Simple machines include the inclined plane, lever, wheel and axle, and pulley. These simple machines have no internal source of energy. More **complex or compound machines** can be formed from them. Simple machines provide a force known as a mechanical advantage and make it easier to accomplish a task. The inclined plane enables a force less than the object's weight to be used to push an object to a greater height. A lever enables a multiplication of force. The wheel and axle allows for movement with less resistance. Single or double pulleys allows for easier direction of force. The wedge and screw are forms of the inclined plane. A wedge turns a smaller force working over a greater distance into a larger force. The screw is similar to an incline that is wrapped around a shaft.

Friction

Friction is a force that arises as a **resistance to motion** where two surfaces are in contact. The maximum magnitude of the frictional force (f)can be calculated as $f = F_c\mu$, where F_c is the contact force between the two objects and μ is a coefficient of friction based on the surfaces' material composition. Two types of friction are static and kinetic. To illustrate these concepts, imagine a book resting on a table. The force of its weight (W) is equal and opposite to the force of the table on the book, or the normal force (N). If we exert a small force (F) on the book, attempting to push it to one side, a frictional force (f) would arise, equal and opposite to our force. At this point, it is a **static frictional force** because the book is not moving. If we increase our force on the book, we will eventually cause it to move. At this point, the frictional force opposing us will be a **kinetic frictional force**. Generally, the kinetic frictional force is lower than static frictional force (because the frictional coefficient for static friction is larger), which means that the amount of force needed to maintain the movement of the book will be less than what was needed to start it moving.

Sound

Sound is a pressure disturbance that moves through a medium in the form of mechanical waves, which transfer energy from one particle to the next. Sound requires a medium to travel through, such as air, water, or other matter since it is the vibrations that transfer energy to adjacent particles, not the actual movement of particles over a great distance. Sound is transferred through the movement of atomic particles, which can be atoms or molecules. Waves of sound energy move outward in all directions from the source. Sound waves consist of compressions (particles are forced together) and rarefactions (particles move farther apart and their density decreases). A wavelength consists of one compression and one rarefaction. Different sounds have different wavelengths. Sound is a form of kinetic energy.

Pitch, Loudness, Sound Intensity, Timbre, and Oscillation

Pitch — Pitch is the quality of sound determined by frequency. For example, a musical note can be tuned to a specific frequency. A, for instance, has a frequency of 440 Hz, which is a higher frequency than middle C. Humans can detect frequencies between about 20 Hz to 20,000 Hz.

Copyright © Mometrix Media. You have been licensed one copy of this document for personal use only. Any other reproduction or redistribution is strictly prohibited. All rights reserved.

Loudness — Loudness is a human's perception of sound intensity.

Sound intensity — Sound intensity is measured as the sound power per unit area, and can be expressed in decibels.

Timbre — This is a human's perception of the type or quality of sound.

Oscillation — This is a measurement, usually of time, against a basic value, equilibrium, or rest point.

Doppler Effect

The **Doppler effect** refers to the effect the relative motion of the source of the wave and the location of the observer has on waves. The Doppler effect is easily observable in **sound waves**. What a person hears when a train approaches or a car honking its horn passes by are examples of the Doppler effect. The pitch of the sound is different not because the emitted frequency has changed, but because the received frequency has changed. The frequency is higher (as is the pitch) as the train approaches, the same as emitted just as it passes, and lower as the train moves away. This is because the wavelength changes. The Doppler effect can occur when an observer is stationary, and can also occur when two trains approach and pass each other. **Electromagnetic waves** are also affected in this manner. The motion of the medium can also affect the wave. For waves that do not travel in a medium, such as light waves, it is the difference in velocity that determines the outcome.

Waves

Waves have energy and can transfer energy when they interact with matter. Although waves transfer energy, they do not transport matter. They are a disturbance of matter that transfers energy from one particle to an adjacent particle. There are many types of waves, including sound, seismic, water, light, micro, and radio waves. The two basic categories of waves are mechanical and electromagnetic. **Mechanical waves** are those that transmit energy through matter. **Electromagnetic waves** can transmit energy through a vacuum. A **transverse wave** provides a good illustration of the features of a wave, which include crests, troughs, amplitude, and wavelength.

Electromagnetic Spectrum

The **electromagnetic spectrum** is defined by frequency (f) and wavelength (λ). Frequency is typically measured in hertz and wavelength is usually measured in meters. Because light travels at a fairly constant speed, frequency is inversely proportional to wavelength, a relationship expressed by the formula $f = c/\lambda$, where c is the speed of light (about 300 million meters per second). Frequency multiplied by wavelength equals the speed of the wave; for electromagnetic waves, this is the speed of light, with some variance for the medium in which it is traveling. Electromagnetic waves include (from largest to smallest wavelength) radio waves, microwaves, infrared radiation (radiant heat), visible light, ultraviolet radiation, x-rays, and gamma rays. The energy of electromagnetic waves is carried in packets that have a magnitude inversely proportional to the wavelength. **Radio waves** have a range of wavelengths, from about 10^{-3} to 10^{5} meters, while their frequencies range from about 10^{3} to 10^{11} Hz.

Visible Light

Light is the portion of the electromagnetic spectrum that is visible because of its ability to stimulate the retina. It is absorbed and emitted by electrons, atoms, and molecules that move from one

Copyright © Mometrix Media. You have been licensed one copy of this document for personal use only. Any other reproduction or redistribution is strictly prohibited. All rights reserved.

energy level to another. **Visible light** interacts with matter through molecular electron excitation (which occurs in the human retina) and through plasma oscillations (which occur in metals). Visible light is between ultraviolet and infrared light on the spectrum. The wavelengths of visible light cover a range from 380 nm (violet) to 760 nm (red). Different wavelengths correspond to different colors.

Reflection and Refraction

Reflection is the rebound of a light wave from a surface back toward the medium from where it came. A light wave that hits a reflecting surface at a 90-degree angle retraces its original path back to its source. Striking the surface at any other angle results in reflection of the wave at an angle in the opposite direction. Reflectance is the amount of light a material reflects; metals have high reflectance. The smoother a surface, the higher its reflectance. **Refraction** is the change in the direction of a light wave when it passes through a transparent medium with a different optical density from the one in which the wave had been traveling. This results in a change in the wave's velocity. The ratio of the sine of the angle of the incoming ray to the sine of the angle of refraction is equal to the ratio of the speed of light in the original medium to the speed of light in the refracting medium.

Science,Technology, and Society

Debate over Science and Ethics

Debates over issues paramount to **science and ethics** are rarely resolved unambiguously. Ethical conclusions should be based on reason, logic, and accepted principles that represent a consensus of current thinking on a question. Education and debate are important in clarifying issues and allowing intelligent participation in a democratic process. Deciding issues of science and society usually requires an examination of individual cases. Generalizations in these areas tend to lead to extreme positions that exclude mainstream opinions. Both intrinsic and consequential arguments for or against any question may be advanced. There are no blanket solutions to most problems involving science, technology, and societal ethics.

Major Effects of Improvements in Scientific and Technological Knowledge on Human and Other Life

Since the Industrial Revolution, **technological improvements** to agricultural production have made agriculture productive on an industrial scale, while advances in medical knowledge have brought about the cures for many diseases. People in many parts of the world live longer and enjoy a higher standard of living than ever before. However, this progress does not come without a price. The effects on the **environment** of industrialization are almost exclusively negative. Monoculture farming practices resulting from industrialization mean that farming no longer exists as a closed ecosystem; the chemical fertilizers that create record crop yields have changed the nutrient environment, and the waste products of industrial agriculture pollute the water rather than fertilizing the soil. Increased travel creates dangerous carbon dioxide emissions and depletes the earth's limited store of fossil fuels. Water pollution means limited access to potable water, and deforestation has begun to change the makeup of ecosystems and cause the extinction of many species. Through the increased contact made available by improved technology, however, humans are also collaborating on solutions to these new problems.

Copyright © Mometrix Media. You have been licensed one copy of this document for personal use only. Any other reproduction or redistribution is strictly prohibited. All rights reserved.

Major Energy Issues

Since the Industrial Revolution, **energy** for industrialized human needs has come from fossil fuels, particularly coal and petroleum, but increased use means that this source of fuel is quickly being depleted, in addition to causing pollution. The search for **alternative, safe sources** of energy for an increasingly industrialized world population is therefore increasingly important to scientists. An ideal source of energy would be efficient, renewable, and sustainable. Various sources of alternative energy have been proposed, including wind, water, solar, nuclear, geothermal, and biomass, but thus far none have been made practically available on a large scale. Some, such as wind and water, blight the landscape, while the conversion methods for other sources, such as solar and biomass, are still relatively inefficient. The scientific community is still unclear on the best way to harness the power of photosynthesis and biomass for energy needs in a way that would allow a large-scale energy industry to use it. Scientists remain at work studying the long-term solutions to an increasingly urgent problem for humanity.

Controversies Surrounding Use of Nuclear Power

Nuclear fission power, while sustainable, has a host of attendant controversial problems. Among them is the incredibly dangerous transportation and long-term storage of its radioactive waste products, for which there is still no safe long-term solution. Its effects on those environments and creatures that come in contact with nuclear waste are still largely unknown. In addition, nuclear materials can be used in weaponry, and accidents at nuclear power plants like the one at Chernobyl can be devastating for thousands of years. Scientists continue their study of the process of **nuclear fusion**, hoping that if humans can learn to harness the energy produced by smashing atoms rather than splitting them, the attendant problems of nuclear waste storage will be minimized.

Review Video: Nuclear Fusion
Visit mometrix.com/academy and enter code: 381782

Effects of Increased Production of Consumer Goods After Industrial Revolution

Electric-based, industrial production of **manufactured goods** has led to an increase in the standard of living for many, especially those in the industrialized world. Consumer goods are produced more cheaply than ever before, since the means of production is not as dependent on the physical abilities of human beings. Scientific advancements have led to a huge number of new synthetic materials from which goods can be made, including plastics and nylon. However, this increased production damages the **environment**. Waste products are now created of which humans can make no use, a new phenomenon. Trash created from these new products is buried in landfills, where it has no access to the air, water, and sunlight that are a necessary part of biodegradation; trash made from some synthetic materials does not biodegrade at all. While some waste products can be recycled, many byproducts of industrial manufacturing are hazardous, with no safe way to dispose of them. The long-term sustainability of the environment as a result of massively increased consumer production is an issue of increasing urgency for scientists.

Issues Concerning Management of Renewable Resources

Natural resources can be divided into two types, renewable and non-renewable. **Renewable resources** include plants and animals, along with water, air, and soil. A pre-industrial earth was a self-sustaining system, maintaining a natural balance among plants, animals, and non-living elements in which waste products from one natural process were the fuel for another. Modern humans have intervened in this process in a way that upsets the natural balance of life. Humans

Copyright © Mometrix Media. You have been licensed one copy of this document for personal use only. Any other reproduction or redistribution is strictly prohibited. All rights reserved.

have introduced non-native species from one part of the world to another, resulting in the devastation of local populations. Industrial-scale buildings can create disasters for local ecosystems, ruining habitats for animal populations. Humans remove an increasing amount of the world's resources for industrial use, too quickly for nature to recover from easily. Renewable resources must be carefully managed to maintain a balanced ecosystem; over-harvesting of forests or over-hunting of animal populations can be devastating. Pollution of the air and water with chemical pollutants has far-reaching effects on the ecosystems of the earth, including the depletion of the ozone layer that protects earth life from ultraviolet rays, as does the removal of forests that produce the earth's oxygen.

Issues Concerning Management of Non-Renewable Resources

Non-renewable resources include minerals, which are created naturally over millions of years. The industrialized world extracts minerals for fuel as well as for use in electronic equipment and medicine. Increased human extraction of non-renewable resources has endangered their availability, and over-mining has created other ecological problems, including runoff and water pollution. The use of fossil fuels for energy and transportation causes air pollution and is unsustainable. Fossil fuels cannot be replaced once depleted, and they are being depleted at an increasing rate. The need to find a sustainable alternative to the use of non-renewable fossil fuels is imperative.

Recent Applications of Science and Technology to Health Care, the Environment, Agriculture, and Information Technology

Scientific and technological developments have led to the widespread availability of **technologies** heretofore unheard of, including cellular phones, satellite-based applications, and a worldwide network of connected computers. Some of the notable recent applications include:

- **Health care**: Antibiotics, genetic screening for diseases, the sequencing of the human genome. Issues include problems with health care distribution on an increasingly industrialized planet.
- **The environment**: Computerized models of climate change and pollution monitoring. Issues include increased pollution of the water, air, and soil, and the over-harvesting of natural resources with mechanized equipment.
- **Agriculture**: Genetic improvements in agricultural practices, including increased output on the same amount of arable land. Issues include unknown environmental effects of hybrid species, cross-pollination with organic species, and pollution caused by synthetic chemical fertilizers.
- **Information technology**: New Internet-based industries, increased worldwide collaboration, and access to information. Issues include the depletion of natural resources for electronics production.

Social Impacts of Recent Developments in Science and Technology

Recent **developments in science and technology** have had both positive and negative effects on human society. The issue of sustainable growth is an increasingly important one, as humans realize that the resources they use are not unlimited. Genetic research into diseases, stem cell research, and cloning technology have created great controversies as they have been introduced, and an increasing number of people reject the morality of scientific practices like animal testing in the pursuit of scientific advancement. In addition, an increasingly technology-based world has produced a new social inequality based on access to computers and Internet technology. These

Copyright © Mometrix Media. You have been licensed one copy of this document for personal use only. Any other reproduction or redistribution is strictly prohibited. All rights reserved.

issues are beginning to be debated at all levels of human government, from city councils to the United Nations. Does science provide the authoritative answer to all human problems, or do ethics carry weight in scientific debates as well? Ultimately, humans must weigh the competing needs of facilitating scientific pursuits and maintaining an ethical society as they face new technological questions.

Human Impacts on Ecosystems

Human impacts on ecosystems take many forms and have many causes. They include widespread disruptions and specific niche disturbances. Humans practice many forms of environmental manipulation that affect plants and animals in many biomes and ecosystems. Many human practices involve the consumption of natural resources for food and energy production, the changing of the environment to produce food and energy, and the intrusion on ecosystems to provide shelter. These general behaviors include a multitude of specific behaviors, including the use and overuse of pesticides, the encroachment upon habitat, over hunting and over fishing, the introduction of plant and animal species into non-native ecosystems, not recycling, and the introduction of hazardous wastes and chemical byproducts into the environment. These behaviors have led to a number of consequences, such as acid rain, ozone depletion, deforestation, urbanization, accelerated species loss, genetic abnormalities, endocrine disruption in populations, and harm to individual animals.

Greenhouse Effect

The **greenhouse effect** refers to a naturally occurring and necessary process. **Greenhouse gasses**, which are ozone, carbon dioxide, water vapor, and methane, trap infrared radiation that is reflected toward the atmosphere. This is actually beneficial in that warm air is trapped. Without the greenhouse effect, it is estimated that the temperature on Earth would be 30 degrees less on average. The problem occurs because human activity generates more greenhouse gases than necessary. The practices that increase the amount of greenhouse gases are the burning of natural gas and oil, farming practices that result in the release of methane and nitrous oxide, factory operations that produce gases, and deforestation practices that decrease the amount of oxygen available to offset greenhouse gases. Population growth also increases the volume of gases released. Excess greenhouse gases cause more infrared radiation to become trapped, which increases the temperature at the Earth's surface.

<u>Impact</u>

Rising temperatures may lead to an increase in sea levels as polar ice melts, lower amounts of available fresh water as coastal areas flood, species extinction because of changes in habitat, increases in certain diseases, and a decreased standard of living for humans. Less fresh water and losses of habitat for humans and other species can also lead to decreased agricultural production and food supply shortages. Increased desertification leads to habitat loss for humans and certain other species. Decreases in animal populations from losses of habitat and increased hunting by other species can lead to extinction. Increases in severe weather, such as huge sustained snowstorms, may also occur at unlikely latitudes. Even though global warming results in weather that is drier and warmer overall, it still gets cold enough to snow. There may be more moisture in the atmosphere due to evaporation. **Global warming** may cause the permanent loss of glaciers and permafrost. There might also be increases in air pollution and acid rain.

Impact of Science and Technology on Environment and Human Affairs

Since the industrial revolution, science and technology have had a profound impact on **human affairs**. There has been a rapid increase in the number of discoveries in many fields. Many major

Copyright © Mometrix Media. You have been licensed one copy of this document for personal use only. Any other reproduction or redistribution is strictly prohibited. All rights reserved.

and minor discoveries have led to a great improvement in the quality of life of many people. This includes longer life spans because of better nutrition, access to medical care, and a decrease in workplace health hazards. Not all of these problems have been solved, and many still exist in one form or another. For example, even though there are means to recycle, not every business does so because of economic factors. These advances, while improving the lives of many humans, have also taken their toll on the environment. A possible solution may arise when the carrying capacity for humans on Earth is reached. The population will decline, and solutions will have to be found. Otherwise, an immediate halt or decrease in the human behaviors that are causing environmental damage will need to happen.

Purpose of Studying Interactions Among Humans, Natural Hazards, and the Environment

In science class, students will learn that the **human population** on earth can be affected by various factors from both their natural environments and from the technologies they use in their daily lives. These factors can be positive or negative, so students need to learn how to prepare for, respond to, and evaluate the consequences of environmental occurrences over a long period of time. Natural disasters are a negative experience, but so are human-made disasters such as pollution and deforestation. Students need to understand that science is involved in the interactions between the human population, natural hazards, and the environment. They should know that the aim of science is to make these interactions **balanced and positive**. Science is a discipline that can help find ways to increase safety during and remediate after natural disasters, advance technology and transportation in an environmentally safe manner, prevent and cure diseases, and remediate the environmental damage that has already been done.

Subjects Covered in Personal Health Portion of Science Class

Among the personal and social perspectives of science are the issues of **personal and public health care**. In this area, students learn such things as:

- The importance of regular **exercise** to the maintenance and improvement of health
- The need for **risk assessment** and educated decisions to prevent injuries and illnesses because of the potential for accidents and the existence of hazards
- The risk of illness and the social and psychological factors associated with the use of **tobacco products**
- The dangers of abusing **alcohol and other drug substances**, including addiction and damage to body functions
- The energy and nutrition values of various **foods**, their role in growth and development, and the requirements of the body according to variable factors
- The complexities of **human sexuality** and the dangers of sexually transmitted diseases
- The relationship between **environmental and human health**, and the need to monitor soil, water, and air standards

Risk and Benefit Analysis as Studied in Personal and Social Perspectives of Science

Risk analysis considers the type of hazard and estimates the number of people who might be exposed and the number likely to suffer consequences. The results are used to determine options for reducing or eliminating risks. For example, the Center for Disease Control must analyze the risk of a certain new virus strain causing a pandemic, how many people and what age groups need to be vaccinated first, and what precautions can be taken to guard against the spread of the disease. **Risk and benefit analysis** involves having students consider the dangers of natural (major storms), chemical (pollution), biological (pollen and bacteria), social (occupational safety and

Copyright © Mometrix Media. You have been licensed one copy of this document for personal use only. Any other reproduction or redistribution is strictly prohibited. All rights reserved.

transportation), and personal (smoking, dieting, and drugs) hazards. Students then use a systematic approach to think critically about these hazards, apply probability estimates to the risks, and compare them to estimated and perceived personal and social benefits.

Interactions of Science and Technology with Society

The interactions of science and technology with society include:

- **Scientific knowledge** and the procedures used by scientists influence the way many people think about themselves, others, and the environment.
- **Technology** influences society through its products and processes. It influences quality of life and the ways people act and interact. Technological changes are often accompanied by social, political, and economic changes. Science and technology contribute enormously to economic growth and productivity. The introduction of the cell phone into society is a perfect example of technology influencing society, quality of life, human interaction, and the economy.
- **Societal challenges** often inspire questions for scientific research, and social priorities often influence research priorities through the availability of research funding.

Science and technology have been advanced through the contributions of many different people in a variety of cultures during different time periods in history. Scientists and engineers work in colleges, businesses and industries, research institutes, and government agencies, touching many lives in a variety of settings.

Components of Scientific Experimentation

- A **hypothesis** is a tentative supposition about a phenomenon (or a fact or set of facts) made in order to examine and test its logical or empirical consequences through investigation or methodological experimentation.
- A **theory** is a scientifically proven, general principle offered to explain phenomena. A theory is derived from a hypothesis and verified by experimentation and research.
- A **scientific law** is a generally accepted conclusion about a body of observations to which no exceptions have been found. Scientific laws explain things, but do not describe them.
- A **control** is a normal, unchanged situation used for comparison against experimental data.
- **Constants** are factors in an experiment that remain the same.
- **Independent variables** are factors, traits, or conditions that are changed in an experiment. A good experiment has only one independent variable so that the scientist can track one thing at a time. The independent variable changes from experiment to experiment.
- **Dependent variables** are changes that result from variations in the independent variable.

Review Video: Experimental Science
Visit mometrix.com/academy and enter code: 283092

Review Video: Experimental Science Project
Visit mometrix.com/academy and enter code: 584444

Science as a Series of Processes

Science is not just the steps of experimentation. While the process of posing a question, forming a hypothesis, testing the hypothesis, recording data, and drawing a conclusion is at the heart of **scientific inquiry**, there are other processes that are important as well. Once the scientist has

Copyright © Mometrix Media. You have been licensed one copy of this document for personal use only. Any other reproduction or redistribution is strictly prohibited. All rights reserved.

completed the testing of a hypothesis and possibly come up with a theory, the scientist should then go through the process of getting feedback from colleagues, publishing an article about the work in a peer-reviewed journal, or otherwise reporting the results to the scientific community, replicating the experiment for verification of results (by the original scientist or others), and developing new questions. Science is not just a means of satisfying curiosity, but is also a process for developing technology, addressing social issues, building knowledge, and solving everyday problems.

Review Video: Scientific Hypothesis and Theories
Visit mometrix.com/academy and enter code: 918083

Drawing Conclusions After Experiments

Conclusions are based on data analysis and background research. The scientist has to take a hard look at the results of an experiment and check the accuracy of the data to draw preliminary conclusions. These should be compared to the background research to find out if the preliminary conclusion can be supported by previous research experiments. If the results do not support the hypothesis, or if they are contrary to what the background research predicted, then further research is needed. The focus should be on finding a reason for the different results. Finally, the scientist provides a discussion of findings that includes a summary of the results of the experiment, a statement as to whether the hypothesis was proven or disproven, a statement of the relationship between the independent and dependent variable, a summary and evaluation of the procedures of the experiment (including comments about successes and effectiveness), and suggestions for changes/modifications in procedures for further studies.

Steps of the Scientific Method

The steps of the **scientific method** are as follows:

1. The scientific method begins with, and absolutely depends upon, the **observation** of objective, unbiased data. Any prejudice or bias in the observed data nullifies its validity. Thus the basic input from the observations must be rigorously screened to ensure objectivity.
2. The development of a **theory or hypotheses** based on objective data is the next step in the scientific method. These theories or hypotheses pose logical expectations that the experiment may yield.
3. Construction of a rigorous and valid **experimental method** designed to test the theories is the next phase of the scientific method. This experimental method must be carefully constructed to give objective, unbiased conclusions based on the hypotheses posited.
4. Careful and statistically correct **analysis and evaluation** of the experimental results make up the next stage.
5. **Modification and replication** of the experiment must then follow to provide a statistically accurate demonstration of the validity of the hypotheses. Equivalent results must be shown from a number of repetitions of the experiment.

Review Video: The Scientific Method
Visit mometrix.com/academy and enter code: 191386

Copyright © Mometrix Media. You have been licensed one copy of this document for personal use only. Any other reproduction or redistribution is strictly prohibited. All rights reserved.

Steps of the Scientific Inquiry

Scientific inquiry is the impetus and catalyst for all scientific research and experimentation. It grows from questions about the observed world and gives us a template with which to apply the scientific method. Steps in scientific inquiry include the following principles:

- Determination and scope of the questions to be investigated are the first step. These may range from simple to extremely complex questions to be explored by scientists.
- The design, strategy, and method of the inquiry are then carefully considered, and a model for the inquiry is constructed.
- The formulation of theories and models based on the careful observation of objective, unbiased data then follows. This formulation is derived from the scope of the scientific inquiry and the questions to be investigated.
- Analysis of possible alternative conclusions drawn from the models and results of experimentation follows.
- Postulating a theory or constructing a scientific statement based on conclusions is the next logical step.
- Defending the scientific statement against alternative hypotheses is a critical function of scientific inquiry.
- Defense of the theory or conclusion against critical analysis is the final step in the process.

Science

Science is a method of acquiring and obtaining knowledge. It is the process of gaining reliable information about the real world, including the explanation of phenomena. It is the development of a body of knowledge about observable phenomena, using the best capabilities humans have at their disposal. The process of organizing and classifying knowledge, through objective observation and evaluation, is a major goal of science. Science can be considered *reliable*, but it is not *infallible*. The limits of human knowledge are constantly growing, often making yesterday's science obsolete and simplistic. Science is thus never fixed; it is always subject to change as new information is gained and synthesized with existing knowledge. Ultimately, science is the sum total of knowledge in any period of time, based on the current abilities of man to understand the world of phenomena, verifiable by observable data.

Limitations of Science

There are clear **limits** on what science can explain. The demand for objectivity both strengthens knowledge we gain from scientific experiments and limits what we can explore. Beyond the realm of scientific inquiry are such questions as "Why does anything exist?" or "What is the meaning of life?" These are subjective questions that do not lend themselves easily to scientific inquiry. These questions, and others like them, come from within, and their conclusions, not validated by science, shape the very fabric of a society. They attempt to give meaning to what may be viewed as chaos.

Periodically, science will impact these **subjective conclusions** with new evidence. For example, the theory of evolution is regarded as blasphemy by many religious fundamentalists. These conflicts may cause great upheavals in society, leaving many to wonder how science and religious belief can be reconciled. Ultimately, observation of the external world must stand as the true test of science.

Copyright © Mometrix Media. You have been licensed one copy of this document for personal use only. Any other reproduction or redistribution is strictly prohibited. All rights reserved.

Hypothetico-Deductive Process

The **hypothetico-deductive process** states that to have an idea and then formulate a hypothesis are essentially creative processes, driven by eons of human experience. Statements about reality are the logical conclusions of observed experience. Such creative propositions are the basis for scientific inquiry. Empirical evidence must then validate these hypotheses. Creative inspiration and scientific validation are interdependent aspects of scientific inquiry. New observations often are the catalyst for creative new theories. Science thus proceeds through creative thinking and scientific validation. There are criticisms of the hypothetico-deductive process: The problem of deduction points out that the original hypothesis may be proved wrong in the future, thus invalidating all subsequent conclusions. The problem of induction, building a theory from generalizations, is that any generalization may be proved wrong by future objective observations. This hypothetico-deductive process, and its problems, is a fascinating subject to philosophers of science.

Hypothesis

It is important to form a **hypothesis** in order to make a tentative explanation that accounts for an unbiased observation. To be scientific, the hypothesis must be testable through experimentation. Careful construction of the experiment provides that predictions derived from the hypothesis are valid. The hypothesis must be formulated in a manner designed to provide a framework for evaluating the results of an experiment. In many scientific experiments, a hypothesis is posited in negative terms because scientists may accept logically plausible ideas until they are proven false. It is more difficult to prove that a hypothesis is true because its validity must be proven in all possible situations under endless variable conditions. Scientists tend to construct hypotheses for testing by creating experiments that might prove them false. If they succeed, the hypothesis must be modified or discarded.

Review Video: Fact, Conclusion, Cause and Effect, Model, and Scientific Law
Visit mometrix.com/academy and enter code: 534217

Review Video: Hypothesis and Null Hypothesis
Visit mometrix.com/academy and enter code: 133239

Basic Science and Applied Science

Basic science and applied science share many attributes but are generally motivated by different influences:

- **Basic science** is spurred on by scientific inquiry, the human need to explain the observed physical world. It may have no specific goal, but is man's response to questions that arise from human curiosity and interest. It is usually an attempt to explain the laws of nature by using the scientific method.
- **Applied science** has a specific practical goal or application: It is designed to solve a problem. Industry and government are institutions that use applied science regularly.

Thus, basic and applied science share many qualities, including scientific inquiry and the scientific method. The goals of each can be very different. It should be pointed out that basic science very often provides results that have uses in applied science.

Copyright © Mometrix Media. You have been licensed one copy of this document for personal use only. Any other reproduction or redistribution is strictly prohibited. All rights reserved.

Benefits of Basic Science

Although **basic science** may have no stated goal or target, it provides many benefits to society:

- Basic science contributes greatly to human understanding and culture, enriching society in many ways.
- Basic science has been responsible for major breakthroughs that have great social and economic impact.
- Basic science provides derivative solutions that can be used in applied science. For example, basic science was critical to the development of the space program, from which countless valuable applications have been derived.
- Basic science contributes to education and research across the broad spectrum of society.

Measuring, Organizing, and Classifying Data

Measuring data is a crucial part of the scientific process. Measurements are most useful if they are quantified—expressed in numbers. Measuring is the process of determining variables such as time, space, and temperature of objects and processes in precise numbers. The metric system is the universal standard of measurement in science. Data must be **organized** in a practical, useful manner to be valuable. Scientists use graphs, charts, tables, and other organizational tools to make data more useful. Data must then be **classified**—grouped into organizational schemes for easy access and use. These schemes attempt to organize the maximum amount of useful data in a format that scientists can use. Although these steps may be less glamorous than other areas of science, they are essential.

Review Video: Variables in an Experiment
Visit mometrix.com/academy and enter code: 648641

Review Video: Terminology for Tables and Graphs
Visit mometrix.com/academy and enter code: 355505

Review Video: Understanding Charts and Tables
Visit mometrix.com/academy and enter code: 882112

Scientific Laws

Scientific principles must meet a high standard to be classified as laws; scientific laws are identified as follows:

- **Scientific laws** must be true, not just probable. A highly probable principle may still be proven false.
- Laws are statements of patterns found in nature.
- Laws may have a universal form but be stated conditionally. For example, the statement "All living human beings breathe," may be restated "If a thing is a living human being it must breathe."
- Laws refer to a general, not a particular, class.
- Laws have purely qualitative predicates.
- Laws must have a formal language of expression to be fully understood. Such a language does not exist now.
- Laws may be probabilistic. For example, a law may state "Eight percent of all dogs are terriers."

Copyright © Mometrix Media. You have been licensed one copy of this document for personal use only. Any other reproduction or redistribution is strictly prohibited. All rights reserved.

Common Criticisms of Deductive Model

The **deductive model** of the scientific method has the following criticisms:

- The deductive model fails to make logical distinctions among explanations, predictions, and descriptions of things to be explained.
- The deductive model is restrictive: It excludes most scientific examples.
- The deductive model is too inclusive: It admits data that cannot be explained.
- The deductive model requires an account of cause, law, and probability, which are basically unsound.
- The deductive model leaves out the elements of context, judgment, and understanding.

Prediction

These are the two widely accepted definitions of **scientific prediction**:

1. In the language of science, prediction is stating in advance the outcome from testing a theory or hypothesis in a controlled experiment. Based on objective observation of data, scientists move from observation of facts to a general explanation, or hypothesis, which must be confirmed by testing through experimentation.
2. Another definition of prediction favored by scientific philosophers is the ability of a hypothesis to lead to deductions of scientific statements that could not be anticipated when the hypothesis was posited. In this sense, prediction means what the scientist can verify from what he or she has deduced from the hypothesis.

Laboratory Safety

The following basic rules should be supplemented by standards appropriate to individual laboratories:

- Hazardous areas must be identified and warnings posted regarding risks.
- A hazard containment plan must be in effect and readily available.
- Safe control of airflow must be maintained at all times.
- Safe work practices must be taught to all who work in the lab.
- Proper maintenance of laboratory equipment must be enforced.
- Safe storage of hazardous material must be implemented.
- Procedures for safe disposal of hazardous wastes must be followed at all times.
- An updated emergency procedure manual must be available.
- A complete emergency first aid kit should be accessible at all times.
- Regular education on the basics of lab safety should be implemented.

Verification and Confirmation of Data in Valid Science

A critical distinction should be made between confirmation and verification of scientific data. **Verification** establishes once and for all the truth of the statement. **Confirmation** is the testing of claims to see how true they are. For a claim to be testable, an experiment must be devised to ensure the validity of the results. A claim can only be confirmed when we know the conditions for verification. A claim confirmation is always relative to the testing procedures. Test results must always be objective and observable. Actually, no factual claim can ever be verified because there is always the possibility of new evidence appearing that proves the claim false. A scientific law must also be confirmed by making predictions based on unbiased, observable data.

Copyright © Mometrix Media. You have been licensed one copy of this document for personal use only. Any other reproduction or redistribution is strictly prohibited. All rights reserved.

Scientific Measurement and Unit Systems

The basis of quantitative measurement is the **unit system**. In order to properly describe how large, how heavy, or how hot something is, it is necessary to have some reference unit. The most commonly used unit system in the world is the **SI**, short for the Systeme International d'Unites, although the English system is still in popular use in the United States. In SI, there are base units and derived units. Derived units may be stated as some combination of the base units. The SI base units for length, mass, time, temperature, and electric current are meter (m), kilogram (kg), second (s), kelvin (K), and ampere (A), respectively. Some common derived units are newtons ($kg\text{-}m/s^2$) and pascals ($kg/m\text{-}s^2$). Most SI units can be scaled up or down by adding a prefix. To alter a unit by 10^3, 10^6, or 10^9, add a prefix of kilo (k), mega (M), or giga (G). For instance, a kilometer (km) is 10^3 meters. To change the unit by a factor of 10^{-3}, 10^{-6}, or 10^{-9}, add a prefix of milli (m), micro (μ), or nano (n). For instance, a microsecond (μs) is 10^{-6} seconds. It is important to note that the SI base unit kilogram has already employed a prefix to scale up the smaller unit, gram (g). *Order of magnitude* is a concept that deals with comparison between two values. If one value differs from the other by a factor of 10^n, it may be said that it differs by n orders of magnitude. Other SI base units include the mole and the candela. Some lesser used prefixes include: hecto (h), 10^2; deca (da), 10^1; deci (d), 10^{-1}; and centi (c), 10^{-2}.

Data Collection and Analysis

In order to take **data measurements** from their experimental setups, scientists will often use measurement devices wired to a computer running data-acquisition software. This allows them to take numerous readings per second if necessary. Once the data is collected, it will often be organized using a spreadsheet, such as Microsoft Excel. This multipurpose program contains several options for displaying the data in graphs or charts, as well as tools for performing statistical analyses or linear regressions. Linear regression is a technique used to determine whether gathered data fits a particular trend or equation. It attempts to fit a common line or curve equation to the data set. A very important concept to understand when taking data is that of **significant figures**. Significant figures, or significant digits, indicate how precisely a quantity is known. Each non-zero digit is always significant. A zero is significant if either: 1) it is to the right of both a non-zero digit and the decimal point; or 2) it is between two other significant digits. For instance, 1.0230 has five significant figures while 0.0230 has only three because the trailing zero is the only zero to the right of both a non-zero and the decimal. When multiplying (or dividing), the product (quotient) has as many significant figures as the factor (dividend or divisor) with the fewest. When adding (or subtracting), the sum (difference) should be rounded to the highest final decimal place of the involved terms.

(3.4 + 56.78 = 60.18 --> 60.2, three significant figures)

Interpretation and Drawing of Conclusions from Data Presented in Tables, Charts, and Graphs

One of the reasons data are so often plotted on graphs is that this format makes it much easier to see **trends** and draw **conclusions**. For instance, on a simple position vs. time graph, the slope of the curve indicates the object's velocity at each point in time. If the curve becomes level, this means the object is not moving. In a simple velocity vs. time graph, the slope of the curve indicates the object's acceleration at each point in time. Additionally, the area contained under the curve indicates the total distance traveled. For instance, if the object is traveling at a constant 5 m/s for 10 s, the velocity vs. time graph will be a straight line at y = 5 between x = 0 and x = 10. The area under this curve is (5 m/s)(10 s) = 50 m. Thus, the object traveled 50 meters. Nearly any type of

Copyright © Mometrix Media. You have been licensed one copy of this document for personal use only. Any other reproduction or redistribution is strictly prohibited. All rights reserved.

quantity may be graphed, so it is important to always check the axis labels to ensure that you know what the graph represents and what units are being used.

Data Errors and Error Analysis

No measurements are ever 100% accurate. There is always some amount of **error** regardless of how careful the observer or how good his equipment. The important thing for the scientist to know is how much error is present in a given measurement. Two commonly misunderstood terms regarding error are accuracy and precision. **Accuracy** is a measure of how close a measurement is to the true value. **Precision** is a measure of how close repeated measurements are to one another. Error is usually quantified using a confidence interval and an uncertainty value. For instance, if the quantity is measured as 100 ± 2 on a 95% confidence interval, this means that there is a 95% chance that the actual value falls between 98 and 102. When looking for the uncertainty in a derived quantity such as density, the errors in the constituent quantities, mass and volume in this case, are propagated to the derived quantity. The percent uncertainty in the density, U_ρ/ρ, can be found by the equation:

$$U_\rho/\rho = \text{sqrt}((U_m/m)^2 + (U_V/V)^2).$$

Importance of Studying Science in Context of Personal and Social Perspectives

Learning must be **relevant**, so when students study science in the context of personal and social perspectives, they see the practical application of the textbook knowledge. They are given an understanding of the issues around them that can be solved by science and the means to act on those issues. Science should be taught within the **social context of history** so that students can see where society has been and how far it has come thanks to scientific advancements related to tools, medicine, transportation, and communication. Students should also understand how these advances developed in response to resources, needs, and values. Students need to review the **process of scientific inquiry** through the centuries to get a sense of the benefits of intellectual curiosity, the inter-relatedness of science, and the development of civilization. Students should question the role science has played in the development of various cultures by considering how computers, refrigeration, vaccines, microscopes, fertilizers, etc. have improved the lives of people.

Inquiry-Based Science

If learning in the science classroom is **inquiry based**, children should see themselves as being involved in the process of learning. They should feel free to express curiosity and skepticism, change ideas and procedures, take risks, and exchange information with their classmates. Inquiry-based learning in science begins with observations of details, sequences, events, changes, similarities and differences, etc. Observations are followed by investigations based on scientific standards and safety that are designed by students. Designs should allow for verification, extension, or dismissal of ideas. Investigations should involve choosing tools, handling materials, measuring, observing, and recording data. The results of an investigation can take the form of a journal, report, drawing, graph, or chart. The summary of the observations and investigation should include explanations, solutions, and connections to other ideas, as well as further questions, an assessment of the quality of the work, a description of any problems encountered, and a description of the strengths and weaknesses of the investigation. Finally, students should reflect together about the lessons learned from the investigation.

Copyright © Mometrix Media. You have been licensed one copy of this document for personal use only. Any other reproduction or redistribution is strictly prohibited. All rights reserved.

Research-Based Teaching Strategies for Science

Research-based teaching strategies for science emphasize student-centered learning and encourage that all new concepts be connected to prior knowledge. Research suggests that having students connect new concepts to prior knowledge allows for new information to be comprehended more easily and retained more frequently. To ensure that activities are developmentally appropriate, teachers must take into consideration the prior knowledge of students, along with students' maturity and ability levels. Students must be mature enough to handle all necessary materials and must also have the ability to complete the tasks assigned to them, with an appropriate level of scaffolding.

Considering Reading Strategies and Mathematical Practices when Choosing Science Content Material

For students to understand and make sense of science materials, certain **reading and math skills** must be attained. For example, when learning about a new science concept, students must have the ability to identify a main idea, analyze new information, interpret findings, and use decoding strategies (as well as context clues) for unknown words or phrases. During labs, students must have the ability to draw conclusions, identify cause and effect, follow written directions and answer questions. When working through specific science topics, students must use their math skills to make sense of problems, persevere through challenging scenarios, reason abstractly, model their findings, and construct arguments to explain why things happen the way they do. When choosing appropriate science content, teachers must gauge the reading and mathematical abilities of their students to ensure that developmentally appropriate materials are provided.

Differentiated Science Instruction and Assessment

Differentiated instruction is the way in which teachers modify the delivery of lessons and assessment of learning to meet the needs of all ability levels. In a science classroom, all students are exposed to the same concepts; however, the delivery of those concepts may look different for each student. Accelerated learners may be expected to read an excerpt from a science journal and answer questions based on their reading, whereas struggling learners may be given a video to watch or listen to a read-aloud to complete a guided note sheet. As an assessment, accelerated learners may be given a task with written directions and the expectation of written responses and explanations. Struggling learners might demonstrate learning of the same concept through the completion of smaller tasks, broken into more manageable chunks, where responses can be written or sketched.

Developmentally Appropriate Assessments in Science Classroom

The three types of assessments in the science classroom are diagnostic, formative, and summative. **Diagnostic assessments** are given at the start of each unit or topic in an effort to determine prior knowledge. This prior knowledge is then used as a way of making a connection to new concepts in a meaningful way. **Formative assessments** are ongoing throughout each unit of study. These assessments are used to track each student's learning and direct future instruction. **Summative assessments** occur at the end of each unit of study to measure each student's comprehension and mastery of the skills and concepts that are being evaluated.

Copyright © Mometrix Media. You have been licensed one copy of this document for personal use only. Any other reproduction or redistribution is strictly prohibited. All rights reserved.

Social Studies

U.S. History

Contributions of Early French Explorers

The **French** never succeeded in attracting settlers to their territories. Those who came were more interested in the fur and fish trades than in forming colonies. Eventually, the French ceded their southern possessions and New Orleans, founded in 1718, to Spain. However, the French made major contributions to the exploration of the new continent, including:

- **Giovanni da Verrazano** and **Jacques Cartier** explored the North American coast and the St. Lawrence Seaway for France.
- **Samuel de Champlain**, who founded Quebec and set up a fur empire on the St. Lawrence Seaway, also explored the coasts of Massachusetts and Rhode Island between 1604 and 1607.
- **Fr. Jacques Marquette**, a Jesuit missionary, and **Louis Joliet** were the first Europeans to travel down the Mississippi in 1673.
- **Rene-Robert de la Salle** explored the Great Lakes and the Illinois and Mississippi Rivers from 1679-1682, claiming all the land from the Great Lakes to the Gulf of Mexico and from the Appalachians to the Rockies for France.

Earliest Spanish Explorers

The **Spanish** claimed and explored huge portions of the United States after the voyages of Christopher Columbus. Among them were:

- **Juan Ponce de Leon** – In 1513, he became the first European in Florida; established the oldest European settlement in Puerto Rico; discovered the Gulf Stream; and searched for the fountain of youth.
- **Alonso Alvarez de Pineda** – He charted the Gulf Coast from Florida to Mexico in 1519. Probably the first European in Texas, he claimed it for Spain.
- **Panfilo de Narvaez** – He docked in Tampa Bay with Cabeza de Vaca in 1528, claimed Florida for Spain, and then sailed the Gulf Coast.
- **Alvar Nuñez Cabeza de Vaca** – He got lost on foot in Texas and New Mexico. Estevanico, or Esteban, a Moorish slave, was a companion who guided them to Mexico.
- **Francisco Vásquez de Coronado** – While searching for gold in 1540, he became the first European to explore Kansas, Oklahoma, Texas, New Mexico, and Arizona.
- **Hernando De Soto** – He was the first European to explore the southeastern United States from Tallahassee to Natchez.

Colonization of Virginia and the Virginia Company

In 1585, **Sir Walter Raleigh** landed on Roanoke Island and sent Arthur Barlow to the mainland, which they named **Virginia**. Two attempts to establish settlements failed. The first permanent English colony was founded by Captain John Smith in **Jamestown** in 1607. The **Virginia Company** and the **Chesapeake Bay Company** successfully colonized other Virginia sites. By 1619, Virginia had a House of Burgesses. The crown was indifferent to the colony, so local government grew strong and tobacco created wealth. The First Families of Virginia dominated politics there for two centuries, and four of the first five United States presidents came from these families. The Virginia

Copyright © Mometrix Media. You have been licensed one copy of this document for personal use only. Any other reproduction or redistribution is strictly prohibited. All rights reserved.

Company sent 24 Puritan families, known as **Pilgrims**, to Virginia on the **Mayflower**. In 1620, it landed at Plymouth, Massachusetts instead. The **Plymouth Plantation** was established and survived with the help of natives. This is where the first Thanksgiving is believed to have occurred.

Colonization in Massachusetts, Maryland, Rhode Island, and Pennsylvania

In 1629, 400 Puritans arrived in **Salem**, which became an important port and was made famous by the witch trials in 1692. In 1628, the self-governed **Massachusetts Bay Company** was organized, and the Massachusetts Indians sold most of the land to the English. **Boston** was established in 1630 and **Harvard University** was established in 1636.

Maryland was established by Lord Baltimore in 1632 in the hopes of providing refuge for English Catholics. The Protestant majority, however, opposed this religious tolerance.

Roger Williams was banished from Massachusetts in 1636 because he called for separation of church and state. He established the **Rhode Island** colony in 1647 and had 800 settlers by 1650, including Anne Hutchinson and her "Antinomians," who attacked clerical authority.

In 1681, **William Penn** received a royal charter for the establishment of **Pennsylvania** as a colony for Quakers. However, religious tolerance allowed immigrants from a mixed group of denominations, who prospered from the beginning.

Reasons for American Revolution

The English colonies **rebelled** for the following reasons:

- England was remote yet **controlling**. By 1775, few Americans had ever been to England. They considered themselves Americans, not English.
- During the Seven Years' War (aka French and Indian War) from 1754-1763, Americans, including George Washington, served in the British army, but were treated as **inferiors**.
- It was feared that the Anglican Church might try to expand in the colonies and **inhibit religious freedom**.
- Heavy **taxation** such as the Sugar and Stamp Acts, which were created solely to create revenue for the crown, and business controls such as restricting trade of certain products to England only, were burdensome.
- The colonies had no official **representation** in the English Parliament and wanted to govern themselves.
- There were fears that Britain would block westward expansion and independent enterprise.
- **Local government**, established through elections by property holders, was already functioning.

Important Events and Groups Leading up to American Revolution

Over several years, various events and groups contributed to the rebellion that became a revolution:

- **Sons of Liberty** – This was the protest group headed by Samuel Adams that incited the Revolution.
- **Boston Massacre** – On March 5, 1770, soldiers fired on a crowd and killed five people.
- **Committees of Correspondence** – These were set up throughout the colonies to transmit revolutionary ideas and create a unified response.

Copyright © Mometrix Media. You have been licensed one copy of this document for personal use only. Any other reproduction or redistribution is strictly prohibited. All rights reserved.

- **The Boston Tea Party** – On December 6, 1773, the Sons of Liberty, dressed as Mohawks, dumped tea into the harbor from a British ship to protest the tea tax. The harsh British response further aggravated the situation.
- **First Continental Congress** – This was held in 1774 to list grievances and develop a response, including boycotts. It was attended by all the colonies with the exception of Georgia.
- **The Shot Heard Round the World** – In April, 1775, English soldiers on their way to confiscate arms in Concord passed through Lexington, Massachusetts and met the colonial militia called the Minutemen. A fight ensued. In Concord, a larger group of Minutemen forced the British to retreat.

Review Video: The First and Second Continental Congress
Visit mometrix.com/academy and enter code: 835211

Original 13 Colonies and Major Turning Points of the Revolution

The original **13 colonies** were: Connecticut, Delaware, Georgia, Maryland, Massachusetts, New Hampshire, New Jersey, New York, North Carolina, Pennsylvania, Rhode Island, South Carolina, and Virginia. Delaware was the first state to ratify the constitution.

The major turning points of the American Revolution were:

- The actions of the **Second Continental Congress** – This body established the Continental Army and chose George Washington as its commanding general. They allowed printing of money and created government offices.
- "**Common Sense**" – Published in 1776 by Thomas Paine, this pamphlet calling for independence was widely distributed.
- The **Declaration of Independence** – Written by Thomas Jefferson, it was ratified on July 4, 1776 by the Continental Congress assembled in Philadelphia.
- **Alliance with France** – Benjamin Franklin negotiated an agreement with France to fight with the Americans in 1778.
- **Treaty of Paris** – In 1782, it signaled the official end of the war, granted independence to the colonies, and gave them generous territorial rights.

Review Video: Declaration of Independence
Visit mometrix.com/academy and enter code: 256838

Review Video: Colonization of the Americas
Visit mometrix.com/academy and enter code: 438412

Articles of Confederation and the Constitution

The **Articles of Confederation**, designed to protect states' rights over those of the national government and sent to the colonies for ratification in 1777, had two major elements that proved unworkable. First, there was no centralized national government. Second, there was no centralized power to tax or regulate trade with other nations or between states. With no national tax, the Revolution was financed by printing more and more money, which caused inflation. In 1787, a convention was called to write a new **constitution**. This constitution created the three branches of government with checks and balances of power: **executive, legislative, and judicial**. It also created a **bicameral legislature** so that there would be equal representation for the states in the Senate and representation for the population in the House. Those who opposed the new

Copyright © Mometrix Media. You have been licensed one copy of this document for personal use only. Any other reproduction or redistribution is strictly prohibited. All rights reserved.

constitution, the **Anti-Federalists**, wanted a bill of rights included. The **Federalist** platform was explained in the "Federalist Papers," written by James Madison, John Jay, and Alexander Hamilton. The Constitution went into effect in 1789, and the **Bill of Rights** was added in 1791.

Review Video: Articles of Confederation
Visit mometrix.com/academy and enter code: 927401

Louisiana Purchase

The **Louisiana Purchase** in 1803 for $15 million may be considered **Thomas Jefferson's** greatest achievement as president. The reasons for the purchase were to gain the vital port of New Orleans, remove the threat of French interference with trade along the Mississippi River, and double the territory of the United States. The purchase both answered and raised new questions about the use of federal power, including the constitutionality of the president making such a purchase, Jefferson asking Congress for permission, and Jefferson taking the biggest federalist action up to that time, even though he was an anti-federalist. Jefferson sent **Meriwether Lewis and William Clark** to map the new territory and find a means of passage all the way to the Pacific Ocean. Although there was no river that flowed all the way west, their expedition and the richness of the land and game started the great western migration of settlers.

War of 1812

A war between **France and Britain** caused blockades that hurt American trade and caused the British to attack American ships and impress sailors on them. An embargo against France and Britain was imposed by Jefferson, but rescinded by Madison with a renewed demand for respect for American sovereignty. However, Britain became more aggressive and war resulted. Native Americans under the leadership of **Tecumseh** sided with the British. The British captured Washington, D.C., and burned the White House, but Dolly Madison had enough forethought to save priceless American treasures, such as the Gilbert Stuart portrait of George Washington. Most battles, however, came to a draw. As a result, in 1815, when the British ended the war with France, they negotiated for peace with the United States as well under the **Treaty of Ghent**. A benefit of the war was that it motivated Americans to become more **self-sufficient** due to increased manufacturing and fewer imports.

Monroe Doctrine, Manifest Destiny, and Missouri Compromise

Three important political actions in the 19th century were:

- The **Monroe Doctrine** – Conceived by President James Monroe in 1823, this foreign policy warned European powers to cease colonization of Central and South America or face military intervention by the United States. In return, the United States would not meddle in the political affairs or standing colonies of Europe.
- The **Missouri Compromise** – In 1820, there were 11 free states and 11 slave states. The fear of a power imbalance between slave and free states when Missouri petitioned to become a slave state brought about this agreement. Maine was brought in as a free state; the southern border of Missouri was set as the northernmost line of any slave territory; and the western states could come in as free states, while Arkansas and Florida could be slave states.
- **Manifest Destiny** – This was a popular belief during the 1840s that it was the right and duty of the United States to expand westward to the Pacific. The idea became a slogan for the flood of settlers and expansionist power grabs.

Copyright © Mometrix Media. You have been licensed one copy of this document for personal use only. Any other reproduction or redistribution is strictly prohibited. All rights reserved.

Review Video: Monroe Doctrine
Visit mometrix.com/academy and enter code: 953021

Review Video: Missouri Compromise
Visit mometrix.com/academy and enter code: 848091

Review Video: Manifest Destiny
Visit mometrix.com/academy and enter code: 957409

Andrew Jackson Presidency

A number of important milestones occurred in American history during the presidency of **Andrew Jackson**. They included:

- Jackson's election is considered the beginning of the modern political party system and the start of the **Democratic Party**.
- Jeffersonian Democracy, a system governed by middle and upper class educated property holders, was replaced by **Jacksonian Democracy**, a system that allowed universal white male suffrage.
- The **Indian Removal Act of 1830** took natives out of territories that whites wanted to settle, most notably the Trail of Tears that removed Cherokees from Georgia and relocated them to Oklahoma.
- The issue of **nullification**, the right of states to nullify any federal laws they thought unconstitutional, came to a head over tariffs. However, a strong majority vote in Congress supporting the Tariff Acts cemented the policy that states must comply with federal laws.

Whig Party

The **Whig Party** existed from 1833 to 1856. It started in opposition to Jackson's **authoritarian policies** and was particularly concerned with defending the supremacy of Congress over the executive branch, states' rights, economic protectionism, and modernization. Notable members included: Daniel Webster, Henry Clay, Winfield Scott, and a young Abraham Lincoln. The Whigs had four presidents: William Henry Harrison, Zachary Taylor, John Tyler (expelled from the party), and Millard Fillmore. However, the Whigs won only two presidential elections. Harrison and Taylor were elected in 1840 and 1848, respectively. However, both died in office, so Tyler and Fillmore assumed the presidency. In 1852, the anti-slavery faction of the party kept Fillmore from getting the nomination. Instead, it went to Scott, who was soundly defeated. In 1856, the Whigs supported Fillmore and the National American Party, but lost badly. Thereafter, the **split over slavery** caused the party to dissolve.

Important 19th Century American Writers

In the 19th century, American literature became an entity of its own and provided a distinct voice for the American experience. **James Fenimore Cooper** was a great writer from this time period. He was the first to write about Native Americans, and was the author of the Leatherstocking series, which includes *The Last of the Mohicans* and *The Deerslayer*.

- **Ralph Waldo Emerson** – He was an essayist, philosopher, and poet, and also the leader of the Transcendentalist movement. His notable works include "Self-Reliance" and "The American Scholar."

Copyright © Mometrix Media. You have been licensed one copy of this document for personal use only. Any other reproduction or redistribution is strictly prohibited. All rights reserved.

- **Nathaniel Hawthorne** – This novelist and short story writer wrote *The Scarlet Letter, The House of Seven Gables*, "Young Goodman Brown," and "The Minister's Black Veil."
- **Herman Melville** – He was a novelist, essayist, short story writer, and poet who wrote *Moby Dick, Billy Budd*, and "Bartleby the Scrivener." **Edgar Allan Poe** – He was a poet, literary critic, and master of the short story, especially horror and detective stories. His notable works include "The Tell-Tale Heart," "The Pit and the Pendulum," "Annabel Lee," and "The Raven."
- **Harriet Beecher Stowe** – She was the author of *Uncle Tom's Cabin.*
- **Henry David Thoreau** – He was a poet, naturalist, and Transcendentalist who wrote *Walden* and *Civil Disobedience.*
- **Walt Whitman** – He was a poet, essayist, and journalist who wrote *Leaves of Grass* and "O Captain! My Captain!"

19th Century Social and Religious Leaders

Some of the important social and religious leaders from the 19th century were:

- **Susan B. Anthony** – A women's rights and abolition activist, she lectured across the nation for suffrage, property and wage rights, and labor organizations for women.
- **Dorothea Dix** – She created the first American asylums for the treatment of mental illness and served as the Superintendent of Army Nurses during the War Between the States.
- **Frederick Douglass** –An escaped slave who became an abolitionist leader, government official, and writer.
- **William Lloyd Garrison** –An abolitionist and the editor of the *Liberator*, the leading anti-slavery newspaper of the time.
- **Joseph Smith** – He founded the Latter-Day Saints (Mormonism) in 1829.
- **Horace Mann** – A leader of the common school movement that made public education a right of all Americans.
- **Elizabeth Cady Stanton** – With Lucretia Mott, she held the Seneca Falls Convention in 1848, demanding women's suffrage and other reforms.
- **Brigham Young** –The leader of the Mormons when they fled religious persecution, built Salt Lake City, and settled much of the West. He was the first governor of the Utah Territory.

Compromise of 1850, Fugitive Slave Law, Kansas-Nebraska Act, Bleeding Kansas, and Dred Scott Case

- The **Compromise of 1850**, calling upon the principle of popular sovereignty, allowed those who lived in the Mexican cession to decide for themselves whether to be a free or slave territory.
- The **Fugitive Slave Law of 1850** allowed slave owners to go into free states to retrieve their escaped slaves.
- The **Kansas-Nebraska Act of 1854** repealed the Missouri Compromise of 1820 to allow the lands from the Louisiana Purchase to settle the slavery issue by popular sovereignty. Outraged Northerners responded by defecting from the Whig Party and starting the Republican Party.
- **Bleeding Kansas** was the name applied to the state when a civil war broke out between pro- and anti-slavery advocates while Kansas was trying to formalize its statutes before being admitted as a state.

Copyright © Mometrix Media. You have been licensed one copy of this document for personal use only. Any other reproduction or redistribution is strictly prohibited. All rights reserved.

- The **Dred Scott vs. Sandford case** was decided by the Supreme Court in 1857. It was ruled that Congress had no authority to exclude slavery from the territories, which in effect meant that the Missouri Compromise had been unconstitutional.

States Forming the Confederacy and Leaders of the War Between the States

The states that **seceded** from the Union to form the Confederacy were: Georgia, Arkansas, South Carolina, North Carolina, Virginia, Florida, Mississippi, Alabama, Louisiana, Texas, and Tennessee. The slave-holding states that were kept in the Union were Delaware, Maryland, Kentucky, and Missouri.

- **Jefferson Davis** of Mississippi, a former U. S. senator and cabinet member, was the president of the Confederacy.
- **Abraham Lincoln** of Illinois was the President of the United States. His election triggered the secession of the south. He was assassinated shortly after winning a second term.
- **Robert E. Lee** of Virginia was offered the position of commanding general of the Union Army, but declined because of loyalty to his home state. He led the Army of Northern Virginia and the central Confederate force, and is still considered a military mastermind.
- **Ulysses S. Grant** of Ohio wasn't appointed to command the Union Army until 1864, after a series of other commanders were unsuccessful. He received Lee's surrender at the Appomattox Court House in Virginia in April, 1865, and went on to become President from 1869 to 1877.

Reconstruction and 13th, 14th, and 15th Amendments

Reconstruction was the period from 1865 to 1877, during which the South was under strict control of the U.S. government. In March, 1867, all state governments of the former Confederacy were terminated, and **military occupation** began. Military commanders called for constitutional conventions to reconstruct the state governments, to which delegates were to be elected by universal male suffrage. After a state government was in operation and the state had **ratified the 14th Amendment**, its representatives were admitted to Congress. Three constitutional amendments from 1865 to 1870, which tried to rectify the problems caused by slavery, became part of the Reconstruction effort. The **13th Amendment** declared slavery illegal. The **14th Amendment** made all persons born or naturalized in the country U.S. citizens, and forbade any state to interfere with their fundamental civil rights. The **15th Amendment** made it illegal to deny individuals the right to vote on the grounds of race. In his 1876 election campaign, President **Rutherford B. Hayes** promised to withdraw the troops, and did so in 1877.

Major Changes in Industry in the Late 1800s

Important events during this time of enormous business growth and large-scale exploitation of natural resources were:

- **Industrialization** – Like the rest of the world, the United States' entry into the Industrial Age was marked by many new inventions and the mechanization of factories.
- **Railroad expansion** – The Transcontinental Railroad was built from 1865 to 1969. Railroad tracks stretched over 35,000 miles in 1865, but that distance reached 240,000 miles by 1910. The raw materials and manufactured goods needed for the railroads kept mines and factories very busy.
- **Gold and silver mining** – Mines brought many prospectors to the West from 1850 to about 1875, but mining corporations soon took over.

Copyright © Mometrix Media. You have been licensed one copy of this document for personal use only. Any other reproduction or redistribution is strictly prohibited. All rights reserved.

- **Cattle ranching** – This was a large-scale enterprise beginning in the late 1860s, but by the 1880s open ranges were being fenced and plowed for farming and pastures. Millions of farmers moved into the high plains, establishing the "Bread Basket," which was the major wheat growing area of the country.

Gilded Age and Infamous Robber Barons

The **Gilded Age**, from the 1870s to 1890, was so named because of the enormous wealth and grossly opulent lifestyle enjoyed by a handful of powerful families. This was the time when huge mansions were built as summer "cottages" in Newport, Rhode Island, and great lodges were built in mountain areas for the pleasure of families such as the Vanderbilts, Ascots, and Rockefellers. Control of the major industries was held largely by the following men, who were known as **Robber Barons** for their ruthless business practices and exploitation of workers: Jay Gould, railroads; Andrew Carnegie, steel; John D. Rockefeller, Sr., oil; Philip Danforth Armour, meatpacking; J. P. Morgan, banking; John Jacob Astor, fur pelts; and Cornelius Vanderbilt, steamboat shipping. Of course, all of these heads of industry diversified and became involved in multiple business ventures. To curb cutthroat competition, particularly among the railroads, and to prohibit restrained trade, Congress created the **Interstate Commerce Commission** and the **Sherman Anti-Trust Act**. Neither of these, however, was enforced.

Review Video: The Gilded Age: An Overview
Visit mometrix.com/academy and enter code: 684770

Review Video: The Gilded Age: Chinese Immigration
Visit mometrix.com/academy and enter code: 624166

Review Video: The Gilded Age: Labor Strikes
Visit mometrix.com/academy and enter code: 683116

Review Video: The Gilded Age: Labor Unions
Visit mometrix.com/academy and enter code: 749692

Immigration Trends in Late 1800s

The population of the United States doubled between 1860 and 1890, the period that saw 10 million **immigrants** arrive. Most lived in the north. Cities and their **slums** grew tremendously because of immigration and industrialization. While previous immigrants had come from Germany, Scandinavia, and Ireland, the 1880s saw a new wave of immigrants from Italy, Poland, Hungary, Bohemia, and Greece, as well as Jewish groups from central and eastern Europe, especially Russia. The Roman Catholic population grew from 1.6 million in 1850 to 12 million in 1900, a growth that ignited an anti-Catholic backlash from the anti-Catholic Know-Nothing Party of the 1880s and the Ku Klux Klan. Exploited immigrant workers started **labor protests** in the 1870s, and the **Knights of Labor** was formed in 1878, calling for sweeping social and economic reform. Its membership reached 700,000 by 1886. Eventually, this organization was replaced by the **American Federation of Labor**, headed by Samuel Gompers.

Effects of Progressive Movement on Foreign Affairs

The **Progressive Era**, which was the time period from the 1890s to the 1920s, got its name from progressive, reform-minded political leaders who wanted to export a just and rational social order to the rest of the world while increasing trade with foreign markets. Consequently, the United States interfered in a dispute between Venezuela and Britain. America invoked the **Monroe**

Copyright © Mometrix Media. You have been licensed one copy of this document for personal use only. Any other reproduction or redistribution is strictly prohibited. All rights reserved.

Doctrine and sided with Cuba in its independence struggle against Spain. The latter resulted in the **Spanish-American Wars** in 1898 that ended with Cuba, Puerto Rico, the Philippines, and Guam becoming American protectorates at the same time the United States annexed Hawaii. In 1900, America declared an **Open Door policy** with China to support its independence and open markets. In 1903, Theodore Roosevelt helped Panama become independent of Columbia, and then secured the right to build the **Panama Canal**. Roosevelt also negotiated the peace treaty to end the Russo-Japanese War, which earned him the Nobel Peace prize. He then sent the American fleet on a world cruise to display his country's power.

Review Video: The Progressive Era
Visit mometrix.com/academy and enter code: 722394

Domestic Accomplishments of Progressive Era

To the Progressives, promoting law and order meant cleaning up city governments to make them honest and efficient, bringing more democracy and humanity to state governments, and establishing a core of social workers to improve slum housing, health, and education. Also during the **Progressive Era**, the national government strengthened or created the following regulatory agencies, services, and acts to oversee business enterprise:

- Passed in 1906, the **Hepburn A**ct reinforced the Interstate Commerce Commission. In 1902, Roosevelt used the Justice Department and lawsuits to try to break monopolies and enforce the **Sherman Anti-Trust Act**. The **Clayton Anti-Trust Act** was added in 1914.
- From 1898 to 1910, the **Forest Service** guided lumber companies in the conservation and more efficient use of woodland resources under the direction of Gifford Pinchot.
- In 1906, the **Pure Food and Drug Act** was passed to protect consumers from fraudulent labeling and adulteration of products.
- In 1913, the **Federal Reserve System** was established to supervise banking and commerce. In 1914, the **Fair Trade Commission** was established to ensure fair competition.

US Involvement in World War I

When World War I broke out in 1914, America declared **neutrality**. The huge demand for war goods by the Allies broke a seven-year industrial stagnation and gave American factories full-time work. The country's sympathies lay mostly with the Allies, and before long American business and banking were heavily invested in an Allied victory. In 1916, **Woodrow Wilson** campaigned on the slogan "He kept us out of war." However, when the British ship the ***Lusitania*** was torpedoed in 1915 by a German submarine and many Americans were killed, Wilson had already warned the Germans that the United States would enter the war if Germany interfered with neutral ships at sea. Eventually, when it was proven that Germany was trying to incite Mexico and Japan into attacking the United States, Wilson declared war in 1917, even though America was unprepared.

Copyright © Mometrix Media. You have been licensed one copy of this document for personal use only. Any other reproduction or redistribution is strictly prohibited. All rights reserved.

Nonetheless, America quickly armed and transferred sufficient troops to Europe, bringing the **Allies** to victory in 1918.

> **Review Video: WWI Overview**
> Visit mometrix.com/academy and enter code: 659767
>
> **Review Video: World War I: European Alliances**
> Visit mometrix.com/academy and enter code: 257458
>
> **Review Video: World War I: Outcomes**
> Visit mometrix.com/academy and enter code: 278666

Decade of Optimism

After World War I, **Warren Harding** ran for President on the slogan "return to normalcy" and concentrated on domestic affairs. The public felt optimistic because life improved due to affordable automobiles from Henry Ford's mass production system, better roads, electric lights, airplanes, new communication systems, and voting rights for women (19th Amendment, 1920). Radio and movies helped develop a national culture. For the first time, the majority of Americans lived in **cities**. Young people shortened dresses and haircuts, and smoked and drank in public despite Prohibition (18th Amendment, 1919). Meantime, the **Russian Revolution** caused a **Red Scare** that strengthened the already strong Ku Klux Klan that controlled some states' politics. In 1925, the **Scopes trial** in Tennessee convicted a high school teacher for presenting Darwinian theories. The **Teapot Dome scandal** rocked the Harding administration. After Harding died in 1923, **Calvin Coolidge** became president. He was followed by **Herbert Hoover**, a strong proponent of capitalism under whom unregulated business led to the 1929 stock crash.

Great Depression and Dust Bowl

In the 1920s, the rich got richer. After World War I, however, farmers were in a depression when foreign markets started growing their own crops again. Increased credit buying, bank war debts, a huge gap between rich and poor, and a belief that the stock market would always go up got the nation into financial trouble. The **Stock Market Crash** in October 1929 that destroyed fortunes dramatized the downward spiral of the whole economy. Banks failed, and customers lost all their money. By 1933, 14 million were unemployed, industrial production was down to one-third of its 1929 level, and national income had dropped by half. Adding to the misery of farmers, years of breaking sod on the prairies without adequate conservation techniques caused the topsoil to fly away in great **dust storms** that blackened skies for years, causing deaths from lung disease and failed crops.

US Role in World War II

World War II began in 1939. As with World War I, the United States tried to stay out of World War II, even though the **Lend-Lease program** transferred munitions to Great Britain. However, on December 7, 1941, Japan attacked **Pearl Harbor** in Hawaii. Since Japan was an ally of Germany, the United States declared war on all the Axis powers. Although there was fighting in both Europe and the Pacific, the decision was made to concentrate on defeating Hitler first. Since it did not have combat within its borders, the United States became the great manufacturer of goods and munitions for the war effort. Women went to work in the factories, while the men entered the military. All facets of American life were centered on the war effort, including rationing, metal collections, and buying war bonds. The benefit of this production was an **end to the economic**

Copyright © Mometrix Media. You have been licensed one copy of this document for personal use only. Any other reproduction or redistribution is strictly prohibited. All rights reserved.

depression. The influx of American personnel and supplies eventually brought victory in Europe in April of 1945, and in Asia the following August.

> **Review Video:** World War II
> Visit mometrix.com/academy and enter code: 759402
>
> **Review Video:** World War II: Germany
> Visit mometrix.com/academy and enter code: 951452
>
> **Review Video:** World War II: Japan
> Visit mometrix.com/academy and enter code: 313104

Major Programs and Events Resulting from the Cold War

After World War II, the Soviet Union kept control of Eastern Europe, including half of Germany. **Communism** spread around the world. Resulting fears led to:

- The **Truman Doctrine** (1947) – This was a policy designed to protect free peoples everywhere against oppression.
- The **Marshall Plan** (1948) – This devoted $12 billion to rebuild Western Europe and strengthen its defenses.
- The **Organization of American States** (1948) – This was established to bolster democratic relations in the Americas.
- The **Berlin Blockade** (1948-49) – The Soviets tried to starve out West Berlin, so the United States provided massive supply drops by air.
- The **North Atlantic Treaty Organization** (1949) – This was formed to militarily link the United States and western Europe so that an attack on one was an attack on both.
- The **Korean War** (1950-53) – This divided the country into the communist North and the democratic South.
- The **McCarthy era** (1950-54) – Senator Joseph McCarthy of Wisconsin held hearings on supposed Communist conspiracies that ruined innocent reputations and led to the blacklisting of suspected sympathizers in the government, Hollywood, and the media.

> **Review Video:** The Cold War: The United States and Russia
> Visit mometrix.com/academy and enter code: 981433

Major Events of 1960s

The 1960s were a tumultuous time for the United States. Major events included:

- The **Cuban Missile Crisis** (1961) – This was a stand-off between the United States and the Soviet Union over a build-up of missiles in Cuba. Eventually, the Soviets stopped their shipments and a nuclear war was averted.
- The assassinations of President Kennedy (1963), Senator Robert Kennedy (1968), and Dr. Martin Luther King, Jr. (1968).
- The **Civil Rights Movement** – Protest marches held across the nation to draw attention to the plight of black citizens. From 1964 to 1968, race riots exploded in more than 100 cities.
- The **Vietnam War** (1964-73) – This resulted in a military draft. There was heavy involvement of American personnel and money. There were also protest demonstrations, particularly on college campuses. At Kent State, several students died after being shot by National Guardsmen.

Copyright © Mometrix Media. You have been licensed one copy of this document for personal use only. Any other reproduction or redistribution is strictly prohibited. All rights reserved.

- **Major legislation** – Legislation passed during this decade included the Civil Rights Act, the Clean Air Act, and the Water Quality Act. This decade also saw the creation of the Peace Corps, Medicare, and the War on Poverty, in which billions were appropriated for education, urban redevelopment, and public housing.

Presidents and Vice Presidents from 1972 to 1974

In a two-year time span, the United States had two presidents and two vice presidents. This situation resulted first from the resignation of Vice President **Spiro T. Agnew** in October of 1973 because of alleged kickbacks. President **Richard M. Nixon** then appointed House Minority Leader **Gerald R. Ford** to be vice president. This was accomplished through Senate ratification, a process that had been devised after Harry Truman succeeded to the presidency upon the death of Franklin Roosevelt and went through nearly four years of his presidency without a vice president. Nixon resigned the presidency in August of 1974 because some Republican party members broke into Democratic headquarters at the **Watergate** building in Washington, DC, and the president participated in covering up the crime. Ford succeeded Nixon, and had to appoint another vice president. He chose **Nelson Rockefeller**, former governor of New York.

U.S. Government

Principles of the Constitution

The six basic principles of the Constitution are:

1. **Popular Sovereignty** – The people establish government and give power to it; the government can function only with the consent of the people.
2. **Limited Government** – The Constitution specifies limits on government authority, and no official or entity is above the law.
3. **Separation of Powers** – Power is divided among three government branches: the legislative (Congress), the executive (President), and the judicial (federal courts).
4. **Checks and Balances** – This is a system that enforces the separation of powers and ensures that each branch has the authority and ability to restrain the powers of the other two branches, thus preventing tyranny.
5. **Judicial Review** – Judges in the federal courts ensure that no act of government is in violation of the Constitution. If an act is unconstitutional, the judicial branch has the power to nullify it.
6. **Federalism** – This is the division of power between the central government and local governments, which limits the power of the federal government and allows states to deal with local problems.

Classic Forms of Government

Forms of government that have appeared throughout history include:

- **Feudalism** – This is based on the rule of local lords who are loyal to the king and control the lives and production of those who work on their land.
- **Classical republic** – This form is a representative democracy. Small groups of elected leaders represent the interests of the electorate.
- **Absolute monarchy** – A king or queen has complete control of the military and government.

Copyright © Mometrix Media. You have been licensed one copy of this document for personal use only. Any other reproduction or redistribution is strictly prohibited. All rights reserved.

- **Authoritarianism** – An individual or group has unlimited authority. There is no system in place to restrain the power of the government.
- **Dictatorship** – Those in power are not held responsible to the people.
- **Autocracy** – This is rule by one person (despot), not necessarily a monarch, who uses power tyrannically.
- **Oligarchy** – A small, usually self-appointed elite rules a region.
- **Liberal democracy** – This is a government based on the consent of the people that protects individual rights and freedoms from any intolerance by the majority.
- **Totalitarianism** – All facets of the citizens' lives are controlled by the government.

Influences of Philosophers on Political Study

Ancient Greek philosophers **Aristotle** and **Plato** believed political science would lead to order in political matters, and that this scientifically organized order would create stable, just societies.

Thomas Aquinas adapted the ideas of Aristotle to a Christian perspective. His ideas stated that individuals should have certain rights, but also certain duties, and that these rights and duties should determine the type and extent of government rule. In stating that laws should limit the role of government, he laid the groundwork for ideas that would eventually become modern constitutionalism. **Niccolò Machiavelli**, author of *The Prince*, was a proponent of politics based solely on power.

Parliamentary and Democratic Systems of Government

In a **parliamentary system**, government involves a legislature and a variety of political parties. The head of government, usually a Prime Minister, is typically the head of the dominant party. A head of state can be elected, or this position can be taken by a monarch, such as in Great Britain's constitutional monarchy system.

In a **democratic system** of government, the people elect their government representatives. The term democracy is a Greek term that means "for the rule of the people." There are two forms of democracy—direct and indirect. In a direct democracy, each issue or election is decided by a vote where each individual is counted separately. An indirect democracy employs a legislature that votes on issues that affect large number of people whom the legislative members represent. Democracy can exist as a Parliamentary system or a Presidential system. The US is a presidential, indirect democracy.

Bill of Rights

The **United States Bill of Rights** was based on principles established by the **Magna Carta** in 1215, the 1688 **English Bill of Rights**, and the 1776 **Virginia Bill of Rights**. In 1791, the federal government added 10 amendments to the United States Constitution that provided the following **protections**:

- Freedom of speech, religion, peaceful assembly, petition of the government, and petition of the press
- The right to keep and bear arms
- No quartering of soldiers on private property without the consent of the owner
- Regulations on government search and seizure
- Provisions concerning prosecution
- The right to a speedy, public trial and the calling of witnesses

Copyright © Mometrix Media. You have been licensed one copy of this document for personal use only. Any other reproduction or redistribution is strictly prohibited. All rights reserved.

- The right to trial by jury
- Freedom from excessive bail or cruel punishment
- These rights are not necessarily the only rights
- Powers not prohibited by the Constitution are reserved to the states.

Review Video: Bill of Rights
Visit mometrix.com/academy and enter code: 585149

Making a Formal Amendment to the Constitution

So far, there have been only **27 amendments** to the federal Constitution. There are four different ways to change the wording of the constitution: two methods for proposal and two methods for ratification:

1. An amendment is proposed by a two-thirds vote in each house of Congress and ratified by three-fourths of the state legislatures.
2. An amendment is proposed by a two-thirds vote in each house of Congress and ratified by three-fourths of the states in special conventions called for that purpose.
3. An amendment is proposed by a national convention that is called by Congress at the request of two-thirds of the state legislatures and ratified by three-fourths of the state legislatures.
4. An amendment is proposed by a national convention that is called by Congress at the request of two-thirds of the state legislatures and ratified by three-fourths of the states in special conventions called for that purpose.

Review Video: Amending the Constitution
Visit mometrix.com/academy and enter code: 147023

Division of Powers

The division of powers in the federal government system is as follows:

- **National** – This level can coin money, regulate interstate and foreign trade, raise and maintain armed forces, declare war, govern United States territories and admit new states, and conduct foreign relations.
- **Concurrent** – This level can levy and collect taxes, borrow money, establish courts, define crimes and set punishments, and claim private property for public use.
- **State** – This level can regulate trade and business within the state, establish public schools, pass license requirements for professionals, regulate alcoholic beverages, conduct elections, and establish local governments.

There are three types of delegated powers granted by the Constitution:

1. **Expressed or enumerated powers** – These are specifically spelled out in the Constitution.
2. **Implied** – These are not expressly stated, but are reasonably suggested by the expressed powers.
3. **Inherent** – These are powers not expressed by the Constitution but ones that national governments have historically possessed, such as granting diplomatic recognition.

Copyright © Mometrix Media. You have been licensed one copy of this document for personal use only. Any other reproduction or redistribution is strictly prohibited. All rights reserved.

Powers can also be classified or reserved or exclusive. **Reserved powers** are not granted to the national government, but not denied to the states. **Exclusive powers** are those reserved to the national government, including concurrent powers.

Stages of Extending Suffrage in US

Originally, the Constitution of 1789 provided the right to vote only to white male property owners. Through the years, suffrage was extended through the following five stages.

1. In the early1800s, states began to eliminate **property ownership** and **tax payment qualifications**.
2. By 1810, there were no more **religious tests** for voting. In the late 1800s, the 15th Amendment protected citizens from being denied the right to vote because of **race or color**.
3. In 1920, the 19th Amendment prohibited the denial of the right to vote because of **gender**, and women were given the right to vote.
4. Passed in 1961 and ratified in 1964, the 23rd Amendment added the voters of the **District of Columbia** to the presidential electorate and eliminated the poll tax as a condition for voting in federal elections. The **Voting Rights Act of 1965** prohibited disenfranchisement through literacy tests and various other means of discrimination.
5. In 1971, the 26th Amendment set the minimum voting age at **18 years of age**.

Major Supreme Court Cases

Out of the many Supreme Court rulings, several have had critical historical importance. These include:

- **Marbury v. Madison** (1803) – This ruling established judicial review as a power of the Supreme Court.
- **Dred Scott v. Sandford** (1857) – This decision upheld property rights over human rights in the case of a slave who had been transported to a free state by his master, but was still considered a slave.
- **Brown v. Board of Education** (1954) – The Court ruled that segregation was a violation of the Equal Protection Clause and that the "separate but equal" practice in education was unconstitutional. This decision overturned the 1896 Plessy v. Ferguson ruling that permitted segregation if facilities were equal.
- **Miranda v. Arizona** (1966) – This ruling made the reading of Miranda rights to those arrested for crimes the law. It ensured that confessions could not be illegally obtained and that citizen rights to fair trials and protection under the law would be upheld.

Review Video: Landmark Supreme Court Cases
Visit mometrix.com/academy and enter code: 753011

Famous Speeches in US History That Defined Government Policy, Foreign Relations, and American Spirit

Among the best-known speeches and famous lines known to modern Americans are the following:

- The **Gettysburg Address** – Made by Abraham Lincoln on November 19, 1863, it dedicated the battleground's cemetery.
- The **Fourteen Points** – Made by Woodrow Wilson on January 18, 1918, this outlined Wilson's plans for peace and the League of Nations.

Copyright © Mometrix Media. You have been licensed one copy of this document for personal use only. Any other reproduction or redistribution is strictly prohibited. All rights reserved.

- **Address to Congress** – Made by Franklin Roosevelt on December 8, 1941, it declared war on Japan and described the attack on Pearl Harbor as "a day which will live in infamy."
- **Inaugural Address** – Made by John F. Kennedy on January 20, 1961, it contained the famous line: "Ask not what your country can do for you, ask what you can do for your country."
- **Berlin Address** – Made by John F. Kennedy on June 26, 1963, it contained the famous line "Ich bin ein Berliner," which expressed empathy for West Berliners in their conflict with the Soviet Union.
- "**I Have a Dream**" and "**I See the Promised Land**" – Made by Martin Luther King, Jr. on August 28, 1963 and April 3, 1968, respectively, these speeches were hallmarks of the Civil Rights Movement.
- **Brandenburg Gate speech** – Made by Ronald Reagan on June 12, 1987, this speech was about the Berlin Wall and the end of the Cold War. It contained the famous line "Tear down this wall."

Closed and Open Primaries in a Direct Primary System

The **direct primary system** is a means for members of a political party to participate in the selection of a candidate from their party to compete against the other party's candidate in a general election. A **closed primary** is a party nominating election in which only declared party members can vote. Party membership is usually established by registration. Currently, 26 states and the District of Columbia use this system. An **open primary** is a party nominating election in which any qualified voter can take part. The voter makes a public choice at the polling place about which primary to participate in, and the choice does not depend on any registration or previous choices. A **blanket primary**, which allowed voters to vote in the primaries of both parties, was used at various times by three states. The Supreme Court ruled against this practice in 2000.

Important Documents in United States History and Government

The following are among the greatest **American documents** because of their impact on foreign and domestic policy:

- Declaration of Independence (1776)
- The Articles of Confederation (1777)
- The Constitution (1787) and the Bill of Rights (1791)
- The Northwest Ordinance (1787)
- The Federalist Papers (1787-88)
- George Washington's Inaugural Address (1789) and Farewell Address (1796)
- The Alien and Sedition Act (1798)
- The Louisiana Purchase Treaty (1803)
- The Monroe Doctrine (1823); The Missouri Compromise (1830)
- The Compromise of 1850
- The Kansas-Nebraska Act (1854)
- The Homestead Act (1862)
- The Emancipation Proclamation (1863)
- The agreement to purchase Alaska (1866)
- The Sherman Anti-Trust Act (1890)
- Theodore Roosevelt's Corollary to the Monroe Doctrine (1905)

Copyright © Mometrix Media. You have been licensed one copy of this document for personal use only. Any other reproduction or redistribution is strictly prohibited. All rights reserved.

- The Social Security Act (1935) and other acts of the New Deal in the 1930s; The Truman Doctrine (1947); The Marshall Plan (1948)
- The Civil Rights Act (1964)

Federal Taxes

The four types of **federal taxes** are:

- **Income taxes on individuals** – This is a complex system because of demands for various exemptions and rates. Further, the schedule of rates can be lowered or raised according to economic conditions in order to stimulate or restrain economic activity. For example, a tax cut can provide an economic stimulus, while a tax increase can slow down the rate of inflation. Personal income tax generates about five times as much as corporate taxes. Rates are based on an individual's income, and range from 10 to 35 percent.
- **Income taxes on corporations** – The same complexity of exemptions and rates exists for corporations as individuals. Taxes can be raised or lowered according to the need to stimulate or restrain the economy.
- **Excise taxes** – These are taxes on specific goods such as tobacco, liquor, automobiles, gasoline, air travel, and luxury items, or on activities such as highway usage by trucks.
- **Customs duties** – These are taxes imposed on imported goods. They serve to regulate trade between the United States and other countries.

United States Currency System

The Constitution of 1787 gave the United States Congress the central authority to **print or coin money** and to **regulate its value**. Before this time, states were permitted to maintain separate currencies. The currency system is based on a **modified gold standard**. There is an enormous store of gold to back up United States currency housed at Fort Knox, Kentucky. Paper money is actually **Federal Reserve notes** and coins. It is the job of the Bureau of Engraving and Printing in the Treasury Department to design plates, special types of paper, and other security measures for bills and bonds. This money is put into general circulation by the Treasury and Federal Reserve Banks, and is taken out of circulation when worn out. Coins are made at the Bureau of the Mint in Philadelphia, Denver, and San Francisco.

Employment Act of 1946

The **Employment Act of 1946** established the following entities to combat unemployment:

- The **Council of Economic Advisers** (CEA) – Composed of a chair and two other members appointed by the President and approved by the Senate, this council assists the President with the development and implementation of U.S. economic policy. The Council members and their staff, located in the Executive Office, are professionals in economics and statistics who forecast economic trends and provide analysis based on evidence-based research.
- The **Economic Report of the President** – This is presented every January by the President to Congress. Based on the work of the Council, the report recommends a program for maximizing employment, and may also recommend legislation.
- **Joint Economic Committee** (JEC) – This is a committee composed of 10 members of the House and 10 members of the Senate that makes a report early each year on its continuous study of the economy. Study is conducted through hearings and research, and the report is made in response to the president's recommendations.

Copyright © Mometrix Media. You have been licensed one copy of this document for personal use only. Any other reproduction or redistribution is strictly prohibited. All rights reserved.

Qualifications of a US Citizen

Anyone born in the US, born abroad to a US citizen, or who has gone through a process of **naturalization** to become a citizen, is considered a **citizen** of the United States. It is possible to lose US citizenship as a result of conviction of certain crimes such as treason. Citizenship may also be lost if a citizen pledges an oath to another country or serves in the military of a country engaged in hostilities with the US. A US citizen can also choose to hold dual citizenship, work as an expatriate in another country without losing US citizenship, or even renounce citizenship if he or she so chooses.

Rights, Duties, and Responsibilities Granted to or Expected from US Citizens

Citizens are granted certain rights under the US government. The most important of these are defined in the **Bill of Rights**, and include freedom of speech, religion, assembly, and a variety of other rights the government is not allowed to remove.

Duties of a US citizen include:

- Paying taxes
- Loyalty to the government, though the US does not prosecute those who criticize or seek to change the government
- Support and defend the Constitution
- Serve in the Armed Forces as required by law
- Obeying laws as set forth by the various levels of government.

Responsibilities of a US citizen include:

- Voting in elections
- Respecting one another's rights and not infringing upon them
- Staying informed about various political and national issues
- Respecting one another's beliefs

Representative Democracy

In a system of government characterized as a representative democracy, voters elect **representatives** to act in their interests. Typically, a representative is elected by and responsible to a specific subset of the total population of eligible voters; this subset of the electorate is referred to as a representative's constituency. A **representative democracy** may foster a more powerful legislature than other forms of government systems; to compensate for a strong legislature, most constitutions stipulate that measures must be taken to balance the powers within government, such as the creation of a separate judicial branch. Representative democracy became popular in post-industrial nations where increasing numbers of people expressed an interest in politics, but where technology and census counts remained incompatible with systems of direct democracy. Today, the majority of the world's population resides in representative democracies, including constitutional monarchies that possess a strong representative branch.

Democracy

Democracy, or rule by the people, is a form of government in which power is vested in the people and in which policy decisions are made by the majority in a decision-making process such as an election that is open to all or most citizens. Definitions of democracy have become more generalized and include aspects of society and political culture in democratic societies that do not necessarily represent a form of government. What defines a democracy varies, but some of the

Copyright © Mometrix Media. You have been licensed one copy of this document for personal use only. Any other reproduction or redistribution is strictly prohibited. All rights reserved.

characteristics of a democracy could include the presence of a middle class, the presence of a civil society, a free market, political pluralism, universal suffrage, and specific rights and freedoms. In practice however, democracies do have limits on specific freedoms, which are justified as being necessary to maintain democracy and ensure democratic freedoms. For example, freedom of association is limited in democracies for individuals and groups that pose a threat to government or to society.

Presidential/Congressional System

In a **presidential system**, also referred to as a **congressional system**, the legislative branch and the executive branches are elected separately from one another. The features of a presidential system include a *president* who serves as both the head of state and the head of the government, who has no formal relationship with the legislative branch, who is not a voting member, who cannot introduce bills, and who has a fixed term of office. *Elections* are held at scheduled times. The president's *cabinet* carries out the policies of the executive branch and the legislative branch.

Political Parties

A **political party** is an organization that advocates a particular ideology and seeks to gain power within government. The tendency of members of political parties to support their party's policies and interests relative to those of other parties is referred to as partisanship. Often, a political party is comprised of members whose positions, interests and perspectives on policies vary, despite having shared interests in the general ideology of the party. As such, many political parties will have divisions within them that have differing opinions on policy. Political parties are often placed on a political spectrum, with one end of the spectrum representing conservative, traditional values and policies and the other end of the spectrum representing radical, progressive value and policies.

Review Video: Political Parties
Visit mometrix.com/academy and enter code: 640197

Types of Party Systems

There is a variety of **party systems**, including single-party systems, dominant-party systems, and dual-party systems. In a **single-party system**, only one political party may hold power. In this type of system, minor parties may be permitted, but they must accept the leadership of the dominant party. **Dominant-party systems** allow for multiple parties in opposition of one another, however the dominant party is the only party considered to have power. A **two-party system**, such as in the United States, is one in which there are two dominant political parties. In such a system, it is very difficult for any other parties to win an election. In most two-party systems, there is typically one right wing party and one left wing party.

Democratic Party

The **Democratic Party** was founded in 1792. In the United States, it is one of the two dominant political parties, along with the Republican Party. The Democratic Party is to the left of the Republican Party. The Democratic Party began as a conservative party in the mid-1800s, shifting to the left during the 1900s. There are many factions within the Democratic Party in the United States. The **Democratic National Committee (DNC)** is the official organization of the Democratic Party, and it develops and promotes the party's platform and coordinates fundraising and election strategies. There are Democratic committees in every U.S. state and most U.S. counties. The official symbol of the Democratic Party is the donkey.

Copyright © Mometrix Media. You have been licensed one copy of this document for personal use only. Any other reproduction or redistribution is strictly prohibited. All rights reserved.

Republican Party

The **Republican Party** is often referred to as the **GOP**, which stands for *Grand Old Party*. The Republican Party is considered socially conservative and economically neoliberal relative to the Democratic Party. Like the Democratic Party, there are factions within the Republic Party that agree with the party's overall ideology, but disagree with the party's positions on specific issues. The official symbol of the Republican Party is the elephant. The **Republican National Committee (RNC)** is the official organization of the Republican Party, and it develops and promotes the party's platform and coordinates fundraising and election strategies. There are Republican committees in every U.S. state and most U.S. counties.

Political Campaigns

A **political campaign** is an organized attempt to influence the decisions of a particular group of people . Examples of campaigns could include elections or efforts to influence policy changes. One of the first steps in a campaign is to develop a **campaign message**. The message must then be delivered to the individuals and groups that the campaign is trying to reach and influence through a campaign plan. There are various ways for a campaign to communicate its message to the intended audience, including public media; paid media such as television, radio and newspaper ads, billboards and the internet; public events such as protests and rallies; meetings with speakers; mailings; canvassing; fliers; and websites. Through these efforts, the campaign attempts to attract additional support and, ultimately, to reach the goal of the campaign.

Review Video: Political Campaigns
Visit mometrix.com/academy and enter code: 838608

Voting

Voting is a method of decision making that allows people to express their opinion or preference for a candidate or for a proposed resolution of an issue. In a democratic system, voting typically takes place as part of an **election**. An individual participates in the voting process by casting a vote, or a **ballot**; ballots are produced by states A *secret ballot* can be used at polls to protect voters' privacy. Individuals can also vote via *absentee ballot*. In some states voters can write-in a name to cast a vote for a candidate that is not on the ballot. Some states also use *straight ticket voting*, allowing the voter to vote for one party for all the elected positions on the ballot.

US Elections

In the United States, **officials** are elected at the federal, state and local levels. The first two articles of the Constitution, as well as various amendments, establish how **federal elections** are to be held. The **President** is elected indirectly, by electors of an electoral college. Members of the electoral college nearly always vote along the lines of the popular vote of their respective states. Members of **Congress** are directly elected. At the state level, state law establishes most aspects of how elections are held. There are many elected offices at the state level, including a governor and state legislature. There are also elected offices at the local level.

Voter Eligibility

The United States Constitution establishes that individual people are permitted to **vote** in elections if they are citizens of the United States and are at least eighteen years old. The **fifteenth** and **nineteenth amendments** of the United States Constitution stipulate that the right to vote cannot be denied to any United States citizen based on race or sex, respectively. States regulate voter

Copyright © Mometrix Media. You have been licensed one copy of this document for personal use only. Any other reproduction or redistribution is strictly prohibited. All rights reserved.

eligibility beyond the minimum qualifications stipulated by the United States Constitution. Depending on the regulations of individual states, individuals may be denied the right to vote if they are convicted criminals.

Review Video: Voter Behavior
Visit mometrix.com/academy and enter code: 976272

Advantages and Disadvantages to Two-Party System

Advocates of the **two-party system** argue that its advantages are that they are stable because they enable policies and government to change slowly rather than rapidly due to the relative lack of influence from small parties representing unconventional ideologies. In addition, they seem to drive voters toward a middle ground and are less susceptible to revolutions, coups, or civil wars. Among the critiques of the two-party system is the claim that stability in and of itself is not necessarily desirable, as it often comes at the expense of democracy. Critics also argue that the two-party system promotes negative political campaigns, in which candidates and their respective parties only take positions on issues that will differentiate themselves from their opponents, rather than focusing on policy issues that are of significance to citizens. Another concern is that if one of the two major parties becomes weak, a dominant-party system may develop.

Campaign Message

Political campaigns consist of three main elements, which are the campaign message, the money that is necessary to run the campaign and "machine," or the capital that is necessary run the campaign. A campaign message is a succinct statement expressing why voters should support the campaign and the individual or policy associated with that campaign. The message is one of the most significant aspects of a political campaign, and a considerable amount of time, money and effort is invested in devising a successful campaign message, as it will be repeated throughout the campaign and will be one of the most identifying factors of the campaign.

Modern Election Campaigns in US

Political campaigns in the U.S. have changed and continue to change as advances in technology permit varied campaign methods. Campaigns represent a civic practice, and today they are a high profit industry. The U.S. has an abundance of professional political consultants that employ highly sophisticated campaign management strategies and tools. The election process varies widely between the federal, state and local levels. Campaigns are typically controlled by individual candidates, rather than by the parties that they are associated with. Larger campaigns utilize a vast array of media to reach their targeted audiences, while smaller campaigns are typically limited to direct contact with voters, direct mailings and other forms of low-cost advertising to reach their audiences. In addition to fundraising and spending done by individual candidates, party committees and political action committees also raise money and spend it in ways that will advance the cause of the particular campaign they are associated with.

Voter Registration

Individuals have the responsibility of **registering to vote**. Every state except North Dakota requires citizens to register to vote. In an effort to increase voter turnout, Congress passed the **National Voter Registration Act** in 1993. The Act is also known as "Motor Voter," because it required states to make the voter registration process easier by providing registration services through drivers' license registration centers, as well as through disability centers, schools, libraries,

Copyright © Mometrix Media. You have been licensed one copy of this document for personal use only. Any other reproduction or redistribution is strictly prohibited. All rights reserved.

and mail-in registration. Some states are exempt because they permit same-day voter registration, which enables voters to register to vote on the day of the election.

Presidential Elections

The President of the United States is elected **indirectly**, by members of an **electoral college**. Members of the electoral college nearly always vote along the lines of the popular vote of their respective states. The winner of a presidential election is the candidate with at least 270 electoral college votes. It is possible for a candidate to win the electoral vote, and lose the popular vote. Incumbent Presidents and challengers typically prefer a balanced ticket, where the President and Vice President are elected together and generally balance one another with regard to geography, ideology, or experience working in government. The nominated Vice Presidential candidate is referred to as the President's *running mate*.

Electoral College

Electoral college votes are cast by state by a group of electors; each elector casts one electoral college vote. State law regulates how states cast their electoral college votes. In all states except Maine and Nebraska, the candidate winning the most votes receives all the state's electoral college votes. In Maine and Nebraska two electoral votes are awarded based on the winner of the statewide election, and the rest go to the highest vote-winner in each of the state's congressional districts. Critics of the electoral college argue that it is undemocratic because the President is elected indirectly as opposed to directly, and that it creates inequality between voters in different states because candidates focus attention on voters in swing states who could influence election results. Critics argue that the electoral college provides more representation for voters in small states than large states, where more voters are represented by a single electoral than in small states and discriminates against candidates that do not have support concentrated in a given state.

Congressional Elections

Congressional elections are every two years. Members of the **House of Representatives** are elected for a two year term and elections occur every two years on the first Tuesday after November 1st in even years. A Representative is elected from each of 435 House districts in the U.S. House elections usually occur in the same year as Presidential elections. Members of the **Senate** are elected to six year terms; one-third of the Senate is elected every two years. Per the Seventeenth Amendment to the Constitution, which was passed in 1913, Senators are elected by the electorate of states. The country is divided into **Congressional districts**, and critics argue that this division eliminates voter choice, sometimes creating areas in which Congressional races are uncontested. Every ten years **redistricting** of Congressional districts occurs. However, redistricting is often partisan and therefore reduces the number of competitive districts. The division of voting districts resulting in an unfair advantage to one party in elections is known as gerrymandering. Gerrymandering has been criticized as being undemocratic.

State and Local Elections

State elections are regulated by state laws and constitutions. In keeping with the ideal of separation of powers, the legislature and the executive are elected separately at the state level, as they are at the federal level. In each state, a **Governor** and a **Lieutenant Governor** are elected. In some states, the Governor and Lieutenant Governor are elected on a joint ticket, while in other states they are elected separately from one another. In some states, executive positions such as Attorney General and Secretary of State are also elected offices. All members of state legislatures are elected, including state senators and state representatives. Depending on the state, members of

Copyright © Mometrix Media. You have been licensed one copy of this document for personal use only. Any other reproduction or redistribution is strictly prohibited. All rights reserved.

the state supreme court and other members of the state judiciary may be chosen in elections. Local government can include the governments of counties and cities. At this level, nearly all government offices are filled through an election process. Elected local offices may include sheriffs, county school boards, and city mayors.

Campaign Finance and Independent Expenditures

An individual or group is legally permitted to make unlimited **independent expenditures** in association with federal elections. An independent expenditure is an expenditure that is made to pay for a form of communication that supports the election or defeat of a candidate; the expenditure must be made independently from the candidate's own campaign. To be considered independent, the communication may not be made with the cooperation or consultation with, or at the request or suggestion of, any candidate, any committees or political party associated with the candidate, or any agent that acts on behalf of the candidate. There are no restrictions on the amount that anyone may spend on an independent expenditure, however, any individual making an independent expenditure must report it and disclose the source of the funds they used.

Campaign Finance and Activities of Political Parties

Political parties participate in federal elections at the local, state and national levels. Most **party committees** must register with the **Federal Election Committee** and file reports disclosing federal campaign activities. While party committees may contribute funds directly to federal candidates, the amounts that they contribute are restricted by the campaign finance contribution limits. National and state party committees are permitted to make additional **coordinated expenditures,** within limits, to assist their nominees in general elections. However, national party committees are not permitted to make unlimited **independent expenditures** to support or oppose federal candidates using soft money. State and local party committees are also not permitted to use soft money for the purpose of supporting or opposing federal candidates, but they are allowed to spend soft money, up to a limit of $10,000 per source, on voter registration and on efforts aimed at increasing voter participation. All party committees are required to register themselves and file disclosure reports with the Federal Election Committee once their federal election activities exceed specified monetary limits.

Public Opinion

Public opinion represents the collective attitudes of individual members of the adult population in the United States of America. There are many varied forces that may influence public opinion. These forces include *public relations efforts* on the part of political campaigns and political parties. Another force affecting political opinion is the *political media* and the *mass media*. Public opinion is very important during elections, particularly Presidential elections, as it is an indicator of how candidates are perceived by the public and of how well candidates are doing during their election campaigns. Public opinion is often measured and evaluated using survey sampling.

Mass Media and Public Opinion

The **mass media** is critical in developing public opinion. In the short term people generally evaluate information they receive relative to their own beliefs; in the long term the media may have a considerable impact on people's beliefs. Due to the impact of the media on an individual's beliefs, some experts consider the effects of the media on an individual's independence and autonomy to be negative. Others view the impact of the media on individuals as a positive one, because the media provides information that expands worldviews and enriches life, and fosters the development of opinions that are informed by many sources of information. A critical aspect of the relationship

Copyright © Mometrix Media. You have been licensed one copy of this document for personal use only. Any other reproduction or redistribution is strictly prohibited. All rights reserved.

between the media and public opinion is who is in control of the knowledge and information that is disseminated through the media. Whoever controls the media can propagate their own agenda. The extent to which an individual interprets and evaluates information received through the media can influence behaviors such as voting patterns or consumer behavior, as well as social attitudes.

Geography

Important Terms Related to Maps

The most important terms used when describing items on a map or globe are:

- **Latitude and longitude** – Latitude and longitude are the imaginary lines (horizontal and vertical, respectively) that divide the globe into a grid. Both are measured using the 360 degrees of a circle.
- **Coordinates** – These are the latitude and longitude measures for a place.
- **Absolute location** – This is the exact spot where coordinates meet. The grid system allows the location of every place on the planet to be identified.
- **Equator** – This is the line at 0° latitude that divides the earth into two equal halves called hemispheres.
- **Parallels** – This is another name for lines of latitude because they circle the earth in parallel lines that never meet.
- **Meridians** – This is another name for lines of longitude. The Prime Meridian is located at 0° longitude, and is the starting point for measuring distance (both east and west) around the globe. Meridians circle the earth and connect at the Poles.

Review Video: 5 Elements of any Map
Visit mometrix.com/academy and enter code: 437727

Four Hemispheres, North and South Poles, Tropics of Cancer and Capricorn, and Arctic and Antarctic Circles

The definitions for these terms are as follows:

- **Northern Hemisphere** – This is the area above, or north, of the equator.
- **Southern Hemisphere** – This is the area below, or south, of the equator.
- **Western Hemisphere** – This is the area between the North and South Poles. It extends west from the Prime Meridian to the International Date Line.
- **Eastern Hemisphere** – This is the area between the North and South Poles. It extends east from the Prime Meridian to the International Date Line.
- **North and South Poles** – Latitude is measured in terms of the number of degrees north and south from the equator. The North Pole is located at 90°N latitude, while the South Pole is located at 90°S latitude.
- **Tropic of Cancer** – This is the parallel, or latitude, 23½° north of the equator.
- **Tropic of Capricorn** – This is the parallel, or latitude, 23½° south of the equator. The region between these two parallels is the tropics. The subtropics is the area located between 23½° and 40° north and south of the equator.
- **Arctic Circle** – This is the parallel, or latitude, 66½° north of the equator.
- **Antarctic Circle** – This is the parallel, or latitude, 66½° south of the equator.

Copyright © Mometrix Media. You have been licensed one copy of this document for personal use only. Any other reproduction or redistribution is strictly prohibited. All rights reserved.

Review Video: Geographical Features
Visit mometrix.com/academy and enter code: 773539

GPS

Global Positioning System (GPS) is a system of satellites that orbit the Earth and communicate with mobile devices to pinpoint the mobile device's position. This is accomplished by determining the distance between the mobile device and at least three satellites. A mobile device might calculate a distance of 400 miles between it and the first satellite. The possible locations that are 400 miles from the first satellite and the mobile device will fall along a circle. The possible locations on Earth relative to the other two satellites will fall somewhere along different circles. The point on Earth at which these three circles intersect is the location of the mobile device. The process of determining position based on distance measurements from three satellites is called **trilateration**.

Review Video: Cartography and Technology
Visit mometrix.com/academy and enter code: 642071

Types of Maps

- A **physical map** is one that shows natural features such as mountains, rivers, lakes, deserts, and plains. Color is used to designate the different features.
- A **topographic map** is a type of physical map that shows the relief and configuration of a landscape, such as hills, valleys, fields, forest, roads, and settlements. It includes natural and human-made features.
- A **topological map** is one on which lines are stretched or straightened for the sake of clarity, but retain their essential geometric relationship. This type of map is used, for example, to show the routes of a subway system.
- A **political map** uses lines for state, county, and country boundaries; points or dots for cities and towns; and various other symbols for features such as airports and roads.

Physical and Cultural Features of Geographic Locations and Countries

Physical features:

- **Vegetation zones, or biomes** – Forests, grasslands, deserts, and tundra are the four main types of vegetation zones.
- **Climate zones** – Tropical, dry, temperate, continental, and polar are the five different types of climate zones. Climate is the long-term average weather conditions of a place.

Cultural features:

- **Population density** – This is the number of people living in each square mile or kilometer of a place. It is calculated by dividing population by area.
- **Religion** – This is the identification of the dominant religions of a place, whether Christianity, Hinduism, Judaism, Buddhism, Islam, Shinto, Taoism, or Confucianism. All of these originated in Asia.
- **Languages** – This is the identification of the dominant or official language of a place. There are 12 major language families. The Indo-European family (which includes English, Russian, German, French, and Spanish) is spoken over the widest geographic area, but Mandarin Chinese is spoken by the most people.

Copyright © Mometrix Media. You have been licensed one copy of this document for personal use only. Any other reproduction or redistribution is strictly prohibited. All rights reserved.

Review Video: Physical vs. Cultural Geography
Visit mometrix.com/academy and enter code: 912136

Coral Reefs

Coral reefs are formed from millions of tiny, tube-shaped **polyps**, an animal life form encased in tough limestone skeletons. Once anchored to a rocky surface, polyps eat plankton and miniscule shellfish caught with poisonous tentacles near the mouth. Polyps use calcium carbonate absorbed from chemicals given off by algae to harden their body armor and cement themselves together in fantastic shapes of many colors. Polyps reproduce through eggs and larvae, but the reef grows by branching out shoots of polyps. There are three types of coral reefs:

- **Fringing reefs** – These surround, or "fringe," an island.
- **Barrier reefs** – Over the centuries, a fringe reef grows so large that the island sinks down from the weight, and the reef becomes a barrier around the island. Water trapped between the island and the reef is called a lagoon.
- **Atolls** – Eventually, the sinking island goes under, leaving the coral reef around the lagoon.

Formation of Mountains

Mountains are formed by the movement of geologic plates, which are rigid slabs of rocks beneath the earth's crust that float on a layer of partially molten rock in the earth's upper mantle. As the plates collide, they push up the crust to form mountains. This process is called **orogeny**. There are three basic forms of orogeny:

- If the collision of continental plates causes the crust to buckle and fold, a chain of **folded mountains**, such as the Appalachians, the Alps, or the Himalayas, is formed.
- If the collision of the plates causes a denser oceanic plate to go under a continental plate, a process called **subduction**; strong horizontal forces lift and fold the margin of the continent. A mountain range like the Andes is the result.
- If an oceanic plate is driven under another oceanic plate, **volcanic mountains** such as those in Japan and the Philippines are formed.

Harmful or Potentially Harmful Interaction with Environment

Wherever humans have gone on the earth, they have made **changes** to their surroundings. Many are harmful or potentially harmful, depending on the extent of the alterations. Some of the changes and activities that can harm the **environment** include:

- Cutting into mountains by machine or blasting to build roads or construction sites
- Cutting down trees and clearing natural growth
- Building houses and cities
- Using grassland to graze herds
- Polluting water sources
- Polluting the ground with chemical and oil waste
- Wearing out fertile land and losing topsoil
- Placing communication lines cross country using poles and wires or underground cable
- Placing railway lines or paved roads cross country
- Building gas and oil pipelines cross country
- Draining wetlands

Copyright © Mometrix Media. You have been licensed one copy of this document for personal use only. Any other reproduction or redistribution is strictly prohibited. All rights reserved.

- Damming up or re-routing waterways
- Spraying fertilizers, pesticides, and defoliants
- Hunting animals to extinction or near extinction

Adaptation to Environmental Conditions

The environment influences the way people live. People **adapt** to **environmental conditions** in ways as simple as putting on warm clothing in a cold environment; finding means to cool their surroundings in an environment with high temperatures; building shelters from wind, rain, and temperature variations; and digging water wells if surface water is unavailable. More complex adaptations result from the physical diversity of the earth in terms of soil, climate, vegetation, and topography. Humans take advantage of opportunities and avoid or minimize limitations. Examples of environmental limitations are that rocky soils offer few opportunities for agriculture and rough terrain limits accessibility. Sometimes, **technology** allows humans to live in areas that were once uninhabitable or undesirable. For example, air conditioning allows people to live comfortably in hot climates; modern heating systems permit habitation in areas with extremely low temperatures, as is the case with research facilities in Antarctica; and airplanes have brought people to previously inaccessible places to establish settlements or industries.

Carrying Capacity and Natural Hazards

Carrying capacity is the maximum, sustained level of use of an environment can incur without sustaining significant environmental deterioration that would eventually lead to environmental destruction. Environments vary in terms of their carrying capacity, a concept humans need to learn to measure and respect before harm is done. Proper **assessment of environmental conditions** enables responsible decision making with respect to how much and in what ways the resources of a particular environment should be consumed. **Energy and water conservation** as well as recycling can extend an area's carrying capacity. In addition to carrying capacity limitations, the physical environment can also have occasional extremes that are costly to humans. **Natural hazards** such as hurricanes, tornadoes, earthquakes, volcanoes, floods, tsunamis, and some forest fires and insect infestations are processes or events that are not caused by humans, but may have serious consequences for humans and the environment. These events are not preventable, and their precise timing, location, and magnitude are not predictable. However, some precautions can be taken to reduce the damage.

Applying Geography to Interpretation of the Past

Space, environment, and chronology are three different points of view that can be used to study history. Events take place within **geographic contexts**. If the world is flat, then transportation choices are vastly different from those that would be made in a round world, for example. Invasions of Russia from the west have normally failed because of the harsh winter conditions, the vast distances that inhibit steady supply lines, and the number of rivers and marshes to be crossed, among other factors. Any invading or defending force anywhere must make choices based on consideration of space and environmental factors. For instance, lands may be too muddy or passages too narrow for certain equipment. Geography played a role in the building of the Panama Canal because the value of a shorter transportation route had to outweigh the costs of labor, disease, political negotiations, and equipment, not to mention a myriad of other effects from cutting a canal through an isthmus and changing a natural land structure as a result.

Copyright © Mometrix Media. You have been licensed one copy of this document for personal use only. Any other reproduction or redistribution is strictly prohibited. All rights reserved.

Applying Geography to Interpretation of the Present and Plans for the Future

The decisions that individual people as well as nations make that may **affect the environment** have to be made with an understanding of spatial patterns and concepts, cultural and transportation connections, physical processes and patterns, ecosystems, and the impact, or "footprint," of people on the physical environment. Sample issues that fit into these considerations are recycling programs, loss of agricultural land to further urban expansion, air and water pollution, deforestation, and ease of transportation and communication. In each of these areas, present and future uses have to be balanced against possible harmful effects. For example, wind is a clean and readily available resource for electric power, but the access roads to and noise of wind turbines can make some areas unsuitable for livestock pasture. Voting citizens need to have an understanding of **geographical and environmental connections** to make responsible decisions.

Spatial Organization

Spatial organization in geography refers to how things or people are grouped in a given space anywhere on earth. Spatial organization applies to the **placement of settlements**, whether hamlets, towns, or cities. These settlements are located to make the distribution of goods and services convenient. For example, in farm communities, people come to town to get groceries, to attend church and school, and to access medical services. It is more practical to provide these things to groups than to individuals. These settlements, historically, have been built close to water sources and agricultural areas. Lands that are topographically difficult, have few resources, or experience extreme temperatures do not have as many people as temperate zones and flat plains, where it is easier to live. Within settlements, a town or city will be organized into commercial and residential neighborhoods, with hospitals, fire stations, and shopping centers centrally located. All of these organizational considerations are spatial in nature.

Themes of Geography

The five themes of geography are:

- **Location** – This includes relative location (described in terms of surrounding geography such as a river, sea coast, or mountain) and absolute location (the specific point of latitude and longitude).
- **Place** – This includes physical characteristics (deserts, plains, mountains, and waterways) and human characteristics (features created by humans, such as architecture, roads, religion, industries, and food and folk practices).
- **Human-environmental interaction** – This includes human adaptation to the environment (using an umbrella when it rains), human modification of the environment (building terraces to prevent soil erosion), and human dependence on the environment for food, water, and natural resources.
- **Movement** –Interaction through trade, migration, communications, political boundaries, ideas, and fashions.
- **Regions** – This includes formal regions (a city, state, country, or other geographical organization as defined by political boundaries), functional regions (defined by a common function or connection, such as a school district), and vernacular regions (informal divisions determined by perceptions or one's mental image, such as the "Far East").

Copyright © Mometrix Media. You have been licensed one copy of this document for personal use only. Any other reproduction or redistribution is strictly prohibited. All rights reserved.

Review Video: Regional Geography
Visit mometrix.com/academy and enter code: 350378

Review Video: Human Geography
Visit mometrix.com/academy and enter code: 195767

Geomorphology

The study of landforms is call **geomorphology** or physiography, a science that considers the relationships between *geological structures* and *surface landscape features*. It is also concerned with the processes that change these features, such as erosion, deposition, and plate tectonics. Biological factors can also affect landforms. Examples are when corals build a coral reef or when plants contribute to the development of a salt marsh or a sand dune. Rivers, coastlines, rock types, slope formation, ice, erosion, and weathering are all part of geomorphology. A **landform** is a landscape feature or geomorphological unit. These include hills, plateaus, mountains, deserts, deltas, canyons, mesas, marshes, swamps, and valleys. These units are categorized according to elevation, slope, orientation, stratification, rock exposure, and soil type. Landform elements include pits, peaks, channels, ridges, passes, pools, and plains. The highest order landforms are continents and oceans. Elementary landforms such as segments, facets, and relief units are the smallest homogenous divisions of a land surface at a given scale or resolution.

Oceans, Seas, Lakes, Rivers, and Canals

- **Oceans** are the largest bodies of water on earth and cover nearly 71% of the earth's surface. There are five major oceans: Atlantic, Pacific (largest and deepest), Indian, Arctic, and Southern (surrounds Antarctica).
- **Seas** are smaller than oceans and are somewhat surrounded by land like a lake, but lakes are fresh water and seas are salt water. Seas include the Mediterranean, Baltic, Caspian, Caribbean, and Coral.
- **Lakes** are bodies of water in a depression on the earth's surface. Examples of lakes are the Great Lakes and Lake Victoria.
- **Rivers** are a channeled flow of water that start out as a spring or stream formed by runoff from rain or snow. Rivers flow from higher to lower ground, and usually empty into a sea or ocean. Great rivers of the world include the Amazon, Nile, Rhine, Mississippi, Ganges, Mekong, and Yangtze.
- **Canals** are artificial waterways constructed by humans to connect two larger water bodies. Examples of canals are the Panama and the Suez.

Mountains, Hills, Foothills, Valleys, Plateaus, and Mesas

The definitions for these geographical features are as follows:

- **Mountains** are elevated landforms that rise fairly steeply from the earth's surface to a summit of at least 1,000-2,000 feet (definitions vary) above sea level.
- **Hills** are elevated landforms that rise 500-2,000 feet above sea level.
- **Foothills** are a low series of hills found between a plain and a mountain range.
- **Valleys** are a long depression located between hills or mountains. They are usually products of river erosion. Valleys can vary in terms of width and depth, ranging from a few feet to thousands of feet.

Copyright © Mometrix Media. You have been licensed one copy of this document for personal use only. Any other reproduction or redistribution is strictly prohibited. All rights reserved.

- **Plateaus** are elevated landforms that are fairly flat on top. They may be as high as 10,000 feet above sea level and are usually next to mountains.
- **Mesas** are flat areas of upland. Their name is derived from the Spanish word for table. They are smaller than plateaus and often found in arid or semi-arid areas.

Plains, Deserts, Deltas, and Basins

- **Plains** are extensive areas of low-lying, flat, or gently undulating land, and are usually lower than the landforms around them. Plains near the seacoast are called lowlands.
- **Deserts** are large, dry areas that receive less than 10 inches of rain per year. They are almost barren, containing only a few patches of vegetation.
- **Deltas** are accumulations of silt deposited at river mouths into the seabed. They are eventually converted into very fertile, stable ground by vegetation, becoming important crop-growing areas. Examples include the deltas of the Nile, Ganges, and Mississippi River.
- **Basins** come in various types. They may be low areas that catch water from rivers; large hollows that dip to a central point and are surrounded by higher ground, as in the Donets and Kuznetsk basins in Russia; or areas of inland drainage in a desert when the water can't reach the sea and flows into lakes or evaporates in salt flats as a result. An example is the Great Salt Lake in Utah.

Marshes and Swamps and Tundra and Taiga

Marshes and swamps are both **wet lowlands**. The water can be fresh, brackish, or saline. Both host important ecological systems with unique wildlife. There are, however, some major differences. **Marshes** have no trees and are always wet because of frequent floods and poor drainage that leaves shallow water. Plants are mostly grasses, rushes, reeds, typhas, sedges, and herbs. **Swamps** have trees and dry periods. The water is very slow-moving, and is usually associated with adjacent rivers or lakes.

Both taiga and tundra regions have many plants and animals, but they have few humans or crops because of their harsh climates. **Taiga** has colder winters and hotter summers than tundra because of its distance from the Arctic Ocean. **Tundra** is a Russian word describing marshy plain in an area that has a very cold climate but receives little snow. The ground is usually frozen, but is quite spongy when it is not. Taiga is the world's largest forest region, located just south of the tundra line. It contains huge mineral resources and fur-bearing animals.

Humid Continental, Prairie, Subtropical, and Marine Climates

- A **humid continental climate** is one that has four seasons, including a cold winter and a hot summer, and sufficient rainfall for raising crops. Such climates can be found in the United States, Canada, and Russia. The best farmlands and mining areas are found in these countries.
- **Prairie climates**, or steppe regions, are found in the interiors of Asia and North America where there are dry flatlands (prairies that receive 10-20 inches of rain per year). These dry flatlands can be grasslands or deserts.
- **Subtropical climates** are very humid areas in the tropical areas of Japan, China, Australia, Africa, South America, and the United States. The moisture, carried by winds traveling over warm ocean currents, produces long summers and mild winters. It is possible to produce a continuous cycle of a variety of crops.

Copyright © Mometrix Media. You have been licensed one copy of this document for personal use only. Any other reproduction or redistribution is strictly prohibited. All rights reserved.

- A **marine climate** is one near or surrounded by water. Warm ocean winds bring moisture, mild temperatures year-round, and plentiful rain. These climates are found in Western Europe and parts of the United States, Canada, Chile, New Zealand, and Australia.

Physical and Cultural Geography and Physical and Political Locations

- **Physical geography** is the study of climate, water, and land and their relationships with each other and humans. Physical geography locates and identifies the earth's surface features and explores how humans thrive in various locations according to crop and goods production.
- **Cultural geography** is the study of the influence of the environment on human behaviors as well as the effect of human activities such as farming, building settlements, and grazing livestock on the environment. Cultural geography also identifies and compares the features of different cultures and how they influence interactions with other cultures and the earth.
- **Physical location** refers to the placement of the hemispheres and the continents.
- **Political location** refers to the divisions within continents that designate various countries. These divisions are made with borders, which are set according to boundary lines arrived at by legal agreements.

Both physical and political locations can be precisely determined by geographical surveys and by latitude and longitude.

Natural Resources, Renewable Resources, Nonrenewable Resources, and Commodities

Natural resources are things provided by nature that have commercial value to humans, such as minerals, energy, timber, fish, wildlife, and the landscape. **Renewable resources** are those that can be replenished, such as wind, solar radiation, tides, and water (with proper conservation and clean-up). Soil is renewable with proper conservation and management techniques, and timber can be replenished with replanting. Living resources such as fish and wildlife can replenish themselves if they are not over-harvested. **Nonrenewable resources** are those that cannot be replenished. These include fossil fuels such as oil and coal and metal ores. These cannot be replaced or reused once they have been burned, although some of their products can be recycled. **Commodities** are natural resources that have to be extracted and purified rather than created, such as mineral ores.

Geography

Geography involves learning about the world's primary **physical and cultural patterns** to help understand how the world functions as an interconnected and dynamic system. Combining information from different sources, geography teaches the basic patterns of climate, geology, vegetation, human settlement, migration, and commerce. Thus, geography is an **interdisciplinary** study of history, anthropology, and sociology. **History** incorporates geography in discussions of battle strategies, slavery (trade routes), ecological disasters (the Dust Bowl of the 1930s), and mass migrations. Geographic principles are useful when reading **literature** to help identify and visualize the setting, and also when studying **earth science**, **mathematics** (latitude, longitude, sun angle, and population statistics), and **fine arts** (song, art, and dance often reflect different cultures). Consequently, a good background in geography can help students succeed in other subjects as well.

Copyright © Mometrix Media. You have been licensed one copy of this document for personal use only. Any other reproduction or redistribution is strictly prohibited. All rights reserved.

Areas Covered by Geography

Geography is connected to many issues and provides answers to many everyday questions. Some of the areas covered by geography include:

- Geography investigates global climates, landforms, economies, political systems, human cultures, and migration patterns.
- Geography answers questions not only about where something is located, but also why it is there, how it got there, and how it is related to other things around it.
- Geography explains why people move to certain regions (climate, availability of natural resources, arable land, etc.).
- Geography explains world trade routes and modes of transportation.
- Geography identifies where various animals live and where various crops and forests grow.
- Geography identifies and locates populations that follow certain religions.
- Geography provides statistics on population numbers and growth, which aids in economic and infrastructure planning for cities and countries.

Globe and Map Projections

A **globe** is the only accurate representation of the earth's size, shape, distance, and direction since it, like the earth, is **spherical**. The flat surface of a map distorts these elements. To counter this problem, mapmakers use a variety of "**map projections**," a system for representing the earth's curvatures on a flat surface through the use of a grid that corresponds to lines of latitude and longitude. Some distortions are still inevitable, though, so mapmakers make choices based on the map scale, the size of the area to be mapped, and what they want the map to show. Some projections can represent a true shape or area, while others may be based on the equator and therefore become less accurate as they near the poles. In summary, all maps have some distortion in terms of the shape or size of features of the spherical earth.

Types of Map Projections

There are three main types of map projections:

- **Conical** – This type of projection superimposes a cone over the sphere of the earth, with two reference parallels secant to the globe and intersecting it. There is no distortion along the standard parallels, but distortion increases further from the chosen parallels. A Bonne projection is an example of a conical projection, in which the areas are accurately represented but the meridians are not on a true scale.
- **Cylindrical** – This is any projection in which meridians are mapped using equally spaced vertical lines and circles of latitude (parallels) are mapped using horizontal lines. A Mercator's projection is a modified cylindrical projection that is helpful to navigators because it allows them to maintain a constant compass direction between two points. However, it exaggerates areas in high latitudes.
- **Azimuthal** – This is a stereographic projection onto a plane so centered at any given point that a straight line radiating from the center to any other point represents the shortest distance. This distance can be measured to scale.

Copyright © Mometrix Media. You have been licensed one copy of this document for personal use only. Any other reproduction or redistribution is strictly prohibited. All rights reserved.

Physical Geographical Features to Know to Perform Well in National Geographic Bee

Organizing place names into categories of physical features helps students learn the type of information they need to know to compete in the **National Geographic Bee**. The physical features students need to be knowledgeable about are:

- The continents (Although everyone has been taught that there are seven continents, some geographers combine Europe and Asia into a single continent called Eurasia.)
- The five major oceans
- The highest and lowest points on each continent (Mt. Everest is the highest point in the world; the Dead Sea is the lowest point.)
- The 10 largest seas (The Coral Sea is the largest.)
- The 10 largest lakes (The Caspian Sea is actually the largest lake.)
- The 10 largest islands (Greenland is the largest island.)
- The longest rivers (The Nile is the longest river.)
- Major mountain ranges
- Earth's extremes such as the hottest (Ethiopia), the coldest (Antarctica), the wettest (India), and the driest (Atacama Desert) places; the highest waterfall (Angel Falls); the largest desert (Sahara); the largest canyon (Grand Canyon); the longest reef (Great Barrier Reef); and the highest tides.

Culture

A **culture** is a comprehensive style of living that is developed in a society and maintained from generation to generation. Culture is manifested in a group's traditions, rituals, language, social norms, technology, and economic structures. Broadly speaking, culture is everything that is learned by a member of a particular society, though it may include things that an individual learns but which are never made explicit either in the individual's mind or in his or her social interactions. For this reason, many sociologists feel it is difficult to properly study one's own culture; they suggest that only the unclouded eyes of a foreign observer can perceive a society's most fundamental values.

Material Culture

A society's **material culture** is the set all of the physical objects that the people of that society have either created or to which they assign cultural meaning. Hence, material culture may include objects like books, jewelry, buildings, and furniture; but it may also include natural areas if those areas are assigned significance by the members of the society. As an example of this latter kind of material culture, a sociologist might point to the Native American society, in which the land itself held immense cultural value. Along with **verbal culture**, material culture makes up the sum total of what sociologists have at their disposal for study.

Nonmaterial Culture

Nonmaterial culture is all of a society's customs, beliefs, political structures, languages, and ways of using material objects. In the United States, for instance, the emphasis placed on religious freedom and individual liberty might be considered an example of nonmaterial culture. The boundary between material and nonmaterial culture is never altogether clear; how, for instance, should one separate the American flag and what it stands for, namely the idea of freedom? **Values** and **norms**, as opposed to the physical things that are used to express values and norms, are what

Copyright © Mometrix Media. You have been licensed one copy of this document for personal use only. Any other reproduction or redistribution is strictly prohibited. All rights reserved.

make up a society's nonmaterial culture. Typically, nonmaterial culture is more difficult to change than material culture, and its change is more difficult to observe.

Values

The **values** of a culture are its highest ideals. In the United States, for example, we would say that freedom and equality are two of our most important values. Values are usually very general concepts. They may be complementary, as for example the values of hard work and material success seem to go together. Values are quite fluid, and a major focus of sociology is observing how they change over time. Values may come into conflict with one another, which can create social conflict and disorganization. An example of this is the conflict in mid-twentieth-century America between the values of equal rights and segregation; ultimately, it was clear that only one of these values could remain.

Sanctions

In sociological terms, **sanctions** are any rewards or consequences given to an individual or group to pursue or renounce a certain course of behavior. Sanctions may be positive, as when a reward is promised for something done properly, or negative, as when a punishment is promised for something done improperly. Although the most common use of the word refers to *international economic pressures* (as in, for instance, the economic restrictions placed on Iraq during the 1990s), all societies place sanctions on their members in order to elicit approved behavior. People who uphold the values and norms of the society are rewarded with preferential treatment from their fellows, while those who transgress can be punished socially, economically, or legally.

Norms

Norms are specific rules regulating behavior in a culture. Norms may or may not be directly codified in the law of a society, but they are intended to encourage behavior that promotes the society's values. Taking again the example of the United States, one might say that treating men and women equally is a social norm, insofar as equality between the sexes is a value aspired to by our culture. Norms, then, depend on values for their justification, and values depend on norms for their enactment. Norms may vary greatly from society to society, such that the same behavior may be approved or condemned depending on where it is performed. Most of the time, norms are so customary for the members of a society that they are performed automatically.

Formal Norms and Informal Norms

Norms may be considered formal or informal, depending on whether they are codified in the laws of the society in which they apply. **Formal norms** are written law; examples of formal norms include the prohibition of murder, the forced payment of taxes, and the sanctity of marriage. **Informal norms**, on the other hand, are unwritten codes of conduct. Examples of informal norms might include the prohibition of spitting in public or the encouragement of deference to women. Typically, a society formalizes the norms which are most important, and for which violators should be punished. Formal norms tend to be much more consistent among different societies than informal norms.

Social Markers, Laws, and Folkways

A **social marker** is any part of behavior that indicates the identity, character, or way of understanding of a particular group of people. Social markers can be laws, folkways, traditions, or other patterns of behavior. **Laws** are simply social norms that have been made explicit and are

Copyright © Mometrix Media. You have been licensed one copy of this document for personal use only. Any other reproduction or redistribution is strictly prohibited. All rights reserved.

enforced by the government. There are plenty of norms, though, that are encoded in law but are also internalized-- the prohibition of murder, for instance. **Folkways** are social norms that have become habitual or traditional in a society. In the United States, we are accustomed to tipping a waiter or waitress for their service: that this is so ingrained in our daily life makes it an American folkway.

Cultural Pluralism and Subculture

Cultural pluralism exists when multiple distinct cultures exist within the same society after a process of accommodation. These self-contained cultures should not be confused with **subcultures**, which are smaller cultures within a large culture. Subcultures usually have a set of norms and values that are different from those held by the larger society of which they are a member. In the United States, we might consider punk rockers or hippies as subcultures, because they have different values than Americans on the whole, but do not really have a self-sustaining or separate society of their own.

Countercultures

A **counterculture** is any group whose values and norms challenge and seek to alter the values and norms of the dominant culture in their society. Although the term when used today evokes memories of the 1960s youth rebellion in Western Europe and the United States, earlier countercultural movements include the Bohemians in nineteenth century France, or even the early Christians. Countercultures typically appear at a time when traditional norms and values are felt to no longer be appropriate or helpful in making sense of the world. As in the case of a social movement, a counterculture tends to have more and stronger adherents at the beginning of its life; once the counterculture's norms have been partially co-opted by the larger society, countercultures tend to lose steam.

Dominant Culture and Ethnocentrism

In any society, the **dominant culture** is the group whose norms, values, and behavior patterns are most widespread and influential on the rest of the society. Many nations, including the United States, have laws to restrain the dominant culture from extinguishing minority cultures. **Ethnocentrism** describes the tendency to view one's own cultural patterns as superior and to judge all others only as they relate to one's own. This philosophy has been at the root of some of humanity's worst atrocities, including the Holocaust, which was perpetrated by Germans who believed they must maintain the purity of their race, and colonial conquests, in which Western nations brutally imposed their customs on various indigenous peoples.

World History

Important Contributions of Ancient Civilizations of Sumer, Egypt, and Indus Valley

These three ancient civilizations are distinguished by their unique contributions to the development of world civilization:

- **Sumer** used the first known writing system, which enabled the Sumerians to leave a sizeable written record of their myths and religion; advanced the development of the wheel and irrigation; and urbanized their culture with a cluster of cities.
- **Egypt** was united by the Nile River. Egyptians originally settled in villages on its banks; had a national religion that held their pharaohs as gods; had a central government that controlled civil and artistic affairs; and had writing and libraries.

Copyright © Mometrix Media. You have been licensed one copy of this document for personal use only. Any other reproduction or redistribution is strictly prohibited. All rights reserved.

- The **Indus Valley** was also called Harappan after the city of Harappa. This civilization started in the 3rd and 4th centuries BC and was widely dispersed over 400,000 square miles. It had a unified culture of luxury and refinement, no known national government, an advanced civic system, and prosperous trade routes.

> **Review Video: Early Mesopotamia: The Sumerians**
> Visit mometrix.com/academy and enter code: 939880
>
> **Review Video: Egyptians**
> Visit mometrix.com/academy and enter code: 398041

Common Traits and Cultural Identifiers of Early Empires of Mesopotamia, Egypt, Greece, and Rome

The common traits of these empires were: a strong military; a centralized government; control and standardization of commerce, money, and taxes; a weight system; and an official language. **Mesopotamia** had a series of short-term empires that failed because of their oppression of subject peoples. **Egypt** also had a series of governments after extending its territory beyond the Nile area. Compared to Mesopotamia, these were more stable and long-lived because they blended different peoples to create a single national identity. **Greece** started as a group of city-states that were united by Alexander the Great and joined to create an empire that stretched from the Indus River to Egypt and the Mediterranean coast. Greece blended Greek values with those of the local cultures, which collectively became known as Hellenistic society. **Rome** was an Italian city-state that grew into an empire extending from the British Isles across Europe to the Middle East. It lasted for 1,000 years and became the foundation of the Western world's culture, language, and laws.

> **Review Video: Ancient Greece**
> Visit mometrix.com/academy and enter code: 800829

Major Deities of Greek and Roman Mythology

The major gods of the **Greek/Roman mythological system** are:

- **Zeus/Jupiter** – Head of the Pantheon, god of the sky
- **Hera/Juno** – Wife of Zeus/Jupiter, goddess of marriage
- **Poseidon/Neptune** – God of the seas
- **Demeter/Ceres** – Goddess of grain
- **Apollo** – God of the sun, law, music, archery, healing, and truth
- **Artemis/Diana** – Goddess of the moon, wild creatures, and hunting
- **Athena/Minerva** – Goddess of civilized life, handicrafts, and agriculture
- **Hephaestus/Vulcan** – God of fire, blacksmith
- **Aphrodite/Venus** – Goddess of love and beauty
- **Ares/Mars** – God of war
- **Dionysus/Bacchus** – God of wine and vegetation
- **Hades/Pluto** – God of the underworld and the dead
- **Eros/Cupid** – Minor god of love
- **Hestia/Vesta** – Goddess of the hearth or home
- **Hermes/Mercury** – Minor god of gracefulness and swiftness

Copyright © Mometrix Media. You have been licensed one copy of this document for personal use only. Any other reproduction or redistribution is strictly prohibited. All rights reserved.

Characteristics of Chinese and Indian Empires

While the Chinese had the world's longest lasting and continuous empires, the Indians had more of a cohesive culture than an empire system. Their distinct characteristics are as follows:

- **China** – Since the end of the Warring States period in 221 BC, China has functioned as an empire. Although the dynasties changed several times, the basic governmental structure remained the same into the 20th century. The Chinese also have an extensive written record of their culture which heavily emphasizes history, philosophy, and a common religion.
- **India** – The subcontinent was seldom unified in terms of government until the British empire controlled the area in the 19th and 20th centuries. In terms of culture, India has had persistent institutions and religions that have loosely united the people, such as the caste system and guilds. These have regulated daily life more than any government.

Middle Ages in European History

The **Middle Ages**, or Medieval times, was a period that ran from approximately 500-1500 AD. During this time, the centers of European civilization moved from the Mediterranean countries to France, Germany, and England, where strong national governments were developing. Key events of this time include:

- **Roman Catholicism** was the cultural and religious center of medieval life, extending into politics and economics.
- **Knights**, with their systems of honor, combat, and chivalry, were loyal to their king. **Peasants**, or serfs, served a particular lord and his lands.
- Many **universities** were established that still function in modern times.
- The **Crusades**, the recurring wars between European Christians and Middle East Muslims, raged over the Holy Lands.
- One of the legendary leaders was Charles the Great, or **Charlemagne**, who created an empire across France and Germany around 800 AD.
- The **Black Death plague** swept across Europe from 1347-1350, leaving between one third and one half of the population dead.

Review Video: The Middle Ages
Visit mometrix.com/academy and enter code: 413133

Protestant Reformation

The dominance of the **Catholic Church** during the Middle Ages in Europe gave it immense power, which encouraged corrupt practices such as the selling of indulgences and clerical positions. The **Protestant Reformation** began as an attempt to reform the Catholic Church, but eventually led to the separation from it. In 1517, Martin Luther posted his *Ninety-Five Theses* on the door of a church in Saxony, which criticized unethical practices, various doctrines, and the authority of the pope. Other reformers such as John Calvin and John Wesley soon followed, but disagreed among themselves and divided along doctrinal lines. Consequently, the Lutheran, Reformed, Calvinist, and Presbyterian churches were founded, among others. In England, King Henry VIII was denied a divorce by the pope, so he broke away and established the **Anglican Church**. The Protestant reformation caused the Catholic Church to finally reform itself, but the Protestant movement continued, resulting in a proliferation of new denominations.

Copyright © Mometrix Media. You have been licensed one copy of this document for personal use only. Any other reproduction or redistribution is strictly prohibited. All rights reserved.

Renaissance

Renaissance is the French word for rebirth, and is used to describe the renewal of interest in ancient Greek and Latin art, literature, and philosophy that occurred in Europe, especially Italy, from the 14th through the 16th centuries. Historically, it was also a time of great scientific inquiry, the rise of individualism, extensive geographical exploration, and the rise of secular values.

Notable figures of the Renaissance include:

- **Petrarch** – An Italian scholar, writer, and key figure in northern Italy, which is where the Renaissance started and where chief patrons came from the merchant class
- **Leonardo da Vinci** – Artist and inventor
- Michelangelo and Raphael – Artists
- **Desiderius Erasmus** – Applied historical scholarship to the New Testament and laid the seeds for the Protestant Reformation
- **Sir Thomas More** – A lawyer and author who wrote *Utopia*
- **Niccolò Machiavelli** – Author of *Prince and Discourses*, which proposed a science of human nature and civil life
- **William Shakespeare** – A renowned playwright and poet

Review Video: Renaissance
Visit mometrix.com/academy and enter code: 123100

Industrial Revolution

The **Industrial Revolution** started in England with the construction of the first **cotton mill** in 1733. Other inventions and factories followed in rapid succession. The **steel industry** grew exponentially when it was realized that cheap, abundant English coal could be used instead of wood for melting metals. The **steam engine**, which revolutionized transportation and work power, came next. Around 1830, a factory-based, **technological era** was ushered into the rest of Europe. Society changed from agrarian to urban. A need for cheap, unskilled labor resulted in the extensive employment and abuse of women and children, who worked up to 14 hours a day, six days a week in deplorable conditions. Expanding populations brought crowded, unsanitary conditions to the cities, and the factories created air and water pollution. Societies had to deal with these new situations by enacting **child labor laws** and creating **labor unions** to protect the safety of workers.

Review Video: The Industrial Revolution
Visit mometrix.com/academy and enter code: 372796

Participants of World War I and World War II

World War I, which began in 1914, was fought by the **Allies** Britain, France, Russia, Greece, Italy, Romania, and Serbia. They fought against the **Central Powers** of Germany, Austria-Hungary, Bulgaria, and Turkey. In 1917, the United States joined the Allies, and Russia withdrew to pursue its own revolution. World War I ended in 1918.

World War II was truly a world war, with fighting occurring on nearly every continent. Germany occupied most of Europe and Northern Africa. It was opposed by the countries of the British Empire, free France and its colonies, Russia, and various national resistance forces. Japan, an **Axis** ally of Germany, had been forcefully expanding its territories in Korea, China, Indonesia, the Philippines, and the South Pacific for many years. When Japan attacked Pearl Harbor in 1941, the

Copyright © Mometrix Media. You have been licensed one copy of this document for personal use only. Any other reproduction or redistribution is strictly prohibited. All rights reserved.

United States joined the **Allied** effort. Italy changed from the Axis to the Allied side mid-war after deposing its own dictator. The war ended in Europe in April 1945, and in Japan in August 1945.

Importance of Cross-Cultural Comparisons in World History Instruction

It is important to make **cross-cultural comparisons** when studying world history so that the subject is **holistic** and not oriented to just Western civilization. Not only are the contributions of civilizations around the world important, but they are also interesting and more representative of the mix of cultures present in the United States. It is also critical to the understanding of world relations to study the involvement of European countries and the United States in international commerce, colonization, and development. **Trade routes** from ancient times linked Africa, Asia, and Europe, resulting in exchanges and migrations of people, philosophies, and religions, as well as goods. While many civilizations in the Americas thrived and some became very sophisticated, many eventually became disastrously entangled in **European expansion**. The historic isolation of China and the modern industrialization of Japan have had huge impacts on relations with the rest of the world. The more students understand this history and its effects on the modern world, the better they will able to function in their own spheres.

Economics

Effects Economy Can Have on Purchasing Decisions of Consumers

The **economy** plays an important role in how careful consumers are when using their resources and what they perceive as needs as opposed to what they perceive as wants. When the economy is doing well, unemployment figures are low, which means that people can easily attain their basic necessities. As a result, consumers are typically more willing to spend their financial resources. Consumers will also be more willing to spend their resources on products and services that are not necessary to their survival, but are instead products and services that consumers enjoy having and believe increase their quality of life. On the other hand, when the economy is in a slump, consumers are much more likely to cut back on their spending because they perceive a significantly higher risk of being unable to acquire basic necessities due to a lack of financial resources.

Supply and Demand, Scarcity and Choice, and Money and Resources

Supply is the amount of a product or service available to consumers. **Demand** is how much consumers are willing to pay for the product or service. These two facets of the market determine the price of goods and services. The higher the demand, the higher the price the supplier will charge; the lower the demand, the lower the price.

Scarcity is a measure of supply in that demand is high when there is a scarcity, or low supply, of an item. **Choice** is related to scarcity and demand in that when an item in demand is scarce, consumers have to make difficult choices. They can pay more for an item, go without it, or go elsewhere for the item.

Money is the cash or currency available for payment. **Resources** are the items one can barter in exchange for goods. Money is also the cash reserves of a nation, while resources are the minerals, labor force, armaments, and other raw materials or assets a nation has available for trade.

Copyright © Mometrix Media. You have been licensed one copy of this document for personal use only. Any other reproduction or redistribution is strictly prohibited. All rights reserved.

Effects of Economic Downturn or Recession

When a **recession** happens, people at all levels of society feel the economic effects. For example:

- High **unemployment** results because businesses have to cut back to keep costs low, and may no longer have the work for the labor force they once did.
- **Mortgage rates** go up on variable-rate loans as banks try to increase their revenues, but the higher rates cause some people who cannot afford increased housing costs to sell or suffer foreclosure.
- **Credit** becomes less available as banks try to lessen their risk. This decreased lending affects business operations, home and auto loans, etc.
- **Stock market prices** drop, and the lower dividends paid to stockholders reduce their income. This is especially hard on retired people who rely on stock dividends.
- **Psychological depression and trauma** may occur in those who suffer bankruptcy, unemployment, or foreclosure during a depression.

Positive and Negative Economic Effects of Abundant Natural Resources

The **positive economic aspects** of abundant natural resources are an increase in **revenue and new jobs** where those resources have not been previously accessed. For example, the growing demand for oil, gas, and minerals has led companies to venture into new regions.

The **negative economic aspects** of abundant natural resources are:

- **Environmental degradation**, if sufficient regulations are not in place to counter strip mining, deforestation, and contamination.
- **Corruption**, if sufficient regulations are not in place to counter bribery, political favoritism, and exploitation of workers as greedy companies try to maximize their profits.
- **Social tension**, if the resources are privately owned such that the rich become richer and the poor do not reap the benefits of their national resources. Class divisions become wider, resulting in social unrest.
- **Dependence**, if the income from the natural resources is not used to develop other industries as well. In this situation, the economy becomes dependent on one source, and faces potential crises if natural disasters or depletion take away that income source.

Economics and Kinds of Economies

Economics is the study of the buying choices that people make, the production of goods and services, and how our market system works. The two kinds of economies are command and market. In a **command economy**, the government controls what and how much is produced, the methods used for production, and the distribution of goods and services. In a market economy, producers make decisions about methods and distribution on their own. These choices are based on what will sell and bring a profit in the marketplace. In a **market economy**, consumers ultimately affect these decisions by choosing whether or not to buy certain goods and services. The United States has a market economy.

Copyright © Mometrix Media. You have been licensed one copy of this document for personal use only. Any other reproduction or redistribution is strictly prohibited All rights reserved.

Market Economy

The five characteristics of a **market economy** are:

- **Economic freedom** – There is freedom of choice with respect to jobs, salaries, production, and price.
- **Economic incentives** – A positive incentive is to make a profit. However, if the producer tries to make too high a profit, the consequences might be that no one will purchase the item at that price. A negative incentive would be a drop in profits, causing the producer to decrease or discontinue production. A boycott, which might cause the producer to change business practices or policies, is also a negative economic incentive.
- **Competition** – There is more than one producer for any given product. Consumers thereby have choices about what to buy, which are usually made based on quality and price. Competition is an incentive for a producer to make the best product at the best price. Otherwise, producers will lose business to the competition.
- **Private ownership** – Production and profits belong to an individual or to a private company, not to the government.
- **Limited government** – Government plays no role in the economic decisions of its individual citizens.

Factors of Production and Types of Markets That Create Economic Flow

The factors of **production** are:

- **Land** – This includes not only actual land, but also forests, minerals, water, etc.
- **Labor** – This is the work force required to produce goods and services, including factors such as talent, skills, and physical labor.
- **Capital** – This is the cash and material equipment needed to produce goods and services, including buildings, property, tools, office equipment, roads, etc.
- **Entrepreneurship** – Persons with initiative can capitalize on the free market system by producing goods and services.

The two types of markets are factor and product markets. The **factor market** consists of the people who exchange their services for wages. The people are sellers and companies are buyers. The **product market** is the selling of products to the people who want to buy them. The people are the buyers and the companies are the sellers. This exchange creates a circular economic flow in which money goes from the producers to workers as wages, and then flows back to producers in the form of payment for products.

Economic Impact of Technology

At the start of the 21st century, the role of **information and communications technologies** (ICT) grew rapidly as the economy shifted to a knowledge-based one. Output is increasing in areas where ICT is used intensively, which are service areas and knowledge-intensive industries such as finance; insurance; real estate; business services, health care, and environmental goods and services; and community, social, and personal services. Meanwhile, the economic share for manufacturers is declining in medium- and low-technology industries such as chemicals, food products, textiles, gas, water, electricity, construction, and transport and communication services. Industries that have traditionally been high-tech, such as aerospace, computers, electronics, and pharmaceuticals are remaining steady in terms of their economic share. Technology has become the strongest factor in determining **per capita income** for many countries. The ease of technology investments as

Copyright © Mometrix Media. You have been licensed one copy of this document for personal use only. Any other reproduction or redistribution is strictly prohibited. All rights reserved.

compared to industries that involve factories and large labor forces has resulted in more foreign investments in countries that do not have natural resources to call upon.

PBA

The acronym **PBA** stands for **performance-based assessment**. A PBA is an alternative assessment, defined as a multistep task or project aligned to meet the specific state standards of any given subject. In social sciences, PBAs are used to assess a student's ability to use the concepts learned in a unit and apply those concepts to complete tasks that require higher-order thinking skills. The goal of most PBAs is to create a product or complete a process in which students connect what they have learned to their own experience or environment. These assessments are typically graded using a rubric, which focuses on both the final product and the process followed throughout the project.

Assessment of Social Sciences

Assessment **social sciences** should be assessed before, during, and after instruction. The data from these assessments should be used to guide, monitor, and revise instruction at both the whole-class and individual levels. Before instruction, assessments should be used to plan for an upcoming unit, whereas assessments that occur during instruction should be used to identify students who may need modified instruction or provide for an expansion of the current curriculum for accelerated learners. Assessments occurring after instruction should be used to gauge whether or not students have mastered the intended standards, at which point reteaching may need to occur.

Copyright © Mometrix Media. You have been licensed one copy of this document for personal use only. Any other reproduction or redistribution is strictly prohibited. All rights reserved.

Praxis Practice Test

Reading/Language Arts

Foundations of Reading

1. *Sea* and *see*, *fair* and *fare*, are called:
   a. Homophones
   b. Antonyms
   c. Homographs
   d. Twin words

2. Another name for a persuasive essay is:
   a. Dynamic essay
   b. Convincing essay
   c. Argumentative essay
   d. Position paper

3. A teacher is working with a group of third graders at the same reading level. Her goal is to improve reading fluency. She asks each child in turn to read a page from a book about mammal young. She asks the children to read with expression. She also reminds them they don't need to stop between each word; they should read as quickly as they comfortably can. She cautions them, however, not to read so quickly that they leave out or misread a word. The teacher knows the components of reading fluency are:
   a. Speed, drama, and comprehension
   b. Cohesion, rate, and prosody
   c. Understanding, rate, and prosody
   d. Rate, accuracy, and prosody

4. "Language load" refers to:
   a. The basic vocabulary words a first grader has committed to memory
   b. The number of unrecognizable words an English Language Learner encounters when reading a passage or listening to a teacher
   c. The damage that carrying a pile of heavy books could cause to a child's physique
   d. The number of different languages a person has mastered.

5. A syllable must contain:
   a. A vowel
   b. A consonant
   c. Both a vowel and a consonant
   d. A meaning

Copyright © Mometrix Media. You have been licensed one copy of this document for personal use only. Any other reproduction or redistribution is strictly prohibited. All rights reserved.

6. A third-grade teacher has several students reading above grade level. Most of the remaining students are reading at grade level. There are also a few students reading below grade level. She decides to experiment. Her hypothesis is that by giving the entire class a chapter book above grade level, high-level readers will be satisfied, grade-level readers will be challenged in a positive way, and students reading below grade level will be inspired to improve. Her method is most likely to:

a. Succeed, producing students reading at an Instructional reading level. High-level readers will be happy to be given material appropriate to their reading level. Grade-level readers will challenge themselves to improve reading strategies in order to master the text. Because only a few of the students are reading below grade level, the other students, who feel happy and energized, will inspire the slower readers by modeling success.
b. Succeed, producing students reading at an Independent reading level. High-level readers will independently help grade-level readers who will, in turn, independently help those below grade level.
c. Fail, producing students at a Frustration reading level. Those reading below grade level are likely to give up entirely. Those reading at grade level are likely to get frustrated and form habits that will actually slow down their development.
d. Fail, producing students reading at a Chaotic reading level. By nature, children are highly competitive. The teacher has not taken into consideration multiple learning styles. The children who are at grade level will either become bitter and angry at those whose reading level is above grade level or simply give up. The children reading below grade level will not be able to keep up and will in all likelihood act out their frustration or completely shut down.

7. Of the three tiers of words, the most important words for direct instruction are:

a. Tier-one words
b. Common words
c. Tier-two words
d. Words with Latin roots

8. At the beginning of each month, Mr. Yi has Jade read a page or two from a book she hasn't seen before. He notes the total number of words in the section, and also notes the number of times she leaves out or misreads a word. If Jade reads the passage with less than 3% error, Mr. Yi is satisfied that Jade is:

a. Reading with full comprehension
b. Probably bored and should try a more difficult book
c. Reading at her Independent reading level
d. Comfortable with the syntactical meaning

9. The purpose of corrective feedback is:

a. To provide students with methods for explaining to the teacher or classmates what a passage was about
b. To correct an error in reading a student has made, specifically clarifying where and how the error was made so that the student can avoid similar errors in the future
c. To provide a mental framework that will help the student correctly organize new information
d. To remind students that error is essential in order to truly understand and that it is not something to be ashamed of

Copyright © Mometrix Media. You have been licensed one copy of this document for personal use only. Any other reproduction or redistribution is strictly prohibited. All rights reserved.

10. Dr. Jenks is working with a group of high school students. They are about to read a science book about fossils. Before they begin, she writes the words *stromatolites, fossiliferous,* and *eocene* on the board. She explains the meaning of each word. These words are examples of:

a. Academic words
b. Alliteration
c. Content-specific words
d. Ionization

11. Which of the following best explains the importance prior knowledge brings to the act of reading?

a. Prior knowledge is information the student gets through researching a topic prior to reading the text. A student who is well-prepared through such research is better able to decode a text and retain its meaning.
b. Prior knowledge is knowledge the student brings from previous life or learning experiences to the act of reading. It is not possible for a student to fully comprehend new knowledge without first integrating it with prior knowledge.
c. Prior knowledge is predictive. It motivates the student to look for contextual clues in the reading and predict what is likely to happen next.
d. Prior knowledge is not important to any degree to the act of reading, because every text is self-contained and therefore seamless. Prior knowledge is irrelevant in this application.

12. A cloze test evaluates a student's:

a. Reading fluency
b. Understanding of context and vocabulary
c. Phonemic skills
d. Ability to apply the alphabetic principle to previously unknown material

13. Sight words are:

a. Common words with irregular spelling
b. Words that can easily be found on educational websites
c. Any word that can be seen, including text words, words on signs, brochures, banners, and so forth
d. There is no such thing; because oral language is learned before written language, all words are ultimately based on sound. The correct term is sound words and includes all words necessary to decode a particular text

14. *Phone, they, church.* The underlined letters in these words are examples of:

a. Consonant blend
b. Consonant shift
c. Continental shift
d. Consonant digraph

15. Phonemic awareness is a type of:

a. Phonological awareness. Phonemic awareness is the ability to recognize sounds within words
b. Phonics. It is a teaching technique whereby readers learn the relationship between letters and sounds
c. Alphabetization. Unless a reader knows the alphabet, phonemic awareness is useless
d. Syntactical awareness. Understanding the underlying structure of a sentence is key to understanding meaning

Copyright © Mometrix Media. You have been licensed one copy of this document for personal use only. Any other reproduction or redistribution is strictly prohibited. All rights reserved.

Language in Writing

16. Reading and writing are usually seen as the two major aspects of literacy that are taught in the classroom. What critical aspect of literacy begins at home but is often neglected in the classroom?

a. oral language development
b. health information
c. math skills
d. science awareness

17. A teacher is trying to assist a student with his scientific vocabulary. The student is also an English Language Learner. What could the teacher suggest to help him improve his scientific vocabulary MOST effectively?

a. Use a glossary of scientific terms for each chapter of the textbook, and discuss these terms with the student as the relevant chapters are referenced.
b. Assign a specific number of scientific terms for the student to look up in a scientific dictionary and share with the class.
c. Explain the scientific terms to this student as concepts are presented and related experiments performed.
d. Ask the student to look for context to define difficult scientific words, and have the student record the definitions in a notebook.

18. If a student were asked to use a similar word to describe someone who was happy, he or she would use

a. an antonym.
b. a homonym.
c. a synonym.
d. an euphemism.

19. Homonyms such as *bare* and *bear* are similar in sound yet have different meanings. What would a teacher suggest a student do to avoid misusing these words?

a. Memorize the definitions of the difficult words.
b. Check a dictionary or thesaurus to verify a word's usage.
c. Avoid encountering difficult words.
d. Ignore being precise in the definition.

20. Where does a prefix appear in a word?

a. at the beginning
b. at the end
c. in the middle
d. any place

21. Where does a suffix appear in a word?

a. at the beginning
b. at the end
c. in the middle
d. any place

Copyright © Mometrix Media. You have been licensed one copy of this document for personal use only. Any other reproduction or redistribution is strictly prohibited. All rights reserved.

22. Consider the following sentence:

Mary is a very gregarious person and has many friends.

Based on the context of this sentence, the word *gregarious* means:

a. shy.
b. angry.
c. friendly.
d. mean.

23. A knowledge of word elements can enable a student to understand the meanings of unfamiliar words. What does the prefix *circum-* mean in the word *circumference?*

a. beyond
b. after
c. around
d. before

24. What does the prefix *poly-* mean in the word *polygon?*

a. few
b. several
c. none
d. many

25. A number of verb forms are used in headlines. These include simple tenses, infinitive forms, and auxiliary verbs dropped in the passive voice. Which headline below uses a simple tense?

a. LOST DOG RETURNS
b. GOVERNOR TO VISIT CITY
c. GRADUATE NAMED VALEDICTORIAN
d. HERO GIVEN AWARD

Communication Skills

26. Oral language development across the curriculum requires

a. teamwork.
b. planning.
c. cooperation.
d. all of the above.

27. A teacher asked his students to prepare a presentation that could be shown in a foreign country. He advised them to

a. use idioms.
b. avoid anecdotes local to the foreign country.
c. avoid quotes from a foreign national of the country.
d. keep the presentation simple and succinct.

28. Ross and Janine were discussing a magazine article about codes, ciphers, and steganography, which their teacher gave as a reading assignment. The article described steganography as the practice of embedding secret messages in other messages, pictures, or music, etc. Janine asked Ross to explain the word *embedded* to her. Here is the conversation they had:

Ross: Steganography is cool!

Copyright © Mometrix Media. You have been licensed one copy of this document for personal use only. Any other reproduction or redistribution is strictly prohibited. All rights reserved.

Janine (rolling her eyes): I've heard the word embedded used to describe reporters being put with the troops overseas, but what does it mean here?
Ross: It means the message is inserted into a bigger message.
Janine: But how does that make the message hard to see? You can see the embedded reporters with the troops on TV.
Ross: The writing or picture is too small to see, so it can be hidden. These messages aren't big like a person. That's why someone who needs to read the information has to use special tools to be able to see the secret message.
Janine: Oh, I understand.

What did Ross say that helped Janine finally understand what *embedded* meant with regard to steganography?

a. *Embedded* means removed into something.
b. *Embedded* means inserted and plainly visible in something.
c. *Embedded* means inserted and hidden in something.
d. *Embedded* means inserted in a foreign language in something.

29. President Lincoln's Gettysburg Address was about:

a. the future of America.
b. a dedication of lives lost on this battlefield.
c. an eloquent expression of democratic ideals.
d. all of the above.

30. Doctors perform surgery and the patient dies. A doctor reporting this says the surgery had a "negative patient outcome." This is *best* identified as an example of...

a. jargon.
b. ambiguity.
c. euphemism.
d. connotation.

Mathematics

Number Sense and Numeration

31. In a group of 48 people, 1/3 claimed to be Christians, 3/16 were followers of Islam, 1/16 were Buddhists, 1/16 were Hindu, 1/48 were Sikh, 1/12 were traditional Native Americans and the remainder claimed no religious affiliation. The number of individuals in each group was:

a. 12, 4, 1, 3, 3, 9, 16
b. 16, 9, 3, 3, 1, 4, 12
c. 12, 1, 4, 3, 3, 9, 16
d. None of the above

32. The factors (x – 3), (x – 4) and (x + 7) expand to give the equation:

a. $x3 - 12x^2 -7x + 84$
b. $x^3 + 84x^2 - 14x + 14$
c. $x^3 - 37x + 84$
d. $x^3 +14x^2 - 7x + 84$

Copyright © Mometrix Media. You have been licensed one copy of this document for personal use only. Any other reproduction or redistribution is strictly prohibited. All rights reserved.

33. When multiplied together the two complex numbers (6 + i5) and (3 – i3) yield:

a. (18 - i15)
b. (33 – i3)
c. (33 - i9)
d. (33 - i15)

34. Given that the value of x is between 0 and 5, but not equal to either 0 or 5, which statement is true?

a. $0 \leq x^2 \leq 5$
b. $0 < x^2 < 25$
c. $0 \leq x^2 \leq 25$
d. $x^2 \leq 25$

35. If $2^n = 6$ and $2^8 = 256$, then $2^8 \text{ X } 2^n =$

a. 262
b. 2^{n+8}
c. 2^{8n}
d. $2^n + 6$

36. The series sum of 1/n for integer values of n such that $1 \leq n \leq 6$ is:

a. 2 1/2
b. 2 9/20
c. 2 5/6
d. 2 3/20

37. The series sum of (n + 1/n) for integer values $1 \leq n \leq 4$ is:

a. 11
b. A rational real number
c. A complex number
d. An integer

38. Tomas held out both hands, clearly showing ten digits – eight fingers and two thumbs – and proclaimed "I actually have nine fingers!" His friend Jerzy replied "No, you only have eight fingers!". To prove that he had nine fingers Tomas counted backward on one hand "8 – 7 – 6 – 5", then said "and 4 on this hand makes 9 fingers". This logic is incorrect because:

a. Tomas counted his thumb as one of the fingers
b. Tomas was mixing ordinal and cardinal numbers
c. Tomas began counting from the left instead of the right
d. Tomas began counting from the right instead of the left

39. The sum of two prime numbers is:

a. Always odd
b. Always a prime number
c. Always even
d. None of the above

Copyright © Mometrix Media. You have been licensed one copy of this document for personal use only. Any other reproduction or redistribution is strictly prohibited. All rights reserved.

40. (x – 6) is a factor of the equation $2x^3 + 4x^2 - 82x - 84 = 0$. The remainder:

a. Negative integral roots
b. Negative complex roots
c. Negative irrational roots
d. Both positive and negative roots

41. The necessary and sufficient condition for a prime number is:

a. Divisible only by itself and 1
b. Divisible only by itself
c. Is not a product of two numbers
d. Is the product of prime numbers

42. The ratio of 10 to 17.5 is:

a. 1.75
b. Real, rational
c. 2/3.5
d. b. and c. are true

Algebraic Concepts

43. The function $f(x) = 2x^2/3 + 2x + 3$ has intercepts at:

a. (0,3) and (2,0)
b. (0,3) only
c. (3,0) and (0,3)
d. None of the above

44. There are three branches in a particular electrical circuit. An indicator light is on (True) if both the first and third branches are active (True) or if the second and third branches are active (True), but not (False) if both the first and second branches are active. The truth table for the indicator light is

a.

1	T	T	T	T	F	F	F	F
2	T	T	T	T	F	F	T	T
3	F	T	F	T	F	T	F	T
Light	F	T	F	F	F	F	F	T

b.

1	T	T	T	T	F	F	T	T
2	F	T	T	T	F	F	F	F
3	F	T	F	T	F	T	F	F
Light	F	T	F	F	T	F	F	F

c.

Copyright © Mometrix Media. You have been licensed one copy of this document for personal use only. Any other reproduction or redistribution is strictly prohibited. All rights reserved.

1	TT	TT	TT	TT	TF	FT	FF	FF
2	FF	FF	TT	TT	FF	FT	TT	TT
3	FF	TT	FF	TT	FF	TT	FF	TT
Light	TT	TT	FF	FF	FF	TF	FF	TT

d.

1	T	T	T	T	F	F	F	F
2	F	F	T	T	F	F	T	T
3	F	T	F	T	F	T	F	T
Light	F	T	F	F	F	F	F	T

45. The graph of the function $y = 3x^2 - 6x + 18$ has a maximum or minimum value at:
    a. (1, 15)
    b. (3, -6)
    c. (6, -3)
    d. (6, 18)

46. The equation $x^2 - 2x + 3$ has roots:
    a. -2, 3
    b. $1 + i\sqrt{2}$, $1 - i\sqrt{2}$
    c. $2 + i\sqrt{3}$, $2 - i\sqrt{3}$
    d. $6 - i\sqrt{2}$, $6 + i\sqrt{2}$

47. The value of 7! Divided by 3! is:
    a. 2.33
    b. 840
    c. 210
    d. 1320

48. The graph of $x^2/2 + y^2/5 = 25$ intersects the line $y = 2x + 3$ at coordinates:
    a. (0.4, 2) and (0.2, 3)
    b. (3.40, 9.80) and (-5.25, -7.5)
    c. (2, 0.4) and (3, 0.2)
    d. (3.40, -9.80) and (5.25, -7.5)

49. A equation of a hyperbola has the form:
    a. $yx = a$
    b. $y = ax^2 + b$
    c. $x^2 - y^2 = a$
    d. $x^2 + y^2 = a$

Copyright © Mometrix Media. You have been licensed one copy of this document for personal use only. Any other reproduction or redistribution is strictly prohibited. All rights reserved.

Informal Geometry and Measurement

50. A round cylinder is 10 cm in diameter and 25 cm in length. It has a total surface area of:

a. pr2h
b. 2pr(h + r)
c. 2pdh
d. $2pr^2 + h$

51. A triangular prism has a right triangle cross-section. The orthogonal sides are each 2 cm wide, and the total length of the prism is 10 cm. The total surface area of the prism and its volume are:

a. (44 + 10√2) cm2 and 20 cm3
b. (64√2) cm2 and 20 cm3
c. 42 cm2 and 22 cm3
d. 2(22 + 10√2) cm^2 and 20 cm^3

52. The vectors A and B begin at the origins and extend to the coordinates (6, 16) and (16, 6) respectively. The value of A●B is:

a. 96
b. 36
c. 192
d. 256

53. A complex right triangle has orthogonal sides of length (6 + i3) and (4 + i√3). The hypotenuse has the length:

a. √(40 + 4i(9 +2√3))
b. √(40 + i(36 + 2√3))
c. (40 + 4i(9 + 2√3))
d. (40 + i(36 + 2√3))

54. A large L-shaped field is 400 m long in its longest side, and 150 m wide at its widest point. The opposite parallel sides are only 1/5 as long. The total perimeter of the field is:

a. 6000 m
b. 900 m
c. 1200 m
d. 1100 m

55. The total perimeter of an L-shaped field is 800 feet. The longest side is 300 feet, and the longest width is 100 feet. The shorter sides are 50 feet and 50 feet respectively. The total area of the field is:

a. 22,500 square feet
b. 30,000 square feet
c. 17,500 square feet
d. 45,000 square feet

Copyright © Mometrix Media. You have been licensed one copy of this document for personal use only. Any other reproduction or redistribution is strictly prohibited. All rights reserved.

Data Organizations and Interpretation

56. A magician has a hat that holds two rabbits. One rabbit is black and the other is white. In his last 16 performances he has randomly pulled the black rabbit from the hat 16 times. The probability that he will pull the white rabbit from the hat in his next performance is:

a. 0.50
b. 1
c. 1/17
d. 0

57. A bag contains 16 coins, each with a different date. The number of possible combinations of three coins from the bag is:

a. 650
b. 48
c. 560
d. 6

58. Ten sample values were found to be 6, 7, 7, 9, 5, 7, 8, 2, 6 and 3. The mean and median values of these samples are:

a. 6 and 6.5
b. 6 and 7
c. 6 and 8
d. 6.5 and 7

59. Seven samples were obtained having the values 21, 22, 26, 29, 27, 26 and 24. The mean and standard deviation values are:

a. 22.4 and 2.6
b. 25 and 2.2
c. 25 and 2.6
d. 25.6 and 2.2

60. A certain special die has eight sides instead of six. The probability of rolling an odd number is:

a. The same as for a six-sided die
b. One-third more than for a six-sided die
c. One-third less than for a six-sided die
d. 25% greater

Social Studies

Geography, Anthropology, Sociology

61. How did Egypt's geographical features most contribute to the stability of ancient Egyptian culture?

a. The Nile River regularly and predictably flooded, irrigating crops.
b. The expanse of the Nile River prevented Egyptians from settling elsewhere.
c. The Valley of the Kings divided Upper Egypt from Lower Egypt.
d. The Mediterranean Sea enabled contact between Egyptians and other ancient peoples.

Copyright © Mometrix Media. You have been licensed one copy of this document for personal use only. Any other reproduction or redistribution is strictly prohibited. All rights reserved.

62. How does the prevalence of ziggurats in ancient Mesopotamia illustrate a central factor of Mesopotamian culture?

a. Intended as lookouts, the number of ziggurats illustrates a Mesopotamian concern for security from invaders.
b. Used for stargazing, the number of ziggurats shows how Mesopotamian culture depended on astrology.
c. Dedicated to Mesopotamian rulers, the ziggurats illustrate the complete control Mesopotamian kings held over their subjects.
d. Structures dedicated to gods, the ziggurats illustrate the importance of religion in Mesopotamian culture.

63. How did Charlemagne's coronation as Holy Roman Emperor influence European politics?

a. It united much of Western Europe under a single ruler.
b. It strengthened papal authority regarding the right of political leaders to rule.
c. It made Catholicism the official religion throughout Charlemagne's empire.
d. It led to Charlemagne's renunciation of conquest by force.

64. Which statement best describes the feudal society of Western Europe in the Middle Ages?

a. Religious institutions owned most of the land and leased portions to vassals.
b. Rulers granted land strictly on the basis of blood relationships.
c. Rulers granted vassals land in exchange for military and political service.
d. Feudalism shifted a spice-based economy to a land-based economy.

65. What effect did the Crusades have on Europe's Jewish population?

a. Entire European Jewish communities were killed during the First Crusade.
b. Persecution of Jewish people declined as the Crusaders focused on Muslims.
c. Most Jewish traders and merchants profited through Crusades-related business.
d. To avoid persecution, some Jewish-only battalions fought in each Crusade.

66. During the 15th century, Johann Gutenberg invented a printing press with moveable type. How did his invention influence science?

a. It did not influence science; the printing of Gutenberg Bibles directed public attention away from science and toward reforming the Catholic Church.
b. It led to scientific advances throughout Europe by spreading scientific knowledge.
c. It influenced scientific advancement in Germany only, where Gutenberg's press was based.
d. It did not influence science; though texts with scientific knowledge were printed, distribution of these texts was limited.

67. In about 1428, the Mesoamerican city-states Tenochtitlan, Texcoco, and Tlacopan formed a Triple Alliance. How did this influence Aztec history?

a. Texcoco and Tlacopan secretly conspired against Tenochtitlan, using the Alliance as a front.
b. Disagreements about strategy between the city-states weakened Aztec resistance to Spanish invaders.
c. The alliance agreed that each city-state would offer a specific number of human sacrifices each year.
d. The allied city-states joined forces to conquer other city-states, incorporating them into an Aztec Empire.

Copyright © Mometrix Media. You have been licensed one copy of this document for personal use only. Any other reproduction or redistribution is strictly prohibited. All rights reserved.

68. Which statement best describes the role of the Catholic Church in medieval Western Europe?

a. Powerful and wealthy, the Church was important to both poor and rich people.
b. The Church concerned itself mainly with the poorer members of medieval society.
c. Weakened by infighting about Church doctrine, the Church struggled to wield power.
d. The Catholic Church served as a neutral force between competing political leaders.

69. In the 16th century, Akbar ruled the Mughal Empire, which covered much of present-day India. Which statement best describes one means by which Akbar maintained control of the Empire?

a. He paid administrative officials with land instead of money.
b. He accommodated the religious practices of Hindus as well as Muslims.
c. He refused to allow certain defeated rulers to keep their land.
d. He refused to allow the construction of Hindu temples.

70. Which statement best describes the role played by the French economy in causing the 1789 French Revolution?

a. France's very large national debt led to heavy tax burdens on the French peasantry.
b. Nearly sixty percent of annual national expenditures financed luxuries for the French nobility.
c. Reforms in the guild system allowed many peasants to rise to the middle class.
d. The king's attempt to curtail free trade led skilled journeymen to rebel against the monarchy.

World History

71. Where was the first great human civilization located?

a. Egypt
b. Greece
c. Mesopotamia
d. Samaria

72. Which of the following was not an ancient Egyptian ruler?

a. Anubis
b. Hatshepsut
c. Ramses' II
d. Tutankhamen

73. How did the Crusader army that went on the First Crusade differ from the Crusader armies that Pope Urban II envisioned?

a. There was no difference. The people of Europe were accustomed to obeying clerical direction and eagerly joined the cause creating an army that was primarily made up of faithful Christians from all social classes led by a select group of knights who were responsible for leading and training their armies.
b. There was no difference. The people of Europe obeyed clerical direction and stayed home to pray for the success of an army composed entirely of knights and professional other military personnel.
c. Pope Urban II had envisioned an army of skilled knights and professional soldiers; instead, men and women from all classes joined together to retake the Holy Land.
d. Pope Urban II had envisioned an army composed of faithful Christians of from all social classes led by a group of select knights; instead the army was primarily made up of knights and other professional military personnel.

Copyright © Mometrix Media. You have been licensed one copy of this document for personal use only. Any other reproduction or redistribution is strictly prohibited. All rights reserved.

United States History

74. Which of the following was not a tax levied on the American colonies by the British government in the 1760's and 70's?

a. The Sugar Act of 1764
b. The Stamp Act of 1765
c. The Lead Act of 1772
d. The Tea Act of 1773

75. To whom was the Declaration of Independence addressed and why?

a. To the British Parliament, because the colonists were opposed to being ruled by a king who had only inherited his throne and only considered the popularly elected Parliament to hold any authority over them
b. To the King of England because the colonists were upset that Parliament was passing laws for them even though they did not have the right to elect members of Parliament to represent their interests.
c. To the Governors of the rebelling colonies so that they would know that they had 30 days to either announce their support of the Revolution or to return to England.
d. To the colonial people as a whole. The Declaration of Independence was intended to outline the wrongs that had been inflicted on them by the British military and inspire them to rise up in protest.

76. How did the ruling in Marbury v. Madison alter the Supreme Court's power in the federal government?

a. It lessened it. The Supreme Court was concerned about the possibility of judges overturning laws enacted by voters through referendums and took away that power.
b. It increased it. The decision in Marbury v. Madison gave the Supreme Court it's now traditional right to overturn legislation.
c. It increased it. The decision in Marbury v. Madison strengthened the Supreme Court's Constitutional right to overturn legislation.
d. There was no change. Marbury v. Madison was a case involving a president who was unwilling to obey laws enacted by his predecessor; there was nothing about the case or decision that would have more than a cursory connection to federal powers of government

77. Which President of the United States changed the date of Thanksgiving from the last Thursday of November to the fourth Thursday of November?

a. George Washington
b. Andrew Jackson
c. Abraham Lincoln
d. Franklin D. Roosevelt

78. Which of the following is considered to be the largest cause of death among Native Americans following the arrival of European colonists in North America?

a. Wounds from wars with the European settlers
b. Wounds from wars with the other Native American tribes
c. European diseases
d. Exposure during the wintry, forced marches on which the European settlers forced them

Copyright © Mometrix Media. You have been licensed one copy of this document for personal use only. Any other reproduction or redistribution is strictly prohibited. All rights reserved.

79. Which group(s) of people were originally responsible for selecting the members of the U.S. Senate?

a. State legislatures
b. State governors
c. State electors
d. State residents, subject to voting eligibility

80. The Erie Canal is 363 miles long and connects which body of water to Lake Erie?

a. The Mississippi River
b. The Hudson River
c. The Susquehanna River
d. The Lehigh River

81. The telephone was a solution to which of the following problems with the telegraph?

a. Telegraph lines were thick and difficult to maintain.
b. Telegraph messages could only be received by people who had specialized equipment.
c. Telegraphs could only relay one message at a time.
d. Telegraphs frequently broke down if subject to extended use.

82. Who was Lewis and Clark's guide?

a. Pocahontas
b. Sacagawea
c. Squanto
d. Wauwatosa

83. What was the purpose of Lyndon Johnson's Great Society?

a. To eliminate poverty and racial injustice in America
b. To erase the last vestiges of the Great Depression from the American economic landscape.
c. To encourage economic prosperity through trickledown economics.
d. To increase educational standards in the United States.

Government, Citizenship, and Democracy

84. Which of the following is a significant structural similarity between the government of the Iroquois Confederacy and the government of the United States?

a. Many decisions require compromise between two separate entities. In the Iroquois Confederacy, those entities were two different sets of Lords; in the U.S. government, those entities are the House of Representatives and the Senate.
b. A single leader has significant executive powers: in the Iroquois Confederacy, a chief, and in the U.S. government, the president.
c. The level of representation in at least one legislative body depended on population. In the Iroquois Confederacy, the population of tribes partially determined representation, and in the United States, the population of states partially determines representation.
d. A third judicial branch served as a check on the executive power in both the Iroquois Confederacy and the U.S. government.

Copyright © Mometrix Media. You have been licensed one copy of this document for personal use only. Any other reproduction or redistribution is strictly prohibited. All rights reserved.

85. One of the earliest political parties in the United States was the Federalist Party. Its decline is best explained by:

a. a failure to organize state political parties.
b. the enmity of wealthy Americans.
c. its opposition to the War of 1812.
d. its advocacy of a strong central government.

86. In 1777, the United States Congress adopted the Articles of Confederation. The Articles of Confederation limited the power of the federal government by denying it:

a. the power to borrow money.
b. the power to declare war.
c. the power to make international treaties.
d. the power to raise taxes.

Economics

87. The economic theories of John Maynard Keynes are most closely associated with:

a. the view that deficit spending leads to inflation.
b. advocating government action against monopolies.
c. the view that supply creates its own demand.
d. advocating government action to stimulate economic growth.

88. An action's opportunity cost is best explained in terms of:

a. the minimum amount a business must borrow for the action.
b. the opportunities given up in order to pursue that action.
c. the percentage of one's overall budget that the action requires.
d. the cost of a long-term action adjusted for inflation.

Social Studies as Inquiry and Social Studies Processes

89. In social sciences, reification is best understood as:

a. using qualitative data instead of quantitative data.
b. treating an abstraction as a concrete thing.
c. the use of heuristic devices.
d. mistaking subjectivity for objectivity.

90. Suppose that every time a cat hears a can opener, it is fed. The cat runs to the kitchen to be fed every time it hears a can opener. In psychology, this kind of association is called:

a. Operant conditioning
b. Habituation
c. Classical conditioning
d. Conformity

Copyright © Mometrix Media. You have been licensed one copy of this document for personal use only. Any other reproduction or redistribution is strictly prohibited. All rights reserved.

Science

Earth Science

91. If an astronomer observing the stars detects a blue shift, what could he conclude?
    a. The star is moving farther away from him.
    b. The star is moving closer or toward him.
    c. The star is cooling down and becoming smaller.
    d. The star is heating up and becoming larger.

92. Salts are made from a combination of what two types of elements?
    a. A metal and a nonmetal
    b. A nonmetal and an alkaline earth metal
    c. A cation from a base and an anion from an acid
    d. A metal and a halogen

93. What group of the periodic table makes up the alkaline earth metals?
    a. Group 1
    b. Group 2
    c. Group 13
    d. Group 17

94. Which of the following words is not connected to the process of mountain building?
    a. Folding
    b. Faulting
    c. Transform
    d. Convergent

95. The formation of sedimentary rock includes all of the following processes except
    a. layering.
    b. cementation.
    c. compaction.
    d. heat.

96. Which of the following is an example of chemical weathering?
    a. Rain freezing on the roadway.
    b. Ivy growing on the side of a wooden house.
    c. Vinegar fizzing when poured on a rock.
    d. A river carrying sediment downstream.

97. Which of the following situations would result in the generation of new crust?
    a. Two crustal plates converge.
    b. Two crustal plates move apart.
    c. Two crustal plates slide past one another.
    d. A crustal plate is pushed down into the mantle.

Copyright © Mometrix Media. You have been licensed one copy of this document for personal use only. Any other reproduction or redistribution is strictly prohibited. All rights reserved.

98. Which of the following terms describes an intrusion of magma injected between two layers of sedimentary rock, forcing the overlying strata upward to create a dome-like form?

a. Sill
b. Dike
c. Laccolith
d. Caldera

99. Which statement best describes the process of absolute dating?

a. It compares the amount of radioactive material in a rock to the amount that has decayed into another element.
b. It measures the age of a rock by comparing it to fossils found in the same stratigraphic layer as the rock.
c. It measures the amount of daughter elements that have broken down by half.
d. It measures the mass loss of a rock by estimating the amount of material that has eroded due to catastrophic events.

Life Science

100. Most organic molecules have all of the following properties except

a. high solubility in water.
b. a tendency to melt.
c. covalently bonded.
d. high flammability.

101. The main function of _______ is it to reduce the number of chromosomes to half the number of parent cells?

a. mitosis
b. telophase
c. meiosis I
d. meiosis II

102. This organelle contains digestive enzymes that break down food and unneeded substances. They are also thought to be linked to the aging process. What part of a cell does this describe?

a. Lysosomes
b. Chromatin
c. Plastids
d. Golgi Apparatus

103. Which of the following describes the difference between an anabolism reaction and a catabolism reaction?

a. Anabolism undergoes ionic reactions, while catabolism undergoes covalent reactions.
b. Anabolism undergoes condensation reactions, while catabolism undergoes hydrolysis.
c. Anabolism reactions use water, while catabolism reactions do not.
d. Anabolism reactions release glucose, while catabolism reactions release water.

Copyright © Mometrix Media. You have been licensed one copy of this document for personal use only. Any other reproduction or redistribution is strictly prohibited. All rights reserved.

104. Plant A undergoes C4 photosynthesis. What type of environment would the plant most likely live in?

a. Plant A lives in a very moist environment.
b. Plant A lives in a very arid environment.
c. Plant A lives in a marine environment.
d. Plant A lives in a dark environment that lacks solar energy.

105. Where is the type of RNA that carries and positions amino acids for further assembly located in the cell?

(Sill 3.2)

a. Cytoplasm
b. Nucleus
c. Ribosome
d. Mitochondria

106. The following is the anticodon sequence formed during translation. What is the original codon sequence?

A C G U A C G C U

a. T G C A T G C G A
b. U G C T U G C G T
c. U G C A U G C G A
d. U C G A U C G C A

107. A dihybrid cross is made between the dominant genes for Brown eyes (B) and Blonde hair (S), and the recessive genes for blue eyes (b) and red hair (s). What fraction of offspring would have the genotype BbSs in the F2 generation?

a. 1/16
b. 3/16
c. 4/16
d. 9/16

108. What type of mutation is represented by the following sequence?

1 5 4 3 2 6

a. Breakage
b. Deletion
c. Insertion
d. Inversion

Physical Science

109. The volume of water in a bucket is 2.5 liters. When an object with an irregular shape and a mass of 40 grams is submerged in the water, the volume of the water is 4.5 liters. What is the density of the object?

a. 1/10 g/L
b. 2 g/L
c. 20 g/L
d. 80 g/L

Copyright © Mometrix Media. You have been licensed one copy of this document for personal use only. Any other reproduction or redistribution is strictly prohibited. All rights reserved.

110. Which of the following represents a chemical change?

a. Sublimation of water
b. A spoiling apple
c. Dissolution of salt in water
d. Pulverized rock

111. The amount of potential energy an object has depends on all of the following except its

a. mass.
b. height above ground.
c. gravitational attraction.
d. temperature.

112. Elements on the periodic table are arranged into groups and periods and ordered according to

a. atomic number.
b. number of protons.
c. reactivity.
d. All of the above

113. The specific heat capacity of ice is half as much as that of liquid water. What is the result of this?

a. It takes half the amount of energy to increase the temperature of a 1 kg sample of ice by 1°C than a 1 kg sample of water.
b. It takes twice the amount of energy to increase the temperature of a 1 kg sample of ice by 1°C than a 1 kg sample of water.
c. It takes a quarter the amount of energy to increase the temperature of a 1 kg sample of ice by 1°C than a 1 kg sample of water.
d. It takes the same amount of energy to increase the temperature of a 1 kg sample of ice and a 1 kg sample of water by 1°C.

114. What happens to the temperature of a substance as it is changing phase from a liquid to a solid?

a. Its temperature increases due to the absorption of latent heat.
b. Its temperature decreases due to the heat of vaporization.
c. Its temperature decreases due to the latent heat of fusion.
d. Its temperature remains the same due to the latent heat of fusion.

115. A long nail is heated at one end. After a few seconds, the other end of the nail becomes equally hot. What type of heat transfer does this represent?

a. Radiation
b. Conduction
c. Convection
d. Entropy

116. Which of the following statements about heat transfer is not true?

a. As the energy of a system changes, its thermal energy must change or work must be done.
b. Heat transfer from a warmer object to a cooler object can occur spontaneously.
c. Heat transfer can never occur from a cooler object to a warmer object.
d. If two objects reach the same temperature, energy is no longer available for work.

Copyright © Mometrix Media. You have been licensed one copy of this document for personal use only. Any other reproduction or redistribution is strictly prohibited. All rights reserved.

Science in Personal and Social Perspectives

117. Why would it be ethical for local and state governments to conduct a risk-benefit analysis in making decisions about city planning and development?

a. Governments must know what the benefits of a new development are for people and the economy in order to persuade opponents and the public who are against it.
b. Knowledge of the environmental risks and benefits to humans is required for gaining building permits.
c. The benefits to people and the economy must outweigh the risks to determine whether their decision to build is fair.
d. The benefits to people and the economy can be used to ignore the risks associated with any new development.

118. Which of the following ethical questions regarding biotechnology would be answered and regulated by the FDA (the Food and Drug Administration)?

a. Should the packaging of meat products that come from cloned animals be labeled?
b. Should nitrate or sulfate fertilizers be added to oil spills to assist the decomposition of crude oil by bacteria?
c. Should parents be allowed to genetically alter an embryo by choosing its physical characteristics?
d. Should cells or components of cells be used to create industrially useful products?

Science as Inquiry and Science Processes

119. A student is working on a science project and is going through each step of the scientific method. After the student conducts his or her first experiment and records the results of the experimental test, what should the student do next?

a. Communicate the results
b. Draw a conclusion
c. Repeat the experiment
d. Create a hypothesis

120. Once a hypothesis has been verified and accepted, it becomes a ________.

a. fact
b. law
c. conclusion
d. theory

Copyright © Mometrix Media. You have been licensed one copy of this document for personal use only. Any other reproduction or redistribution is strictly prohibited. All rights reserved.

Answers and Explanations

Reading/Language Arts

Foundations in Reading

1. A: Homophones. Homophones are a type of homonym that sound alike, but are spelled differently and have different meanings. Other examples are *two, to,* and *too; their, they're,* and *there.*

2. C: Argumentative essay. The goal of a persuasive essay is to convince the reader that the author's position or opinion on a controversial topic is correct. That opinion or position is called the argument. A persuasive essay argues a series of points, supported by facts and evidence.

3. D: Rate, accuracy, and prosody. Fluent readers are able to read smoothly and comfortably at a steady pace (rate). The more quickly a child reads, the greater the chance of leaving out a word or substituting one word for another (for example, *sink* instead of *shrink*). Fluent readers are able to maintain accuracy without sacrificing rate. Fluent readers also stress important words in a text, group words into rhythmic phrases, and read with intonation (prosody).

4. B: The number of unrecognizable words an English Language Learner encounters when reading a passage or listening to a teacher. Language load is one of the barriers English Language Learners face. To lighten this load, a teacher can rephrase, eliminate unnecessary words, divide complex sentences into smaller units, and teach essential vocabulary before the student begins the lesson.

5. A: A vowel. A syllable is a minimal sound unit arranged around a vowel. For example, *academic* has four syllables: *a/ca/dem/ic.* It is possible for a syllable to be a single vowel, as in the above example. It is not possible for a syllable to be a single consonant.

6. C: Fail, producing students at a Frustration reading level. Those reading below grade level are likely to give up entirely. Those reading at grade level are likely to get frustrated and form habits that will actually slow down their development. Giving students texts that are too far beyond their reach produces frustrated readers. In an effort to succeed, frustrated writers are likely to apply strategies that have worked for them in the past but cannot work in this case because the text is simply beyond them. Looking for contextual clues to understand the meaning of unfamiliar words requires that most of the words in the passage are familiar. Breaking unfamiliar words into individual phonemes or syllables can be effective, but not if the number of such words is excessive. In this case, students below reading level and students at reading level will become frustrated when the skills that have worked for them in the past now fail.

7. C: Tier-two words. Tier-two words are words that are used with high frequency across a variety of disciplines or words with multiple meanings. They are characteristic of mature language users. Knowing these words is crucial to attaining an acceptable level of reading comprehension and communication skills.

8. C: Reading at her Independent reading level. When reading independently, students are at the correct level if they read with at least 97% accuracy.

9. B: To correct an error in reading a student has made, specifically clarifying where and how the error was made so that the student can avoid similar errors in the future. A reading teacher offers corrective feedback to a student in order to explain why a particular error in reading is, in fact, an

Copyright © Mometrix Media. You have been licensed one copy of this document for personal use only. Any other reproduction or redistribution is strictly prohibited. All rights reserved.

error. Corrective feedback is specific; it locates where and how the student went astray so that similar errors can be avoided in future reading.

10. C: Content-specific words. Because these words are specific to paleontology, it's unlikely the students know their meanings. Without understanding what these words mean, the students would not be able to understand the content of the passage they were about to read.

11. B: Prior knowledge is knowledge the student brings from previous life or learning experiences to the act of reading. It is not possible for a student to fully comprehend new knowledge without first integrating it with prior knowledge. Prior knowledge, which rises from experience and previous learning, provides a framework by which new knowledge gained from the act of reading can be integrated. Every act of reading enriches a student's well of prior knowledge and increases that student's future ability to comprehend more fully any new knowledge acquired through reading.

12. B: Understanding of context and vocabulary. In a cloze test, a reader is given a text with certain words blocked out. The reader must be able to determine probable missing words based on contextual clues. In order to supply these words, the reader must already know them.

13. A: Common words with irregular spelling. Sight words occur in many types of writing; they are high-frequency words. Sight words are also words with irregular spelling. Some examples of sight words include *talk, some,* and *the.* Fluent readers need to recognize these words visually.

14. D: Consonant digraph. A consonant digraph is group of consonants in which all letters represent a single sound.

15. A: Phonological awareness. Phonemic awareness is the ability to recognize sounds within words. Segmenting words and blending sounds are components of phonemic awareness. Phonological awareness includes an understanding of multiple components of spoken language. Ability to hear individual words within a vocalized stream and ability to identify spoken syllables are types of phonological awareness.

Language in Writing

16. A: is correct because oral language development begins during infancy and develops until a child has an extensive vocabulary.

17. C: is the MOST effective strategy because it relates concepts to experiments. The student will not only hear and read the definitions of scientific terms, he will also see them in action, and take part in them. This is likely to be far more effective than the other methods.

18. C: A synonym is a word that has a similar meaning. A n antonym is a word that means the opposite. A homonym is a word that sounds the same but has different spelling and meaning.

A euphemism is an inoffensive word used in place of an offensive word.

19. B: is correct. In cases of words that sound alike but have different meanings, checking a dictionary or thesaurus will ensure correct usage of a word.

20. A: Prefixes appear at the beginning of words, while suffixes appear at the end of words.

21. B: Suffixes appear at the end of words, while prefixes appear at the beginning of words.

Copyright © Mometrix Media. You have been licensed one copy of this document for personal use only. Any other reproduction or redistribution is strictly prohibited. All rights reserved.

22. C: Gregarious means easy to get along with, or friendly. If one didn't know the meaning of the word, the fact that Mary has many friends would be a clue to decipher the meaning.

23. C: Circum is Latin for "around." Post is the prefix for "after." Pre is the prefix for "before." There are several prefixes for "beyond", such as trans, hyper, extra.

24. D: Poly means "many." Although the first thing many people might think of when it comes to this prefix is the word polyester, a man-made material that's often used in clothing because it's cheaper than natural materials, it does not mean "artificial."

25. A: This headline uses the simple tense. In this case, it's the simple present tense. B uses the infinitive form, while C and D both drop the auxiliary verb in the passive voice.

Communication Skills

26. D: Oral language development requires teamwork, planning, and cooperation

27. D: For the vast majority of people attending a presentation in a foreign country, English will not be their native language, and many of them will struggle to keep up with a presentation in English, so it should not be complex, or very long. It would be wise to include, not avoid, anecdotes from the country, and quotes from nationals. American idioms should be avoided, as idioms by their nature do not translate well.

28. C: Ross told Janine that the secret message is inserted into a bigger message, but isn't seen by anyone who isn't looking for it because it's so small. It's effectively hidden.

29. D: President Lincoln's Gettysburg Address was about all three of these elements. Its primary purpose was a dedication of lives lost on this battlefield, but it was also about the future of America, and it is now famous as an eloquent expression of democratic ideals.

30. C: A euphemism is an expression used instead of more literal words to make a harsh expression sound softer, to make an impolite description sound more polite, or to make a description less polite (such as saying "bit the dust" instead of "died" in a formal setting). Jargon (A) is the specialized terminology of a specific field or group. This example, however, is NOT medical jargon; a better example might be "expired" or "deceased." Ambiguity (B) means unclear and/or open to multiple interpretations.

Mathematics

Number Sense and Numeration

31. B: One-third of 48 = 16; one-sixteenth of 48 = 3, therefore 3/16 = 9, 1/48 of 48 = 1, 1/12 of 48 = 4. This accounts for 36 individuals in the group, leaving a remainder of 12.

32. C: Multiplication of (x – 3) by (x – 4) yields the quadratic formula (x2 – 7x + 12). When multiplied by the third factor (x + 7), this produces the formula x3 – 37x + 84.

33. B: Complex numbers are multiplied in exactly the same manner as algebraic factors. Here (6 + i5) (3 – i3) = 18 – i18 + i15 -15i2 = 18 + 15 – i3 – 15(-1) = 18 – i3 + 15 = 33 – i3

34. B: Since x is not equal to either 0 or 5, the value of x2 also cannot be equal to either 0 or 25. Of the four possible answers, a, c and d have conditions of equality with the forbidden values.

Copyright © Mometrix Media. You have been licensed one copy of this document for personal use only. Any other reproduction or redistribution is strictly prohibited. All rights reserved.

35. B: The general rule for the multiplication of indices is axay = ax+y.

36. B: The series expands to 1 + 1/2 + 1/3 + 1/4 + 1/5 + 1/6

= 1 + (3/6 + 2/6 + 1/6) + 1/4 + 1/5 = 2 + 1/4 + 1/5 = 2 + 5/20 + 4/20 = 2 9/20

37. B: The series expands to 1 + 1/1 + 2 + 1/2 + 3 + 1/3 + 4 + 1/4 = 12 1/12 = 12.08333, an infinitely repeating decimal value. It is therefore a real, rational number.

38. B: When mixing ordinal and cardinal numbers the point of reference shifts by one unit. Ordinal numbering begins from 1, while cardinal numbering begins from 0.

39. D: The first three answers are easily disproved. Two, three and five are all prime numbers. The sum of three and five is eight, an even number and not a prime number. The sum of two and three is five, an odd number.

40. A: Factoring out (x – 6) leaves 2x2 + 16x + 14 = 0. Using the general formula for finding the roots of a quadratic equation x = (-b ± √(b2 – 4ac.) / (2a. where a = 2, b = 16 and c = 14, substitute the values of a, b and c and complete the calculation to obtain the root values x = -1 and x = -7, which are negative integers.

41. A: A prime number is by definition any number that can be divided integrally only by itself and 1. It therefore has no factors and so is not the product of any other numbers, prime or otherwise.

42. D: The ratio of 17.5 to 10 is 1.75. The ratio of 10 to 17.5 is 4/7 = 0.5714285, a real, rational number that is equivalent to the ratio of 2/3.5

Algebraic Concepts

43. B: The y-intercept at x = 0 has the value f(x) = +3. For an x-intercept, the value of f(x) must be 0 for some real value of x, but f(x) in this case never has a value less than +3.

44. D: The first and third or the second and third branches of the circuit are represented as active in the second, fourth and eighth columns. But in the fourth column the first and second branches are indicated as active, negating the 'Light on' signal.

45. A: A maximum or minimum value of a function coincides with a point at which the slope of the tangent to the function is zero; that is, at the points at which the value of the derivative of the function is zero. For this function. dy/dx = 6x – 6, and dy/dx = 0 at x = 1. The value of the function y at x = 1 is 15.

46. B: Using the general formula for finding the roots of a quadratic equation: x = (-b ± √(b2 – 4ac.) / 2a, where a = 1, b = -2 and c = 3, substitute the values of a, b and c and complete the calculation.

47. B: 7! = 7 x 6 x 5 x 4 x 3 x 2 x 1 and 3! = 3 x 2 x 1. The value of 7!/3! is therefore calculated as 7 x 6 x 5 x 4 = 840

48. B: At the intersection points the two functions must have identical values. Substituting the value of y = (2x + 3) into the other equation and solving the resulting quadratic equation produces the root values of x = 3.40 and -5.25. The corresponding y-coordinate values are determined by substituting these values into the linear equation.

Copyright © Mometrix Media. You have been licensed one copy of this document for personal use only. Any other reproduction or redistribution is strictly prohibited. All rights reserved.

49. C: The first formula describes a straight line that passes through the origin at (0, 0), the second describes a parabola with y-intercept at +b, and the fourth describes a circle centered on the origin at (0,0) with radius $|\sqrt{a}|$.

Informal Geometry and Measurement

50. B: The total surface area of the cylinder is the sum of the two circular ends plus the outer surface of the body. The outer body can be represented as a plane rectangle of which two opposite sides meet at the same line, with the dimensions of the length and the circumference of the cylinder. The circumference is 2pr and the length is h. The area of each end of the cylinder is the area of a circle, pr2, and there are two ends, so the total area of the ends is 2pr2. The total surface area of the cylinder is therefore 2prh + 2pr2, or 2pr(h + r).

51. D: The cross-section of the prism is a right triangle with orthogonal sides of 2 cm. The hypotenuse side is, by Pythagorean Theorem, $\sqrt{8}$ or $2\sqrt{2}$ cm. The surface area of the two ends is calculated as 2(1/2 bh), or 4 cm2. The surface area of the two orthogonal sides of the prism is 2 (2 X 10) cm, or40 cm2. The surface of the angle face of the prism is $2\sqrt{2}$ X 10, or $20\sqrt{2}$ cm2. Altogether the total surface area of the prism is therefore $(44 + 20\sqrt{2})$ cm2, or $2(22 + 10\sqrt{2})$ cm2. The volume is calculated as (1/2 bh) l = 20 cm3.

52. C: The vector 'dot product' A•B is calculated as A•B = |A||B|cosθ, where |A| and |B| are the magnitudes or absolute values of the vectors A and B, and cosθ is the cosine of the angle between the two vectors A and B. The vectors both begin at the origin (0, 0). Their magnitudes are then calculated using the Pythagorean Theorem, and are found to be equivalent values of 17.09. The ratio of the y-coordinate to the respective calculated values of |A| and |B| determine the sin of the angle formed by the vectors and the x-axis. The difference between these two angles is the angle θ separating the two vectors. Substitution of the appropriate values into the formula A•B = |A||B|cosθ produces the value of the dot product A•B.

53. A: Because the complex triangle is a right triangle, the Pythagorean Theorem applies.

h2 = x2 + y2 = (6 + i3)2 + (4 + i$\sqrt{3}$)2 = (36 + i36 – 9) + (16 + i8$\sqrt{3}$ -3)

= (27 + i36) + (13 + i8$\sqrt{3}$) = 40 + i(36 + 8$\sqrt{3}$) = 40 + 4i(9 + 2$\sqrt{3}$)

Therefore, h = $\sqrt{(40 + 4i(9 +2\sqrt{3}))}$

54. D: The perimeter is the total length of the outside edge of the field. Because the sides of the field are orthogonal and parallel, the indented sides do not change the length of the boundaries of the field, only their relative positions.

55. C: This may be solved in two ways, each of which regards the entire field as being constructed from two smaller fields. In the first, the area of a smaller field that is 250 ft X 50 ft is subtracted from the total area encompassed in 300 ft, X 100 ft:

(300 X 100) = 30,000 sq ft

(250 X 50) = 12,500 sq ft

L-shape = 17,500 sq ft

Copyright © Mometrix Media. You have been licensed one copy of this document for personal use only. Any other reproduction or redistribution is strictly prohibited. All rights reserved.

In the second, the total area of the L-shaped field is the sum of the areas of one field that is (250 ft X 50 ft, and a second field that is (50 ft X 100 ft):

(250 X 50) = 12,500 sq ft

(50 X 100) = 5000 sq ft

L-shape = 17,500 sq ft

Data Organizations and Interpretation

56. A: The events, if truly random, are independent of each other. There is therefore an equal probability of pulling the black rabbit or the white rabbit from the hat each time. The probability is therefore 0.50.

57. C: The exact method of calculating the number of ways of choosing three different items from a group of 16 different items, without repeats, is stated as "16 choose 3". The calculation is: N = 16! / ((16 – 3)!3!) = 16! / 13!3! = (16 x 15 x 14) / (3 x 2 x 1) = 560

58. A: The average is the sum of the values (60) divided by the number of values (10). The median value is the value at which there are equal numbers of greater and lesser values.

59. C: The mean value is calculated as the sum of the values (175) divided by the number of values (7). The standard deviation, s, of the sample set is calculated as the square root of the difference between the average of the actual values squared and the square of the average value.

60. A: A six-sided die has an equal number of odd and even numbers on the six faces. The probability that an odd number will appear when the die is rolled is equal to the probability that an even number will appear, or 0.5. The eight-sided die also has an equal number of odd and even numbers on its eight faces. The probability that an odd number will appear when the die is rolled is therefore also equal to the probability that an even umber will appear, or 0.5.

Social Studies

Geography, Anthropology, Sociology

61. A: The Nile River flooded regularly and reliably, irrigating the crops of the ancient Egyptians. This best explains the stability of Egyptian culture. Answer B can be rejected because though the Nile River is expansive; its size did not prevent the Egyptian people from settling elsewhere. Answer C can be rejected because the Valley of the Kings, an ancient Egyptian city, did not separate Upper and Lower Egypt. Answer D can be rejected because, even if true, interaction with other cultures is more likely to lead to a dynamic, changing culture than a stable, unchanging culture.

62. D: Ziggurats were towers dedicated to gods; their prevalence indicates the importance of religion in Mesopotamian culture. The other options can be rejected because they pair accurate facts about Mesopotamia with inaccurate summaries of the purposes of the ziggurats. For example, while rulers of Mesopotamian cities fought among themselves, ziggurats were not used as lookouts. This eliminates option A. Although astrology was practiced in Mesopotamia, ziggurats did not function as places for stargazing or observing the sky. Finally, Mesopotamian cities were ruled by kings, but the ziggurats were not dedicated to them. This eliminates options B and C.

Copyright © Mometrix Media. You have been licensed one copy of this document for personal use only. Any other reproduction or redistribution is strictly prohibited. All rights reserved.

63. B: Although Charlemagne himself may not have believed his authority was conferred by the Pope, Charlemagne's successors sometimes used the title "Holy Roman Emperor" (given to them by the Pope) as a basis for their authority. Thus, the title "Holy Roman Emperor" strengthened the notion that political authority was conferred by the Pope. Charlemagne united much of Europe under a single ruler prior to being named Holy Roman Emperor. While Catholicism may have been the recognized religion, the naming of Charlemagne as Holy Roman Emperor did not make it so. After being so named, Charlemagne did not renounce his conquests. This eliminates options A, C, and D respectively.

64. C: Under the Western European feudal system, rulers granted vassals land in exchange for military and political service. Although the right to use land would often pass from father to son, it was not on the basis of blood relations that a ruler granted land to a vassal; this eliminates option B. Religious institutions such as monasteries did indeed own land, but did not own most of it, eliminating option A. Finally, feudalism was a land-based economy that made a shift from a spice-based economy to a gold-based economy. Therefore, option D can be eliminated.

65. A: The Crusades' biggest impact upon Europe's Jewish population was that entire Jewish communities were killed during the First Crusade. This is the only option that accurately describes historical effects of the Crusades on the Jewish population. Rather than diminishing anti-Jewish sentiment, the Crusades seemed to inflame it, eliminating option B. One specific example of Crusades-era anti-Semitism is that many Jewish people were excluded from particular trades, and thus did not profit from the Crusades. This fact eliminates option C. Finally, there were no Jewish-only battalions during the Crusades, eliminating option D.

66. B: Johann Gutenberg's printing press led to increased scientific knowledge and advancement as scientific texts were printed and dispersed throughout Europe. Because the distribution of such texts extended outside of Germany, options C and D may be eliminated. Gutenberg Bibles were printed using Gutenberg's press, and thus Gutenberg's invention was likely a factor in the Reformation of the Catholic Church. In fact, Martin Luther's Ninety-Five Theses (against the Catholic Church) were printed using a printing press. However, this reformation occurred alongside, rather than in place of, the advancement of scientific knowledge. This eliminates option A.

67. D: The Triple Alliance allowed the city-states to conquer city-states and land by combining forces against mutual enemies. The Triple Alliance and its conquered areas are commonly thought of as the Aztec Empire. While some conquered areas did rebel against the Aztec Empire at the time the Spanish conquistadores arrived, such rebellion did not specifically concern the city-states of the Triple Alliance. Texcoco and Tlacopan did not use the Alliance as a front against Tenochtitlan. The Triple Alliance had nothing to do with the number of annual human sacrifices. This eliminates options A, B, and C.

68. A: The Catholic Church was both powerful and wealthy in medieval Europe. It affected the lives of both the rich and poor; for example, wealthy families often donated to monasteries in exchange for prayers on the donors' behalf. This eliminates option B. Because of these donations, some monasteries became quite wealthy. Rather than being a neutral force, the Catholic Church wielded political power. In medieval times, some claimed that rulers derived their authority to rule from the Catholic Church itself. These facts eliminate options C D.

69. B: Akbar allowed the practice of both Hinduism and Islam, despite pressure from Islamic religious leaders to do otherwise. Akbar specifically permitted the construction of Hindu temples, which freed Akbar from Hindu resistance that he might otherwise have faced. This fact eliminates

Copyright © Mometrix Media. You have been licensed one copy of this document for personal use only. Any other reproduction or redistribution is strictly prohibited. All rights reserved.

answer D. Breaking from some past practices, Akbar also used cash instead of land to pay empire officials, allowing him to control more land. Because of this, option A can be rejected. Option C can be rejected because Akbar allowed certain defeated princes to keep their lands.

70. A: In the 1780s, the French national debt was very high. The French nobility adamantly resisted attempts by King Louis XVI to reform tax laws, which led to a high tax burden on the French peasantry. The French government spent almost 50% of its national expenditures on debt-related payments during the 1780s; thus it could not and did not spend almost 60% to finance luxuries for the French nobility. This eliminates choice B. King Louis XVI temporarily banned the guild system to bolster, rather than stifle, free trade. Because this system gave skilled craftsmen economic advantages, journeymen opposed ending the system. This eliminates choice D. Regardless of the status of guilds before the French Revolution, French society did not offer many opportunities for upward social mobility. Few peasants were able to advance. This eliminates choice C.

World History

71. C: The first great human civilization was the Sumerian civilization which was located in Mesopotamia. Mesopotamia encompasses the area between the Tigris and Euphrates Rivers in modern-day Iraq and is also referred to as "the Cradle of Civilization," and includes part of the Fertile Crescent.

The Sumerian civilization is credited with being the first to practice serious, year round agriculture. There is question over whether Sumeria or Ancient Egypt was the first to have a written language. Sumeria's writing began hieroglyphically and then developed into a form of writing known as cuneiform.

72. A: Anubis was the Egyptian god of the dead, typically depicted as being half human and half jackal.

Hatshepsut was an Egyptian queen who declared herself king while acting as regent for her stepson (who was also her son-in-law). She was the fifth pharaoh of Egypt's 18th dynasty

Ramesses (or Ramses) II was the third pharaoh of Egypt's 19th Dynasty, and Egypt's greatest, most powerful and most celebrated pharaoh. He is also traditionally considered to be the pharaoh of the Bible's Book of Exodus. His tomb in the Valley of the Kings was discovered in 1881. Tutankhamen was the boy pharaoh whose tomb was found in 1922, intact and untouched by tomb raiders, leading to a surge of popular interest in ancient Egypt.

73. C: Pope Urban II's plan for an army made up of previously trained military personnel was thwarted by the popular excitement concerning the First Crusade. This led to the creation of large armies primarily made up of untrained, unskilled, undisciplined, and ill- or unequipped soldiers, most of whom were recruited from the poorest levels of society. These armies were the first to set forth on the Crusade, which became known as the People's Crusade. Even though some of these armies contained knights, they were ultimately ineffective as fighting forces. These armies were prone to rioting and raiding surrounding areas for food and supplies and were viewed as a destabilizing influence by local leaders. They were defeated in battle and many converted to Islam to avoid being killed.

United States History

74. C: The Sugar Act of 1764 raised import duties on goods which were not of British origin, including sugar, while reducing the import tax on molasses. The Stamp Act of 1765 was a tax of

Copyright © Mometrix Media. You have been licensed one copy of this document for personal use only. Any other reproduction or redistribution is strictly prohibited. All rights reserved.

paper and printed products, intended to help the British government recoup some of the costs of the French and Indian War. It was extremely unpopular with the colonists and was repealed in 1766. Lead was one of the goods taxed under the Townshend Acts, enacted in 1767, but it did not receive its own specific tax act. The Tea Act of 1773 was another unpopular tax and led to tea boycotts and was the catalyst for the Boston Tea Party.

75. B: The Founding Fathers decided that because the colonies did not have the right to elect representatives to the British Parliament they could not be justly ruled by Parliament. They envisioned the British Empire's government as being headed by the King of England, under whom the various local parliaments and legislative bodies served to enact laws for the peoples whom they represented. By addressing their ills to the king, the Founding Fathers sought to prevent the appearance that they acknowledged the British Parliament in London as having any authority over the American colonies.

76. B: Marbury v. Madison started with the election of Thomas Jefferson as third President of the United States. The lame-duck Congress responded by issuing a large number of judicial patents, which the incoming president and Secretary of State refused to deliver to their holders. Marbury, who was to receive a patent as Justice of the Peace, sued to demand delivery. What makes this case important is the decision which declared the judiciary's ability to overturn legislation that conflicted with the Constitution. The case states:

"It is emphatically the province and duty of the judicial department to say what the law is. Those who apply the rule to particular cases must, of necessity, expound and interpret that rule. If two laws conflict with each other, the courts must decide on the operation of each.

"So if a law be in opposition to the Constitution; if both the law and the constitution apply to a particular case, so that the court must either decide that case conformably to the law, disregarding the Constitution; or conformably to the Constitution, disregarding the law; the court must determine which of these conflicting rules governs the case. This is of the very essence of judicial duty.

"If, then, the courts are to regard the Constitution, and the Constitution is superior to any ordinary act of the legislature, the Constitution, and not such ordinary act, must govern the case to which they both apply."

Later the ruling states: "The judicial power of the United States is extended to all cases arising under the Constitution." It was in this way that the Supreme Court achieved its now traditional ability to strike down laws and to act as the final arbitrator of what is and is not allowed under the U.S. Constitution.

77. D: Abraham Lincoln issued the Thanksgiving Proclamation on October 3, 1863, in which he specified the last Thursday of November as a day of thanksgiving. The last Thursday in November was the traditional date for the Thanksgiving holiday for the next 76 years.

In 1939, President Roosevelt tried to change the holiday's date from the last Thursday in November to the second to last Thursday in November in order to stimulate the economy by creating a longer Christmas shopping season. This action met with resistance in some parts of the country, and a compromise was reached in 1941, setting the date of Thanksgiving as the fourth Thursday in November.

78. C: While wounds from war most certainly killed more than a few, European disease laid waste to vast swaths of Native American people who has no immunity to the foreign diseases which the

Copyright © Mometrix Media. You have been licensed one copy of this document for personal use only. Any other reproduction or redistribution is strictly prohibited. All rights reserved.

Europeans carried. The forced marches took place in the mid-19th century under Andrew Jackson's presidency and are thus removed from the time frame in question.

79. A: The U.S. Constitution, Article I, Section 3 states that: "The Senate of the United States shall be composed of two Senators from each state, chosen by the legislature thereof, for six years; and each Senator shall have one vote." This was the practice until the Seventeenth Amendment was ratified on April 8, 1913. The Seventeenth Amendment states that U.S. Senators are to be elected by the people of the states which they serve and that the state executive branches may appoint replacement Senators if a Senate seat becomes vacant mid-term, until the state legislature can arrange for a popular election.

80. B: The Erie Canal opened in 1825 and created a water route between the Hudson River and Lake Erie. Water routes have historically been cheaper and easier than overland ones and the Erie Canal was originally proposed in the 1700s as a means of providing a shipping route to assist in settling the areas west of the Appalachian Mountains.

The Mississippi River is to the west of the Great Lakes, its source is in Minnesota and it discharges into the Gulf of Mexico approximately 100 miles downstream of New Orleans, Louisiana.

The Susquehanna River runs through New York, Pennsylvania and Maryland and is the home of Three Mile Island, the site of the United States' largest nuclear disaster.

The Lehigh River is located in eastern Pennsylvania.

81. C: The telegraph was a gigantic leap forward in the realm of communications. Before the telegraph, messages could take days, weeks or months to reach their intended recipient, based upon the distance that they had to travel. The telegraph allowed people to send methods through use of electric signals transmitted over telegraph wires, allowing for instantaneous communications. The main drawbacks to the telegraph included the need to "translate" the message into and out of the appropriate telegraphic code and that the telegraph could only relay one message at a time. In contrast, the telephone allowed for spoken communication between people at different locations, increasing the efficiency and speed as the people on each end of the conversation could communicate multiple messages quickly and in one telephone conversation.

82. B: Sacagawea acted as Lewis and Clark's guide during their exploration of the Louisiana Purchase. She had been separated from her family at a young age and was reunited with her brother on the course of the expedition. Pocahontas was the daughter of Powhatan, the leader of the Algonquian tribes at the beginning of the 17th Century when the colony of Jamestown was founded in modern-day Virginia. Squanto's actual name was Tisquantum. He was the Native American who helped the Pilgrims after their first winter in Massachusetts. Wauwatosa is a suburb of Milwaukee, Wisconsin.

83. A: Lyndon Johnson became president following the assassination of John F. Kennedy on November 22, 1963. The Great Society was a series of social programs implemented under the direction of Lyndon Johnson. The Great Society's goal was to eliminate poverty and racial injustice in America. The Great Society began with economic reforms including a tax cut and the creation of the Office of Economic Opportunity. From there, it grew to include the enacting of laws creating the Medicare and Medicaid systems to assist the elderly and poor with their health care costs, respectively. Educational and Housing reforms followed.

Copyright © Mometrix Media. You have been licensed one copy of this document for personal use only. Any other reproduction or redistribution is strictly prohibited. All rights reserved.

Government, Citizenship, and Democracy

84. A: The Iroquois Confederacy was a confederacy of originally five (and later six) Native American Tribes, founded in 1570. Many decisions involved compromise between two sets of Lords from different tribes, analogous to the compromise involved in decision-making between the U.S. House of Representatives and the U.S. Senate. For the Confederacy to accept a decision, Mohawk and Seneca Lords needed to come to an agreement with Oneida and Cayuga Lords. Option B can be rejected because there is no chief in the Iroquois Confederacy analogous to the U.S. President. Option C can be rejected because the Iroquois Confederacy did not involve representation based upon a tribe's population. Option D can be rejected because there was no judicial branch in the Iroquois Confederacy analogous to that of the U.S. government.

85. C: The Federalist Party advocated a pro-British foreign policy and therefore opposed the War of 1812. This made the Federalists unpopular with many Americans; this unpopularity deepened when the war ended with American victory. The Federalist Party did advocate a strong central government; however, this position was not a key factor in the Party's decline. This eliminates option D. Option A can be rejected because the Federalist Party did organize state political parties in states such as Connecticut, Delaware, and Maryland. Many members of the Federalist Party were pro-trade and pro-business, as many members were well-to-do businessmen. This eliminates option B.

86. D: After the American Revolution, the framers of the American government were concerned that a strong central government could lead to abuses of power. Accordingly, The Articles of Confederation did not grant the federal government the ability to raise taxes. Another restriction was the inability to regulate interstate commerce. Options A, B, and C can all be eliminated because, though the federal government was generally weak under the Articles of Confederation, the Articles granted the federal government each of the powers given in those options.

Economics

87. D: Keynes was an influential advocate of government intervention in a domestic economy for the purpose of stimulating economic growth. Keynes believed that appropriate government action could help end a recession more quickly; such measures might involve deficit spending. Because of this, and because Keynes is not associated with the view that deficit spending leads to inflation, option A can be eliminated. Additionally, Keynes is not closely associated with advocating government action to break up monopolies; this eliminates option A. Finally, option C can be eliminated because it describes Say's Law, which is in fact the opposite of Keynes's law: demand creates its own supply.

88. B: Economists understand the true cost of an action as not only its monetary cost but the cost of other opportunities missed as a result of pursuing that action. For example, if a person chooses to go to school rather than working, the cost of the action involves not only tuition and other associated fees and expenses, but the money one would have earned working, as well as the time one could have spent pursuing other activities. The concept of opportunity cost is not described by options A, C, or D, each of which is concerned only with monetary costs. Each of these answers can be rejected on that basis.

Social Studies as Inquiry and Social Studies Processes

89. B: Reification is the act of treating an abstraction as a real, concrete thing. For example, the concept of society might be useful, but it is not an actual, concrete thing separate from the components (such as people and infrastructure) that make up society. Options A, C, and D can all be

Copyright © Mometrix Media. You have been licensed one copy of this document for personal use only. Any other reproduction or redistribution is strictly prohibited. All rights reserved.

rejected because none accurately capture the concept of reification. Social scientists might indeed be concerned with relative appropriateness of qualitative data and quantitative data, but using one over the other is not reification. Social scientists might use heuristic devices, but this is not simply reification (not all cases of reification are cases of using heuristic devices). Reification is not mistaking subjectivity for objectivity.

90. C: Learning such an association is classical conditioning. Generally, classical conditioning is the process of learning an association between two stimuli, one of which is neutral (in this instance, the sound of the can opener) and one to which an organism responds automatically (in this instance, food). Habituation occurs when an organism becomes desensitized to a repeated stimulus; this eliminates option B. Operant conditioning differs from classical conditioning in that, in the former, an organism changes its behavior in response to reinforcement (that is, an organism can change the outcome of an event by changing its behavior). This eliminates option A. Conformity is the process by which an organism changes its behavior to match others' behavior. This eliminates option D.

Science

Earth Science

91. B: The star is moving closer or toward him. When an astronomer observing stars detects a blue shift, he can conclude the star is moving closer or toward him. This is an example of the practical application of the Doppler effect in astronomy as applied to electromagnetic waves. The Doppler effect explains the change of wavelength caused by motion of the source or the relative difference in velocity between the observer and the source. When observing stars, a red shift or blue shift can be used to measure the speed that stars and galaxies are approaching or receding. Blue light has a higher frequency than red light. A red shift indicates a receding source.

92. C: A cation from a base and an anion from an acid. A salt is a general term for the neutral ionic product of a neutralization reaction between an acid and a base. Often, table salt, or sodium chloride, is mistakenly characterized as "salt", indicating that all salts are this compound. Although it is very common for a salt to be composed of a metal and a nonmetal, this is not always true, as in the case of the salt ammonium chloride. The ammonium ion (NH4+) is a polyatomic ion composed of non-metals. Likewise, many salts are composed of an alkali or alkaline earth metal and a halogen, but this is not always the case.

93. B: Group 2. Group 2 makes up the alkaline earth metals on the periodic chart of elements. There are 18 groups, or vertical columns, on the periodic table. In general, Group 2, alkaline earth metals, are characterized by silver colored, soft metals that melt at high temperatures. They also combine well with halogens to form salts and have two electrons in their valence level. Answer A, Group 1, are called the alkali metals or lithium family. Answer C, Group 13, is the boron family. Answer D, Group 17, are known as the halogens or fluorine family.

94. C: Transform. Transform is not connected to the process of mountain building. Orogeny, or mountain building, occurs at the Earth's lithosphere or crust. Answer A, Folding, or deformation, is a process that occurs to make mountains where two portions of the lithosphere collide. One is subducted and the other is pushed upward forming a mountain. This action produces various types of folding. Answer B, Faulting, can be characterized by a brittle deformation where the rock breaks abruptly (compared with folding). Faulting and fault types are associated with earthquakes and relatively rapid deformation. D, Convergent, is a more general term used to describe plates converging.

Copyright © Mometrix Media. You have been licensed one copy of this document for personal use only. Any other reproduction or redistribution is strictly prohibited. All rights reserved.

95. D: heat. The formation of sedimentary rock does not include heat. Of the three types of rock igneous, sedimentary and metamorphic, heat is essential to two: igneous and metamorphic. Sedimentary rocks are formed by sediments that get deposited and then compacted or cemented together. Sedimentary rocks are classified into detrital, organic or chemical sediments. Answer A, layering, is correct since sediments can be deposited or otherwise formed in layers. Answer B, cementation, is also called lithification. Answer C, compaction, refers to the pressure forming sedimentary rock leading to cementation.

96. C: Vinegar fizzing when poured on a rock, is an example of chemical weathering. Mechanical and chemical weathering are processes that break down rocks. Mechanical weathering breaks down rocks physically, but does not change their chemical composition. Frost and abrasion are examples. Water, oxygen, carbon dioxide and living organisms can lead to the chemical weathering of rock. Vinegar is a weak acid and will undergo a chemical reaction, evidenced by fizzing, with the rock. Answer A, Rain freezing on the roadway, is an example of the phase change of water from a liquid to a solid and may lead to physical weathering. Answer B, Ivy growing on the side of a wooden house, is incorrect since the house is not a rock. Answer D, A river carrying sediment downstream, is an example of erosion.

97. B: Two crustal plates move apart. When two crustal plates move apart, magma welling up could result in the formation of new crust. This has been shown to be occurring on the ocean floor where places of the crust are weaker. The crust spreads apart at these trenches, pushing outward and erupting at the ridges. Answer A, When two crustal plates converge, sublimation occurs as one plate runs under another pushing it up. Answer C, Two crustal plates slide past one another, is an example of a transform fault, which does not create new crust. Answer D, A crustal plate is pushed down into the mantle, does not form new crust but perhaps recycles the old one.

98. C: Laccolith. A laccolith is formed when an intrusion of magma injected between two layers of sedimentary rock forces the overlying strata upward to create a dome-like form. Eventually, the magma cools, the sedimentary rock wears away and the formation is exposed. Answer A, Sill, and Answer B, Dike, are both examples of sheet intrusions: where magma has inserted itself into other rock. Sills are horizontal and dikes are vertical. Answer D, Caldera, is a crater-like feature that was formed from the collapse of a volcano after erupting.

99. A: It compares the amount of radioactive material in a rock to the amount that has decayed into another element. This best describes the process of absolute dating. Answer B, It measures the age of a rock by comparing it to fossils found in the same stratigraphic layer as the rock, is not usually done. Usually the stratigraphic layer of rock is used to date the fossils, which is referred to as relative dating. Answer C, It measures the amount of daughter elements that have broken down by half, is incorrect as this would not lead to a correct date since the daughter elements may have a different half life than the parent material.

Life Science

100. A: high solubility in water. Most organic molecules have all of the following properties except high solubility in water. Answer B, a tendency to melt, Answer C, covalently bonded, and Answer D, high flammability, are all characteristics of organic molecules. Organic molecules are those that contain carbon molecules, with a few exceptions. Organic molecules tend to be less soluble in water than inorganic salts. They are good at forming unique structures and there are many organic compounds. Examples of organic compounds include hydrocarbons, carbohydrates, lipids and proteins.

Copyright © Mometrix Media. You have been licensed one copy of this document for personal use only. Any other reproduction or redistribution is strictly prohibited. All rights reserved.

101. C: meiosis I. In humans, diploid cells are those that contain 46 chromosomes. There are 23 pairs of chromosomes each made up of one chromosome from the father and one from the mother. In meiosis I, each chromosome replicates itself and lines up, or synapses, with its homologous chromosome, and each of the daughter cells ends up with one copy of each of the chromosomes. The two daughter cells at the end of meiosis I are haploid because they contain half of the chromosomes of the parent cell. In humans, this would be 23 chromosomes. However, each of these chromosomes are made of two sister chromatids. In meiosis II, the sister chromatids in the daughter cells separate and result in the production of the gametes. These are also haploid cells because they contain one copy of half of the genetic material of the parent cell. Four haploid cells result from meiosis. Answer A, mitosis, can be eliminated as it refers to the process of cell division where each daughter cell contains exactly the same genetic material as the parent cell. Answer B, telophase, refers to phases of both mitosis and meiosis, during which chromosomes move toward the opposite ends of the cell.

102. A: Lysosomes. A lysosome is an organelle that contains digestive enzymes that break down food and unneeded substances and are thought to be linked to the aging process. Answer B, Chromatin, is the structure created by DNA and various proteins in the cell nucleus during interphase and condenses to form chromosomes. Plastids, Answer C, are found in plants and algae. They often contain pigments and usually help make chemical compounds for the plant. Answer D, Golgi apparatus, gets macromolecules, like proteins and lipids, ready for transport.

103. B: Anabolism undergoes condensation reactions, while catabolism undergoes hydrolysis. Anabolic processes are those that use energy to build larger molecules. In cells, adenosine triphosphate (ATP) is used as a source of energy. A condensation reaction joins two molecules together to make a larger molecule and in the process, produces a water molecule. Condensation reactions are important in protein synthesis. Anabolic processes are often reduction reactions. Catabolism breaks down molecules and usually generates energy. Catabolic reactions are often oxidation reactions. Hydrolysis is a catabolic process where water is added to a molecule and then split, resulting in the molecule breaking apart into two different molecules. Hydrolysis is the opposite of condensation.

104. B: Plant A lives in a very arid environment. Photosynthesis converts carbon dioxide into sugars that plants use. Three types are C3, C4 and CAM. C3 is used by most plants. C4 and CAM are used by desert plants. C4 first forms a four carbon sugar instead of the three carbon sugar formed by C3. Also, the stomata of C4 plants are faster at absorbing carbon dioxide and do not have to open as long, so less water is lost by transpiration. A C4 plant, such as saltbush, corn or some grasses, would live in an arid environment rather than a moist, marine or dark environment. Plants that use the CAM (Crassulacean Acid Metabolism) type of photosynthesis also use water more efficiently as their stomata are closed during the day and open at night. Desert cacti are examples.

105. A: Cytoplasm. The type of RNA described by the question is transfer RNA (tRNA). tRNA is found in the cytoplasm and carries and positions amino acids at the ribosome for protein synthesis. There are two other types of RNA. Messenger RNA (mRNA) contains the coding for the amino acid sequence in the protein. mRNA is first made in the nucleus before traveling through the cytoplasm to a ribosome. Ribosomal RNA (rRNA) is the RNA that is found in the ribosome along with proteins and allow the mRNA and tRNA to bind for protein synthesis. All three types of RNA originate in the nucleus where they are transcribed from DNA. Mitochondria are organelles that harbor mitochondrial DNA (mtDNA).

106. C: U G C A U G C G A. Translation is the process of the tRNA bringing the correct amino acid to the ribosome according to the sequence of the mRNA. Since translation only involves RNA, the four

Copyright © Mometrix Media. You have been licensed one copy of this document for personal use only. Any other reproduction or redistribution is strictly prohibited. All rights reserved.

bases are adenine (A), cytosine (C), guanine (G) and uracil (U). There is no thymine (T) used in RNA. Cytosine (C) and guanine (G) pair and adenine (A) and uracil (U) pair. A codon is the triplet sequence that represents a specific amino acid or a start/stop point. It is on the messenger RNA (mRNA). The anticodon is on tRNA and corresponds to the amino acid used by the ribosome during translation. They are complimentary. UGC becomes AUG; AUG becomes CGA. The original codon sequence is U G C A U G C G A if the anticodon sequence formed during translation is A C G U A C G C U.

107. C: 4/16. The fraction of offspring that that have the genotype BbSs is 4/16. A dihybrid cross considers two traits at a time, in this case, eye color and hair color. In the parent (P) generation, a parent with the genotype BBSS would be crossed with a parent with the genotype bbss. The offspring are considered the F1 generation and all would have the genotype BbSs. This question asks about the F2 generation, which is the offspring between a cross of the F1 generation. Therefore the parent genotypes in this question would be BbSs. To solve, develop a Punnet square of 16 cells. Each parent will produce the following gametes: BS, Bs, bS, bs. Place these across the top and the side. After completing the square, the resulting offspring show that four would have the genotype BbSs.

108. D: Inversion. This type of mutation is represented in the sequence 1 5 4 3 2 6. An inversion error is a type of mutation where an entire sequence of DNA is reversed. In this case, 2 3 4 5 has been reversed to 5 4 3 2. Breakage, Answer A, in a gene can mess up its function entirely or lead to a translocation of genetic information. Answer B, Deletion, is when a section of DNA is omitted or lost. Answer C, Insertion, is when an extra base pair is added to a DNA sequence. Deletions and insertions can lead to a frameshift effect where entire sequences are thrown off because one nucleotide is wrong. This could result in coding for the wrong amino acid and non-functioning proteins.

Physical Science

109. C: 20 g/L. One way to measure the density of an irregularly shaped object is to submerge it in water and measure the displacement. This is done by taking the mass (40 grams), then finding the volume by measuring how much water it displaces. Fill a graduated cylinder with water and record the amount. Put the object in the water and record the water level. Subtract the difference in water levels to get the amount of water displaced, which is also the volume of the object. In this case, 4.5 liters minus 2.5 liters equals 2 liters. Divide mass by volume (40 grams divided by 2 liters) to get 20 g/L (grams per liter).

110. B: A spoiling apple. A spoiling apple is an example of a chemical change. During a chemical change, one substance is changed into another. Oxidation, a chemical change, occurs when an apple spoils. Answer A, Sublimation of water, refers to the conversion between the solid and the gaseous phases of matter, with no intermediate liquid stage. This is a phase change, not a chemical reaction. Answer C, Dissolution of salt in water, refers to a physical change, since the salt and water can be separated again by evaporating the water, which is a physical change. Answer D, Pulverized rock, is an example of a physical change where the form has changed but not the substance itself.

111. D: temperature. The amount of potential energy an object has depends on mass, height above ground and gravitational attraction, but not temperature. The formula for potential energy is $PE = mgh$, or potential energy equals mass times gravity times height. Answers A, B, and C are all valid answers as they are all contained in the formula for potential energy. Potential energy is the amount of energy stored in a system particularly because of its position.

Copyright © Mometrix Media. You have been licensed one copy of this document for personal use only. Any other reproduction or redistribution is strictly prohibited. All rights reserved.

112. D: All of the above. Elements on the periodic table are arranged into periods, or rows, according to atomic number, which is the number of protons in the nucleus. The periodic table illustrates the recurrence of properties. Each column, or group, contains elements that share similar properties, such as reactivity.

113. A: It takes half the amount of energy to increase the temperature of a 1 kg sample of ice by 1°C than a 1 kg sample of water. Heat capacity refers to the amount of heat or thermal energy required to raise the temperature of a specific substance a given unit. A substance with a higher heat capacity requires more heat to raise its temperature than a substance with a lower heat capacity. The comparison here is that the specific heat capacity of ice is half as much as that of liquid water, so it takes half the amount of energy to increase the same amount of ice one temperature unit than it would if it were liquid water.

114. D: Its temperature remains the same due to the latent heat of fusion. The temperature of a substance during the time of any phase change remains the same. In this case, the phase change was from liquid to solid, or freezing. Latent heat of fusion, in this case, is energy that is released from the substance as it reforms its solid form. This energy will be released and the liquid will turn to solid before the temperature of the substance will decrease further. If the substance were changing from solid to liquid, the heat of fusion would be the amount of heat required to break apart the attractions between the molecules in the solid form to change to the liquid form. The latent heat of fusion is exactly the same quantity of energy for a substance for either melting or freezing. Depending on the process, this amount of heat would either be absorbed by the substance (melting) or released (freezing).

115. B: Conduction. A long nail or other type of metal, substance or matter that is heated at one end and then the other end becomes equally hot is an example of conduction. Conduction is energy transfer by neighboring molecules from an area of hotter temperature to cooler temperature. Answer A, Radiation, or thermal radiation, refers to heat being transferred through empty space by electromagnetic radiation. An example is sunlight heating the earth. Answer C, Convection, refers to heat being transferred by molecules moving from one location in the substance to another creating a heat current, usually in a gas or a liquid. Answer D, Entropy, relates to the second law of thermodynamics and refers to how much heat or energy is no longer available to do work in a system. It can also be stated as the amount of disorder in a system.

116. C: Heat transfer can never occur from a cooler object to a warmer object. While the second law of thermodynamics implies that heat never spontaneously transfers from a cooler object to a warmer object, it is possible for heat to be transferred to a warmer object, given the proper input of work to the system. This is the principle by which a refrigerator operates. Work is done to the system to transfer heat from the objects inside the refrigerator to the air surrounding the refrigerator. All other answer choices are true.

Science in Personal and Social Perspectives

117. C: The benefits to people and the economy must outweigh the risks to determine whether their decision to build is fair. This is why governments would conduct a risk-benefit analysis in making decisions about city planning and development. Answer A, Governments must know what the benefits of a new development are for people and the economy in order to persuade opponents and the public who are against it, would be incorrect because the intention would be to build regardless of risk. Answer D, The benefits to people and the economy can be used to ignore the risks associated with any new development, would also be incorrect as it would be unethical to ignore the risks.

Copyright © Mometrix Media. You have been licensed one copy of this document for personal use only. Any other reproduction or redistribution is strictly prohibited. All rights reserved.

118. A: Should the packaging of meat products that come from cloned animals be labeled? This is an issue that would be regulated by the Food and Drug Administration (FDA) as it regulates the packaging of meat products, among many other types of food. Answer B, Should nitrate or sulfate fertilizers be added to oil spills to assist the decomposition of crude oil by bacteria, would not be an issue for the FDA. The Environmental Protection Agency (EPA) regulates issues regarding the environment as well as superfund clean ups. Neither Answer C, about genetic engineering of humans, nor Answer D, about cell use in industry, relate to food and drugs and would not fall under the jurisdiction of the FDA.

Science as Inquiry and Science Processes

119. C: Repeat the experiment. Repeating the experiment validates data. Each separate experiment is called a repetition. Results of experiments or tests should be able to be replicated. Similar data gathered from many experiments can also be used to quantify the validity of the hypothesis. Repeating the experiments allows the student to observe variation in the results. Variation in data can be caused by a variety of errors or may be disproving the hypothesis. Answer D, Create a hypothesis, comes before experiments. Answers A, Communicate the results, and B, Draw a conclusion, occur after testing.

120. D: theory. Once a hypothesis has been verified and accepted, it becomes a theory. A theory is a generally accepted explanation that has been highly developed and tested. A theory can explain data and be expected to predict outcomes of tests. Answer A, fact, is considered to be an objective and verifiable observation; whereas, a scientific theory is a greater body of accepted knowledge, principles, or relationships that might explain a fact. Answer B, law, is an explanation of events by which the outcome is always the same. Answer C, conclusion, is more of an opinion and could be based on observation, evidence, fact, laws or even beliefs.

Copyright © Mometrix Media. You have been licensed one copy of this document for personal use only. Any other reproduction or redistribution is strictly prohibited. All rights reserved.

How to Overcome Test Anxiety

Just the thought of taking a test is enough to make most people a little nervous. A test is an important event that can have a long-term impact on your future, so it's important to take it seriously and it's natural to feel anxious about performing well. But just because anxiety is normal, that doesn't mean that it's helpful in test taking, or that you should simply accept it as part of your life. Anxiety can have a variety of effects. These effects can be mild, like making you feel slightly nervous, or severe, like blocking your ability to focus or remember even a simple detail.

If you experience test anxiety—whether severe or mild—it's important to know how to beat it. To discover this, first you need to understand what causes test anxiety.

Causes of Test Anxiety

While we often think of anxiety as an uncontrollable emotional state, it can actually be caused by simple, practical things. One of the most common causes of test anxiety is that a person does not feel adequately prepared for their test. This feeling can be the result of many different issues such as poor study habits or lack of organization, but the most common culprit is time management. Starting to study too late, failing to organize your study time to cover all of the material, or being distracted while you study will mean that you're not well prepared for the test. This may lead to cramming the night before, which will cause you to be physically and mentally exhausted for the test. Poor time management also contributes to feelings of stress, fear, and hopelessness as you realize you are not well prepared but don't know what to do about it.

Other times, test anxiety is not related to your preparation for the test but comes from unresolved fear. This may be a past failure on a test, or poor performance on tests in general. It may come from comparing yourself to others who seem to be performing better or from the stress of living up to expectations. Anxiety may be driven by fears of the future—how failure on this test would affect your educational and career goals. These fears are often completely irrational, but they can still negatively impact your test performance.

Review Video: 3 Reasons You Have Test Anxiety
Visit mometrix.com/academy and enter code: 428468

Copyright © Mometrix Media. You have been licensed one copy of this document for personal use only. Any other reproduction or redistribution is strictly prohibited. All rights reserved.

Elements of Test Anxiety

As mentioned earlier, test anxiety is considered to be an emotional state, but it has physical and mental components as well. Sometimes you may not even realize that you are suffering from test anxiety until you notice the physical symptoms. These can include trembling hands, rapid heartbeat, sweating, nausea, and tense muscles. Extreme anxiety may lead to fainting or vomiting. Obviously, any of these symptoms can have a negative impact on testing. It is important to recognize them as soon as they begin to occur so that you can address the problem before it damages your performance.

Review Video: 3 Ways to Tell You Have Test Anxiety
Visit mometrix.com/academy and enter code: 927847

The mental components of test anxiety include trouble focusing and inability to remember learned information. During a test, your mind is on high alert, which can help you recall information and stay focused for an extended period of time. However, anxiety interferes with your mind's natural processes, causing you to blank out, even on the questions you know well. The strain of testing during anxiety makes it difficult to stay focused, especially on a test that may take several hours. Extreme anxiety can take a huge mental toll, making it difficult not only to recall test information but even to understand the test questions or pull your thoughts together.

Review Video: How Test Anxiety Affects Memory
Visit mometrix.com/academy and enter code: 609003

Effects of Test Anxiety

Test anxiety is like a disease—if left untreated, it will get progressively worse. Anxiety leads to poor performance, and this reinforces the feelings of fear and failure, which in turn lead to poor performances on subsequent tests. It can grow from a mild nervousness to a crippling condition. If allowed to progress, test anxiety can have a big impact on your schooling, and consequently on your future.

Test anxiety can spread to other parts of your life. Anxiety on tests can become anxiety in any stressful situation, and blanking on a test can turn into panicking in a job situation. But fortunately, you don't have to let anxiety rule your testing and determine your grades. There are a number of relatively simple steps you can take to move past anxiety and function normally on a test and in the rest of life.

Review Video: How Test Anxiety Impacts Your Grades
Visit mometrix.com/academy and enter code: 939819

Copyright © Mometrix Media. You have been licensed one copy of this document for personal use only. Any other reproduction or redistribution is strictly prohibited. All rights reserved.

Physical Steps for Beating Test Anxiety

While test anxiety is a serious problem, the good news is that it can be overcome. It doesn't have to control your ability to think and remember information. While it may take time, you can begin taking steps today to beat anxiety.

Just as your first hint that you may be struggling with anxiety comes from the physical symptoms, the first step to treating it is also physical. Rest is crucial for having a clear, strong mind. If you are tired, it is much easier to give in to anxiety. But if you establish good sleep habits, your body and mind will be ready to perform optimally, without the strain of exhaustion. Additionally, sleeping well helps you to retain information better, so you're more likely to recall the answers when you see the test questions.

Getting good sleep means more than going to bed on time. It's important to allow your brain time to relax. Take study breaks from time to time so it doesn't get overworked, and don't study right before bed. Take time to rest your mind before trying to rest your body, or you may find it difficult to fall asleep.

Review Video: The Importance of Sleep for Your Brain
Visit mometrix.com/academy and enter code: 319338

Along with sleep, other aspects of physical health are important in preparing for a test. Good nutrition is vital for good brain function. Sugary foods and drinks may give a burst of energy but this burst is followed by a crash, both physically and emotionally. Instead, fuel your body with protein and vitamin-rich foods.

Also, drink plenty of water. Dehydration can lead to headaches and exhaustion, especially if your brain is already under stress from the rigors of the test. Particularly if your test is a long one, drink water during the breaks. And if possible, take an energy-boosting snack to eat between sections.

Review Video: How Diet Can Affect your Mood
Visit mometrix.com/academy and enter code: 624317

Along with sleep and diet, a third important part of physical health is exercise. Maintaining a steady workout schedule is helpful, but even taking 5-minute study breaks to walk can help get your blood pumping faster and clear your head. Exercise also releases endorphins, which contribute to a positive feeling and can help combat test anxiety.

When you nurture your physical health, you are also contributing to your mental health. If your body is healthy, your mind is much more likely to be healthy as well. So take time to rest, nourish your body with healthy food and water, and get moving as much as possible. Taking these physical steps will make you stronger and more able to take the mental steps necessary to overcome test anxiety.

Review Video: How to Stay Healthy and Prevent Test Anxiety
Visit mometrix.com/academy and enter code: 877894

Copyright © Mometrix Media. You have been licensed one copy of this document for personal use only. Any other reproduction or redistribution is strictly prohibited. All rights reserved.

Mental Steps for Beating Test Anxiety

Working on the mental side of test anxiety can be more challenging, but as with the physical side, there are clear steps you can take to overcome it. As mentioned earlier, test anxiety often stems from lack of preparation, so the obvious solution is to prepare for the test. Effective studying may be the most important weapon you have for beating test anxiety, but you can and should employ several other mental tools to combat fear.

First, boost your confidence by reminding yourself of past success—tests or projects that you aced. If you're putting as much effort into preparing for this test as you did for those, there's no reason you should expect to fail here. Work hard to prepare; then trust your preparation.

Second, surround yourself with encouraging people. It can be helpful to find a study group, but be sure that the people you're around will encourage a positive attitude. If you spend time with others who are anxious or cynical, this will only contribute to your own anxiety. Look for others who are motivated to study hard from a desire to succeed, not from a fear of failure.

Third, reward yourself. A test is physically and mentally tiring, even without anxiety, and it can be helpful to have something to look forward to. Plan an activity following the test, regardless of the outcome, such as going to a movie or getting ice cream.

When you are taking the test, if you find yourself beginning to feel anxious, remind yourself that you know the material. Visualize successfully completing the test. Then take a few deep, relaxing breaths and return to it. Work through the questions carefully but with confidence, knowing that you are capable of succeeding.

Developing a healthy mental approach to test taking will also aid in other areas of life. Test anxiety affects more than just the actual test—it can be damaging to your mental health and even contribute to depression. It's important to beat test anxiety before it becomes a problem for more than testing.

Review Video: Test Anxiety and Depression
Visit mometrix.com/academy and enter code: 904704

Copyright © Mometrix Media. You have been licensed one copy of this document for personal use only. Any other reproduction or redistribution is strictly prohibited. All rights reserved.

Study Strategy

Being prepared for the test is necessary to combat anxiety, but what does being prepared look like? You may study for hours on end and still not feel prepared. What you need is a strategy for test prep. The next few pages outline our recommended steps to help you plan out and conquer the challenge of preparation.

Step 1: Scope Out the Test

Learn everything you can about the format (multiple choice, essay, etc.) and what will be on the test. Gather any study materials, course outlines, or sample exams that may be available. Not only will this help you to prepare, but knowing what to expect can help to alleviate test anxiety.

Step 2: Map Out the Material

Look through the textbook or study guide and make note of how many chapters or sections it has. Then divide these over the time you have. For example, if a book has 15 chapters and you have five days to study, you need to cover three chapters each day. Even better, if you have the time, leave an extra day at the end for overall review after you have gone through the material in depth.

If time is limited, you may need to prioritize the material. Look through it and make note of which sections you think you already have a good grasp on, and which need review. While you are studying, skim quickly through the familiar sections and take more time on the challenging parts. Write out your plan so you don't get lost as you go. Having a written plan also helps you feel more in control of the study, so anxiety is less likely to arise from feeling overwhelmed at the amount to cover. A sample plan may look like this:

- Day 1: Skim chapters 1–4, study chapter 5 (especially pages 31–33)
- Day 2: Study chapters 6–7, skim chapters 8–9
- Day 3: Skim chapter 10, study chapters 11–12 (especially pages 87–90)
- Day 4: Study chapters 13–15
- Day 5: Overall review (focus most on chapters 5, 6, and 12), take practice test

Step 3: Gather Your Tools

Decide what study method works best for you. Do you prefer to highlight in the book as you study and then go back over the highlighted portions? Or do you type out notes of the important information? Or is it helpful to make flashcards that you can carry with you? Assemble the pens, index cards, highlighters, post-it notes, and any other materials you may need so you won't be distracted by getting up to find things while you study.

If you're having a hard time retaining the information or organizing your notes, experiment with different methods. For example, try color-coding by subject with colored pens, highlighters, or post-it notes. If you learn better by hearing, try recording yourself reading your notes so you can listen while in the car, working out, or simply sitting at your desk. Ask a friend to quiz you from your flashcards, or try teaching someone the material to solidify it in your mind.

Step 4: Create Your Environment

It's important to avoid distractions while you study. This includes both the obvious distractions like visitors and the subtle distractions like an uncomfortable chair (or a too-comfortable couch that makes you want to fall asleep). Set up the best study environment possible: good lighting and a

Copyright © Mometrix Media. You have been licensed one copy of this document for personal use only. Any other reproduction or redistribution is strictly prohibited. All rights reserved.

comfortable work area. If background music helps you focus, you may want to turn it on, but otherwise keep the room quiet. If you are using a computer to take notes, be sure you don't have any other windows open, especially applications like social media, games, or anything else that could distract you. Silence your phone and turn off notifications. Be sure to keep water close by so you stay hydrated while you study (but avoid unhealthy drinks and snacks).

Also, take into account the best time of day to study. Are you freshest first thing in the morning? Try to set aside some time then to work through the material. Is your mind clearer in the afternoon or evening? Schedule your study session then. Another method is to study at the same time of day that you will take the test, so that your brain gets used to working on the material at that time and will be ready to focus at test time.

Step 5: Study!

Once you have done all the study preparation, it's time to settle into the actual studying. Sit down, take a few moments to settle your mind so you can focus, and begin to follow your study plan. Don't give in to distractions or let yourself procrastinate. This is your time to prepare so you'll be ready to fearlessly approach the test. Make the most of the time and stay focused.

Of course, you don't want to burn out. If you study too long you may find that you're not retaining the information very well. Take regular study breaks. For example, taking five minutes out of every hour to walk briskly, breathing deeply and swinging your arms, can help your mind stay fresh.

As you get to the end of each chapter or section, it's a good idea to do a quick review. Remind yourself of what you learned and work on any difficult parts. When you feel that you've mastered the material, move on to the next part. At the end of your study session, briefly skim through your notes again.

But while review is helpful, cramming last minute is NOT. If at all possible, work ahead so that you won't need to fit all your study into the last day. Cramming overloads your brain with more information than it can process and retain, and your tired mind may struggle to recall even previously learned information when it is overwhelmed with last-minute study. Also, the urgent nature of cramming and the stress placed on your brain contribute to anxiety. You'll be more likely to go to the test feeling unprepared and having trouble thinking clearly.

So don't cram, and don't stay up late before the test, even just to review your notes at a leisurely pace. Your brain needs rest more than it needs to go over the information again. In fact, plan to finish your studies by noon or early afternoon the day before the test. Give your brain the rest of the day to relax or focus on other things, and get a good night's sleep. Then you will be fresh for the test and better able to recall what you've studied.

Step 6: Take a practice test

Many courses offer sample tests, either online or in the study materials. This is an excellent resource to check whether you have mastered the material, as well as to prepare for the test format and environment.

Check the test format ahead of time: the number of questions, the type (multiple choice, free response, etc.), and the time limit. Then create a plan for working through them. For example, if you have 30 minutes to take a 60-question test, your limit is 30 seconds per question. Spend less time on the questions you know well so that you can take more time on the difficult ones.

Copyright © Mometrix Media. You have been licensed one copy of this document for personal use only. Any other reproduction or redistribution is strictly prohibited. All rights reserved.

If you have time to take several practice tests, take the first one open book, with no time limit. Work through the questions at your own pace and make sure you fully understand them. Gradually work up to taking a test under test conditions: sit at a desk with all study materials put away and set a timer. Pace yourself to make sure you finish the test with time to spare and go back to check your answers if you have time.

After each test, check your answers. On the questions you missed, be sure you understand why you missed them. Did you misread the question (tests can use tricky wording)? Did you forget the information? Or was it something you hadn't learned? Go back and study any shaky areas that the practice tests reveal.

Taking these tests not only helps with your grade, but also aids in combating test anxiety. If you're already used to the test conditions, you're less likely to worry about it, and working through tests until you're scoring well gives you a confidence boost. Go through the practice tests until you feel comfortable, and then you can go into the test knowing that you're ready for it.

Test Tips

On test day, you should be confident, knowing that you've prepared well and are ready to answer the questions. But aside from preparation, there are several test day strategies you can employ to maximize your performance.

First, as stated before, get a good night's sleep the night before the test (and for several nights before that, if possible). Go into the test with a fresh, alert mind rather than staying up late to study.

Try not to change too much about your normal routine on the day of the test. It's important to eat a nutritious breakfast, but if you normally don't eat breakfast at all, consider eating just a protein bar. If you're a coffee drinker, go ahead and have your normal coffee. Just make sure you time it so that the caffeine doesn't wear off right in the middle of your test. Avoid sugary beverages, and drink enough water to stay hydrated but not so much that you need a restroom break 10 minutes into the test. If your test isn't first thing in the morning, consider going for a walk or doing a light workout before the test to get your blood flowing.

Allow yourself enough time to get ready, and leave for the test with plenty of time to spare so you won't have the anxiety of scrambling to arrive in time. Another reason to be early is to select a good seat. It's helpful to sit away from doors and windows, which can be distracting. Find a good seat, get out your supplies, and settle your mind before the test begins.

When the test begins, start by going over the instructions carefully, even if you already know what to expect. Make sure you avoid any careless mistakes by following the directions.

Then begin working through the questions, pacing yourself as you've practiced. If you're not sure on an answer, don't spend too much time on it, and don't let it shake your confidence. Either skip it and come back later, or eliminate as many wrong answers as possible and guess among the remaining ones. Don't dwell on these questions as you continue—put them out of your mind and focus on what lies ahead.

Be sure to read all of the answer choices, even if you're sure the first one is the right answer. Sometimes you'll find a better one if you keep reading. But don't second-guess yourself if you do immediately know the answer. Your gut instinct is usually right. Don't let test anxiety rob you of the information you know.

Copyright © Mometrix Media. You have been licensed one copy of this document for personal use only. Any other reproduction or redistribution is strictly prohibited. All rights reserved.

If you have time at the end of the test (and if the test format allows), go back and review your answers. Be cautious about changing any, since your first instinct tends to be correct, but make sure you didn't misread any of the questions or accidentally mark the wrong answer choice. Look over any you skipped and make an educated guess.

At the end, leave the test feeling confident. You've done your best, so don't waste time worrying about your performance or wishing you could change anything. Instead, celebrate the successful completion of this test. And finally, use this test to learn how to deal with anxiety even better next time.

Review Video: 5 Tips to Beat Test Anxiety
Visit mometrix.com/academy and enter code: 570656

Important Qualification

Not all anxiety is created equal. If your test anxiety is causing major issues in your life beyond the classroom or testing center, or if you are experiencing troubling physical symptoms related to your anxiety, it may be a sign of a serious physiological or psychological condition. If this sounds like your situation, we strongly encourage you to seek professional help.

Copyright © Mometrix Media. You have been licensed one copy of this document for personal use only. Any other reproduction or redistribution is strictly prohibited. All rights reserved.

Thank You

We at Mometrix would like to extend our heartfelt thanks to you, our friend and patron, for allowing us to play a part in your journey. It is a privilege to serve people from all walks of life who are unified in their commitment to building the best future they can for themselves.

The preparation you devote to these important testing milestones may be the most valuable educational opportunity you have for making a real difference in your life. We encourage you to put your heart into it—that feeling of succeeding, overcoming, and yes, conquering will be well worth the hours you've invested.

We want to hear your story, your struggles and your successes, and if you see any opportunities for us to improve our materials so we can help others even more effectively in the future, please share that with us as well. **The team at Mometrix would be absolutely thrilled to hear from you!** So please, send us an email (support@mometrix.com) and let's stay in touch.

If you'd like some additional help, check out these other resources we offer for your exam:

http://MometrixFlashcards.com/PraxisII

Copyright © Mometrix Media. You have been licensed one copy of this document for personal use only. Any other reproduction or redistribution is strictly prohibited. All rights reserved.

Additional Bonus Material

Due to our efforts to try to keep this book to a manageable length, we've created a link that will give you access to all of your additional bonus material.

Please visit http://www.mometrix.com/bonus948/priieeckft to access the information.

Copyright © Mometrix Media. You have been licensed one copy of this document for personal use only. Any other reproduction or redistribution is strictly prohibited. All rights reserved.